# Building Structures ILLUSTRATED

# Building Structures
# ILLUSTRATED
## Second Edition

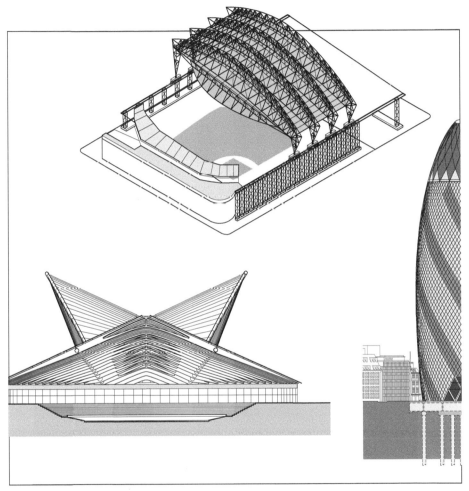

Francis D. K. Ching

Barry Onouye

Douglas Zuberbuhler

# WILEY

Library of Congress Cataloging-in-Publication Data:

Ching, Frank, 1943-
 Building structures illustrated : patterns, systems, and design
/ Francis D.K. Ching, Barry Onouye, Doug Zuberbuhler.
     p. cm.
Includes bibliographical references and index.
 ISBN 978-1-118-45835-8 (pbk.); 978-1-118-80823-8 (ebk); 978-1-118-84830-2 (ebk)
1. Structural design. 2.  Buildings. I. Onouye, Barry. II. Zuberbuhler, Doug. III. Title.

TA658.C49 2009
624.1'771--dc22

               2008047061

# Contents

**Disclaimer**

While this publication is designed to provide accurate and authoritative information regarding the subject matter covered, it is sold with the understanding that neither the publisher nor the authors are engaged in rendering professional services. If professional advice or other expert assistance is required, the services of a competent professional person should be sought.

# Preface

Many reputable books are available that cover the subject of building structures, from ones focusing on statics and strength of materials to others dealing with the design and analysis of structural elements, such as beams and columns, and still others covering specific structural materials. An understanding of the behavior of structural elements under different load conditions is critical to professionals, as is the ability to select, size, and shape appropriate structural materials and their connections. This book assumes the accessibility of these valuable resources and focuses instead on building structures as systems of interrelated parts for creating and supporting the habitable environments we call architecture.

A principal characteristic of this text is its holistic approach to building structures. Beginning with a concise review of how structural systems have evolved over time, the text discusses the idea of structural patterns and how these patterns of supports and spans can not only sustain but reinforce an architectural idea. The core of this book is an examination of the horizontal spanning and vertical support systems that house our activities and contribute to the vertical dimensions of form and space. The discussion then turns to a review of the critical aspects of lateral forces and stability, the unique properties of long-span structures, and current strategies for high-rise structures. The final chapter is a brief but important review of the integration of structural and other building systems.

While this text deliberately avoids a strictly mathematical approach to building structures, it does not neglect the fundamental principles that govern the behavior of structural elements, assemblies, and systems. To better serve as a guide during the preliminary design process, the discussion is accompanied by numerous drawings and diagrams that instruct and perhaps even inspire ideas about how a structural pattern might inform a design concept. The challenge in design is always how to translate principles into action. The major change in this second edition, therefore, is the addition of examples that illustrate the ways in which structural principles can be manifested in examples of real-world architecture.

The authors hope that this richly illustrated work will serve as a desktop resource for design students as well as young professionals and help them view structural systems as essential and integral to the design and building process.

## Metric Equivalents

The International System of Units is an internationally accepted system of coherent physical units, using the meter, kilogram, second, ampere, kelvin, and candela as the base units of length, mass, time, electric current, temperature, and luminous intensity. To reinforce an understanding of the International System of Units, metric equivalents are provided throughout this book according to the following conventions:

- All whole numbers in parentheses indicate millimeters unless otherwise noted.
- Dimensions 3 inches and greater are rounded to the nearest multiple of 5 millimeters.
- Note that 3487 mm = 3.487 m.
- In all other cases, the metric unit of measurement is specified.

# 1
# Building Structures

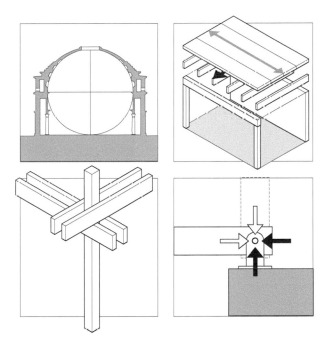

# BUILDING STRUCTURES

Buildings—the relatively permanent constructions we erect on a plot of land for habitable use—have developed over the course of history from simple shelters constructed of sticks, mud-brick, and stones to the more sophisticated constructions of concrete, steel, and glass of today. Throughout this evolution of building technology, what has remained constant is the enduring presence of some form of structural system capable of withstanding the forces of gravity, wind, and oftentimes, earthquakes.

We can define a structural system as a stable assembly of elements designed and constructed to function as a whole in supporting and transmitting applied loads safely to the ground without exceeding the allowable stresses in the members. While the forms and materials of structural systems have evolved with advances in technology and culture, not to mention the lessons learned from numerous building failures, they remain essential to the existence of all buildings, no matter their scale, context, or use.

The brief historical survey that follows illustrates the development of structural systems over time, from the earliest attempts to satisfy the fundamental human need for shelter against sun, wind, and rain, to the longer spans, greater heights, and increasing complexity of modern architecture.

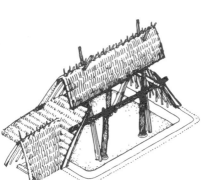

6500 BC: Mehrgarh (Pakistan). Compartmentalized mud-brick structures.

7500 BC: Catal Hüyük (Anatolia). Mud-brick houses with plastered interior walls.

5000 BC: Banpo, China. Pit-style houses using thick pillars to support their roofs.

**5000 BC**                    Bronze Age

The Neolithic period dawned with the advent of farming c. 8500 BC and transitioned to the early Bronze Age with the development of metal tools c. 3500 BC. The practice of using caves for shelter and dwelling had already existed for millennia and continued to develop as an architectural form, ranging from simple extensions of natural caves to carved out temples and churches to entire towns carved into the sides of the mountains.

9000 BC: Göbekli Tepe (Turkey). The world's oldest known stone temples.

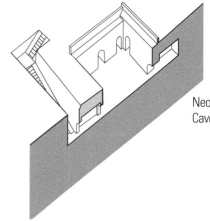

Neolithic Age: China, Northern Shaanxi province. Cave dwelling continues to the present day.

3400 BC: Sumerians introduce kilns.

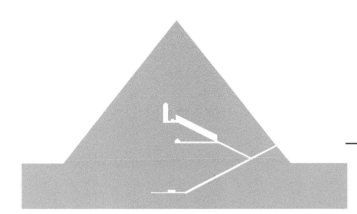

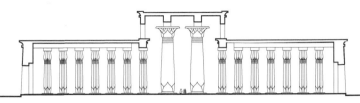

1500 BC: Temple of Amun at Karnak, Egypt. Hypostyle Hall is a stellar example of trabeated (column-and-beam) stone construction.

2500 BC: Great Pyramid of Khufu, Egypt. Until the 19th century, this stone pyramid was the tallest structure in the world.

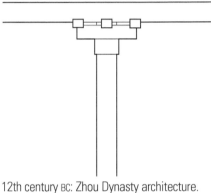

2600 BC: Harappa and Mohenjo-daro, Indus Valley, modern-day Pakistan and India. Fire-baked bricks and corbeled arches.

12th century BC: Zhou Dynasty architecture. Corbel brackets (dougong) on column heads help support projecting eaves.

**2500 BC**                                                                 **1000 BC**        Iron Age

While cave dwelling endures in various forms in different parts of the world, most architecture is created by assembling materials to define the limits of space as well as to provide shelter, house activities, commemorate events, and signify meaning. Early houses consisted of rough timber frames with mud-brick walls and thatched roofing. Sometimes pits were dug in the earth to provide additional warmth and protection; at other times, dwellings were elevated on stilts for ventilation in warm, humid climates or to rise above the shores of rivers and lakes. The use of heavy timber for the structural framing of walls and roof spans continued to develop over time and was refined, especially in the architecture of China, Korea, and Japan.

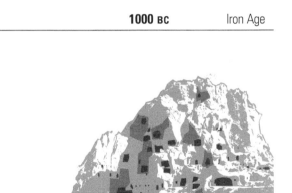

3000 BC: Alvastra (Scandinavia). Houses raised on wood stilts.

1000 BC: Cappadocia, Anatolia. Extensive excavations formed houses, churches, and monasteries.

3000 BC: Egyptians mix straw with mud to bind dried bricks.

1500 BC: Egyptians work molten glass.

1350 BC: Shang Dynasty (China) develops advanced bronze casting.

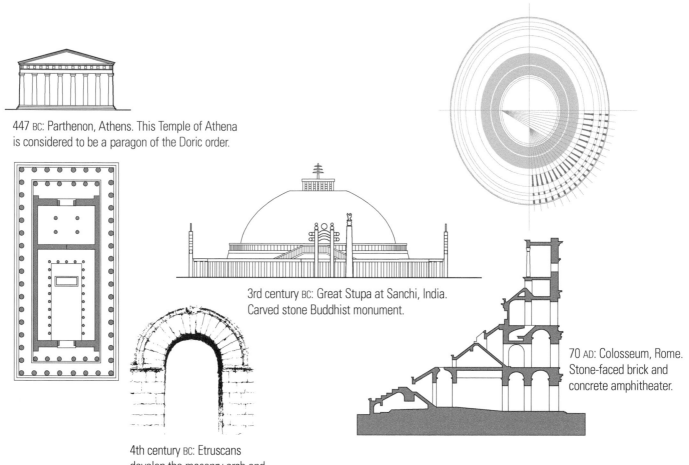

447 BC: Parthenon, Athens. This Temple of Athena is considered to be a paragon of the Doric order.

3rd century BC: Great Stupa at Sanchi, India. Carved stone Buddhist monument.

70 AD: Colosseum, Rome. Stone-faced brick and concrete amphitheater.

4th century BC: Etruscans develop the masonry arch and vault. Porta Pulchra, Perugia.

**500 BC**                                                                 **1 AD**

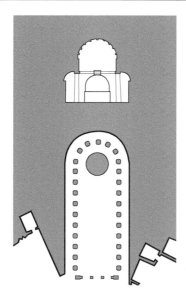

200 BC: India. Numerous examples of Buddhist, Jain, and Hindu cave architecture.

10 BC: Petra, Jordan. Palace tombs half-built, half-carved into the rock.

5th century BC: Chinese cast iron.

4th century BC: Babylonians and Assyrians use bitumen to bind bricks and stones.

3rd century BC: Romans make concrete with pozzolanic cement.

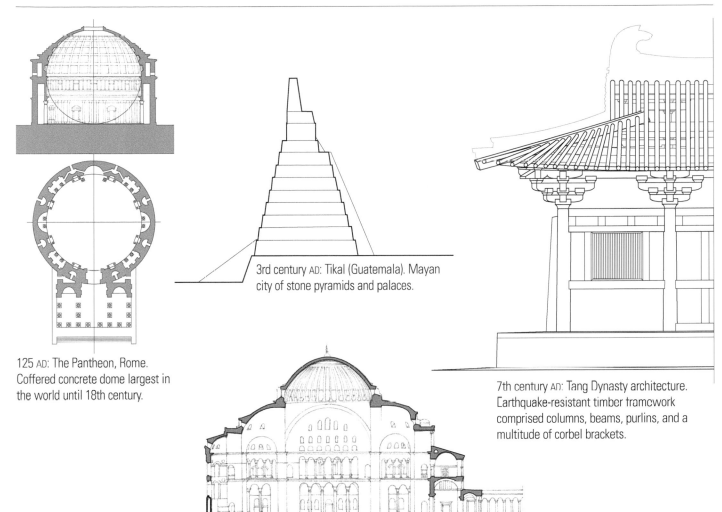

3rd century AD: Tikal (Guatemala). Mayan city of stone pyramids and palaces.

125 AD: The Pantheon, Rome. Coffered concrete dome largest in the world until 18th century.

7th century AD: Tang Dynasty architecture. Earthquake-resistant timber framework comprised columns, beams, purlins, and a multitude of corbel brackets.

**800 AD**

532–37 AD: Hagia Sophia, Istanbul. Central dome carried on pendentives that enable the transition from round dome to square plan. Concrete is used in the construction of the vaulting and arches of the lower levels.

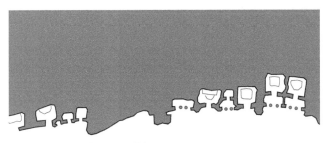

460 AD: Yungang Grottoes, China. Buddhist temples carved into sandstone cliffs.

2nd century AD: Paper is invented in China.

752 AD: Todaiji, Nara. Buddhist temple is world's largest wooden building; present reconstruction is two-thirds of the original temple's size.

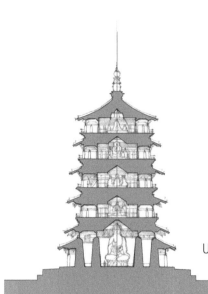

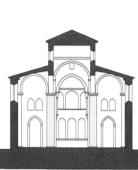

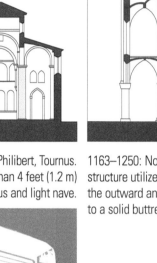

11th century: Abbey church of St-Philibert, Tournus. Unadorned cylindrical pillars more than 4 feet (1.2 m) thick support the spacious and light nave.

1163–1250: Notre Dame Cathedral, Paris. Cut stone structure utilizes external flying buttresses to transmit the outward and downward thrust from a roof or vault to a solid buttress.

1056: Sakyamuni Pagoda, China. Oldest surviving timber pagoda and tallest timber building in the world at a height of 220 feet (67.1 m).

1100: Chan Chan. Citadel walls of stucco-covered mud-brick.

**900** AD

Where stone was available, it was first used to establish defensive barriers and serve as bearing walls to support timber spans for floors and roofs. Masonry vaulting and domes led to higher elevations and greater spans, while the development of pointed arches, clustered columns, and flying buttresses enabled the creation of lighter, more open, skeletal stone structures.

1100: Lalibela, Ethiopia. Site of monolithic, rock-cut churches.

1170: Cast iron is produced in Europe.

15th century: Filippo Brunelleschi develops theory of linear perspective.

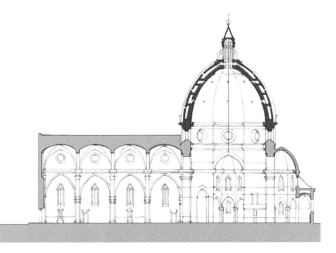

13th century: Cathedral of Florence, Italy. Filippo Brunelleschi designed the double-walled dome, resting on a drum, to allow it to be built without the need for scaffolding from the ground.

1506–1615: St. Peter's Basilica, Rome, Donato Bramante, Michelangelo, Giacomo della Porta. Until recently the largest church ever built, covering an area of 5.7 acres (23,000 m$^2$).

**1400 AD**                                                                                     **1600 AD**

As early as the 6th century AD the main arcades of Hagia Sophia in Istanbul incorporated iron bars as tension ties. During the Middle Ages and the Renaissance, iron was used for both decorative and structural components, such as dowels and ties, to strengthen masonry structures. But it was not until the 18th century that new production methods allowed cast and wrought iron to be produced in large enough quantities to be used as a structural material for the skeletal structures of railway stations, market halls, and other public buildings. The mass of stone walls and columns transitions to the lighter imprint of iron and steel frames.

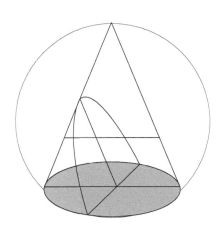

1638: Galileo publishes his first book, *The Discourses and Mathematical Demonstrations Relating to Two New Sciences*, the two sciences referring to the strength of materials and the motion of objects.

Early-16th century: Blast furnaces are able to produce large quantities of cast iron.

1687: Isaac Newton publishes *Philosophiae Naturilis Principia Mathematica*, which describes universal gravitation and the three laws of motion, laying the groundwork for classical mechanics.

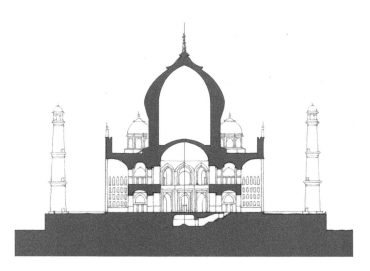

1653: Taj Mahal, Agra, India. Ahmad Lahauri. Iconic white-domed, marble mausoleum built in memory of Mumtaz Mahai, wife of Mughal Emperor Shah Jahan.

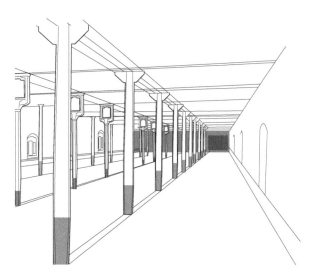

1797: Ditherington Flax Mill, Shrewsbury, England, William Strutt. Oldest steel-framed building in the world, having a structural frame of cast iron columns and beams.

**1700**                                                **1800**

Late-18th and early-19th centuries: The Industrial Revolution introduces major changes in agriculture, manufacturing, and transportation that alter the socioeconomic and cultural climate in Britain and elsewhere.

Central heating was widely adopted in the early-19th century when the Industrial Revolution caused an increase in the size of buildings for industry, residential use, and services.

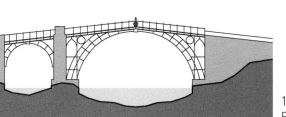

1777–79: Iron Bridge at Coalbrookdale, England. T. M. Pritchard.

1711: Abraham Darby produces high-quality iron smelted with coke and molded in sand.

1801: Thomas Young studies elasticity and gives his name to the elastic modulus.

1735: Charles Maria de la Condamine finds rubber in South America.

1778: Joseph Bramah patents a practical water closet.

1738: Daniel Bernoulli relates fluid flow to pressure.

1779: Bry Higgins patents hydraulic cement for exterior plaster.

1851: Crystal Palace, Hyde Park, London, John Paxton. Prefabricated units of wrought iron and glass were assembled to create 990,000 square feet (91,974 m²) of exhibition space.

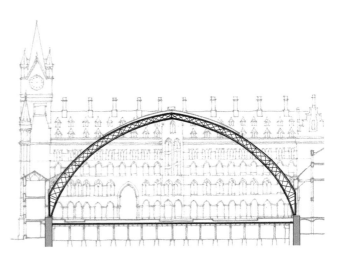

1868: St. Pancras Station, London, William Barlow. Trussed arch structure with tie rods below floor level to resist outward thrust.

**1860**

There is evidence that the Chinese used a mixture of lime and volcanic ash to build the pyramids of Shaanxi several thousand years ago, but it was the Romans who developed a hydraulic concrete from pozzolanic ash similar to the modern concrete made from Portland cement. The formulation of Portland cement by Joseph Aspdin in 1824 and the invention of reinforced concrete, attributed to Joseph-Louis Lambot in 1848, stimulated the use of concrete for architectural structures.

The modern era in steelmaking began when Henry Bessemer described a process for mass-producing steel relatively cheaply in 1856.

1850: Henry Waterman invents the lift.

1853: Elisha Otis introduces the safety elevator to prevent the fall of the cab if the cable is broken. The first Otis elevator is installed in New York City in 1857.

1824: Joseph Aspdin patents the manufacture of Portland cement.

1827: George Ohm formulates the law relating current, voltage, and resistance.

1855: Alexander Parkes patents celluloid, the first synthetic plastic material.

1867: Joseph Monier patents reinforced concrete.

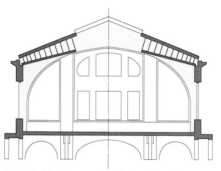

1889: Eiffel Tower, Paris, Gustave Eiffel. The Tower replaced the Washington Monument as the world's tallest structure, a title it retained until the Chrysler Building in New York City was erected in 1930.

1884: Home Insurance Building, Chicago, William Le Baron Jenney. The 10-story structural frame of steel and cast iron carries the majority of the weight of the floors and exterior walls.

1898: Public Natatorium, Gebweiler, France, Eduard Züblin. Reinforced concrete roof vault consists of five rigid frames with thin plates spanning between each frame.

**1875**                                                                 **1900**

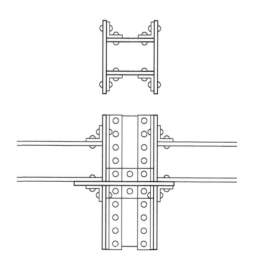

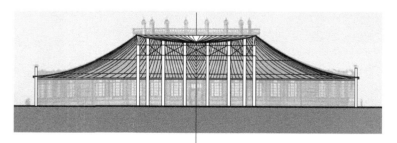

1896: Rotunda-Pavilion, All-Russia Industrial and Art Exhibition, Nizhny Novgorod, Vladimir Shukhov. The world's first steel tensile structure.

1881: Charles Louis Strobel standardizes rolled wrought-iron sections and riveted connections.

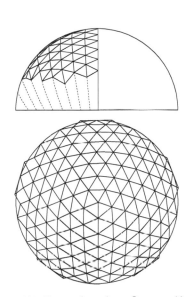

1453 feet (442.9 m)

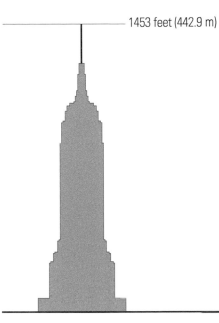

1903: Ingalls Building, Cincinnati, Ohio, Elzner & Anderson. First reinforced concrete high-rise building.

1922: Planetarium, Jena, Germany, Walter Bauerfeld. First contemporary geodesic dome on record, derived from the icosahedron.

1931: Empire State Building, New York City, Shreve, Lamb, and Harmon. World's tallest building until 1972.

**1940**

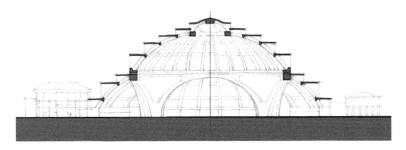

1913: Jahrhunderthalle (Centennial Hall), Breslau, Max Berg. Reinforced concrete structure, including a 213-feet (65-m) diameter dome, influences the use of concrete for enclosing large, public spaces.

With the advent of improved steels and computerized stress analytical techniques, steel structures have become lighter and joints more refined, allowing an array of structural shapes.

1903: Alexander Graham Bell experiments with spatial structural forms, leading to the later development of space frames by Buckminster Fuller, Max Mengeringhausen, and Konrad Wachsmann.

1919: Walter Gropius establishes the Bauhaus.

1928: Eugène Freyssinet invents prestressed concrete.

1960: Palazzo Dello Sport, Rome, Italy, Pier Luigi Nervi. 330-feet (100-m) diameter ribbed reinforced-concrete dome built for the 1960 Summer Olympic Games.

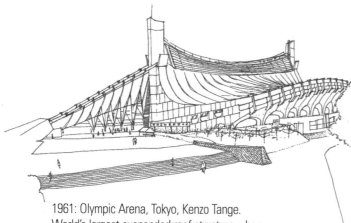

1961: Olympic Arena, Tokyo, Kenzo Tange. World's largest suspended roof structure when built, its steel cables are suspended from two reinforced concrete pillars.

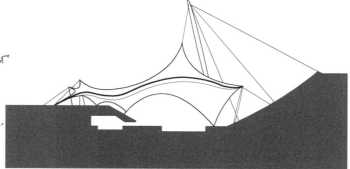

1972: Olympic Swimming Arena, Munich, Germany, Frei Otto. Steel cables combine with fabric membranes to create an extremely lightweight, long-span structure.

**1950**

**1975**

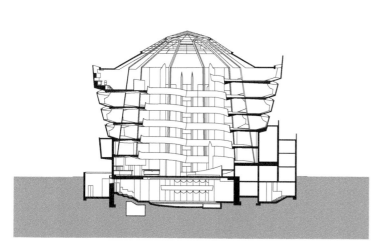

1943–59: Guggenheim Museum, New York City, Frank Lloyd Wright.

1955: The commercial use of computers develops.

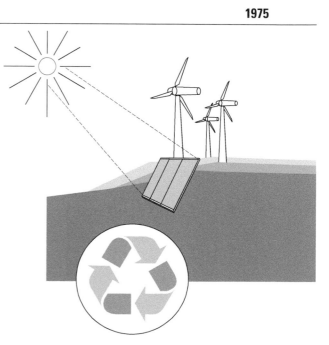

1973: Rise in oil prices stimulates research into alternative sources of energy, leading to energy conservation becoming a major element in architectural design.

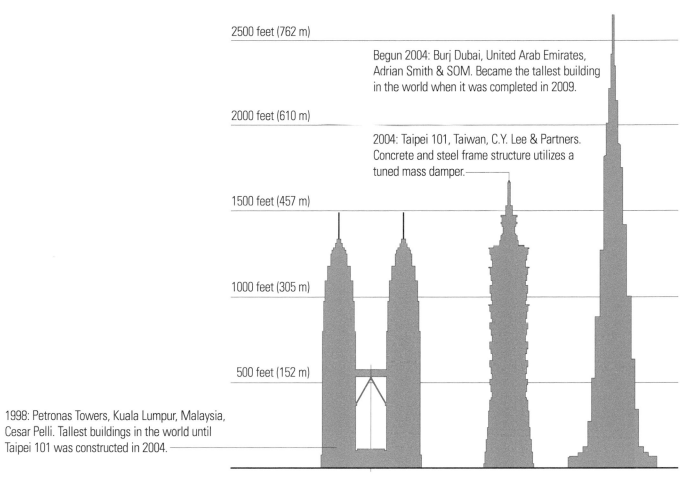

2500 feet (762 m)

Begun 2004: Burj Dubai, United Arab Emirates, Adrian Smith & SOM. Became the tallest building in the world when it was completed in 2009.

2000 feet (610 m)

2004: Taipei 101, Taiwan, C.Y. Lee & Partners. Concrete and steel frame structure utilizes a tuned mass damper.

1500 feet (457 m)

1000 feet (305 m)

500 feet (152 m)

1998: Petronas Towers, Kuala Lumpur, Malaysia, Cesar Pelli. Tallest buildings in the world until Taipei 101 was constructed in 2004.

**2000**

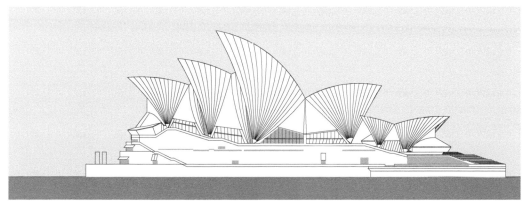

1973: Sydney Opera House, Jørn Utzon. Iconic shell structures consist of prefabricated, cast-on-site concrete ribs.

# ARCHITECTURAL STRUCTURES

The preceding historical review conveys a sense not only of how structural systems have evolved but also how they have had, and will continue to have, an impact on architectural design. Architecture embodies ineffable yet sensible, aesthetic qualities that emerge from a union of space, form, and structure. In providing support for other building systems and our activities, a structural system enables the shape and form of a building and its spaces, similar to the way in which our skeletal system gives shape and form to our body and support to its organs and tissues. So when we speak of architectural structures, we refer to those that unite with form and space in a coherent manner.

Designing an architectural structure therefore involves more than the proper sizing of any single element or component, or even the design of any particular structural assembly. It is not simply the task of balancing and resolving forces. Rather, it requires that we consider the manner in which the overall configuration and scale of structural elements, assemblies, and connections encapsulate an architectural idea, reinforce the architectural form and spatial composition of a design proposal, and enable its constructibility. This then requires an awareness of structure as a system of interconnected and interrelated parts, an understanding of the generic types of structural systems, as well as an appreciation for the capabilities of certain types of structural elements and assemblies.

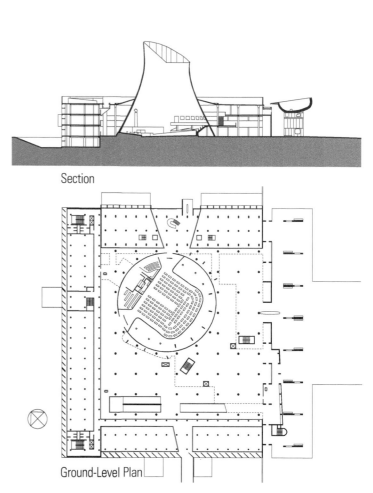

Section

Ground-Level Plan

**Parliament Building**, Chandigarh, India, 1951–1963, Le Corbusier

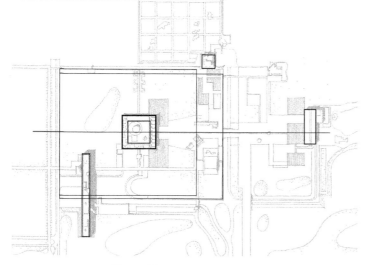

Site and Context

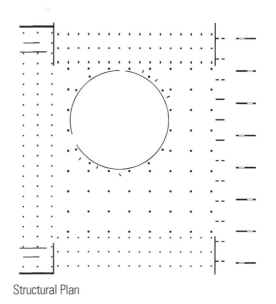

Structural Plan

To understand the impact of structural systems on architectural design, we should be aware of how they relate to the conceptual, experiential, and contextual ordering of architecture.

- Formal and spatial composition
- Definition, scale, and proportions of forms and spaces
- Qualities of shape, form, space, light, color, texture, and pattern
- Ordering of human activities by their scale and dimension
- Functional zoning of spaces according to purpose and use
- Access to and the horizontal and vertical paths of movement through a building
- Buildings as integral components within the natural and built environment
- Sensory and cultural characteristics of place

The remaining sections of this chapter outline major aspects of structural systems that support, reinforce, and ultimately give form to an architectural idea.

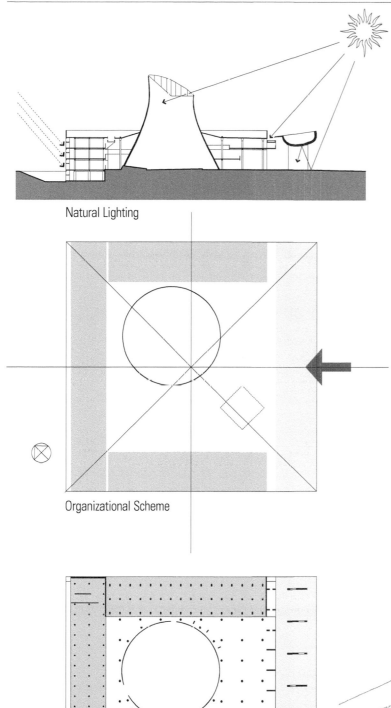

Natural Lighting

Organizational Scheme

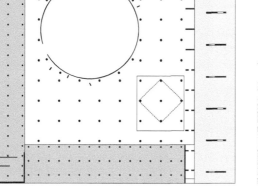

Structure Supporting Organizational Idea

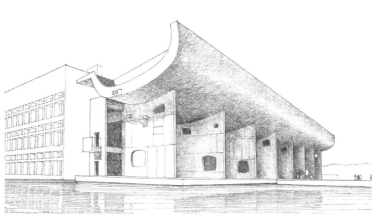

Structure Supporting Formal Idea

# ARCHITECTURAL STRUCTURES

## Formal Intent

There are three fundamental ways in which the structural system can relate to the form of an architectural design. These fundamental strategies are:

- Exposing the structural system
- Concealing the structure
- Celebrating the structure

## Exposing the Structure

Historically, stone- and masonry-bearing wall systems dominated architecture until the advent of iron and steel construction in the late-18th century. These structural systems also functioned as the primary system of enclosure and therefore expressed the form of the architecture, typically in an honest and straightforward manner.

Whatever formal modifications were made were usually a result of molding or carving the structural material in such a way as to create additive elements, subtractive voids, or reliefs within the mass of the structure.

Even in the modern era, there are examples of buildings that exposed their structural systems—whether in timber, steel, or concrete—using them effectively as the primary architectonic form-givers.

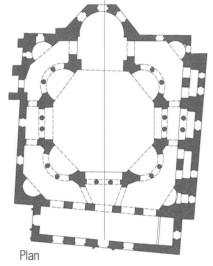

Section

Plan

SS. Sergius and Bacchus, Istanbul, Turkey, 527–536 AD. The Ottomans converted this Eastern Orthodox church into a mosque. Featuring a central dome plan, it is believed by some to be a model for Hagia Sophia.

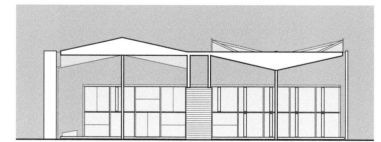

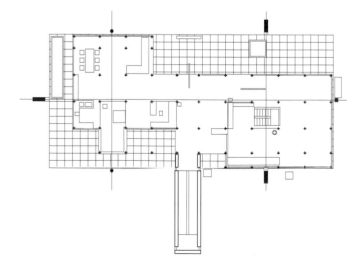

Centre Le Corbusier/Heidi Weber Pavilion, Zurich, 1965, Le Corbusier. A structural steel parasol hovers over a modular steel frame structure with sides of enameled steel panels and glass.

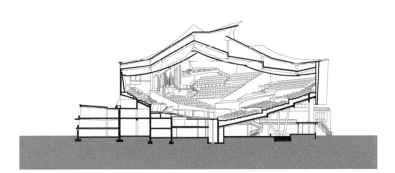

Section

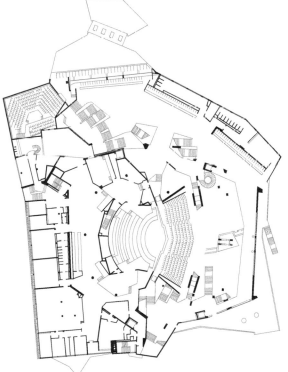

Lower-Level Plan

## Concealing the Structure

In this strategy, the structural system is concealed or obscured by the exterior cladding and roofing of the building. Some reasons for concealing the structure are practical, as when the structural elements must be clad to make them fire-resistant, or contextual, as when the desired exterior form is at odds with interior space requirements. In the latter case, the structure may organize the interior spaces while the form of the exterior shell responds to site conditions or constraints.

The designer may simply want freedom of expression for the shell without considering how the structural system might aid or hinder formal decisions. Or the structural system may be obscured through neglect rather than intent. In both of these cases, legitimate questions arise as to whether the resulting design is intentional or accidental, willful or, dare we say, careless.

◄ Philharmonic Hall, Berlin, Germany, 1960–63, Hans Scharoun. An example of the Expressionist movement, this concert hall has an asymmetric structure with a tent-like concrete roof and a stage in the middle of terraced seating. Its external appearance is subordinate to the functional and acoustic requirements of the concert hall.

Guggenheim Museum, Bilbao, Spain, 1991–97, Frank Gehry. A novelty when completed, this contemporary art museum is known for its sculpted, titanium-clad forms. While difficult to understand in traditional architectural terms, the definition and constructibility of the apparently random forms were made possible through the use of CATIA, an integrated suite of Computer Aided Design (CAD), Computer Aided Engineering (CAE), and Computer Aided Manufacturing (CAM) applications.

▼

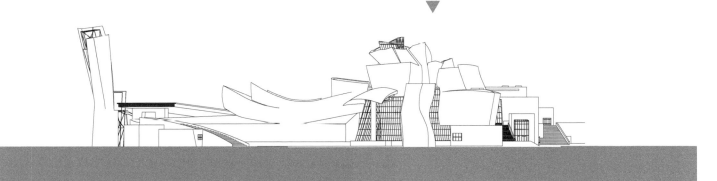

# ARCHITECTURAL STRUCTURES

## Celebrating the Structure

Rather than being merely exposed, the structural system can be exploited as a design feature, celebrating the form and materiality of the structure. The often exuberant nature of shell and membrane structures makes them appropriate candidates for this category.

There are also those structures that dominate by the sheer forcefulness with which they express the way they resolve the forces acting on them. These types of structures often become iconic symbols due to their striking imagery. Think Eiffel Tower or the Sydney Opera House.

When judging whether a building celebrates its structure or not, we should be careful to differentiate structural expression from expressive forms which are not, in truth, structural but only appear to be so.

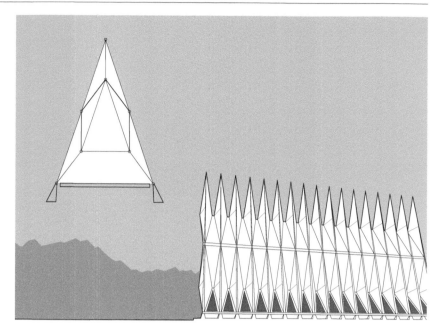

Air Force Academy Chapel, Colorado Springs, Colorado, USA, 1956–62, Walter Netsch/Skidmore, Owings and Merrill. The soaring structure, consisting of 100 identical tetrahedrons, develops stability through the triangulation of individual structural units as well as a triangular section.

Los Manantiales, Xochimilco, Mexico, 1958, Felix Candela. The thin-shell concrete structure consists of a series of intersecting, saddle-shaped hyperbolic paraboloids arranged in a radial plan.

Main Terminal, Dulles International Airport, Chantilly, Virginia, USA, 1958–62, Eero Saarinen. Catenary cables suspended between two long colonnades of outward-leaning and tapered columns carry a gracefully curved concrete roof suggestive of flight.

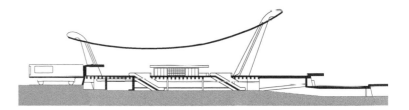

Hong Kong and Shanghai Bank, Hong Kong, China, 1979–85, Norman Foster. Eight groups of four aluminum-clad steel columns rise up from the foundations and support five levels of suspension trusses, from which are hung the floor structures.

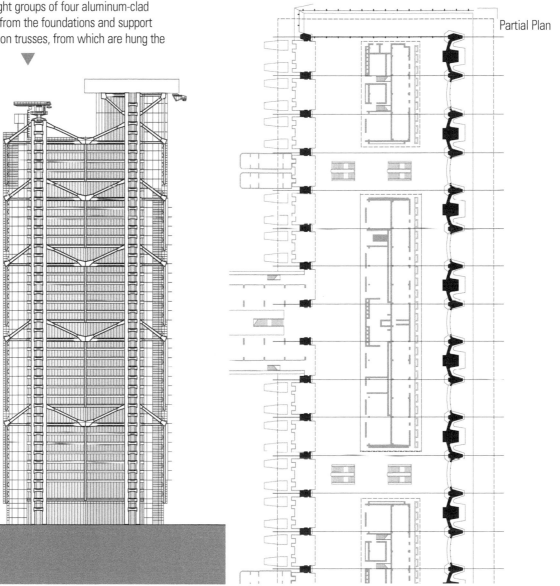

Partial Plan

Elevation and Structural Plan

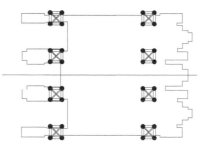

## Spatial Composition

The form of a structural system and the pattern of its supporting and spanning elements can be related to the spatial layout and composition of a design in two fundamental ways. The first is a correspondence between the form of the structural system and that of the spatial composition. The second is a looser fit in which the structural form and pattern allow more freedom or flexibility in spatial layout.

## Correspondence

Where there is a correspondence between structural form and spatial composition, either the pattern of structural supports and spanning systems can prescribe the disposition of spaces within a building or the spatial layout can suggest a certain type of structural system. In the design process, which comes first?

In ideal cases, we consider both space and structure together as co-determinants of architectural form. But composing spaces according to needs and desires often precedes thinking about structure. On the other hand, there are times when structural form can be the driving force in the design process.

In either case, structural systems that prescribe a pattern of spaces of certain sizes and dimensions, or even a pattern of use, may not allow for flexibility in future use or adaptation.

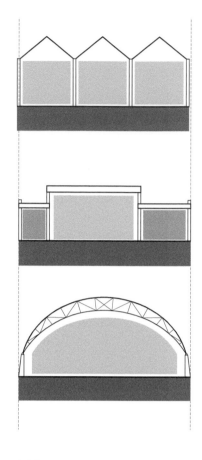

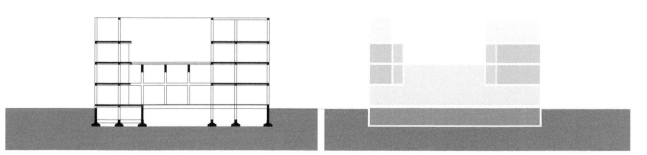

Structural and Spatial Diagrams in Plan and Section. Casa del Fascio, Como, Italy, 1932–36, Giuseppe Terragni.

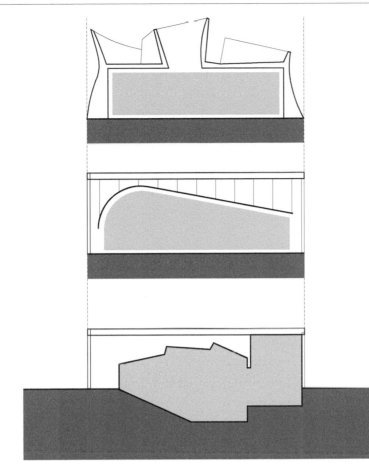

### Contrast

When there is a lack of correspondence between structural form and spatial composition, either may take precedence. The structure may be large enough to shelter or encompass a series of spaces within its volume, or the spatial composition may dominate a concealed structure. An irregular or asymmetrical structural system may envelop a more regular spatial composition, or a structural grid may provide a uniform set or network of points against which a freer spatial composition can be gauged or contrasted.

A distinction between space and structure may be desirable to provide flexibility of layout; allow for growth and expansion; make visible the identity of different building systems; or express differences between interior and exterior needs, desires, and relationships.

Sala Sinopoli, Parco della Musica, Rome, Italy, 1994–2002, Renzo Piano. A secondary structure supports a lead-clad roof intended to reduce the penetration of exterior noise into the auditorium while the primary structure supports cherry-wood interior surfaces that are adjustable for tuning of the acoustic environment.

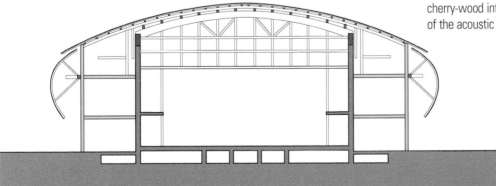

# STRUCTURAL SYSTEMS

A system can be defined as an assembly of interrelated or interdependent parts forming a more complex and unified whole and serving a common purpose. A building can be understood to be the physical embodiment of a number of systems and subsystems that must necessarily be related, coordinated, and integrated with each other as well as with the three-dimensional form and spatial organization of the building as a whole.

The structural system of a building, in particular, consists of a stable assembly of structural elements designed and constructed to support and transmit applied loads safely to the ground without exceeding the allowable stresses in the members. Each of the structural members has a unitary character and exhibits a unique behavior under an applied load. But before individual structural elements and members can be isolated for study and resolution, it is important for the designer to understand how the structural system accommodates and supports in a holistic manner the desired programmatic and contextual forms, spaces, and relationships of an architectural scheme.

Regardless of the size and scale of a building, it comprises physical systems of structure and enclosure that define and organize its forms and spaces. These elements can be further categorized into a substructure and a superstructure.

## Substructure

The substructure is the lowest division of a building—its foundation—constructed partly or wholly below the surface of the ground. Its primary function is to support and anchor the superstructure above and transmit its loads safely into the earth. Because it serves as a critical link in the distribution and resolution of building loads, the foundation system, while normally hidden from view, must be designed to both accommodate the form and layout of the superstructure above and respond to the varying conditions of soil, rock, and water below.

The principal loads on a foundation are the combination of dead and live loads acting vertically on the superstructure. In addition, a foundation system must anchor the superstructure against wind-induced sliding, overturning, and uplift, withstand the sudden ground movements of an earthquake, and resist the pressure imposed by the surrounding soil mass and groundwater on basement walls. In some cases, a foundation system may also have to counter the thrust from arched or tensile structures.

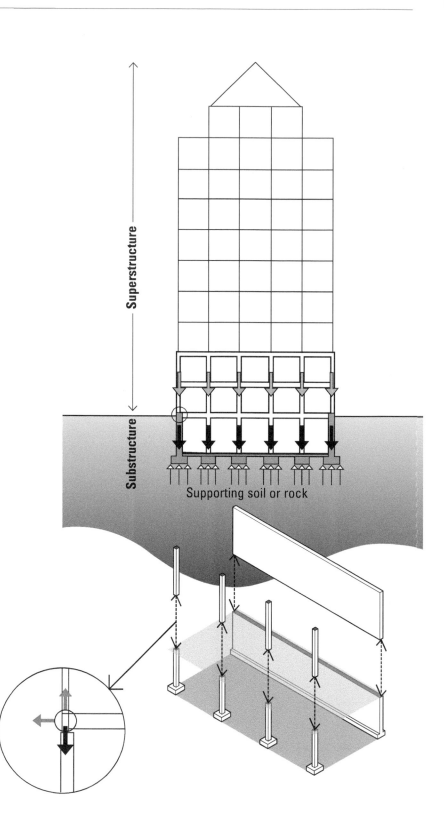

Superstructure

Substructure

Supporting soil or rock

An important influence on the type of substructure we select, and consequently, the structural pattern we design, is the site and context for a building.

• Relation to superstructure: The type and pattern of required foundation elements impact, if not dictate, the layout of supports for the superstructure. Vertical continuity in load transmission should be maintained as much as possible for structural efficiency.
• Soil type: The integrity of a building structure depends ultimately on the stability and strength under loading of the soil or rock underlying the foundation. The bearing capacity of the underlying soil or rock may therefore limit the size of a building or require deep foundations.
• Relation to topography: The topographic character of a building site has both ecological and structural implications and consequences, requiring that any site development be sensitive to natural drainage patterns, conditions conducive to flooding, erosion, or slides, and provisions for habitat protection.

## Shallow Foundations

Shallow or spread foundations are employed when stable soil of adequate bearing capacity occurs relatively near to the ground surface. They are placed directly below the lowest part of a substructure and transfer building loads directly to the supporting soil by vertical pressure. Shallow foundations can take any of the following geometric forms:

• Point: Column footings
• Line: Foundation walls and footings
• Plane: Mat foundations—thick, heavily reinforced concrete slabs that serve as a single monolithic footing for a number of columns or an entire building—are used when the allowable bearing capacity of a foundation soil is low relative to building loads and interior column footings become so large that it becomes more economical to merge them into a single slab. Mat foundations may be stiffened by a grid of ribs, beams, or walls.

## Deep Foundations

Deep foundations consist of caissons or piles that extend down through unsuitable soil to transfer building loads to a more appropriate bearing stratum of rock or dense sands and gravels well below the superstructure.

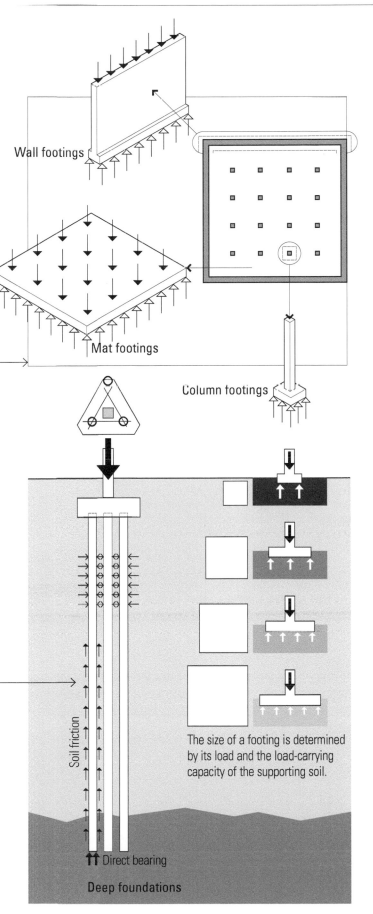

Wall footings

Mat footings

Column footings

Soil friction

The size of a footing is determined by its load and the load-carrying capacity of the supporting soil.

↑↑ Direct bearing

Deep foundations

# STRUCTURAL SYSTEMS

### Superstructure
The superstructure, the vertical extension of a building above the foundation, consists of a shell and interior structure that defines the form of a building and its spatial layout and composition.

### Shell
The shell or envelope of a building, consisting of the roof, exterior walls, windows, and doors, provides protection and shelter for the interior spaces of a building.

- The roof and exterior walls shelter interior spaces from inclement weather and control moisture, heat, and air flow through the layering of construction assemblies.
- Exterior walls and roofs also dampen noise and provide security and privacy for the occupants of a building.
- Doors provide physical access.
- Windows provide access to light, air, and views.

### Structure
A structural system is required to support the shell of a building as well as its interior floors, walls, and partitions, and to transfer the applied loads to the substructure.

- Columns, beams, and loadbearing walls support floor and roof structures.
- Floor structures are the flat, level base planes of interior space that support our interior activities and furnishings.
- Interior structural walls and nonloadbearing partitions subdivide the interior of a building into spatial units.
- Lateral-force-resisting elements are laid out to provide lateral stability.

In the construction process, the superstructure rises from the substructure, following the same paths along which the superstructure transmits its loads down to the substructure.

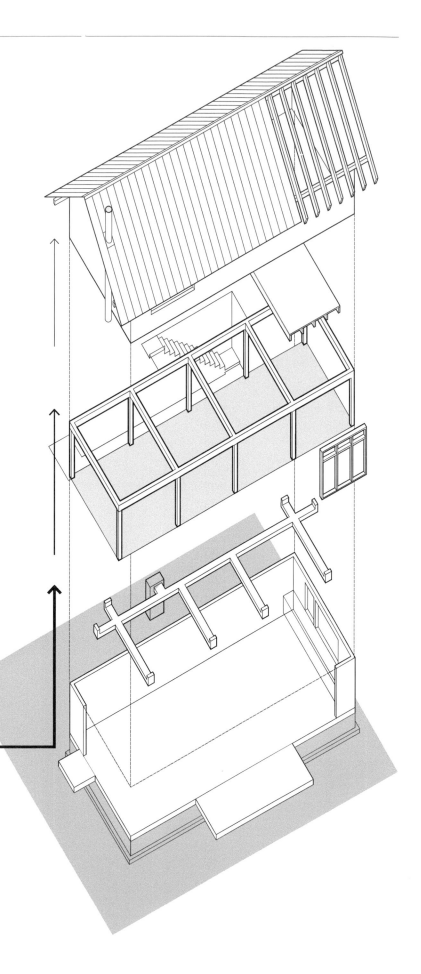

The formal intent of an architectural design may be offered, given, suggested, or mandated by the site and context, the program and function, or by purpose and meaning. Concurrent with thinking about formal and spatial options, we should also begin to consider our structural options—the palette of materials, the types of support, spanning, and lateral-force-resisting systems—and how these choices might influence, support, and reinforce the formal and spatial dimensions of a design idea.

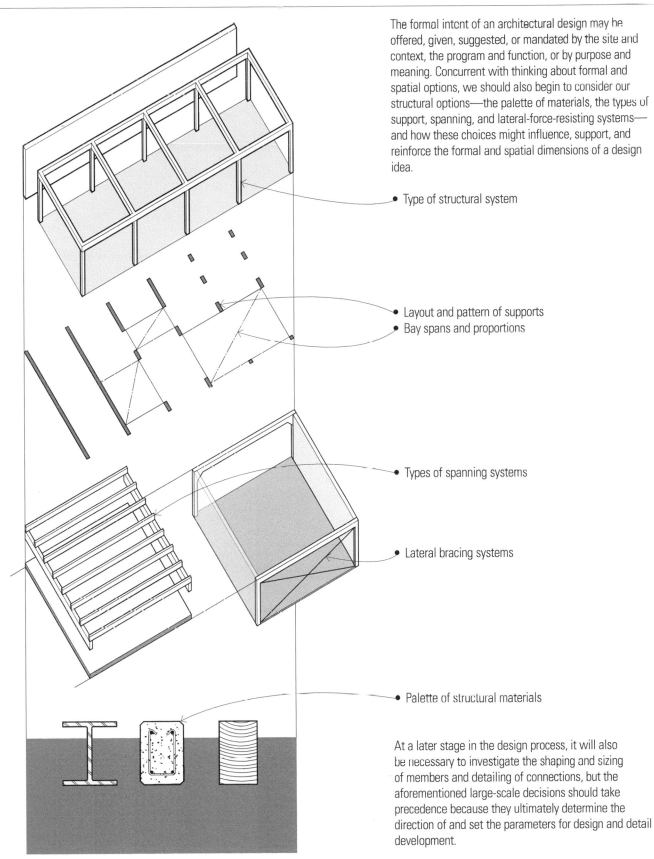

• Type of structural system

• Layout and pattern of supports
• Bay spans and proportions

• Types of spanning systems

• Lateral bracing systems

• Palette of structural materials

At a later stage in the design process, it will also be necessary to investigate the shaping and sizing of members and detailing of connections, but the aforementioned large-scale decisions should take precedence because they ultimately determine the direction of and set the parameters for design and detail development.

### Types of Structural Systems

Given a specific attitude toward the expressive role of the structural system and the desired spatial composition, appropriate choices for a structural system can be made if one understands the formal attributes the various systems develop in responding to applied forces and redirecting these forces to their foundations.

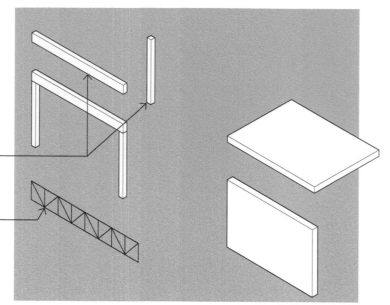

- Bulk-active structures redirect external forces primarily through the bulk and continuity of its material, such as beams and columns. ————

- Vector-active structures redirect external forces primarily through the composition of tension and compression members, such as a truss. ————

- The proportions of structural elements, such as bearing walls, floor and roof slabs, vaults and domes, give us visual clues to their role in a structural system as well as the nature of their material. A masonry wall, being strong in compression but relatively weak in bending, will be thicker than a reinforced concrete wall doing the same work. A steel column will be thinner than a wood post supporting the same load. A 4-inch reinforced concrete slab will span farther than 4-inch wood decking.

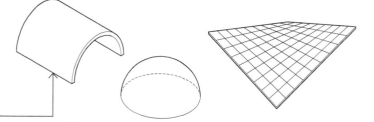

- Surface-active structures redirect external forces primarily along the continuity of a surface, such as a plate or shell structure. ————

- Form-active structures redirect external forces primarily through the form of its material, such as an arch or cable system. ————

- As a structure depends less on the weight and stiffness of a material and more on its geometry for stability, as in the case of membrane structures and space frames, its elements will get thinner and thinner until they lose their ability to give a space scale and dimension.

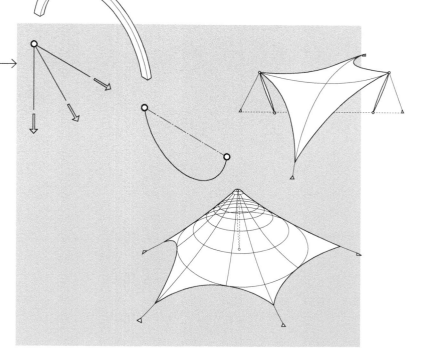

## Structural Analysis and Design

Before proceeding to a discussion of structural design, it might be useful to distinguish between structural design and structural analysis. Structural analysis is the process of determining the ability of a structure or any of its constituent members, either existing or assumed, to safely carry a given set of loads without material distress or excessive deformation, given the arrangement, shape, and dimensions of the members, the types of connections and supports utilized, and the allowable stresses of the materials employed. In other words, structural analysis can occur only if given a specific structure and certain load conditions.

Structural design, on the other hand, refers to the process of arranging, interconnecting, sizing, and proportioning the members of a structural system in order to safely carry a given set of loads without exceeding the allowable stresses of the materials employed. Structural design, similar to other design activities, must operate in an environment of uncertainty, ambiguity, and approximation. It is a search for a structural system that can meet not only the load requirements but also address the architectural, urban design, and programmatic issues at hand.

The first step in the structural design process may be stimulated by the nature of the architectural design, its site and context, or the availability of certain materials.

- The architectural design idea may elicit a specific type of configuration or pattern.
- The site and context may suggest a certain type of structural response.
- Structural materials may be dictated by building code requirements, supply, availability of labor, or costs.

Once the type of structural system, its configuration or pattern, and the palette of structural materials are projected, then the design process can proceed to the sizing and proportioning of assemblies and individual members and the detailing of connections.

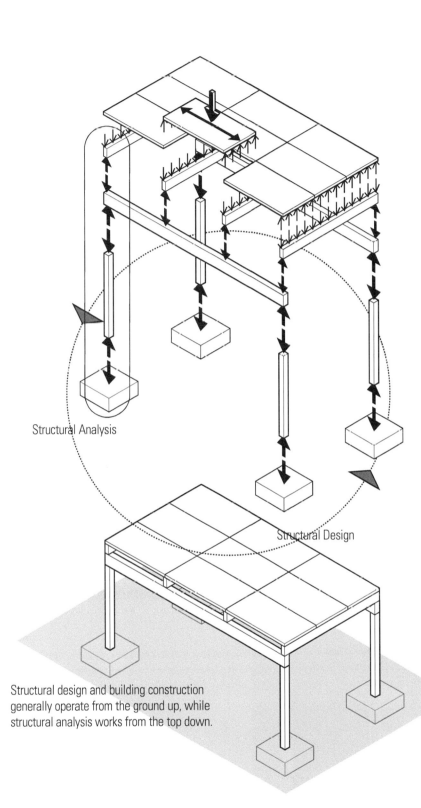

Structural Analysis

Structural Design

Structural design and building construction generally operate from the ground up, while structural analysis works from the top down.

- For clarity, lateral-force-resisting elements have been omitted. See Chapter 5 for lateral-force-resisting systems and strategies.

### Detailing of Connections

The manner in which forces are transferred from one structural element to the next and how a structural system performs as a whole depend to a great extent on the types of joints and connections used. Structural elements can be joined to each other in three ways.

- Butt joints allow one of the elements to be continuous and usually require a third mediating element to make the connection.
- Overlapping joints allow all of the connected elements to bypass each other and be continuous across the joint.
- The joining elements can also be molded or shaped to form a structural connection.

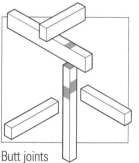
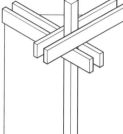
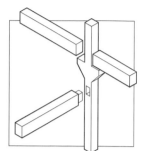

Butt joints      Overlapping joints      Shaped joints

We can also categorize structural connections on a geometric basis.

- Point: bolted connections
- Line: welded connections
- Plane: glued connections

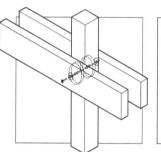
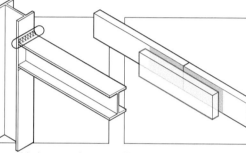

Point: bolted connections      Line: welded connections      Plane: glued connections

There are four fundamental types of structural connections.

- Pin or hinge joints allow rotation but resist translation in any direction.
- Roller joints or supports allow rotation but resist translation in a direction perpendicular into or away from its face.
- Rigid or fixed joints maintain the angular relationship between the joined elements, restrain rotation and translation in any direction, and provide both force and moment resistance.
- Cable supports or anchorages allow rotation but resist translation only in the direction of the cable.

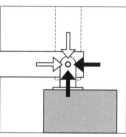
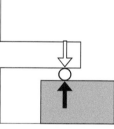
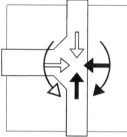

Pin joints      Roller joints      Rigid joints

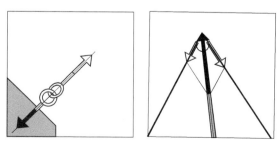

Cable anchorages and supports

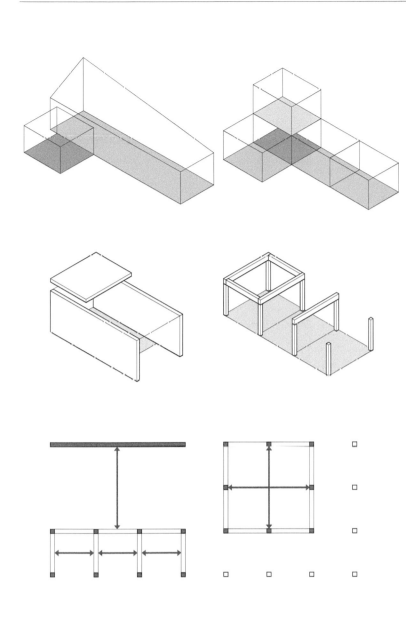

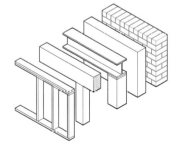

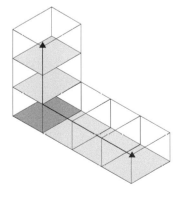

In the design process, we tend to think first of the larger holistic pattern before we consider the elemental structural units that make up the larger whole. So as we strategize to develop a structural plan for a building, we should consider both the essential qualities of the architectural composition and the nature and configuration of the structural elements. This leads to a series of fundamental questions:

### Building Design
- Is there an overarching form required or does the architectural composition consist of articulated parts? If so, are these parts to be hierarchically ordered?
- Are the principal architectural elements planar or linear in nature?

### Building Program
- Are there required relationships between the desirable scale and proportion of the program spaces, the spanning capability of the structural system, and the resulting layout and spacing of supports?
- Is there a compelling spatial reason for one-way or two-way spanning systems?

### Systems Integration
- How might the mechanical and other building systems be integrated with the structural system?

### Code Requirements
- What are the building code requirements for the intended use, occupancy, and scale of building?
- What is the type of construction and what are the structural materials required?

### Economic Feasibility
- How might material availability, fabrication processes, transportation requirements, labor and equipment requirements, and erection time influence the choice of a structural system?

- Is there a need to allow for expansion and growth either horizontally or vertically?

# STRUCTURAL PLANNING

## Legal Constraints

There exists a regulated relationship between the size (height and area) of a building and its intended use, occupancy load, and type of construction. Understanding the projected scale of a building is important because a building's size is related to the type of structural system required and the materials that may be employed for its structure and construction.

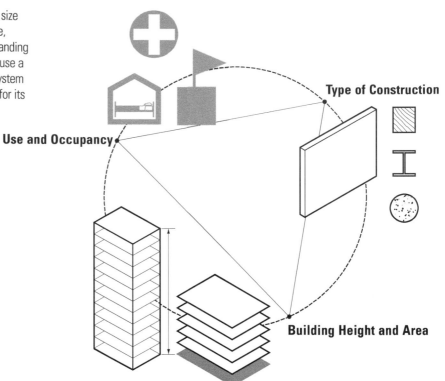

**Type of Construction**

**Use and Occupancy**

**Building Height and Area**

## Zoning Ordinances

Zoning ordinances constrain the allowable bulk (height and area) and shape of a building based on its location in a municipality and position on its site, usually by specifying various aspects of its size.

- How much of the land can be covered by a building structure and the total floor area that may be constructed can be expressed as percentages of the lot area.
- The maximum width and depth a building may have can be expressed as percentages of the dimensions of the site.
- Zoning ordinances can also specify how tall the building structure can be for a particular area in order to provide for adequate light, air, and space, and to enhance the streetscape and pedestrian environment.

The size and shape of a building are also controlled indirectly by specifying the minimum required distances from the structure to the property lines of the site in order to provide for air, light, solar access, and privacy.

- Property lines
- Required front, side, and rear setbacks

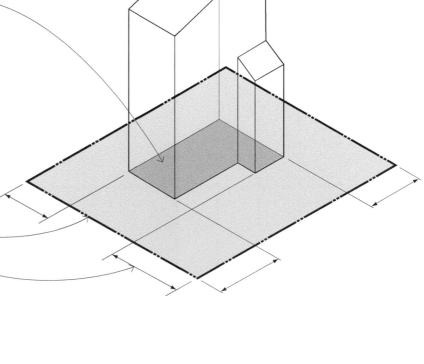

Building codes specify the fire-resistance ratings of materials and construction required for a building, depending on its location, use and occupancy, and height and area per floor.

## Building Height and Area

In addition to zoning ordinances that may limit the use and the overall floor area, height, and bulk of a building, building codes, such as the International Building Code® (IBC), limit the maximum height and area per floor of a building according to construction type and occupancy group, expressing the intrinsic relationship between degree of fire resistance, size of a building, and nature of an occupancy. The larger a building, the greater the number of occupants, and the more hazardous the occupancy, the more fire-resistant the structure should be. The intent is to protect a building from fire and to contain a fire for the time required to safely evacuate occupants and for a firefighting response to occur. The limitation on size may be exceeded if the building is equipped with an automatic fire sprinkler system, or if it is divided by fire walls into areas not exceeding the size limitation.

## Occupancy Classifications

A Assembly
  Auditoriums, theaters, and stadiums
B Business
  Offices, laboratories, and higher education facilities
E Educational
  Child-care facilities and schools through the 12th grade
F Factory and Industrial
  Fabricating, assembling, or manufacturing facilities
H High Hazard
  Facilities handling a certain nature and quantity of hazardous materials
I Institutional
  Facilities for supervised occupants, such as hospitals, nursing homes, and reformatories
M Mercantile
  Stores for the display and sale of merchandise
R Residential
  Homes, apartment buildings, and hotels
S Storage
  Warehousing facilities

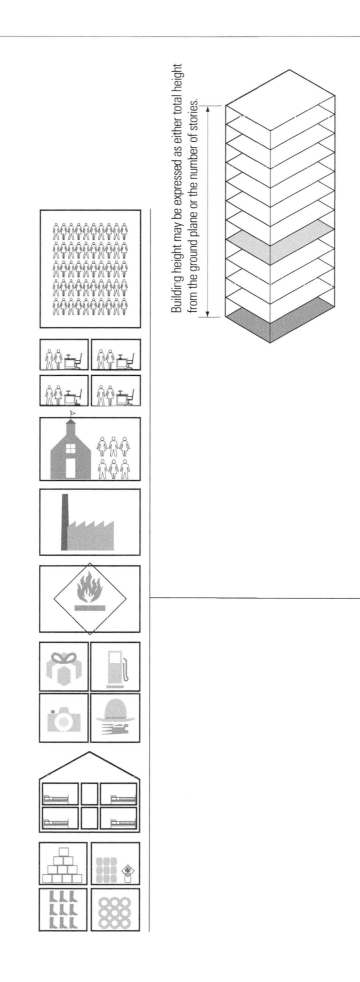

Building height may be expressed as either total height from the ground plane or the number of stories.

# STRUCTURAL PLANNING

## Maximum Height and Area

In IBC Table 503, the allowable height and area of a building are determined by the intersection of occupancy group and construction type. As occupancy is usually determined before heights and areas, the table will typically be entered by reading down the list of occupancy groups to find the occupancy that fits the building design. Reading across leads to the allowable heights and building areas based on types of construction.

Note that the distinction between A and B categories of construction types is one of level of fire resistance. Because category A is of higher fire resistance, Type A buildings of any construction type have higher allowable heights and areas than Type B buildings. Using the principle of classifying occupancies by degree of hazard and building types by fire-resistance, the higher the level of fire and life safety, the larger and taller a building can be.

Heights are expressed in two ways. The first is height in feet above the grade plane and is generally independent of occupancy, but tied to fire-resistance; the second is height in stories and is tied to occupancy. Both sets of criteria apply to each analysis. This is to avoid having high floor-to-floor heights between stories that could generate a building exceeding the height limit in feet above grade plane if heights were not also tabulated.

The illustrations on the facing page show the relationship of occupancy and construction type to allowable heights and building areas. The examples highlight the differences as one proceeds from Type I fire-protected construction to Type V unrated construction.

## IBC Table 503

### Construction Type

Most fire-resistive·················>Least fire-resistive

| Type I | Type II | Type III | Type IV | Type V |
|---|---|---|---|---|
| A  B | A  B | A  B | HT | A  B |

Height in feet above Grade Plane (Building Height) <···············> (55)

### Group (Occupancy)

- A (Assembly)
- B (Business)
- E (Educational)·············>
- F (Factory)
- H (Hazardous)
- I (Institutional)
- M (Mercantile)
- R (Residential)
- S (Storage)
- U (Utility)

2 Stories
14,500 sf (1347 m²)
of floor area per story

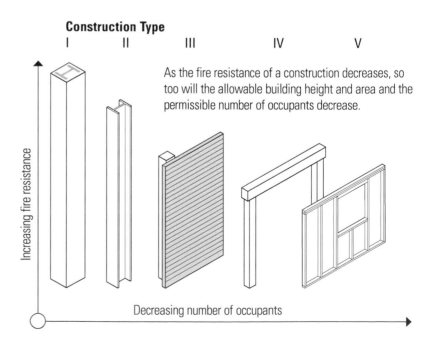

### Construction Type

| I | II | III | IV | V |

As the fire resistance of a construction decreases, so too will the allowable building height and area and the permissible number of occupants decrease.

*Increasing fire resistance*

*Decreasing number of occupants*

**Excerpt from IBC Table 503** (Showing allowable building height, number of stories and proportionate floor areas per story)

| Construction Type<br>From IBC Table 601 | Type I<br>A<br>Fire-Rated | Type II<br>A<br>Fire-Rated | Type III<br>B<br>Partially Rated | Type IV<br>Heavy<br>Timber | Type V<br>B<br>Nonrated |
|---|---|---|---|---|---|
| **Occupancy** | | | | | |
| A-2<br>(Restaurant) | UL/UL/UL | 65/3/15,500 sf<br>19.8 m/3/(1440 m$^2$) | 55/2/9500 sf<br>16.8 m/2/(883 m$^2$) | 65/3/15,000 sf<br>19.8 m/3/(1394 m$^2$) | 40/1/6000 sf<br>12.2 m/1/(557 m$^2$) |
| B<br>(Business) | UL/UL/UL | 65/5/37,500 sf<br>19.8 m/5/(3484 m$^2$) | 55/4/19,000 sf<br>16.8 m/4/(1765 m$^2$) | 65/5/36,000 sf<br>19.8 m/5/(3344 m$^2$) | 40/2/9000 sf<br>12.2 m/2/(836 m$^2$) |
| M<br>(Retail) | UL/UL/UL | 65/4/21,500 sf<br>19.8 m/4/(1997 m$^2$) | 55/4/12,500 sf<br>16.8 m/4/(1161 m$^2$) | 65/4/20,500 sf<br>19.8 m/4/(1904 m$^2$) | 40/1/9000 sf<br>12.2 m/1/(836 m$^2$) |
| R-2<br>(Apartment) | UL/UL/UL | 65/4/24,000 sf<br>19.8 m/4/(2230 m$^2$) | 55/4/16,000 sf<br>16.8 m/4/(1486 m$^2$) | 65/4/20,500 sf<br>19.8 m/4/(1904 m$^2$) | 40/2/7000 sf<br>12.2 m/2/(650 m$^2$) |

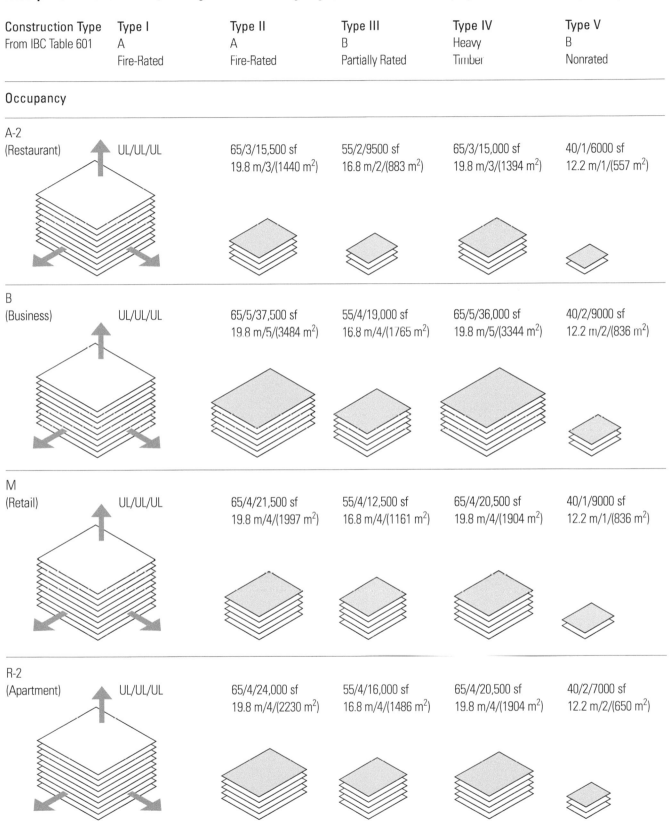

### Types of Construction
The IBC classifies the construction of a building according to the fire resistance of its major elements:

Structural frame •

Exterior and interior bearing walls •

Nonbearing walls and partitions •

Floor and roof assemblies •

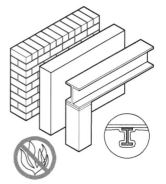

- **Type I** buildings have their major building elements constructed of noncombustible materials, such as concrete, masonry, or steel. Some combustible materials are allowed if they are ancillary to the primary structure of the building.
- **Type II** buildings are similar to Type I buildings except for a reduction in the required fire-resistance ratings of the major building elements.
- **Type III** buildings have noncombustible exterior walls and major interior elements of any material permitted by the code.
- **Type IV** buildings (Heavy Timber, HT) have noncombustible exterior walls and major interior elements of solid or laminated wood of specified minimum sizes and without concealed spaces.
- **Type V** buildings have structural elements, exterior walls, and interior walls of any material permitted by the code.

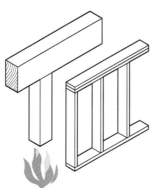

Noncombustible construction        Combustible construction

- Protected construction requires all major building elements, except for nonbearing interior walls and partitions, to be of one-hour fire-resistive construction.
- Unprotected construction has no requirements for fire-resistance except for when the code requires protection of exterior walls due their proximity to a property line.

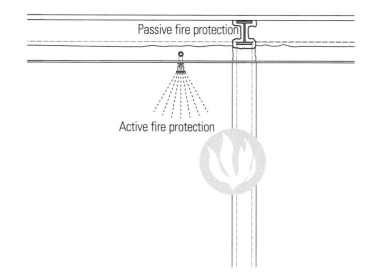

Passive fire protection

Active fire protection

## Required Fire-Resistance Ratings in Hours (Based on IBC Table 601)

| Construction Type | Type I | | Type II | | Type III | | Type IV | Type V | |
| --- | --- | --- | --- | --- | --- | --- | --- | --- | --- |
| | A | B | A | B | A | B | HT | A | B |
| **Building Element** | | | | | | | | | |
| Structural Frame | 3 | 2 | 1 | 0 | 1 | 0 | 2 | 1 | 0 |
| Bearing Walls | | | | | | | | | |
| Exterior | 3 | 2 | 1 | 0 | 2 | 2 | 2 | 1 | 0 |
| Interior | 3 | 2 | 1 | 0 | 1 | 0 | 1/HT | 1 | 0 |
| Nonbearing Walls | | | | | | | | | |
| Exterior | The fire-resistive requirements for nonbearing exterior walls are based on their fire-separation distance from an interior lot line, centerline of a street, or an imaginary line between two buildings on the same property. | | | | | | | | |
| Interior | 0 | 0 | 0 | 0 | 0 | 0 | 1/HT | 0 | 0 |
| Floor Construction | 2 | 2 | 1 | 0 | 1 | 0 | HT | 1 | 0 |
| Roof Construction | 1$^1$/$_2$ | 1 | 1 | 0 | 1 | 0 | HT | 1 | 0 |

Fire-resistance ratings are based on the performance of various materials and construction assemblies under fire-test conditions as defined by the American Society for Testing and Materials (ASTM). However, the building code allows designers to use several alternate methods to demonstrate compliance with fire-resistive criteria. One method allows the use of ratings determined by such recognized agencies as Underwriters Laboratory or Factory Mutual. The International Building Code itself contains a listing of prescriptive assemblies, which describe the protective measures that can be applied to structural members, to floor and roof construction, and to walls to achieve the necessary ratings.

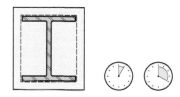

- Steel column protected by cast-in-place lightweight concrete with spirally wound wire tie reinforcement
- 1 to 4 hour rating

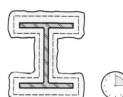

- Steel column protected by perlite or vermiculite gypsum plaster over metal lath
- 3 to 4 hour rating

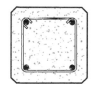

- Reinforced-concrete column with lightweight aggregate
- 1 to 4 hour rating

In planning any structural system, there are two attributes that should be built into the design, guide its development, and ensure its stability, durability, and efficiency. These attributes—redundancy and continuity—apply not to a specific material or to an individual type of structural member, such as a beam, column, or truss, but rather to a building structure viewed as a holistic system of interrelated parts.

The failure of a building structure can result from any fracturing, buckling, or plastic deformation that renders a structural assembly, element, or joint incapable of sustaining the load-carrying function for which it was designed. To avoid failure, structural designs typically employ a factor of safety, expressed as the ratio of the maximum stress that a structural member can withstand to the maximum stress allowed for it in the use for which it is designed.

Under normal conditions, any structural element experiences elastic deformation—deflection or torsion—as a force is applied and as it returns to its original shape when the force is removed. However, extreme forces, such as those generated during an earthquake, can generate inelastic deformation in which the element is unable to return to its original shape. To resist such extreme forces, elements should be constructed of ductile materials.

Ductility is the property of a material that enables it to undergo plastic deformation after being stressed beyond the elastic limit and before rupturing. Ductility is a desirable property of a structural material, since plastic behavior is an indicator of reserve strength and can often serve as a visual warning of impending failure. Further, the ductility of a structural member allows excessive loads to be distributed to other members, or to other parts of the same member.

### Redundancy

In addition to using factors of safety and employing ductile materials, another method for guarding against structural failure is to build redundancy into the structural design. A redundant structure includes members, connections, or supports not required for a statically determinate structure so that if one member, connection, or support fails, others exist to provide alternative paths for the transfer of forces. In other words, the concept of redundancy involves providing multiple load paths whereby forces can bypass a point of structural distress or a localized structural failure.

Redundancy, especially in the lateral-force-resisting systems of a structure, is highly desirable in earthquake-prone regions. It is also an essential attribute of long-span structures in which the failure of a primary truss, arch, or girder could lead to a large portion of the structure failing or even to its total collapse.

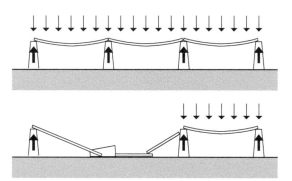

• Simple beams supported at their ends are determinate structures; their support reactions are easily determined through the use of the equations of equilibrium.

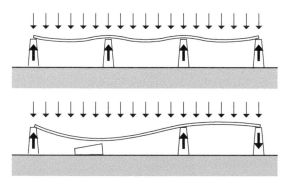

• If the same beam is continuous over four columns along its length, the structural assembly is indeterminate because there are more support reactions than the applicable equations of equilibrium. In effect, the continuity of the beam across multiple supports results in redundant paths for vertical and lateral loads to follow to the support foundations.

Extending structural redundancy to an entire structural system provides protection against progressive collapse of the structure. Progressive collapse can be described as the spread of an initial local failure from one structural member to another, eventually resulting in the collapse of an entire structure or a disproportionately large part of it. This is a major concern because progressive collapse can result in significant structural damage and loss of life.

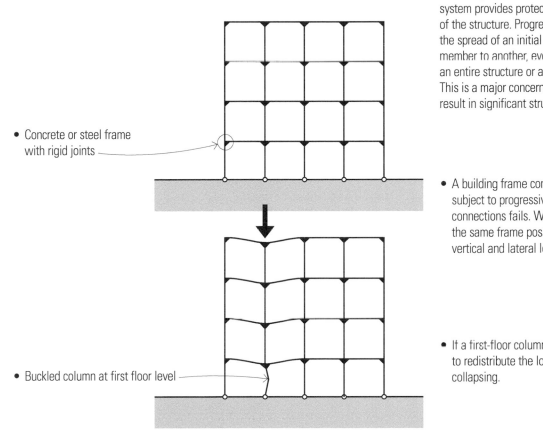

- Concrete or steel frame with rigid joints

- A building frame connected with simple joints is subject to progressive collapse if one of its members or connections fails. With rigid beam-column connections, the same frame possesses ample load paths for both vertical and lateral loads.

- Buckled column at first floor level

- If a first-floor column were to fail, the rigid frame is able to redistribute the loads throughout the frame without collapsing.

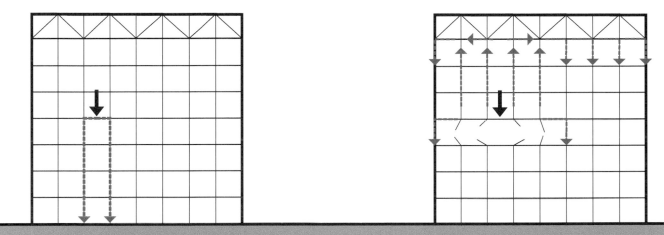

- Vertical loads are normally received by a beam that redirects the load through bending to adjacent columns. The columns, in turn, transfer the loads in a continuous path down to the foundation.

- If columns at a particular story level are damaged or destroyed, the vertical loads are redirected by columns above to a major roof truss or girder. The truss or girder redistributes the loads to columns that are still functional. Redundancy in the overall building structure provides alternate load paths and helps prevent progressive collapse.

## Continuity

Continuity in a structure provides a direct, uninterrupted path for loads through a building's structure, from the roof level down to the foundation. Continuous load paths help to ensure that all forces to which the structure is subjected can be delivered from the point of their application to the foundation. All elements and connections along a load path must have sufficient strength, stiffness, and deformation capability to transfer loads without compromising the building structure's ability to perform as a unit.

- To prevent progressive collapse, structural members and assemblies should be adequately tied together so that forces and displacements can be transferred between vertical and horizontal elements of the structure.
- Strong connections increase the overall strength and stiffness of a structure by enabling all of the building elements to act together as a unit. Inadequate connections represent a weak link in a load path and are a common cause of the damage to and collapse of buildings during earthquakes.
- Rigid, non-structural elements should be isolated properly from the main structure to prevent attracting loads that can cause damage to the non-structural members and, in the process, create unintended load paths that can damage structural elements.

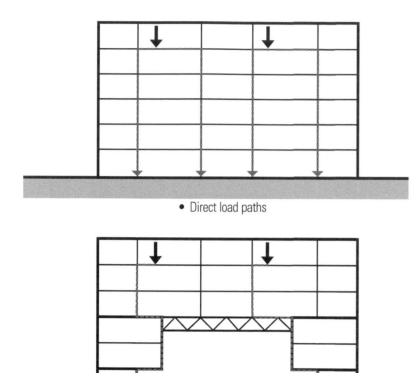

- Direct load paths

- Circuitous load paths

- Load paths through a building's structure should be as direct as possible; offsets should be avoided.
- Disrupting the vertical alignment of columns and bearing walls on successive floors cause vertical loads to be diverted horizontally, inducing large bending stresses on the supporting beam, girder, or truss below and requiring deeper members.

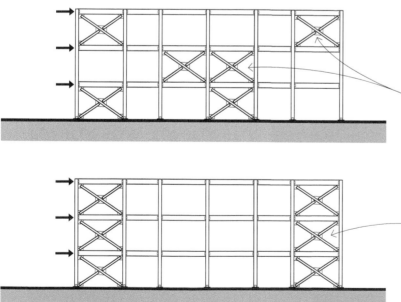

- Lateral forces from the roof are resisted by the diagonal braces at the 3rd floor level. The bracing transmits the lateral forces to the 3rd floor diaphragm, which in turn loads the 2nd floor bracing. Lateral forces collected at the 2nd floor are then transmitted through the 2nd floor diaphragm to the diagonal bracing at the ground floor level. The load path is circuitous because of the vertical discontinuity of the diagonal bracing.
- When the vertical bracing system is arranged in a continuous fashion, in this case as a vertical truss, the loads have a very direct path to the foundation.

# 2
# Structural Patterns

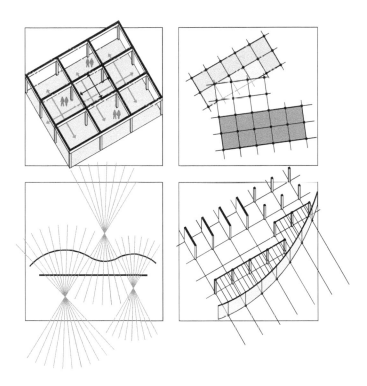

# STRUCTURAL PATTERNS

Critical to thinking about an architectural idea and developing its potential is understanding how it might be structured. The spatial and formal essence of an architectural scheme and the structuring of the idea go hand in hand; each informs the other. To illustrate this symbiotic relationship, this chapter describes the development of structural patterns and how they influence the formal composition and spatial layout embedded in an architectural idea.

This chapter begins with both regular and irregular grid patterns, and then discusses transitional and contextual patterns.

- Structural patterns: patterns of supports, spanning systems, and lateral-force-resisting elements
- Spatial patterns: spatial compositions inferred by the choice of a structural system
- Contextual patterns: arrangements or conditions dictated by the nature and context of a site

Structural patterns can be seen as a two-dimensional layout of supports and spans, as well as three-dimensional arrangements having formal and spatial implications for an architectural design.

Analysis based on the Museum of Modern Art, Gunma Prefecture, Japan, 1971–1974, Arata Isozaki

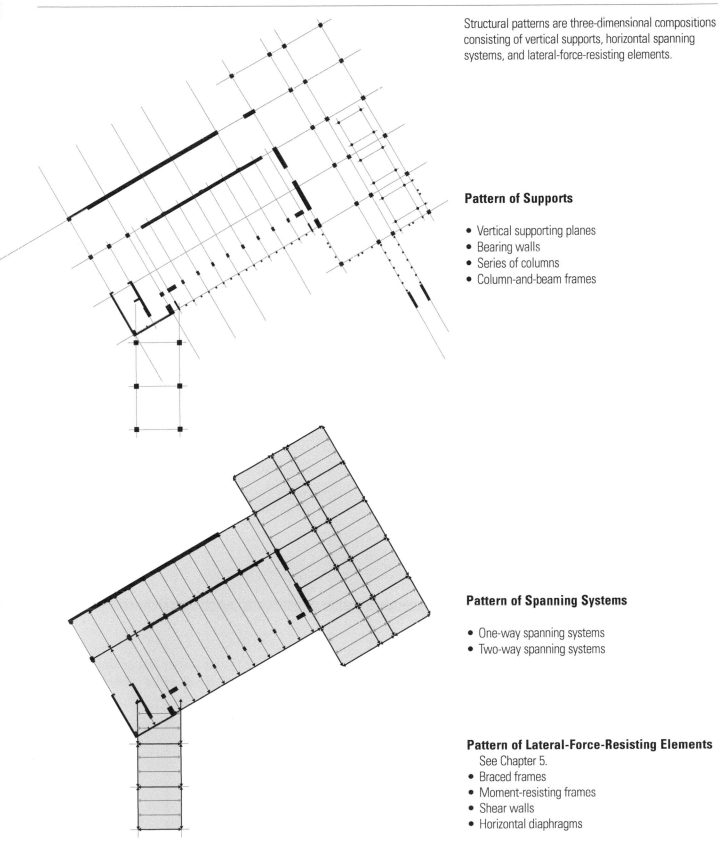

Structural patterns are three-dimensional compositions consisting of vertical supports, horizontal spanning systems, and lateral-force-resisting elements.

### Pattern of Supports

- Vertical supporting planes
- Bearing walls
- Series of columns
- Column-and-beam frames

### Pattern of Spanning Systems

- One-way spanning systems
- Two-way spanning systems

### Pattern of Lateral-Force-Resisting Elements
See Chapter 5.
- Braced frames
- Moment-resisting frames
- Shear walls
- Horizontal diaphragms

### Structural Units

A structural unit is a discrete assembly of structural members capable of forming or marking the boundaries of a single spatial volume. There are several fundamental ways to define a single volume of space.

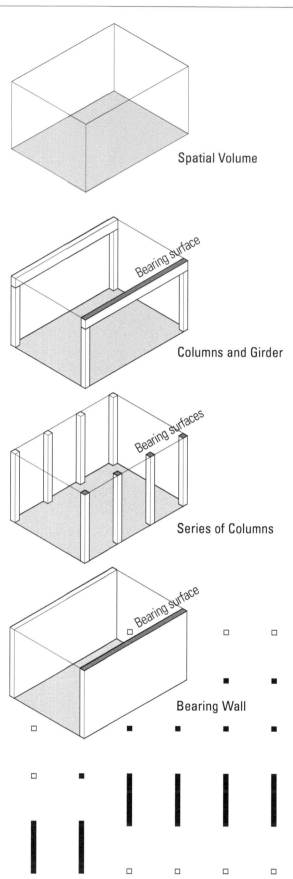

Spatial Volume

Bearing surface

Columns and Girder

Bearing surfaces

Series of Columns

Bearing surface

Bearing Wall

### Support Options

Two columns supporting a beam or girder create an open framework that both separates and unites adjacent spaces. Any enclosure for physical shelter and visual privacy requires the erection of a nonbearing wall, which can either be supported by the structural frame or be self-supporting.

Columns support concentrated loads. As the number of columns increases and the column spacing decreases, the supporting plane becomes more solid than void and approaches the character of a bearing wall, which support distributed loads.

A bearing wall provides support as well as divides a field into separate and distinct spaces. Any opening required to relate the spaces on either side of the wall tends to weaken its structural integrity.

Both column-and-beam frames and bearing walls can be used in combination to develop any number of spatial compositions.

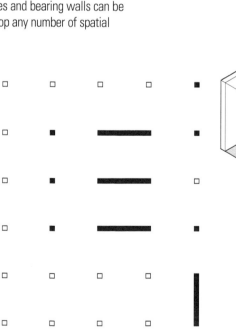

### Spanning Options

Creating a spatial volume requires a minimum of two vertically oriented support planes, be they column-and-beam frames, bearing walls, or a combination thereof. To provide shelter against the vagaries of weather as well as a sense of enclosure, some sort of spanning system is required to bridge the space between the support systems. In looking at the fundamental ways of spanning the space between two support planes, we must consider both the way applied forces are distributed to the supporting planes as well as the form of the spanning system.

### One-Way Spanning Systems

Whether the spanning system transfers and distributes applied forces in one or two (or even multiple) directions will determine the pattern of supports required. As the name implies, one-way systems transfer applied forces to a pair of more or less parallel supporting planes. This configuration naturally leaves two sides of the spatial unit open to adjacent spaces, giving it a strong directional quality.

### Two-Way Spanning Systems

On the other hand, two-way systems transfer applied forces in two directions, requiring two sets of supporting planes or columns, more or less perpendicular to each other and the direction of transfer of forces.

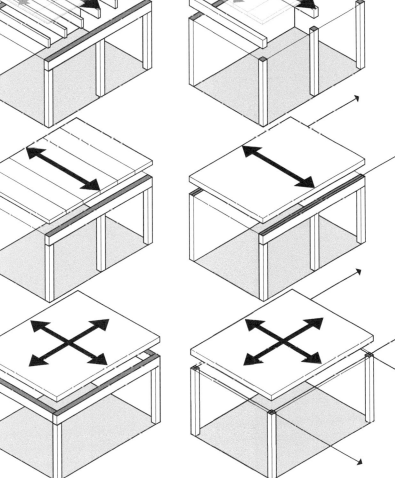

In determining whether to use one-way or two-way systems, consideration must be given to a number of variables:
- Dimensions, scale, and proportions of structural bay
- Structural materials employed
- Depth of construction assembly

For more detailed information, see Chapters 3 and 4.

## Assembling Structural Units

Because most buildings consist of more than a single, solitary space, the structural system must be able to accommodate a number of spaces of varying sizes, uses, relationships, and orientations. To do this, we assemble structural units into a larger holistic pattern that is necessarily related to how spaces are organized in a building and the nature of the building's form and composition.

Because continuity is always a desirable structural condition, it is usually sensible to extend structural units along major support lines and span directions to form a three-dimensional grid. If it is necessary to accommodate spaces of exceptional shape or size, a structural grid can be adapted by distorting, deforming, or enlarging certain bays. Even when a single structural unit or assembly encompasses all of a building's spaces, the spaces themselves must be structured and supported as units or compositional entities.

## Structural Grids

A grid is a pattern of straight lines, usually equally spaced and intersecting at right angles, that serves as a reference for locating points on a map or plan. In architectural design, a grid is often used as an ordering device not only for locating but also for regulating the major elements of a plan. When we speak of a structural grid, therefore, we are referring specifically to a system of lines and points for locating and regulating the position of major structural elements, such as columns and bearing walls.

- The parallel lines of a plan grid indicate the possible location and orientation of vertical supporting planes, which may consist of bearing walls, a frame, or a series of columns, or any combination thereof.

Support spacing = one-way spans

Bearing wall

Frame

Columns

Lines of support can be extended as required or desired.

- Because curved beams are subject to torsion, they are more efficient as straight members. To approximate a curved line of support, a series of columns should support a series of simply spanning beams. Bearing walls, however, can be curved in plan.

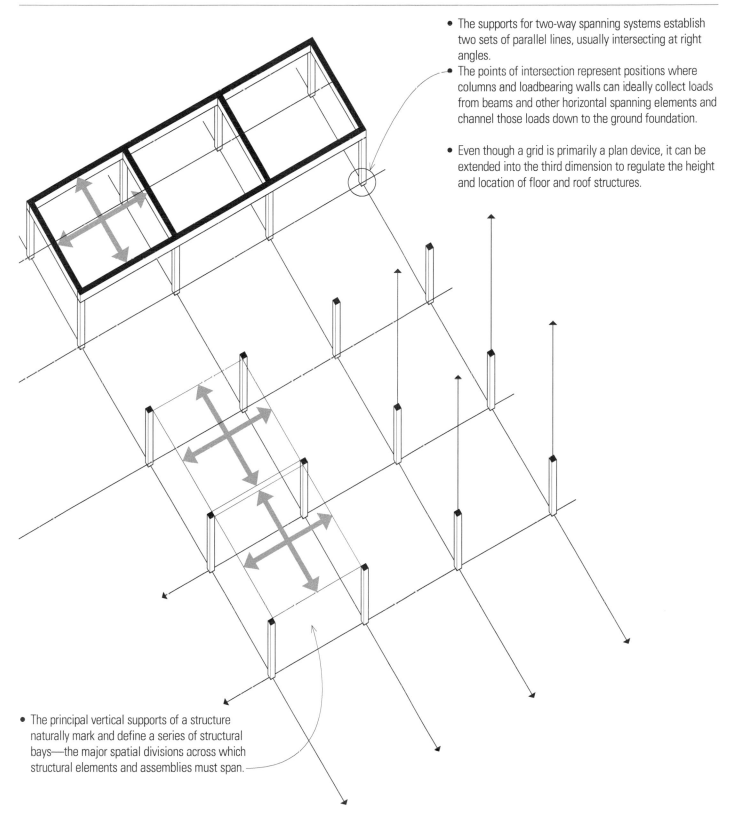

- The supports for two-way spanning systems establish two sets of parallel lines, usually intersecting at right angles.
- The points of intersection represent positions where columns and loadbearing walls can ideally collect loads from beams and other horizontal spanning elements and channel those loads down to the ground foundation.

- Even though a grid is primarily a plan device, it can be extended into the third dimension to regulate the height and location of floor and roof structures.

- The principal vertical supports of a structure naturally mark and define a series of structural bays—the major spatial divisions across which structural elements and assemblies must span.

# STRUCTURAL GRIDS

In developing a structural grid for a building concept, there are important grid characteristics that must be considered for their impact on the architectural idea, the accommodation of program activities, as well as the design of the structure.

## Proportions

The proportions of the structural bays influence, and may limit, the material and structural choices of the horizontal spanning systems. While one-way systems are flexible and can span in either direction of either square or rectangular structural bays, two-way systems are best used to span square or nearly square bays.

## Dimensions

The dimensions of the structural bays obviously impact both the direction and length of the horizontal spans.

- Direction of spans
  The direction of horizontal spans, as determined by the location and orientation of the vertical supporting planes, affects the nature of the spatial composition, the qualities of the spaces defined, and to some extent, the economics of construction.
- Span lengths
  The spacing of the vertical supporting planes determines the length of the horizontal spans, which, in turn, affects the choice of materials and the type of spanning system employed. The greater the span, the deeper the spanning system will have to be.

A bay is a major spatial division, usually one of a series, marked or partitioned off by the principal vertical supports of a structure.

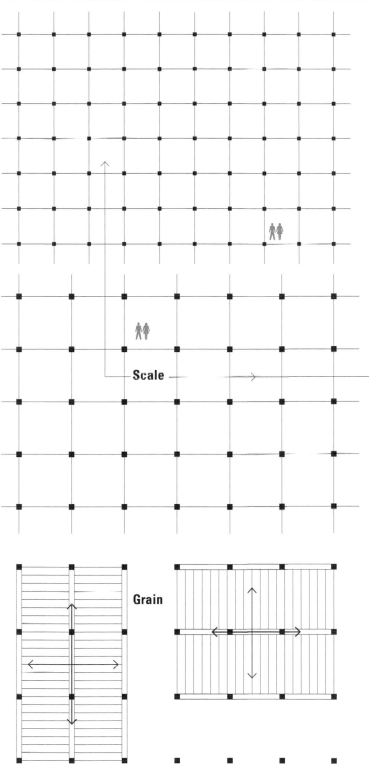

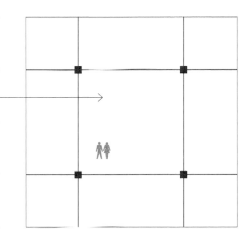

### Scale

In design, scale refers to the proportionate size or extent of an element or composition when judged in relation to some norm or standard. We use such terms as large-scale, small-scale, fine and coarse, to describe how we perceive or judge the relative sizes of things. In developing a structural grid, we can refer to its scale as well, judging the relative fineness or coarseness of the dimensions and proportions of the bays against what we might consider to be normal. The scale of a structural grid is related to:

• the type of human activity to be accommodated;
• the efficient span range for a particular spanning system; and
• the nature of the foundation soil of the building site.

Another aspect of scale is the relative sizes of the members used. Some structures can be seen to be concentrated in nature due to their use of relatively large members carrying concentrated loads. On the other hand, there are some structures that use a multiplicity of small members that distribute their loads among a large number of relatively small members.

A final attribute of some structural systems is its grain, as determined by the direction, size, and arrangement of its spanning elements.

# STRUCTURAL GRIDS

## Spatial Fit

The nature, pattern, and scale of vertical supports suggested by a structural grid not only influence the type of spanning system used but also the arrangement of vertical supports should accommodate the intended patterns and scale of human activity. At a minimum, the vertical support pattern should not limit the usefulness of a space nor constrain its intended activities.

Those activities requiring large clear spans will often dictate the structural approach, but smaller-scale activities can usually be accommodated by a variety of structural approaches. Illustrated on this and the facing page are various types and scales of structural patterns and the pattern and scale of human activity each might be able to accommodate.

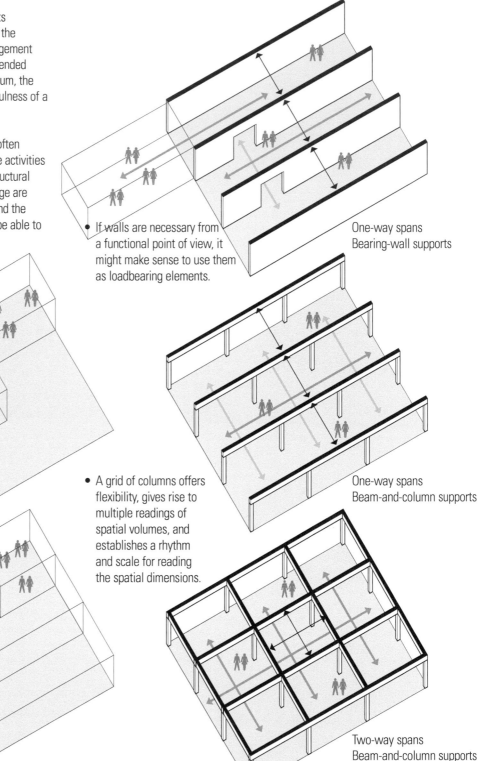

• If walls are necessary from a functional point of view, it might make sense to use them as loadbearing elements.

One-way spans
Bearing-wall supports

• A grid of columns offers flexibility, gives rise to multiple readings of spatial volumes, and establishes a rhythm and scale for reading the spatial dimensions.

One-way spans
Beam-and-column supports

Two-way spans
Beam-and-column supports

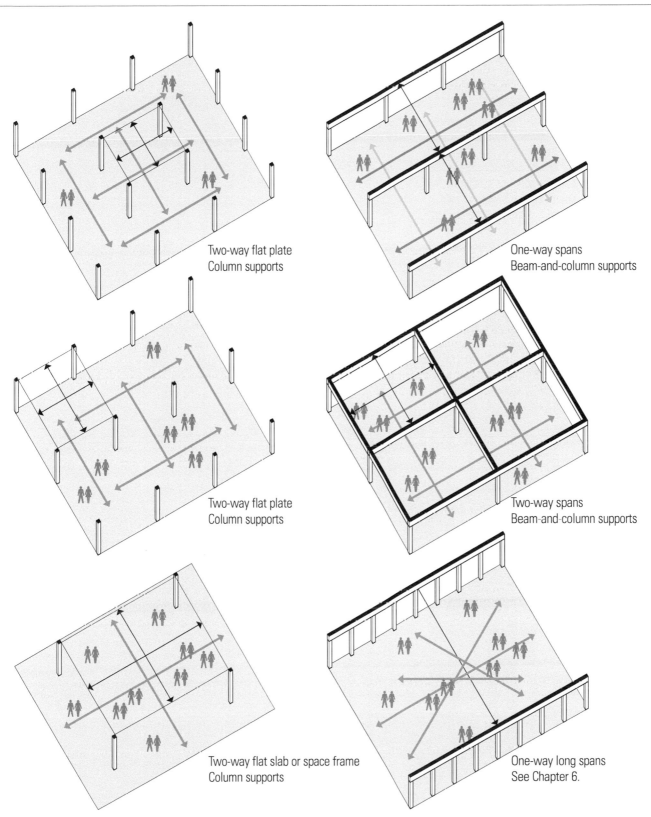

Two-way flat plate
Column supports

One-way spans
Beam-and-column supports

Two-way flat plate
Column supports

Two-way spans
Beam-and-column supports

Two-way flat slab or space frame
Column supports

One-way long spans
See Chapter 6.

# REGULAR GRIDS

Regular grids define equal spans, allow the use of repetitive structural elements, and offer the efficiency of structural continuity across a number of bays. While regular grids cannot be considered the norm, they do provide a useful way to begin thinking about the structural implications of various grid patterns.

## Square Grids

A single square bay can be spanned with either a one-way or two-way system. However, when multiple square bays extend across the field of a square grid, the structural advantage of continuity in two directions suggests the use of concrete two-way spanning systems is appropriate, particularly for small to medium span ranges.

It should be noted that while two-way structural action requires square or very nearly square bays, square bays do not always have to be spanned with two-way systems. For example, a linear arrangement of square bays allows continuity in only one direction, eliminating the structural advantage of two-way spanning systems and suggesting that one-way spanning systems may be more effective than two-way systems. Also, as a square bay grows beyond 60 feet (18 m), more one-way systems and fewer two-way systems become available.

• A single square bay can be spanned with either a one-way or two-way system.

• The bidirectional character of a square grid can be modified by the nature of the spanning and support systems. Bearing walls—and to a lesser extent, column-and-beam frames—can emphasize one axis over the other and suggest the use of a one-way spanning system.

• A linear arrangement of square bays allows continuity in only one direction, eliminating the structural advantage of two-way spanning systems and suggesting that one-way spanning systems may be more effective.

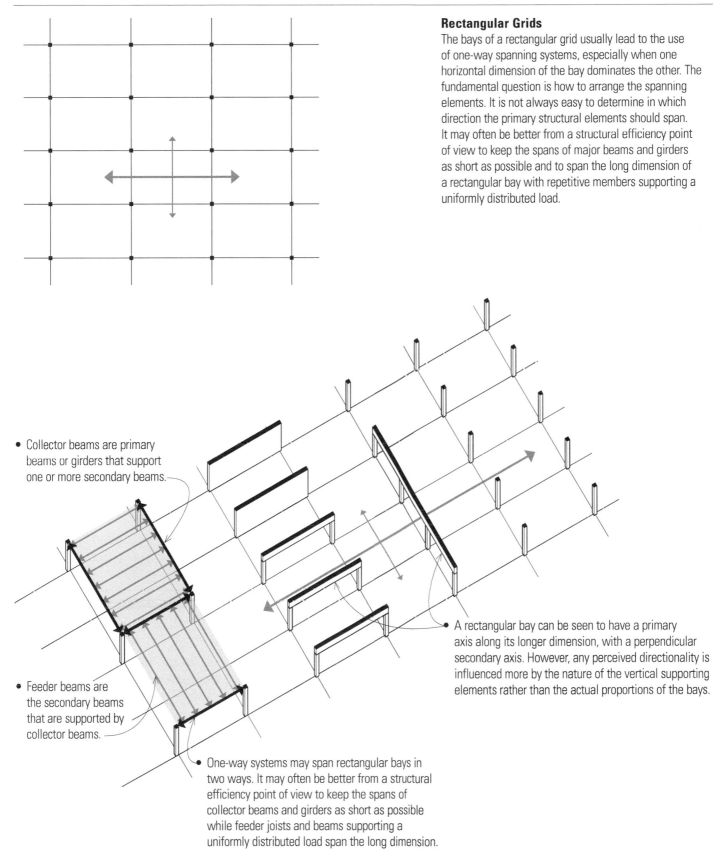

### Rectangular Grids

The bays of a rectangular grid usually lead to the use of one-way spanning systems, especially when one horizontal dimension of the bay dominates the other. The fundamental question is how to arrange the spanning elements. It is not always easy to determine in which direction the primary structural elements should span. It may often be better from a structural efficiency point of view to keep the spans of major beams and girders as short as possible and to span the long dimension of a rectangular bay with repetitive members supporting a uniformly distributed load.

- Collector beams are primary beams or girders that support one or more secondary beams.

- Feeder beams are the secondary beams that are supported by collector beams.

- A rectangular bay can be seen to have a primary axis along its longer dimension, with a perpendicular secondary axis. However, any perceived directionality is influenced more by the nature of the vertical supporting elements rather than the actual proportions of the bays.

- One-way systems may span rectangular bays in two ways. It may often be better from a structural efficiency point of view to keep the spans of collector beams and girders as short as possible while feeder joists and beams supporting a uniformly distributed load span the long dimension.

## Tartan Grids

Both square and rectangular grids may be modified in a number of ways to respond to programmatic needs or contextual requirements. One of these is to offset two parallel grids to produce a tartan or plaid pattern of supports. The resulting interstitial or intervening spaces can be used to mediate between larger spaces, define paths of movement, or house mechanical systems.

While the tartan grid illustrated here is based on the square, rectangular tartan grids are also feasible. In either case, the decision to use one-way or two-way spanning systems depends on the bay proportions, as discussed on page 46.

• Tartan grids provide multiple support points for both collector beams or girders and feeder beams or joists.

• The column clusters can be transformed into a pair of wall-like columns with a strong axis or a single, shaft-like structure.

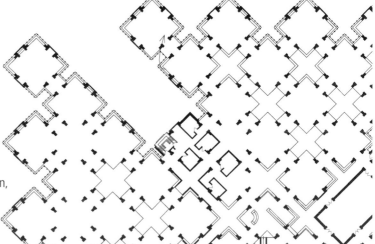

• Partial plan and section: Centraal Beheer Insurance Offices, Apeldoorn, Netherlands, 1967–1972, Herman Hertzberger

### Radial Grids

Radial grids consist of vertical supports arranged in a radial pattern about a real or implied center. The direction of span is influenced by the support spacing, measured both radially and circumferentially.

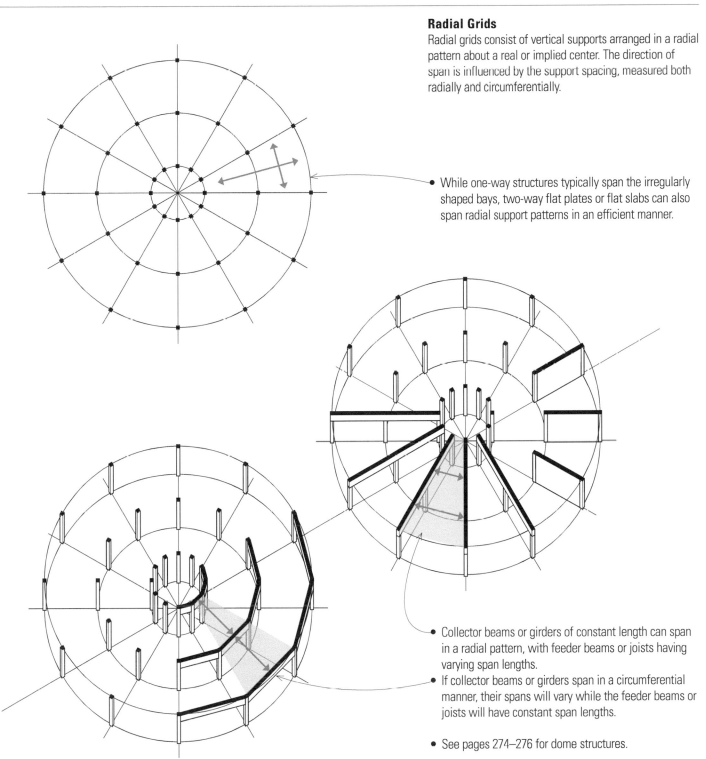

- While one-way structures typically span the irregularly shaped bays, two-way flat plates or flat slabs can also span radial support patterns in an efficient manner.

- Collector beams or girders of constant length can span in a radial pattern, with feeder beams or joists having varying span lengths.
- If collector beams or girders span in a circumferential manner, their spans will vary while the feeder beams or joists will have constant span lengths.

- See pages 274–276 for dome structures.

## Modifying Grids

Square, rectangular, and tartan grids are all regular in the sense that they consist of regularly recurring elements regulated by orthogonal spatial relationships. They are capable of growth in a predictable manner, and even if one or more elements is missing, the pattern of the whole remains recognizable. Even radial grids have recurring relationships defined by their circular geometry.

In architectural design, grids are powerful organizing devices. It should be noted, however, that regular grids are only generalized patterns that can be modified and made specific in response to circumstances of program, site, and materials. The objective is to develop a grid that integrates form, space, and structure into a cohesive whole.

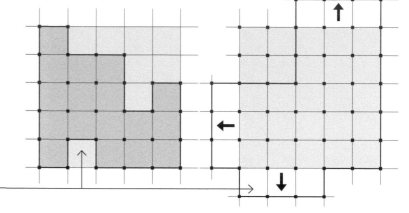

- **Modifying by Addition or Subtraction**
  A regular grid can be modified by selectively removing portions or extending structural bays in one or more directions.

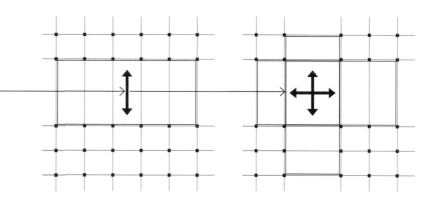

- **Modifying Scale and Proportions**
  A regular grid can be modified by enlarging the bay spans in one or two directions, creating a hierarchical set of modules differentiated by size and proportion.

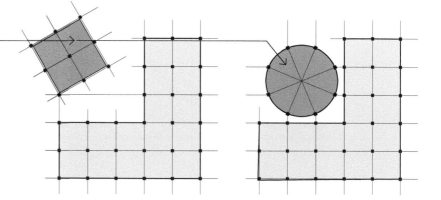

- **Modifying Geometry**
  A regular grid can be modified by incorporating another grid of contrasting orientation or geometry into the composition.

See the example of the Parliament Building by Le Corbusier illustrated on pages 14–15.

### Modifying by Addition or Subtraction

Regular grids can be extended horizontally and vertically to form new compositions of forms and spaces. Such additive compositions can be used to express growth, establish a linear sequence of spaces, or to collect a number of secondary spaces about a major or parent form.

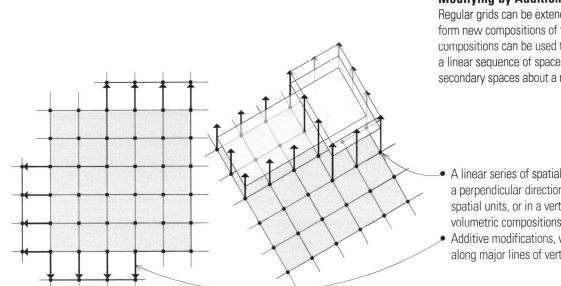

- A linear series of spatial units can be extended in a perpendicular direction to form a planar field of spatial units, or in a vertical direction to form planar or volumetric compositions.
- Additive modifications, whenever possible, should occur along major lines of vertical support and horizontal span.

Subtractive modifications result from the selective removal of a portion of a regular grid. This subtractive process may occur to create:

- A major space larger in scale than that established by the grid, such as a court or atrium, or
- A recessed entry space.

Path or site feature

- A portion of the regular grid can be removed to accommodate or address a unique feature of the site.
- For subtractive modifications, the regular grid should be large enough to encompass the building program and be recognizable as a whole from which parts have been removed.

### Modifying Proportions

To accommodate the specific dimensional requirements of spaces and functions, a grid can be made irregular in one or two directions, creating a hierarchical set of modules differentiated by size, scale, and proportion.

When the structural grid is irregular in only one direction, the collector beams or girders can span uneven bay lengths while the feeder beams or joists retain constant spans. In some cases, it might be more economical to have the collector beams or girders have equal spans while the feeder beams or joists have varying span lengths. In either case, the unequal spans will result in the spanning systems having different depths.

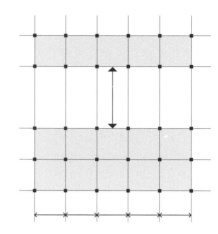
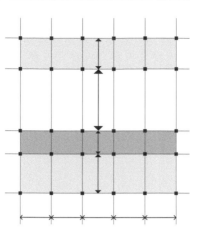

• An unequal grid spacing may result from a desired sectional profile or linear variations in program requirements.

• Equal grid spacing

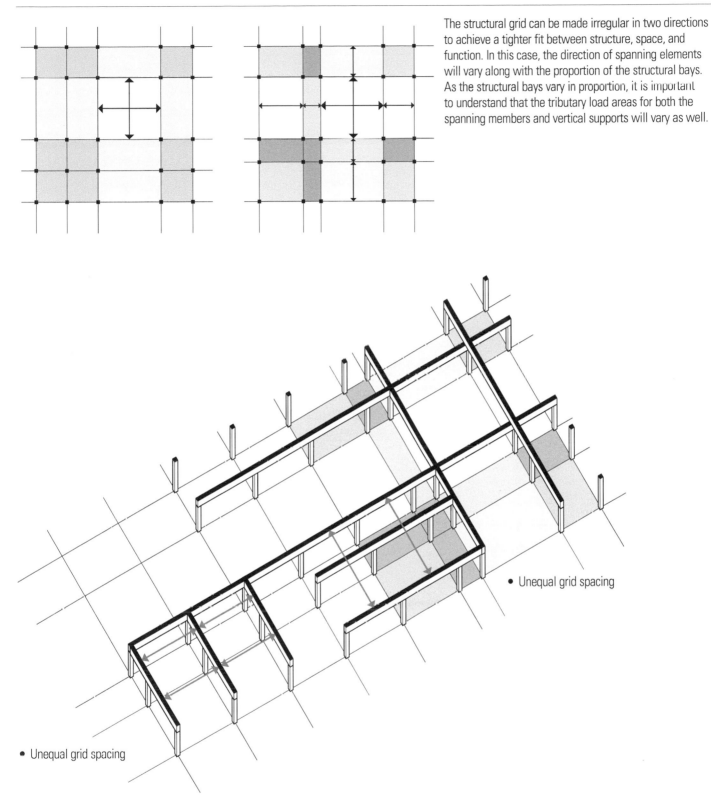

The structural grid can be made irregular in two directions to achieve a tighter fit between structure, space, and function. In this case, the direction of spanning elements will vary along with the proportion of the structural bays. As the structural bays vary in proportion, it is important to understand that the tributary load areas for both the spanning members and vertical supports will vary as well.

• Unequal grid spacing

• Unequal grid spacing

## Accommodating Large-Scale Spaces

When spaces are much larger in scale than those required for typical uses, such as for auditoriums and gymnasiums, they can disrupt the normal rhythm of a structural grid and the increased spans and resulting loads—both gravity and lateral—on vertical supports require special consideration.

Larger-than-normal spaces may be embedded in the structural grid, be separate but attached to the grid, or be large enough to encompass support functions into its volume. In the first two instances, it is usually best to have the vertical supports of the large-scale space be equal to or some multiple of the regular support grid. In this way, horizontal continuity can be maintained throughout the structure.

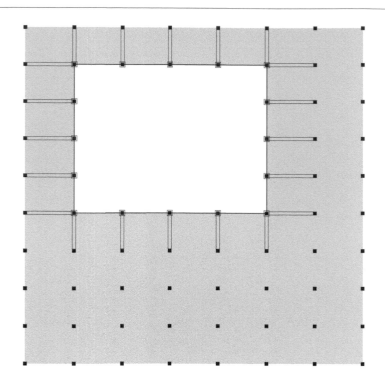

- A large-scale space that is embedded within a grid can be supported and buttressed by the structure of the surrounding spaces. If the grid of the large space does not align with that of the surrounding spaces, then some sort of transitional structure would be necessary to accommodate the shift.

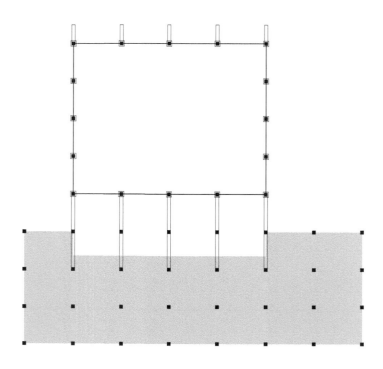

- The desired architectural expression may be that of a large-scale space that is separate from but connected to an adjacent structure. Articulating the large-scale space in this way can alleviate the difficulty that may arise when two different types of structural systems meet or when two structural grids are misaligned. In either case, a third structural system would be required to make the transition.

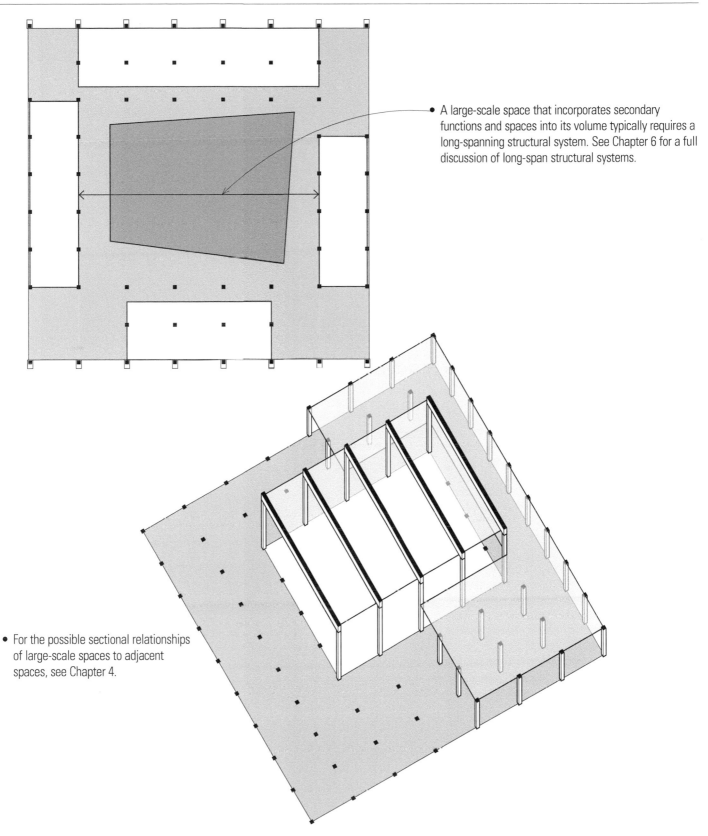

• A large-scale space that incorporates secondary functions and spaces into its volume typically requires a long-spanning structural system. See Chapter 6 for a full discussion of long-span structural systems.

• For the possible sectional relationships of large-scale spaces to adjacent spaces, see Chapter 4.

• See the example of the Parliament Building by Le Corbusier illustrated on pages 14–15.

## Contrasting Geometries

A regular grid can meet a grid of contrasting geometry to reflect differing requirements of interior space and exterior form or to express the importance of a form or space within its context. Whenever this occurs, there are three ways in which to handle the geometric contrast.

- The two contrasting geometries can be kept separate and be linked by a third structural system.

- The two contrasting geometries can overlap with either one dominating the other, or the two combining to form a third geometry.

- One of the two contrasting geometries can incorporate the other into its field.

The transitional or interstitial space formed by the intersection of two contrasting geometries can, if large or unique enough, begin to attain an importance or significance of its own.

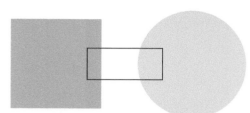

Contrasting geometries separated but connected by a third structure.

Contrasting geometries intersecting or overlapping.

One of two contrasting geometries encompassing the other.

In the latter two cases, the resulting irregular or nonuniform layout of vertical supports and varying span lengths makes it difficult to use repetitive or modular structural members. See pages 70–73 for transitional patterns to mediate between straight and curvilinear structures.

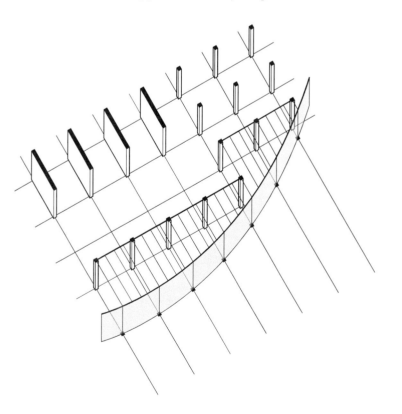

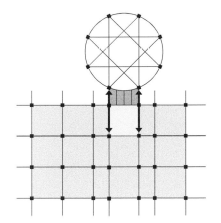

- Contrasting geometries separated but linked

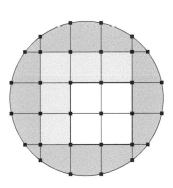

- Rectangular geometry within a circular geometry

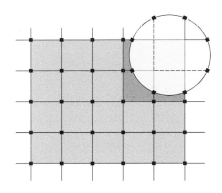

- Overlapping geometries

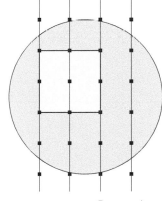

- Rectangular geometry within a circular geometry

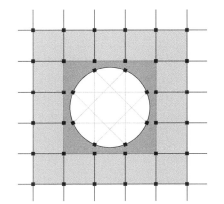

- Circular geometry embedded in a rectangular geometry

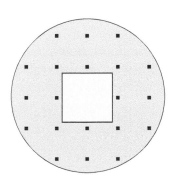

- Rectangular geometry embedded within a circular geometry

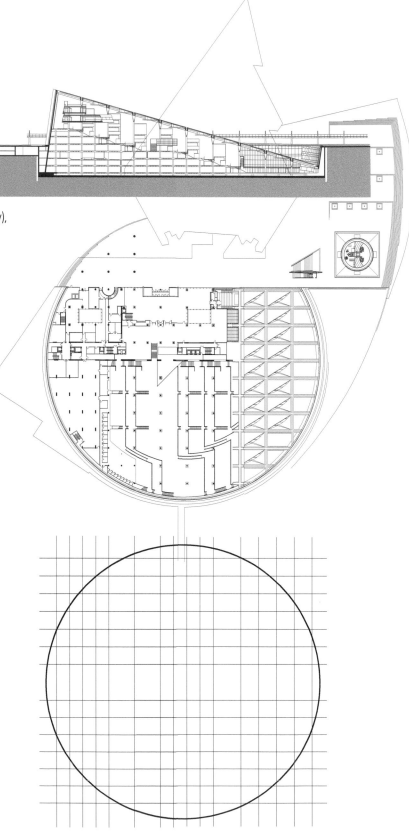

Plan and section: Bibliotheca Alexandrina (Alexandrian Library), Alexandria, Egypt, 1994–2002, Snøhetta

The examples on this and the facing page illustrate ways in which two contrasting geometries—the circular and the rectangular—can be related. The Bibliotheca Alexandrina exhibits a rectangular structural grid within a circular form. The Lister County Courthouse embraces the circular courtroom space partly within the boundaries of a rectangular form. The large, sheltered circular courtyard of the ESO Hotel is separate from but linked by a terrace to the linear block of accommodations.

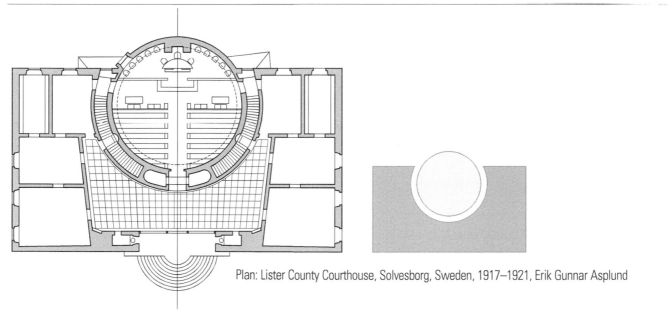

Plan: Lister County Courthouse, Solvesborg, Sweden, 1917–1921, Erik Gunnar Asplund

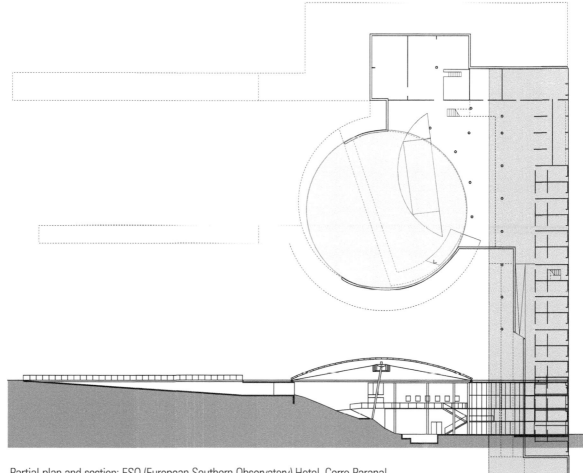

Partial plan and section: ESO (European Southern Observatory) Hotel, Cerro Paranal, Atacama Desert, Chile, 1999–2002, Auer + Weber Associates

## Contrasting Orientation

Just as two structural grids may have contrasting geometries, they also might have differing orientations to address unique features of a site, accommodate an existing pattern of movement, or express contrasting forms or functions within a single composition. And as in the case of contrasting geometries, there are three ways in which to resolve how the two grids that differ in orientation resolve into a single structure.

- The two grids can be kept separate and be linked by a third structural system.

- The two grids can overlap with either one dominating the other, or the two combining to form a third geometry.

- One of the two grids can incorporate the other into its field.

The transitional or interstitial space formed by the intersection of two geometries having contrasting orientations can, if large or unique enough, begin to attain an importance or significance of its own.

In the latter two cases, the resulting irregular or nonuniform layout of vertical supports and varying span lengths make it difficult to use repetitive or modular structural members. See the following page for transitional patterns to mediate between grids having differing orientations.

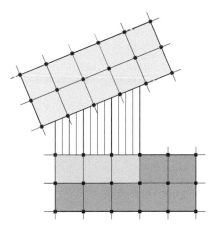

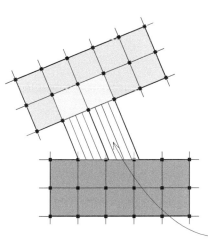

The transitional link between two geometric orientations may reflect either one of the orientations or neither of them. If the linking space conforms to one of the orientations, the contrasting orientation will tend to be emphasized.

• Contrasting orientations can lead to the linking space having unique spanning conditions.

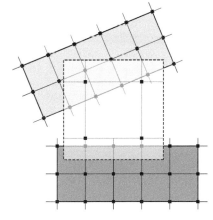

When two grids of contrasting orientation overlap, one will tend to dominate the other. The ascendency of one grid can be further emphasized by a change in vertical scale. Strong structural and architectural emphasis is placed on the exceptional spaces where one can experience both geometries.

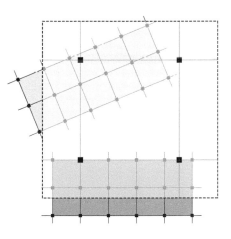

Another way of treating differing orientations is to unify both parts by gathering them under a third dominant structural form. Like the examples above, emphasis occurs at the exceptional condition of two different structural systems are juxtaposed.

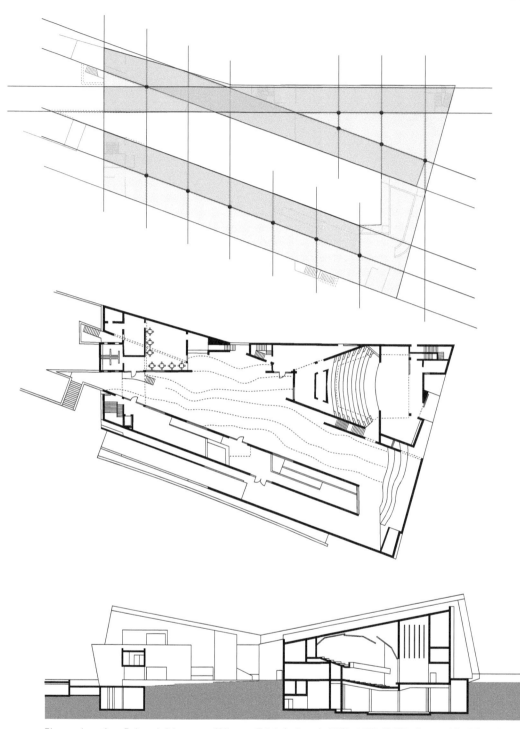

Plan and section: Palmach Museum of History, Tel Aviv, Israel, 1992–1999, Zvi Hecker and Rafi Segal

The examples on this and the previous page illustrate several ways in which contrasting orientations can be accommodated within a single composition.

The Palmach Museum of History consists of three parts, two of which are skewed to preserve an existing cluster of trees and rocks and define an irregularly shaped courtyard. The structure of the Lois & Richard Rosenthal Center for Contemporary Art is based on a regular rectilinear grid but the columns have the shape of parallelograms to reflect the skewed geometry of the full-height, skylit atrium space housing the vertical system of stairways. The Valley Center House uses the main living room as a transitional structure that rises above to visually link the contrasting orientations of two wings.

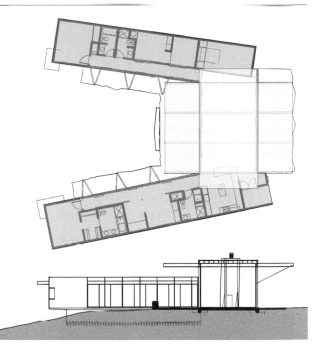

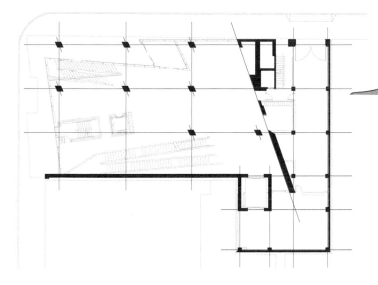

Plan and section: Valley Center House, San Diego County, California, 1999, Daly Genik Architects

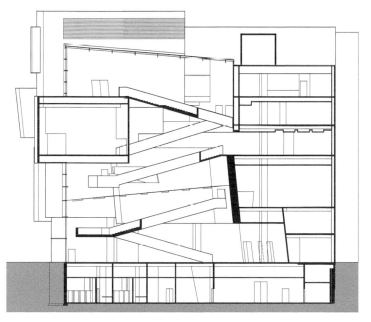

Plan and section: Lois & Richard Rosenthal Center for Contemporary Art, Cincinnati, Ohio, 2001–2003, Zaha Hadid Architects

## Accommodating Irregular Spaces

Design ideas are often generated not from the pattern of structural supports and spanning elements but rather from the desired ordering of program spaces and the formal qualities of the resulting composition. In a typical building program, there are usually requirements for various kinds of spaces. There may be requirements for spaces that are singular and unique in their function or significance to the building organization; others may be flexible in use and can be freely manipulated.

Discrete irregular spaces may be framed by the structure to conform with and reinforce the program requirements of the spatial volume.

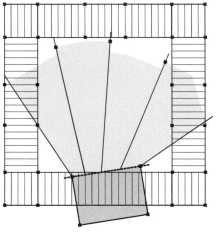

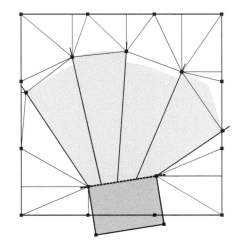

This usually involves working back and forth between a structural concept and the program requirements for the space, searching for an appropriate fit between the structural strategy and the vision for the formal, aesthetic and performance qualities of the resulting spatial environment.

A discrete irregular space may also be developed as an independent structure with a separate structural system and geometry superimposed over the building as a whole. Although appropriate to accommodate the spatial requirements of such spaces as theaters, concert halls, and large galleries, this strategy typically requires long-span spanning systems. For a discussion of long-span structures, see Chapter 6.

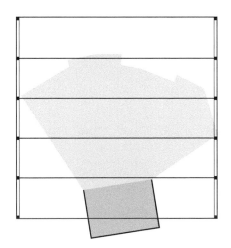

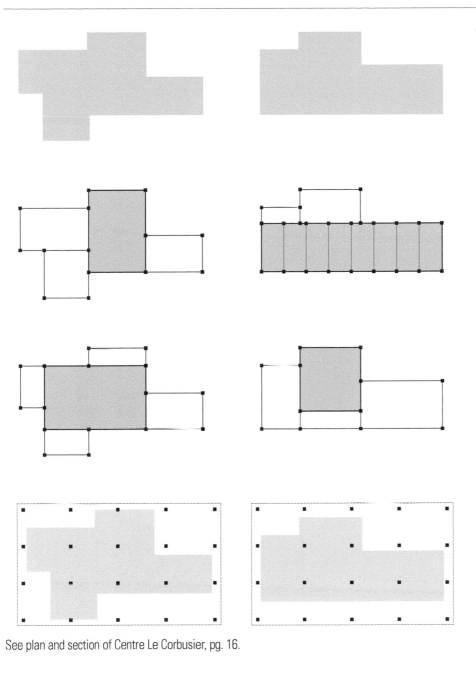

See plan and section of Centre Le Corbusier, pg. 16.

Plan diagrams: Mill Owners' Association Building, Ahmedabad, India, 1952–1954, Le Corbusier.

## Accommodating Irregular Shapes

It is advisable to try to recognize the inherent geometry embedded in irregular plan shapes when attempting to develop a strategy for its structural system. Even the most irregular of plan shapes can often be dissected into parts which can be seen to be transformations of regular geometric shapes.

The manner in which an irregular shape or form might be constructed will often suggest logical options for a framing strategy. This may be as simple as using the center of an arc for a radial framing system or framing parallel or perpendicular to a significant wall or plane within an irregular geometry. Curves, especially, possess a number of properties for establishing the basis for a framing strategy. One might use the radius or center of an arc, a point that is tangent to the arc, or in the case of double curvatures, the inflection point where a change in curvature occurs. The approach one takes will depend on the design intent and how the structural strategy might reinforce the concept.

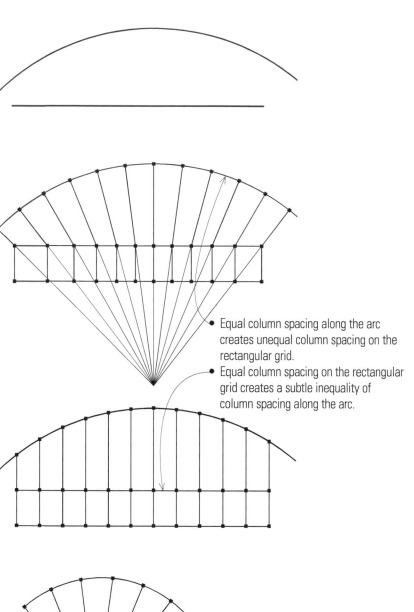

• Equal column spacing along the arc creates unequal column spacing on the rectangular grid.
• Equal column spacing on the rectangular grid creates a subtle inequality of column spacing along the arc.

Although structural framing systems are usually developed in plan, consideration should also be given to the effect of the structure on the vertical aspects of a building—its elevations and the scale of its interior spaces. If column locations will be expressed in the facade, for example, the visible effect of a regular column spacing on a curving exterior wall plane should be considered.

Part of the challenge of structuring irregular plan shapes is to minimize the structural inefficiency that often results from the inevitable variations in span lengths.

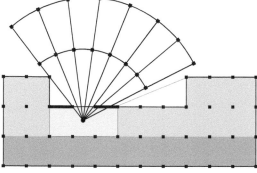

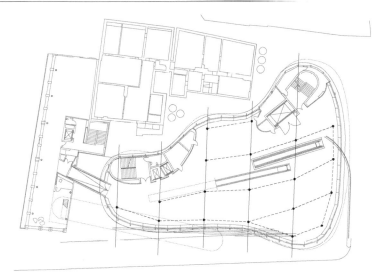

Plan and section: Kunsthaus, Graz, Austria, 1997–2003,
Peter Cook and Colin Fournier

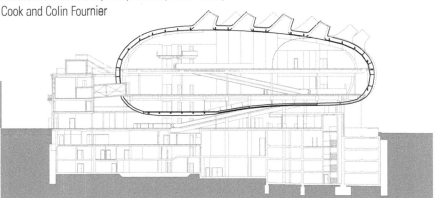

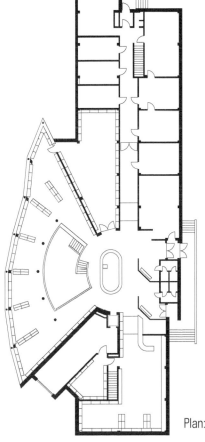

The examples on this page illustrate two ways in which irregular forms have been integrated into the rectilinear geometry of a composition. The bulbous form housing the exhibition spaces and related public facilities in the Kunsthaus is partly a response to an irregular site and the required fire-separation distance from existing adjacent buildings. It appears to float above the geometry of the structural grid that supports it.

The significance of the main reading room of the Seinajoki Library is expressed in both plan and section by its fan-like shape, which is anchored at the circulation desk to the rectilinear geometry of the offices and support spaces.

Plan: Seinajoki Library, Seinajoki, Finland, 1963–1965, Alvar Aalto

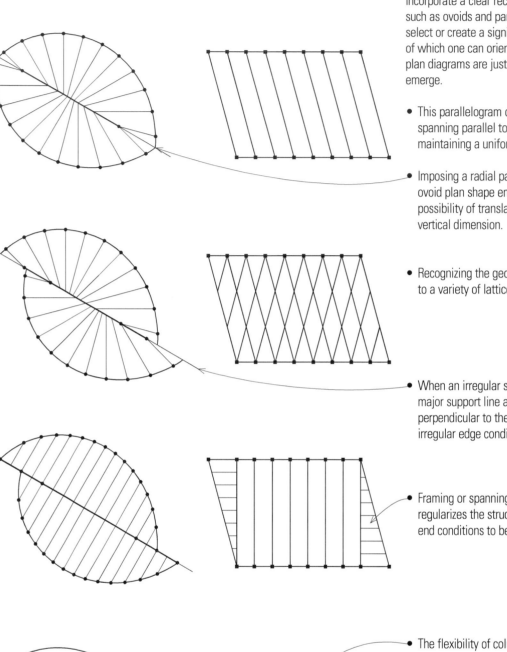

Plan shapes may evolve that do not conform to or incorporate a clear rectilinear or curvilinear geometry, such as ovoids and parallelograms. One approach is to select or create a significant edge or linear condition off of which one can orient the grid or framing pattern. These plan diagrams are just a few of the many possibilities that emerge.

• This parallelogram offers a choice of framing or spanning parallel to one set of edges or the other while maintaining a uniformity of span length.

• Imposing a radial pattern of framing or spans on this ovoid plan shape emphasizes its curvature, with the possibility of translating the curvilinear quality into the vertical dimension.

• Recognizing the geometry of the parallelogram can lead to a variety of lattice-type structures.

• When an irregular shape is sheared, one can create a major support line along the slippage and frame either perpendicular to the slip line or in response to the irregular edge conditions.

• Framing or spanning perpendicular to one set of edges regularizes the structure and leaves triangular shaped end conditions to be spanned in a different manner.

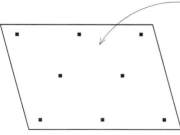

• The flexibility of column location afforded by concrete flat plate structures enables one to create irregular floor shapes as well as respond to a variety of interior space configurations.

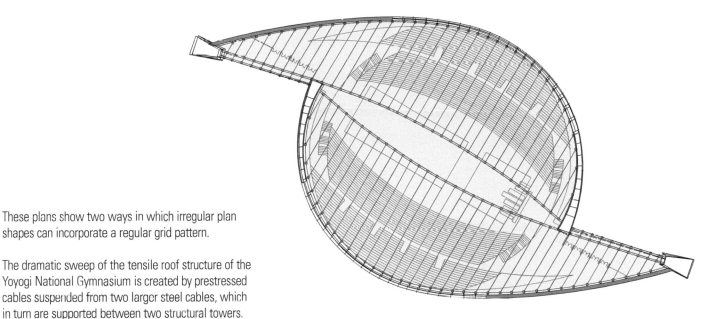

These plans show two ways in which irregular plan shapes can incorporate a regular grid pattern.

The dramatic sweep of the tensile roof structure of the Yoyogi National Gymnasium is created by prestressed cables suspended from two larger steel cables, which in turn are supported between two structural towers. From this central spine, the roof cables drape down and are anchored to curvilinear concrete bases. The plan view, however, shows the regularity of the cable spacing.

The angular, multifaceted nature of the Des Moines Public Library building belies the regularity of the structural grid of columns on the interior. Note how secondary columns define the boundaries of the building facades.

Plan: Arena Maggiore, Yoyogi National Gymnasium, Tokyo, Japan, 1961–1964, Kenzo Tange

Des Moines Public Library, Des Moines, Iowa, 2006, David Chipperfield Architects/HLKB Architecture

## Accommodating Irregular Edge Conditions

Buildings may be shaped by the configuration of the site, the possibilities for view corridors and outlook, the edge conditions of streets and street frontages, or by the desire to preserve unique topographic features. Any of these conditions can lead to an irregular geometry that must be rationalized with the building program and the structural system devised to house it.

One strategy is to reduce the building form into orthogonal shapes with different orientations. This will often result in exceptional conditions that must be resolved at the intersections between the orthogonal parts of the composition. See pages 64–65.

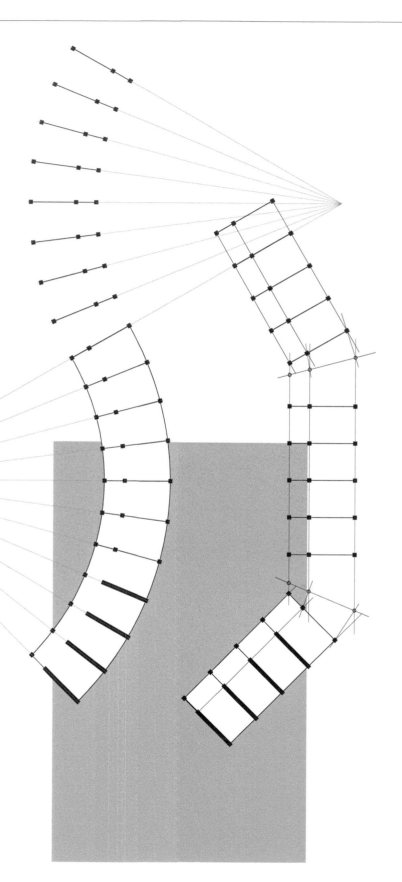

Another approach is to adapt a series of equivalent spatial units or formal elements to an irregular edge condition by bending the linear array along the path of the irregularity. The irregularity can be regularized by visualizing it as a series of curvatures and recognizing the center of radius for each arc segment as well as the points of inflection where changes of curvature occur.

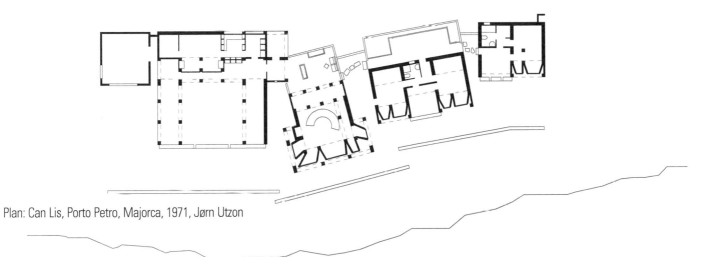

Plan: Can Lis, Porto Petro, Majorca, 1971, Jørn Utzon

These projects show how we can respond to irregular edge conditions. Can Lis, perched high on the edge of a cliff overlooking the Mediterranean, appears to be a loose collection of small, vernacular buildings linked by a circulation spine. The individual nature of the forms or spaces allows each to be oriented independently of each other. The EOS Housing project, on the other hand, is a terrace housing scheme. The sinuous, continuous forms are generated by the radial geometry of the party walls that separate the individual housing units.

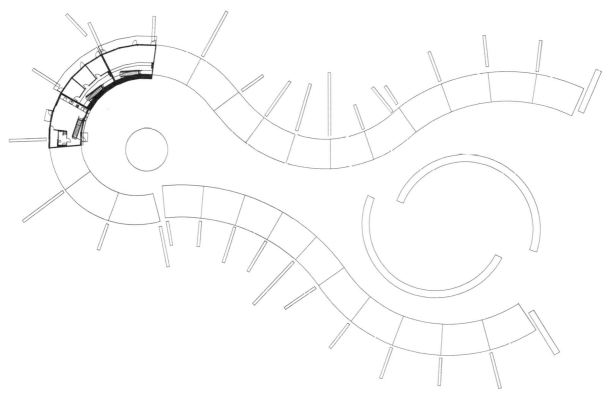

Plan: EOS Housing, Helsingborg, Sweden, 2002, Anders Wilhelmson

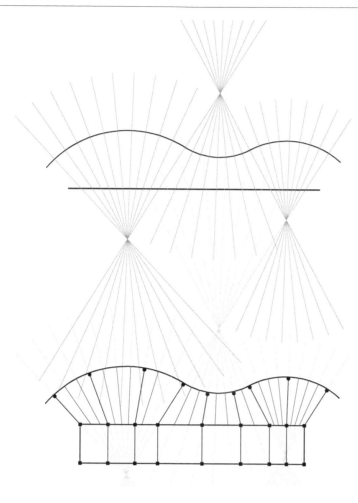

A classic duality in architectural design lies in the opposition between the straight and the curved. Reference has already been made to this opposition on page 70. Presented here are additional approaches to resolving the tension between a curved surface or plane and the rectilinear geometry of a regular structural grid. Each has implications on the design of the structural form as well as the quality of the interior spaces.

One could begin with the geometry that generated the curved surface or plane. This might suggest a framing or spanning pattern that reinforces the curvilinear edge to the space that is generated. The radial nature of the pattern would contrast strongly with the orthogonal grid, which could reinforce a distinction between two parts of the building program. The opposite approach would be to extend the orthogonal relationships established by the regular grid structure to the curved surface or plane.

- In this plan diagram, the radial pattern reinforces the undulating nature of the space enclosed by the curvilinear surface or plane, which is reflected in the irregular spacing of the column supports in the rectangular portion of the structure.

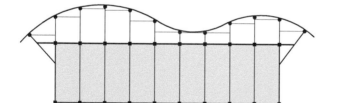

- Extending the orthogonal bay structure to the curvilinear surface or plane creates an irregular series of spaces that mediate between the straight and the curved and unifies the two edge conditions.

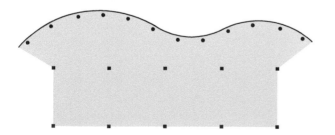

- The flexibility of column location afforded by concrete flat plate structures enables one to create irregular floor shapes as well as respond to a variety of interior space configurations.

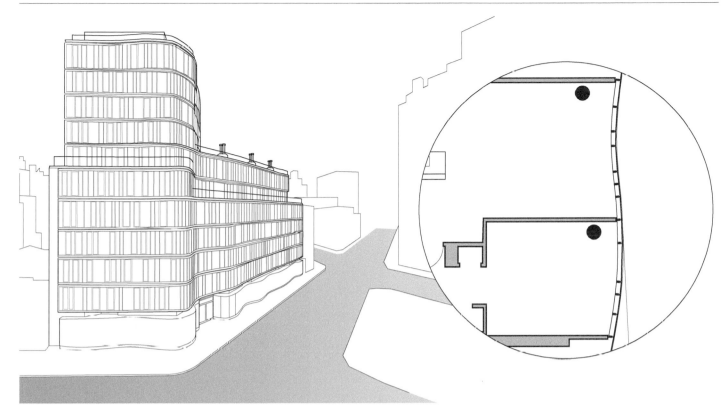

Exterior view and plan detail: One Jackson Square, New York, New York, 2009, Kohn Pedersen Fox

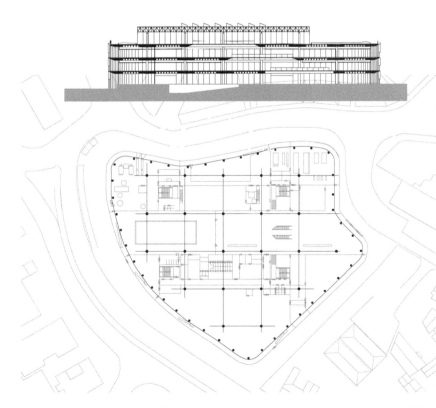

Plan and section: Willis, Faber & Dumas Headquarters, Ipswich, England, 1971–1975, Norman Foster/Foster + Partners

These two examples show how curvilinear curtain walls can be created. The irregular, site-assembled curtain wall panels of One Jackson Square are attached to the curvilinear perimeter of the overhanging concrete slabs. The slab edges had to be formed precisely so that the mullion joints of the curtain wall system would align properly. In a few of the units containing double-height spaces, a large beam replaced the slab edge as a means of support for the curtain wall.

The central portion of Willis, Faber & Dumas Headquarters consists of a square grid of concrete columns spaced at 46-foot (14-m) centers while perimeter columns are set back from the curvilinear slab edges. Dark, solar-tinted glass panes are connected by corner patch fittings and silicone-jointed to form a three-story-high curtain wall, which is suspended from a perimeter edge beam at the roof level. Glass fins provide lateral bracing.

## Sheared Grids

Two portions of a building may be adjacent to each other, each responding in its own way to programmatic or contextual requirements or constraints. Each may also require two different types of structural patterns that meet along a common line of support. Each may have similar structural patterns but one may slip or displace relative to the other. In these situations, differences between the parts may be expressed in the scale or grain of the respective structural patterns.

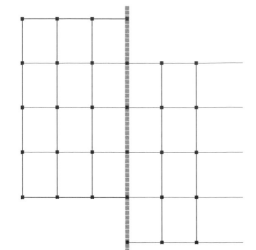

- When the scale and grain of two grids are similar, any differences can be resolved simply by selectively adding or subtracting bays. If there is an established grid structure, this will emphasize the plane along which the shift or shearing occurs.

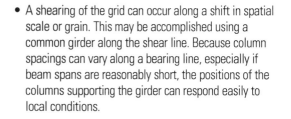

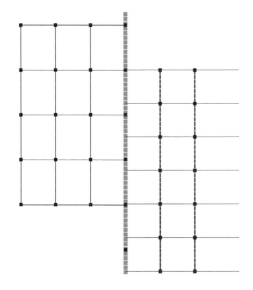

- A shearing of the grid can occur along a shift in spatial scale or grain. This may be accomplished using a common girder along the shear line. Because column spacings can vary along a bearing line, especially if beam spans are reasonably short, the positions of the columns supporting the girder can respond easily to local conditions.

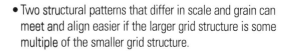

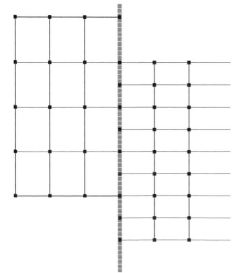

- Two structural patterns that differ in scale and grain can meet and align easier if the larger grid structure is some multiple of the smaller grid structure.

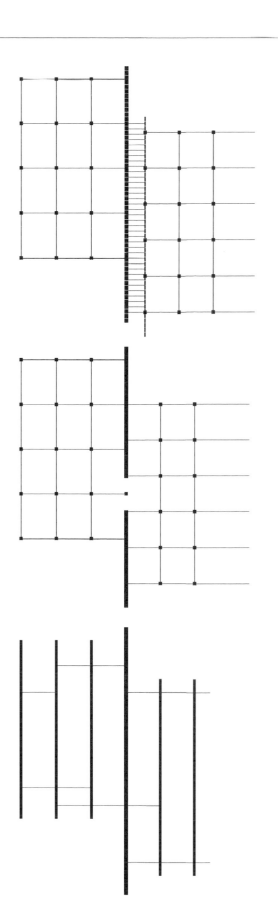

- If two primary grids that differ in scale, proportion, or grain cannot be resolved along a bearing line of columns and beams or girders, a third structure can be introduced to mediate between the two structures. Having a relatively short span, this mediating structure can often have a finer grain, which can help resolve the different spacings and support patterns of the two primary grids.

- If adjacent occupancies can tolerate the degree of separation afforded by a bearing wall, the wall itself can serve to join two contrasting structural grids. The nature of a bearing wall divides a space into two distinct fields. Any penetration through the bearing wall can take on additional significance as a portal or threshold between the two elements.

- A pair of bearing walls defines a field of space distinguished by a strong directional quality toward its open ends. This fundamental type of structural pattern is often used in projects consisting of repetitive units, such as multifamily housing, because they simultaneously serve to isolate the units from one another, curb the passage of sound, and check the spread of fire.
- A series of parallel bearing walls can organize a series of linear spaces, with the solidity of the bearing walls being able to accommodate varying degrees of slippage or offsets, from small to large.

# TRANSITIONAL PATTERNS

Corners define the meeting of two planes. Vertical corners are architecturally significant because they define the edges of building facades in elevation and simultaneously terminate two horizontal directions in plan. Related to the architectural nature of corner conditions are constructibility and structural issues. A decision based on one of these factors inevitably influences the other two. For example, the adjoining sides of a one-way spanning system are inherently different, which would impact the architectural relationship and design expression of adjacent facades.

- If two planes simply touch and the corner remains unadorned, the presence of the corner will depend on the visual treatment of the adjoining surfaces. Unadorned corners emphasize the volume of a form.

- A form or one of its faces can dominate an adjacent mass by continuing to and occupying the corner position, thereby establishing a front for the architectural composition.

- A corner condition can be visually reinforced by introducing a separate and distinct element that is independent of the surfaces it joins. This element emphasizes the corner as a vertical, linear element that defines the edges of the adjoining planes.

- Rounding off the corner emphasizes the continuity of the bounding surfaces of a form, the compactness of its volume, and softness of its contour. The scale of the radius of curvature is important. If too small, it becomes visually insignificant; if too large, it affects the interior space it encloses and the exterior form it describes.

- A void diminishes the primary corner condition, effectively creates two lesser corners, and clarifies the distinction between two separate forms or masses.

The plan diagrams on the following three pages present alternative approaches to structuring these types of corner conditions, each of which has architectural implications.

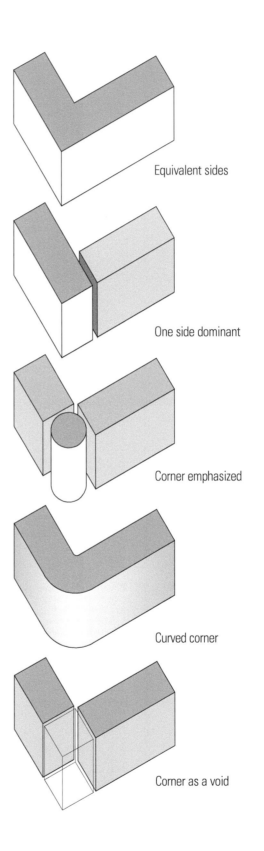

Equivalent sides

One side dominant

Corner emphasized

Curved corner

Corner as a void

- One-way framing or spans of the side bays lead to the two-way framing or span of a square corner bay, establishing an equivalency of the adjacent sides.

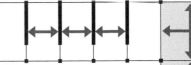
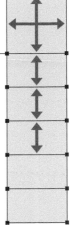

- One-way framing or spans in one wing leads to the two-way span of a square corner bay, diminishing the stature of the other wing. A void between the two wings emphasizes the separation between the two wings.

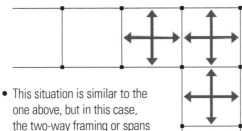

- This situation is similar to the one above, but in this case, the two-way framing or spans of square bays continues along both wings. Note that the continuity that contributes to the efficiency of two-way systems only exists in one direction in each wing.

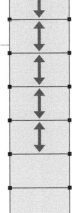

- This situation is similar to the one above, but here the one-way framing or spans in one wing continues unchanged to the corner position, giving the arrangement a definite sidedness.

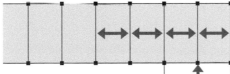
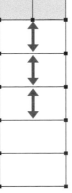

- The one-way framing or spans of one wing of the building continues to the corner position. For the adjoining facades to be equivalent, a column would have to be added to the longer side of the end bay.

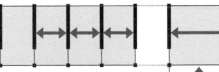
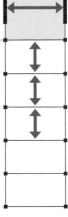

- The one-way framing or spans of one wing, while picking up the spacing of the other wing in one direction, dominates due to its material and type of structure. The corner bay requires a longer one-way spanning system.

**Equivalent Sides**

**One Side Dominant**

## TRANSITIONAL PATTERNS

The three plan diagrams on this page illustrate how a corner condition can be made special or unique through the significant size, distinctive shape, or contrasting orientation of a discrete corner element.

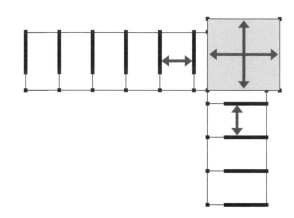

- The square corner bay is enlarged to emphasize its primacy over each wing, which maintains its own one-way framing or spans. Two columns are added to ease the transition from the smaller bay spacing of the wings to the larger corner-bay spans.

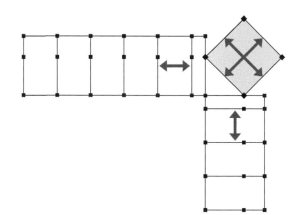

- The square corner bay is rotated to emphasize its corner position while each wing maintains it own one-way framing or spans. Two columns are added to support the corners of the rotated bay.

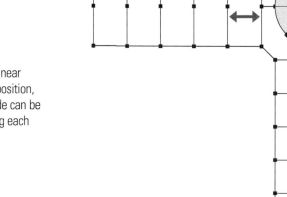

- The circular corner bay contrasts with the rectilinear geometry of each wing, emphasizes its corner position, and requires its own structural pattern. Each side can be framed as a one-way system with beams linking each wing to the corner bay.

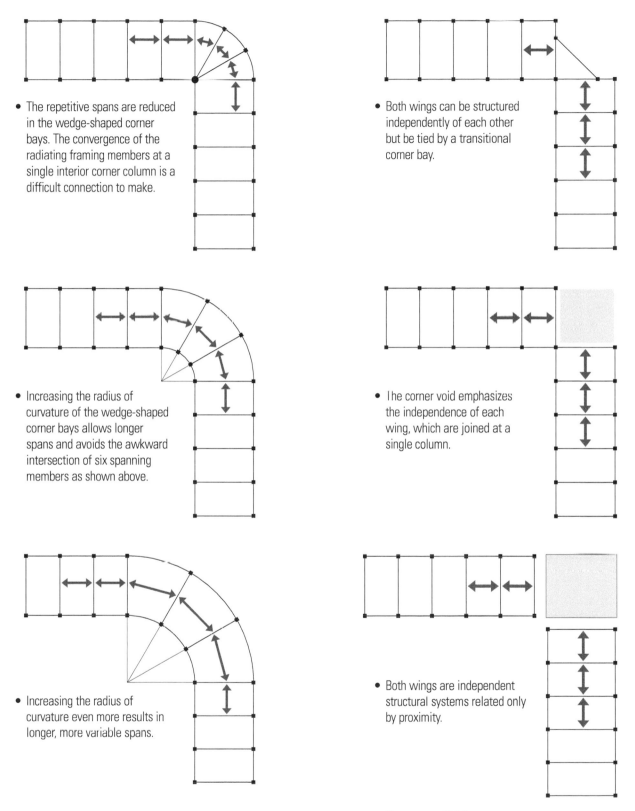

- The repetitive spans are reduced in the wedge-shaped corner bays. The convergence of the radiating framing members at a single interior corner column is a difficult connection to make.

- Increasing the radius of curvature of the wedge-shaped corner bays allows longer spans and avoids the awkward intersection of six spanning members as shown above.

- Increasing the radius of curvature even more results in longer, more variable spans.

- Both wings can be structured independently of each other but be tied by a transitional corner bay.

- The corner void emphasizes the independence of each wing, which are joined at a single column.

- Both wings are independent structural systems related only by proximity.

**Corner as Void**

### Foundation Grids

The primary function of a foundation system is to support and anchor the superstructure above and transmit its loads safely into the earth. Because the foundation serves as a critical link in the distribution and resolution of building loads, its pattern of supports must be designed to both accommodate the form and layout of the superstructure above and respond to the varying conditions of soil, rock, and water below.

The bearing capacity of the supporting soil will impact the choice of a foundation type for a building. Shallow or spread foundations are employed when stable soil of adequate bearing capacity occurs relatively near to the ground surface. Footings are proportioned to distribute their load over a wide enough area that the allowable bearing capacity of the soil is not exceeded. This should ensure that whatever settlement does occur is minimal or is uniformly distributed under all portions of the structure.

When the bearing capacity of the soil on a site varies, spread foundations may be joined by a structural plinth or mat foundation—essentially, a thick, heavily reinforced concrete slab. Mat foundations distribute concentrated loads to areas of higher-capacity soil to avoid the differential settlement that would occur between individual spread footings.

When building loads exceed the bearing capacity of the supporting soil, pile or caisson foundations must be used. Pile foundations consist of steel, concrete, or timber piles that are driven into the ground until they reach a more suitable bearing stratum of dense soil or rock or until the friction of the soil on the piles is sufficient to support the design loads. Individual piles are typically joined with a cast-in-place concrete cap that in turn supports a building column.

Caissons are cast-in-place concrete shafts that are created by drilling the soil to the required depth, placing reinforcing steel, and casting the concrete. Caissons are generally larger in diameter than piling and are particularly suited to slopes where lateral displacement is a major concern.

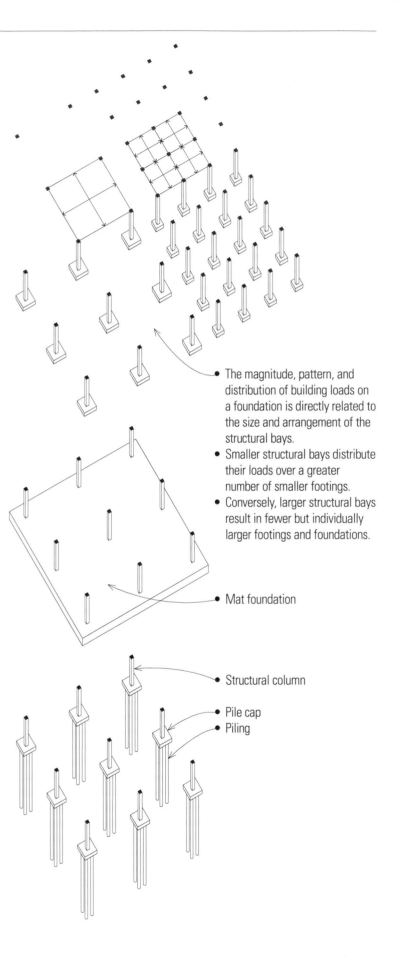

- The magnitude, pattern, and distribution of building loads on a foundation is directly related to the size and arrangement of the structural bays.
- Smaller structural bays distribute their loads over a greater number of smaller footings.
- Conversely, larger structural bays result in fewer but individually larger footings and foundations.

- Mat foundation

- Structural column

- Pile cap
- Piling

### Building on Slopes

Pile foundations can be used on irregular or sloping topography, particularly where the surface soil on the slope may be unstable and the pilings can extend down to bear on or in more stable stratum of soil or rock. In such cases, it may not be necessary to retain soil, and the location of the piles can align with the desired column locations in the building.

When it is desirable or necessary to excavate into a slope, retaining walls are often employed to contain the mass of earth above the grade change. The retained soil is considered to act as a fluid that exerts lateral pressure on the face of the retaining wall, tending to cause the wall to slide laterally or to overturn. The overturning moment created by the lateral soil pressure and the opposing resistance of the wall's foundation is critically dependent on the height of the wall. The moment increases with the square of the height of the earth that is retained. As a retaining wall becomes taller, it may be necessary to install tiebacks to piling or to build in counterforts—cross walls that stiffen the wall slab and add weight to its footing.

A series of retaining walls parallel to the slope can provide continuous support for bearing walls in the superstructure of the building. It is not advisable to add the weight of the building to the soil behind the retaining wall. The location of the retaining walls should therefore coincide with lines of support in the building above.

A retaining wall may fail by overturning, horizontal sliding, or excessive settling.

- Thrust tends to overturn a retaining wall about the toe of the base. To prevent a retaining wall from overturning, the resisting moment of the composite weight of the wall and any soil bearing on the heel of the base must counter the overturning moment created by the soil pressure.
- To prevent a retaining wall from sliding, the composite weight of the wall times the coefficient of friction for the soil supporting the wall must counter the lateral thrust on the wall. The passive pressure of the soil abutting the lower level of the wall aids in resisting the lateral thrust.
- To prevent a retaining wall from settling, the vertical force must not exceed the bearing capacity of the soil.

Toe

For small projects, particularly when the design does not require excavation into a sloping site, grade beams may be used to tie the foundation into a single, rigid unit that is in turn anchored to piling, usually at the upper portion of the site. This has been successful where minimum disruption of the site is desirable and on sites that are primarily accessible from the high side.

Footings •
Grade beams •

When the design does not require excavation into a sloping site, the foundation walls may run perpendicular to the slope and be stepped to follow the topography. Because stepped foundation walls do not retain earth, they will typically not require the reinforcement and large footings of a retaining wall.

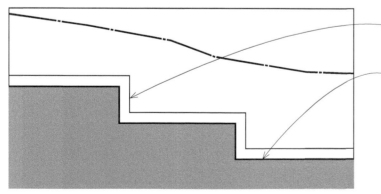

- Footings must be stepped when necessary to keep them in the ground when site slopes exceed 10%.

- Footing thickness should be maintained in its vertical portion.

- Footings are to be placed on undisturbed soil or on properly compacted fill.
- Footings are to be at least 12 inches (305) below grade, except in conditions where frost occurs, in which case the footings must extend below the frost line of the site.
- Footing tops are to be level, whereas the bottom of footings may have a slope of up to 10%.

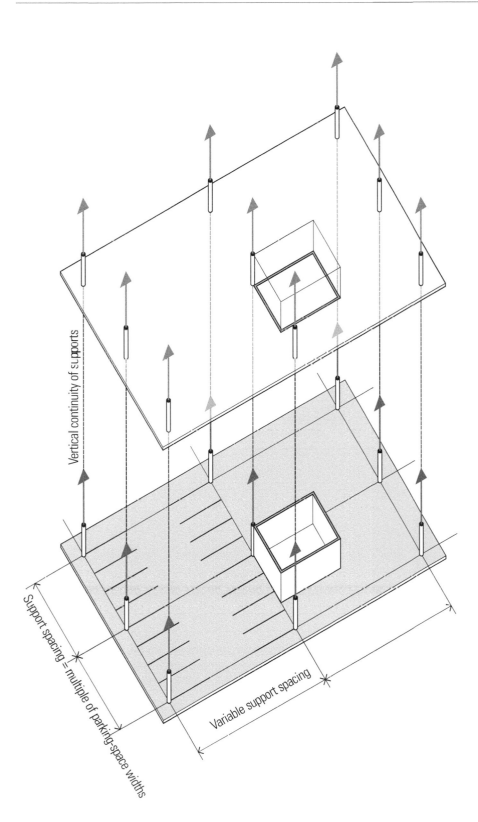

Vertical continuity of supports

Support spacing = multiple of parking-space widths

Variable support spacing

### Parking Structures

When parking is the sole purpose of a structure, the specific dimensions required for maneuvering and parking vehicles dictate the possible column locations for the layout of the structural bays.

When parking is an ancillary function in a building, it is typically located on the lower floors of the structure while other uses occupy the upper floors. It is often difficult to resolve the structural grid that is appropriate for the upper floors with one that effectively accommodates parking. Overlaying the two conditions may identify a possible common grid between the two by taking advantage of the flexibility of column locations suggested in the diagrams on the following page.

Where column alignment is not possible, it may be feasible to use transfer beams or angled struts to carry the loads from the upper floors through the parking floors to the ground foundation. It is always desirable to minimize these conditions.

Mixed-use buildings in which two uses, such as parking and housing, require a specific degree of fire separation, may have the roof of the lower parking structure constructed as a thick, posttensioned concrete plate. The plate is able to transfer column or bearing-wall loads from the upper floors to the parking structure while providing the required fire separation. This is only feasible when the upper structure is subject to relatively light loads and is likely not cost-effective if there are large concentrated loads or when the misalignment between columns creates concentrated loads in the middle third of longer spans.

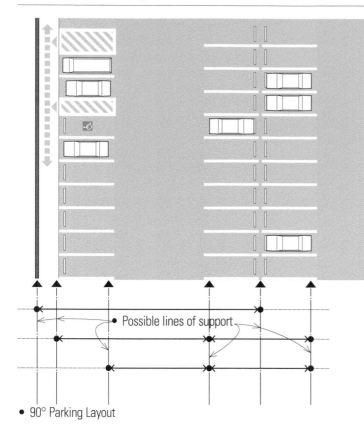

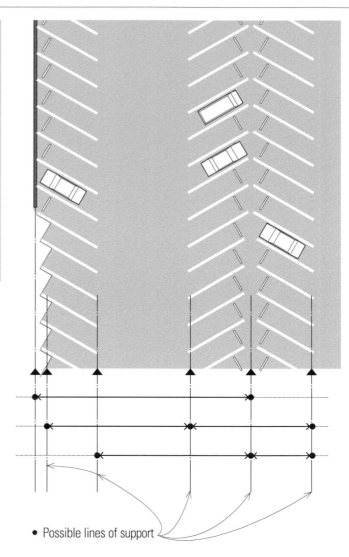

• Possible lines of support

• 90° Parking Layout

• Possible lines of support

• Angled Parking Layout

The columns in a parking structure should, if possible, be placed between adjacent rows of parking spaces in one direction and at some multiple of the width of the parking spaces in the other. The layout should allow sufficient space for cars to maneuver and car doors to open unimpeded. Columns should be visible to drivers when backing up. This will often result in moderately long spans in the range of 60 feet (18 m).

However, as the plan diagrams show, there are alternative locations for column supports. The black triangles indicate possible lines of support along which columns can be spaced in concert with the width of the parking spaces. One can see that a variety of span lengths are feasible, making it possible for a particular layout to be coordinated with the column support pattern in the structure above.

# 3
# Horizontal Spans

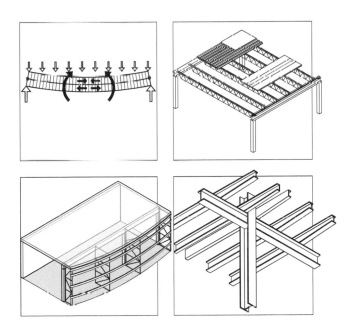

The vertical supports of a building—its columns and loadbearing walls—punctuate space and establish a measurable rhythm and scale that make the spatial dimensions comprehensible. Architectural spaces, however, also require horizontal spans to establish the floor structure that supports our weight, activities, and furnishings, and the overhead roof plane that shelters space and limits its vertical dimension.

## Beams

All floor and roof structures consist of linear and planar elements, such as joists, beams, and slabs, designed to carry and transfer transverse loads across space to supporting elements. To understand the structural behavior of these spanning elements, we begin with a general discussion of beams, which applies as well to joists, girders, and trusses.

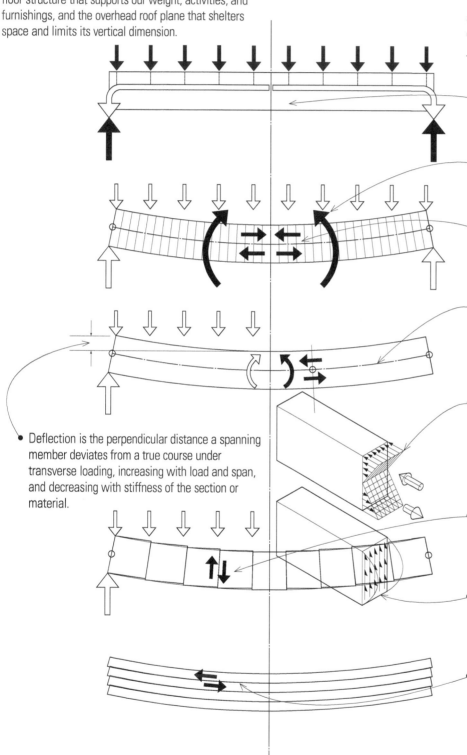

- Span refers to the extent of space between two supports of a structure.

- Bending moment is an external moment tending to cause part of a structure to rotate or bend.

- Resisting moment is an internal moment equal and opposite to a bending moment, generated by a force couple to maintain equilibrium of the section being considered.

- The neutral axis is an imaginary line passing through the centroid—the geometric center—of the cross section of a beam or other member subject to bending, along which no bending stresses occur.

- Bending stress is a combination of compressive and tensile stresses developed at a cross section of a structural member to resist a transverse force, having a maximum value at the surface farthest from the neutral axis.

- Vertical shearing stress is developed along a cross section of a beam to resist transverse shear, having a maximum value at the neutral axis and decreasing nonlinearly toward the outer faces.

- Transverse shear at a cross section of a beam or other member subject to bending is equal to the algebraic sum of transverse forces on one side of the section.

- Horizontal or longitudinal shearing stress is developed along horizontal planes of a beam under transverse loading, equal at any point to the vertical shearing stress at that point.

- Deflection is the perpendicular distance a spanning member deviates from a true course under transverse loading, increasing with load and span, and decreasing with stiffness of the section or material.

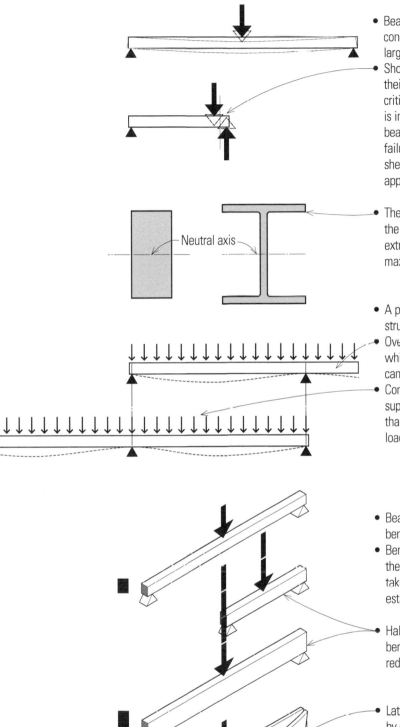

- Beams and girders, having longer spans and supporting concentrated loads near their midspan, are subject to large bending stresses and deflection.
- Short-span beams with large concentrated loads near their supports develop shear stresses that are more critical than the bending stresses. Sufficient beam width is important in reducing these shear stresses. Timber beams, in particular, are very susceptible to shear stress failure. Steel beams are generally more resistant to shear stresses and concrete beams can be detailed with appropriate reinforcement to withstand large shears.

- The efficiency of a beam is increased by making the section deep with most of the material at the extremities—farther from the neutral axis—where the maximum bending stresses occur.

Neutral axis

- A principal objective in the design of spanning structures is to minimize bending and deflection.
- Overhangs reduce the positive moment at midspan while developing a negative moment at the base of the cantilever over the support.
- Continuous beams extending over more than two supports develop greater rigidity and smaller moments than a series of simple beams having similar spans and loading.

- Beam depth is an important consideration for reducing bending stresses and limiting vertical deflection.
- Bending moments in beams increase as the square of the span and deflections increase rapidly with the span taken to a third power. Thus, span is a major factor in establishing beam depth.

- Halving a beam span or doubling its width reduces the bending stresses by a factor of 2, but doubling the depth reduces the bending stresses by a factor of 4.

- Lateral buckling can be induced in a structural member by compressive stresses acting on a slender portion insufficiently rigid in the lateral direction.
- Increasing the beam width—or in the case of a steel beam, the flange width—increases the beam's resistance to lateral buckling.

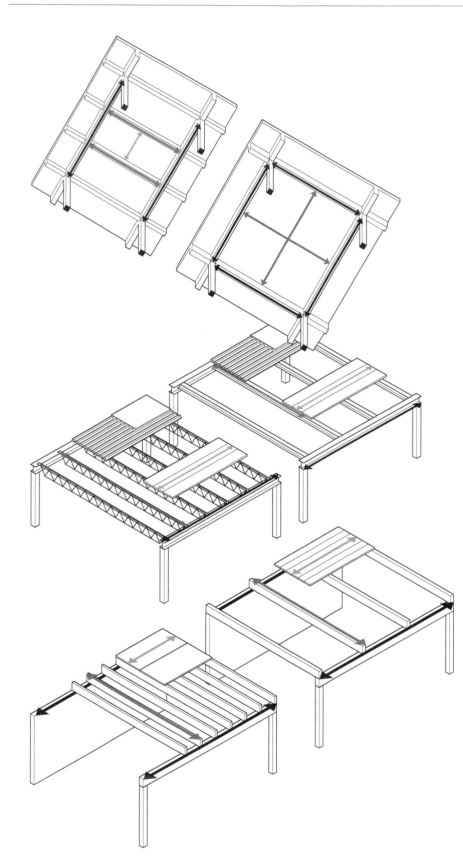

Horizontal spans may be traversed by nearly homogeneous slabs of reinforced concrete or by hierarchical layers of steel or wood girders, beams, and joists supporting a plane of structural sheathing or decking.

### Concrete

- Cast-in-place concrete floor slabs are classified according to their span and cast form; see pages 102–115.
- Precast concrete planks may be supported by beams or loadbearing walls.

### Steel

- Steel beams support steel decking or precast concrete planks.
- Beams may be supported by girders, columns, or loadbearing walls.
- Beam framing is typically an integral part of a steel skeleton frame system.

- Closely spaced light-gauge or open-web joists may be supported by beams or loadbearing walls.
- Steel decking or wood planks have relatively short spans.
- Joists have limited overhang potential.

### Wood

- Wood beams support structural planking or decking.
- Beams may be supported by girders, posts, or loadbearing walls.
- Concentrated loads and floor openings may require additional framing.
- Underside of floor structure may be left exposed; an applied ceiling is optional.

- Relatively small, closely spaced joists may be supported by beams or loadbearing walls.
- Subflooring, underlayment, and applied ceiling finishes have relatively short spans.
- Joist framing is flexible in shape and form.

### Types of Construction

The preceding page describes the major types of reinforced concrete, steel, and wood spanning systems. The material requirements for spanning structures are generally determined by the magnitude of the loads and the lengths of the spans. Another important consideration in selecting a structural material is the type of construction required by the building code for the size and occupancy of the building. Building codes classify the construction of a building according to the fire resistance of its major elements: structural frame, exterior and interior bearing walls, nonbearing walls and partitions, and floor and roof assemblies.

**Concrete**
- Noncombustible
- Types I, II, or III construction

**Steel**
- Noncombustible
- The application of fire-resistive materials can increase the durability of even noncombustible materials in a fire. Even steel or concrete, if unprotected, can lose strength under fire exposure.
- Types I, II, and III construction

**Wood**
- Combustible
- Wood can be made more fire-resistant by applying fire-retardant coverings to impede the spread of fire and extend the durability of the building structure in a fire.
- Types IV and V construction

- Type I buildings have their major building elements constructed of noncombustible materials, such as concrete, masonry, or steel. Some combustible materials are allowed if they are ancillary to the primary structure of the building. Type II buildings are similar to Type I buildings except for a reduction in the required fire-resistance ratings of the major building elements.

- Type III buildings have noncombustible exterior walls and major interior elements of any material permitted by the code.

- Type IV buildings (Heavy Timber) have noncombustible exterior walls and major interior elements of solid or laminated wood of specified minimum sizes and without concealed spaces.

- Type V buildings have structural elements, exterior walls, and interior walls of any material permitted by the code.

- Protected construction requires all major building elements, except for nonbearing interior walls and partitions, to be of one-hour fire-resistive construction.
- Unprotected construction has no requirements for fire-resistance except for when the code requires protection of exterior walls due to their proximity to a property line.

### Structural Layers

When supporting uniformly distributed loads, the first or surface-forming layer should be selected for greatest efficiency. Thus, the selection of structural members for a spanning system and the spacing between them begins at the point of application of the live load. The load is gathered through successive layers of structure until it is resolved at the foundation. Typically, greater spans will result in more layers to reduce the amount of material used, resulting in greater efficiency.

- Each layer of one-way spanning elements is supported by the layer below, requiring the span direction to alternate in each successive layer.

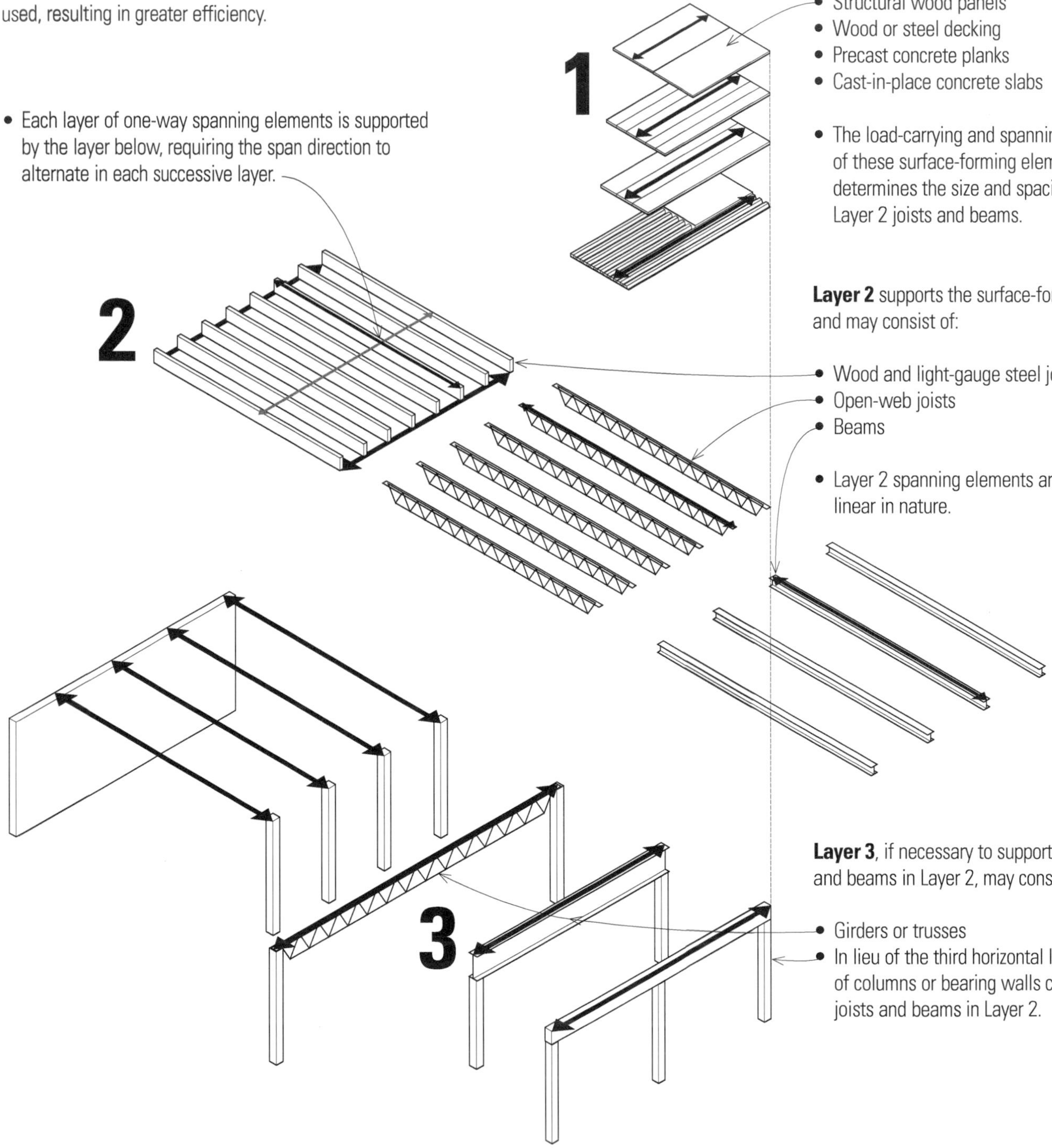

**Layer 1** is the uppermost surface-forming layer and may consist of:

- Structural wood panels
- Wood or steel decking
- Precast concrete planks
- Cast-in-place concrete slabs

- The load-carrying and spanning capability of these surface-forming elements determines the size and spacing of Layer 2 joists and beams.

**Layer 2** supports the surface-forming layer and may consist of:

- Wood and light-gauge steel joists
- Open-web joists
- Beams

- Layer 2 spanning elements are larger and linear in nature.

**Layer 3**, if necessary to support the joists and beams in Layer 2, may consist of:

- Girders or trusses
- In lieu of the third horizontal layer, a series of columns or bearing walls can carry the joists and beams in Layer 2.

### Construction Depth

The depth of a floor or roof system is directly related to the size and proportion of the structural bays it must span, the magnitude of the live loads, and the strength of the materials used. The structural depth of floor and roof systems becomes critical in areas where zoning ordinances restrict building heights and maximizing the usable floor area is important to the economic feasibility of a project. For floor systems between habitable spaces stacked one above the other, additional factors to consider are the blockage of both airborne and structure-borne sound and the fire-resistance rating of the assembly.

The following points can be applied to both steel and timber spanning systems.

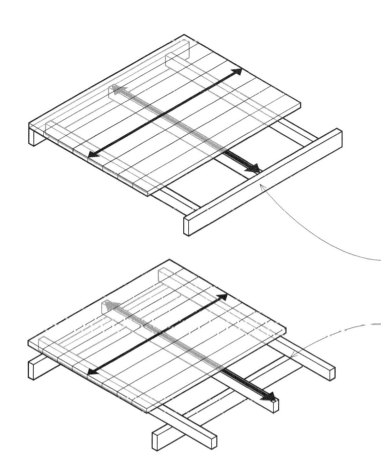

- The structural layers of a spanning system either can be stacked atop of one another or be formed or framed in the same plane.

- Stacking the layers increases the construction depth but enables one-way spanning elements to overhang in the direction of their span.
- Stacking one layer atop the supporting layer below provides space for other systems to cross over the supporting layer between members of the supported layer.

- The layers may be formed or framed in plane to minimize the construction depth. In this case, the depth of the largest spanning elements, such as girders or trusses, establishes the overall depth of the system.

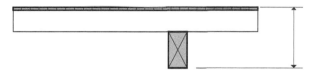

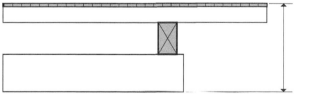

- In some cases, the overall depth of a spanning structure can be reduced further by integrating the mechanical and structural systems so that they occupy the same volume rather than exist in separate layers. This, however, requires careful study since this may require penetrating structural members, which can cause localized stresses.

The sizing and proportioning of structural elements and assemblies requires an understanding of the context in which each element or assembly is used—the type of loads being carried and what is supporting the element or assembly.

## Distributed and Concentrated Loading

Building structures are designed to withstand a combination of dead loads, live loads, and lateral loads. Just as important as the magnitude of these loads is the manner in which the loads are applied to a spanning structure. Loads may be applied either in a distributed or a concentrated manner. Understanding this distinction is important because some structural systems are better suited for carrying relatively light, uniformly distributed loads while others are more appropriate for supporting a set of concentrated loads.

Many floor and roof structures are subject to relatively light, distributed loading. In these cases, when stiffness and resistance to deflection tend to govern the design of the structure, it is usually appropriate to select a distributed type of structure using a number of relatively smaller, more closely spaced spanning elements, such as joists. Distributed structural systems, however, are not well suited to carrying concentrated loads, which require fewer and larger one-way spanning elements such as girders and trusses for their support.

- A uniformly distributed load is one of uniform magnitude extending over the length or area of the supporting structural element, as in the case of the self-weight of the structure, the live load on a floor deck, snow load on a roof, or a wind load on a wall. Building codes specify minimum uniformly distributed unit loads for various uses and occupancies.

- A concentrated load acts on a very small area or particular point of a supporting structural element, as when a beam bears on a column, a column bears on a girder, or a truss bears on a bearing wall.

- Concentrated loads are of particular concern because the effect of concentrating a distributed load in the center of a span doubles the bending moment on the spanning member. For this reason it is always preferable to locate a column or bearing wall directly under a concentrated load.
- When this is not possible, a transfer beam is used to transfer the load to vertical supports.

- Because it must safely support moving loads, a floor system should be relatively stiff while maintaining its elasticity. Due to the detrimental effects that excessive deflection and vibration would have on finish flooring and ceiling materials, as well as on human comfort, deflection rather than bending often becomes the critical controlling factor in the design of floor systems.

- Dead loads are static loads acting vertically downward on a structure, comprising the self-weight of the structure and the weight of building fixtures and equipment permanently attached to it.
- Live loads comprise moving or movable loads on a structure resulting from occupancy, collected snow and water, or portable equipment.

**Load Tracing**

Load tracing is the process of modeling how a structure collects, channels, and redirects the loads resulting from external forces through the hierarchy of its members to the foundation and underlying soil. The analysis usually starts at the roof level with the smallest members actually picking up the loading, and proceeds by tracing the loads through each collecting member. The reactions of each member to its loading become forces on the supporting members in the next layer.

- The hierarchical sequence of load tracing is generally the same for concrete, steel, and timber spanning systems.

- Surface-forming structures, such as structural sheathing or decking, distribute the applied load to its supporting joists or beams in the form of a distributed load.

- Beams transfer the applied distributed load horizontally to supporting girders, trusses, columns, or bearing wall.

- Tributary area is the portion of a structure contributing to the load on a structural element or member.
- Load strip is the tributary area per unit length of a supporting structural member.
- Tributary load is the load on a structural element or member collected from its tributary area.
- Bearing refers to a point, surface, or mass that supports weight, especially the area of contact between a bearing member, as a beam or truss, and a column, wall, or other underlying support.

- Support condition refers to the manner in which a structural member is supported and connected to other members, affecting the nature of the reactive forces developed on the loaded member.
- Anchorage refers to the means for binding a structural member to another or to its foundation, often to resist uplifting and horizontal forces.

- Rigid floor planes can also be designed to serve as horizontal diaphragms which act as thin, wide beams in transferring lateral forces to shear walls. See Chapter 5 for a more detailed discussion of the various methods for providing lateral stability.

The dimensions and proportions of the bays defined by a structural grid influence—and may often limit—the material and structural choices of the horizontal spanning systems.

- The orientation and length of overhangs and size and location of openings within the floor plane should be considered in the layout of the structural supports for the floor. The edge conditions of the floor structure and its connection to supporting foundation and wall systems affect both the structural integrity of a building and its physical appearance.

## Material

- Both wood and steel spanning elements lend themselves to one-way systems, while concrete is appropriate for both one-way and two-way spanning systems.

## Bay Proportion

- Two-way systems are best used to span square or nearly square bays.
- While two-way spanning systems require square or nearly square bays, the converse is not necessarily true. One-way systems are flexible and can span in either direction of either square or rectangular structural bays.

## Span Direction

- The direction of horizontal spans, as determined by the location and orientation of the vertical supporting planes, affects the nature of the spatial composition, the qualities of the spaces defined, and to some extent, the economics of construction.
- One-way joists and beams can span in either the short or long direction of rectangular bays, with their supporting beams, columns, or bearing walls spanning in an alternate, usually perpendicular direction.

## Span Length

- The spacing of supporting columns and bearing walls determines the length of horizontal spans.
- Certain materials have an appropriate range of bay spans. For example, the various types of cast-in-place concrete slabs have bay spans in the range from 6 to 38 feet (1.8 to 12 m). Steel is a more flexible material because its spanning elements are manufactured in different forms, from beams to open-web joists and trusses, which can span from 15 to 80 feet (5 to 24 m).

- One-way systems of joists, planks, or slabs are more efficient when structural bays are rectangular—that is, when the ratio of the long to the short dimensions is greater than 1.5:1—or when the structural grid generates a linear pattern of spaces.

- The parallel nature of loadbearing walls leads naturally to the use of one-way spanning systems.
- Because loadbearing walls are most effective when supporting a uniformly distributed load, they typically support a series of joists, planks, or a one-way slab.

- The most common two-way systems are reinforced concrete slabs used to span square or nearly square bays.
- A two-way slab supported by four columns defines a horizontal layer of space.

- A linear framework of columns and beams defines a three-dimensional module of space capable of being expanded both horizontally and vertically.

- Two loadbearing walls naturally define an axial, bidirectional space. Secondary axes can be developed perpendicular to the primary axis with openings within the loadbearing walls.

# HORIZONTAL SPANNING SYSTEMS

## ONE-WAY SYSTEMS

Listed on this page are appropriate ranges for basic types of spanning elements.

### Decking

- Timber     Wood decking
- Steel     Steel decking

### Joists

- Timber     Solid wood joists

       I-joists

       Trussed joists

- Steel     Light-gauge joists

       Open-web joists

### Beams

- Timber     Solid wood beams

       LVL and PSL beams

       Laminated beams

- Steel     Wide-flange beams
- Concrete     Concrete beams

### Slabs

- Concrete     One-way slab and beam

       Joist slabs

       Precast slabs

For structures spanning beyond 60 feet (18 m), see Chapter 6. ▶▶

## TWO-WAY SYSTEMS

### Slabs

- Concrete     Flat plates

       Flat slabs

       Two-way slab and beam

       Waffle slabs

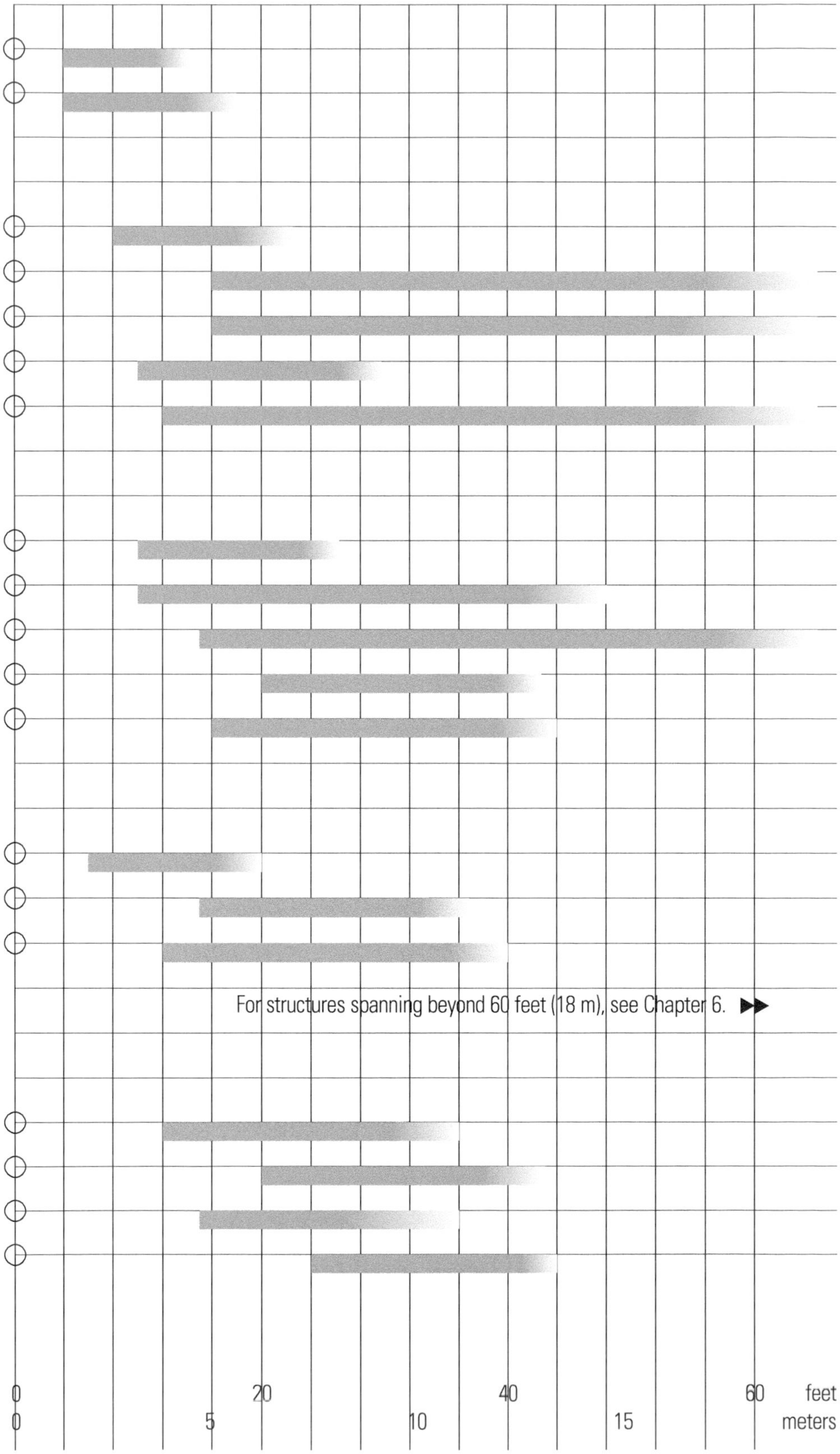

| 0 | 20 | 40 | 60 feet |
| 0 | 5 | 10 | 15 | meters |

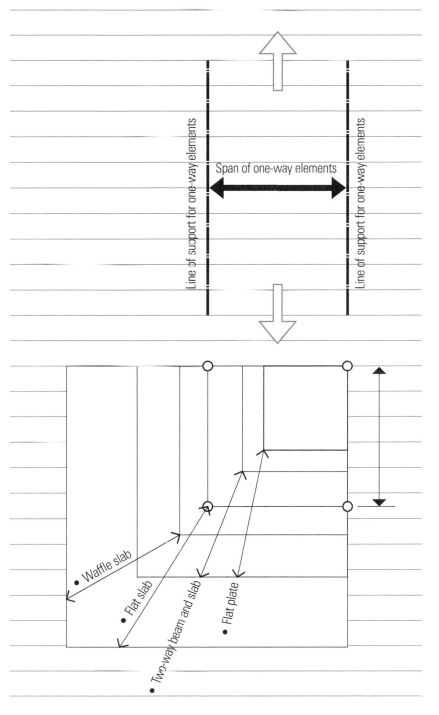

- Bay width is limited in one direction by the span of the one-way elements. In the perpendicular direction, the bay length is determined by the structural elements used to support the one-way elements—either bearing walls, or a beam or girder supported by a series of columns, or a combination thereof.

- The bay dimensions of two-way systems are determined by the spanning capability of each type of two-way reinforced concrete slab. See chart on previous page.

- Grid is based on a 4-foot (1220) square.

## Concrete Slabs

Concrete slabs are plate structures that are reinforced to span either one or both directions of a structural bay. They are classified according to their method of spanning and the form in which they are cast. Because of their noncombustibility, concrete slabs can be used in all types of construction.

## Concrete Beams

Reinforced concrete beams are designed to act together with longitudinal and web reinforcement in resisting applied forces. Cast-in-place concrete beams are almost always formed and placed along with the slab they support. Because a portion of the slab acts as an integral part of the beam, the depth of the beam is measured to the top of the slab.

- Rule of thumb for estimating beam depth: Span/16, including the slab depth, in 2" (51) increments.
- Beam width is 1/3 to 1/2 of beam depth in 2" or 3" (51 or 75) multiples.

## One-Way Slabs

One-way slabs are uniformly thick and structurally reinforced to span in one direction between supports. They are suitable for light to moderate load conditions over relatively short spans of 6 to 18 feet (1.8 to 5.5 m).

While one-way slabs can be supported by concrete- or masonry-bearing walls, they are more typically cast integrally with parallel supporting beams, which in turn are supported by girders or bearing walls. These beams allow for greater bay sizes and flexibility of layout.

- Direction of slab span is usually in the short direction of rectangular bays.
- Tensile reinforcement in the span direction

- Shrinkage and temperature reinforcement perpendicular to main tensile reinforcement

- Rule of thumb for estimating slab thickness:
  Span/28 for floor slabs; 4" (100) minimum
  Span/35 for roof slabs

- Slab is supported on two sides by parallel intermediate beams or loadbearing walls.
- Beams, in turn, may be supported by girders or columns.
- The slab and beams are formed in a continuous pour, allowing the thickness of the slab to contribute to the depth of the beam and reduce the overall depth of the structure.

- Continuity between columns, beams, slabs, and walls is required to minimize bending moments at these junctures.
- Continuous spans over three or more supports are more efficient than simple spans. This is easily attainable in cast-in-place concrete construction.

- Beams and girders can extend beyond the column line to provide overhangs where necessary.

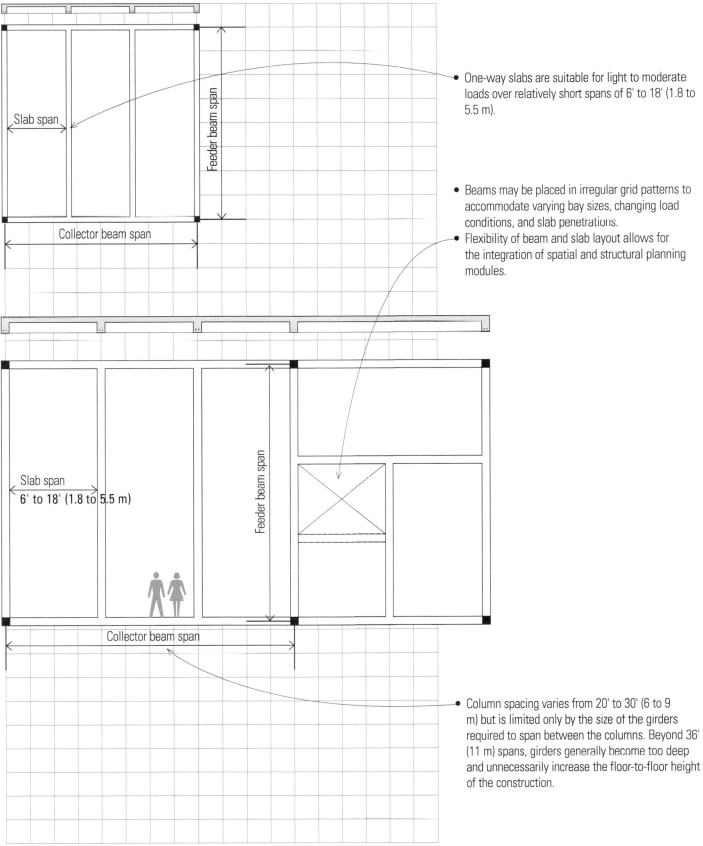

- One-way slabs are suitable for light to moderate loads over relatively short spans of 6' to 18' (1.8 to 5.5 m).

- Beams may be placed in irregular grid patterns to accommodate varying bay sizes, changing load conditions, and slab penetrations.
- Flexibility of beam and slab layout allows for the integration of spatial and structural planning modules.

- Column spacing varies from 20' to 30' (6 to 9 m) but is limited only by the size of the girders required to span between the columns. Beyond 36' (11 m) spans, girders generally become too deep and unnecessarily increase the floor-to-floor height of the construction.

- Grid is based on a 3-foot (915) square.

### Joist Slabs

Joist slabs are cast integrally with a series of closely spaced joists, which in turn are supported by a parallel set of beams. Designed as a series of T-beams, joist slabs are more suitable for longer spans and heavier loads than one-way slabs.

- Tensile reinforcement occurs in the ribs.
- Shrinkage and temperature reinforcement is placed in the slab.

- 3" to 4 1/2" (75 to 115) slab depth
- Rule of thumb for total depth: span/24

- 5" to 9" (125 to 230) joist width

- The pan joist system provides the necessary depth and stiffness while reducing the self-weight of the slab construction.
- The pans used to form the joists are reusable metal or fiberglass molds, available in 20" and 30" (510 and 760) widths and from 6" to 20" (150 to 510) depths in 2" (51) increments. Tapered sides allow for easier removal.
- Tapered endforms are used to thicken joist ends for greater shear resistance.

- Overhanging joists can be formed in-plane with the supporting beam.
- A wider module system can be created by removing alternate joists and thickening the slab, resulting in joists spacing from 5' to 6' (1525 to 1830) o.c. This skip-joist or wide-module system is an economical and efficient system for longer spans and light to medium distributed loading.

- Distribution ribs are formed perpendicular to the joists in order to distribute possible load concentrations over a larger area. One is required for spans between 20' and 30' (6 and 9 m), and not more than 15' (4.5 m) o.c. for spans over 30' (9 m).

- Joist bands are the broad, shallow supporting beams that are economical to form because their depth is the same as that of the joists.

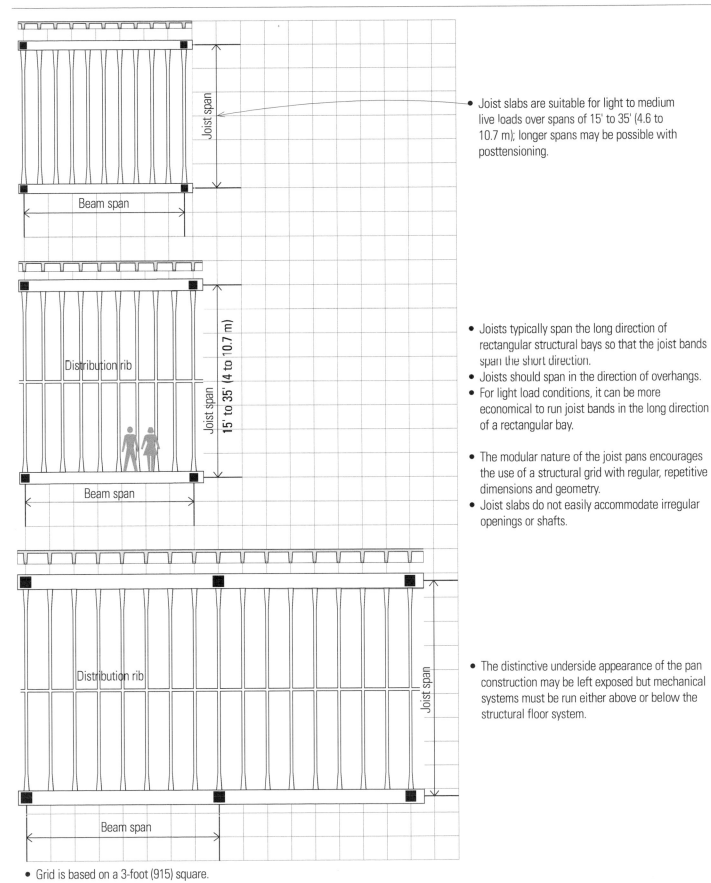

Joist span

Beam span

Distribution rib

Joist span

15' to 35' (4 to 10.7 m)

Beam span

Distribution rib

Joist span

Beam span

- Joist slabs are suitable for light to medium live loads over spans of 15' to 35' (4.6 to 10.7 m); longer spans may be possible with posttensioning.

- Joists typically span the long direction of rectangular structural bays so that the joist bands span the short direction.
- Joists should span in the direction of overhangs.
- For light load conditions, it can be more economical to run joist bands in the long direction of a rectangular bay.

- The modular nature of the joist pans encourages the use of a structural grid with regular, repetitive dimensions and geometry.
- Joist slabs do not easily accommodate irregular openings or shafts.

- The distinctive underside appearance of the pan construction may be left exposed but mechanical systems must be run either above or below the structural floor system.

- Grid is based on a 3-foot (915) square.

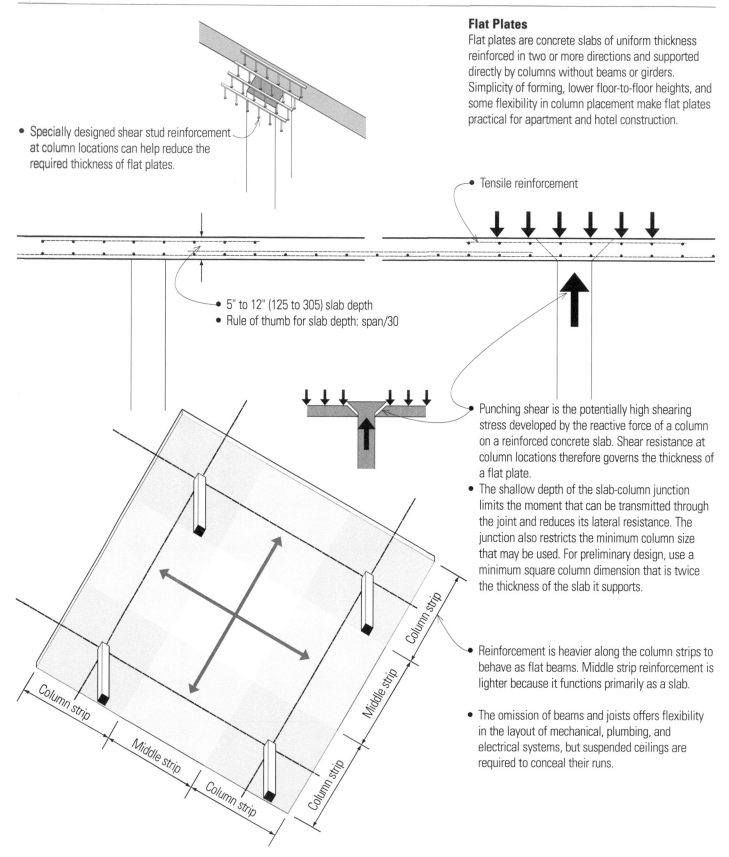

## Flat Plates

Flat plates are concrete slabs of uniform thickness reinforced in two or more directions and supported directly by columns without beams or girders. Simplicity of forming, lower floor-to-floor heights, and some flexibility in column placement make flat plates practical for apartment and hotel construction.

- Specially designed shear stud reinforcement at column locations can help reduce the required thickness of flat plates.

- Tensile reinforcement

- 5" to 12" (125 to 305) slab depth
- Rule of thumb for slab depth: span/30

- Punching shear is the potentially high shearing stress developed by the reactive force of a column on a reinforced concrete slab. Shear resistance at column locations therefore governs the thickness of a flat plate.
- The shallow depth of the slab-column junction limits the moment that can be transmitted through the joint and reduces its lateral resistance. The junction also restricts the minimum column size that may be used. For preliminary design, use a minimum square column dimension that is twice the thickness of the slab it supports.

- Reinforcement is heavier along the column strips to behave as flat beams. Middle strip reinforcement is lighter because it functions primarily as a slab.

- The omission of beams and joists offers flexibility in the layout of mechanical, plumbing, and electrical systems, but suspended ceilings are required to conceal their runs.

Column strip

Middle strip

Column strip

Middle strip

Column strip

Column strip

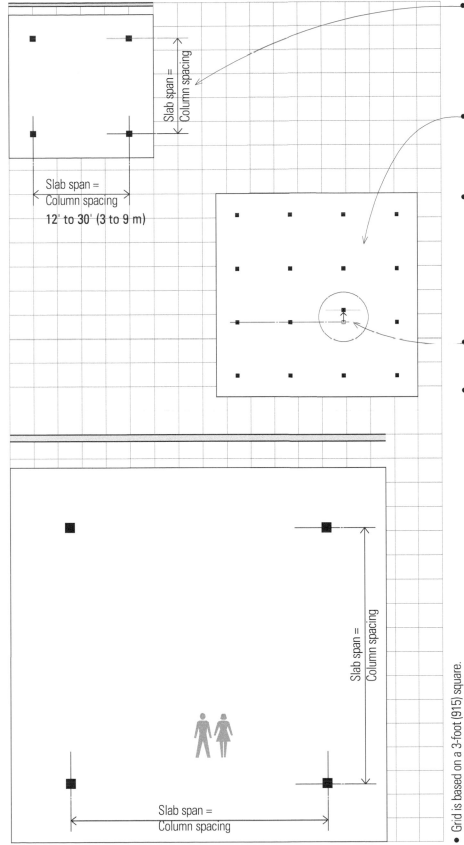

Slab span =
Column spacing
**12' to 30' (3 to 9 m)**

Slab span =
Column spacing

Slab span =
Column spacing

Slab span =
Column spacing

Slab span =
Column spacing

Grid is based on a 3-foot (915) square.

- Flat plates are suitable for light to moderate loads over relatively short spans of 12' to 30' (3.6 to 9.1 m). Greater spans and/or reduced slab thicknesses can be achieved with post-tensioning. Post-tensioning also offers increased control of deflection and cracking.

- Two-way systems are most efficient when spanning square or nearly square bays. The ratio of the long to the short dimensions should not be greater than 1.5:1.

- For maximum efficiency, flat plates should have a continuous span of at least three bays in both directions, and successive span lengths should not differ by more than a third of the longer span.

- While a regular column grid is most appropriate, some flexibility in column placement is possible.

- Individual columns may be offset by as much as 10 percent of the span from the regular column lines, but any shift should occur on all levels so that columns on successive floors remain vertically aligned.

## Flat Slabs

Flat slabs are flat plates thickened at their column supports to increase their shear strength and moment-resisting capacity.

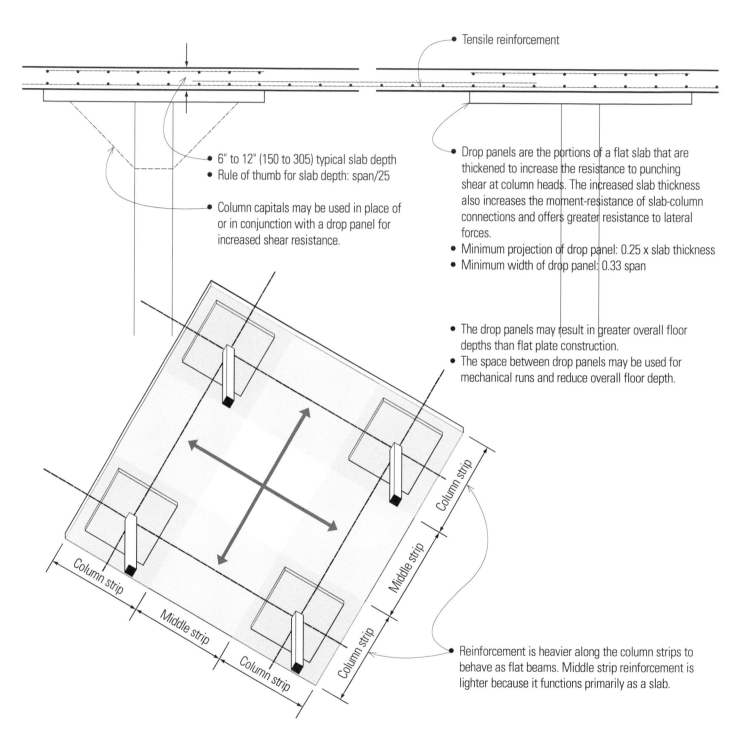

- Tensile reinforcement

- 6" to 12" (150 to 305) typical slab depth
- Rule of thumb for slab depth: span/25

- Column capitals may be used in place of or in conjunction with a drop panel for increased shear resistance.

- Drop panels are the portions of a flat slab that are thickened to increase the resistance to punching shear at column heads. The increased slab thickness also increases the moment-resistance of slab-column connections and offers greater resistance to lateral forces.
- Minimum projection of drop panel: 0.25 x slab thickness
- Minimum width of drop panel: 0.33 span

- The drop panels may result in greater overall floor depths than flat plate construction.
- The space between drop panels may be used for mechanical runs and reduce overall floor depth.

Column strip

Middle strip

Column strip

Column strip

Middle strip

Column strip

- Reinforcement is heavier along the column strips to behave as flat beams. Middle strip reinforcement is lighter because it functions primarily as a slab.

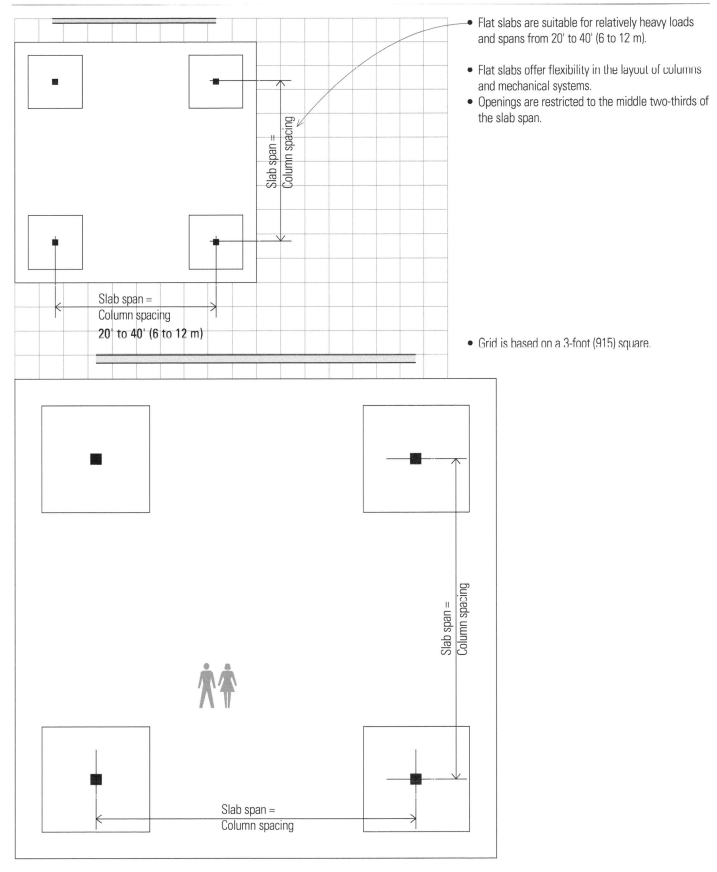

- Flat slabs are suitable for relatively heavy loads and spans from 20' to 40' (6 to 12 m).

- Flat slabs offer flexibility in the layout of columns and mechanical systems.
- Openings are restricted to the middle two-thirds of the slab span.

- Grid is based on a 3-foot (915) square.

Slab span = Column spacing

Slab span = Column spacing
20' to 40' (6 to 12 m)

Slab span = Column spacing

Slab span = Column spacing

## Two-Way Slabs with Beams

A two-way slab of uniform thickness may be reinforced in two directions and cast integrally with supporting beams and columns on all four sides of square or nearly square bays. Two-way slab and beam construction is effective for medium spans and heavy loads. A principal advantage of concrete slab-and-beam systems over flat slabs and plates is the rigid frame action that is made possible by the column-beam interaction for resisting lateral loads. The principal disadvantages are the increased cost of formwork and greater construction depth, particularly when mechanical ductwork must run below the beam structure.

- Because the slab and beams are cast contiguously, the thickness of the slab contributes to the structural depth of the beams.
- Rule of thumb for estimating beam depth: span/16, including the slab depth

- Rule of thumb for slab depth: slab perimeter/180
- 4" (100) minimum slab depth

- Tensile reinforcement

- Beam-column connections can provide moment resistance for increased lateral stability.

- Mechanical systems must run below the beams in both directions, increasing the overall depth of the floor or roof construction. Using a raised floor system and locating the mechanical systems above the structural floor can alleviate this difficulty.

- To simplify the placement of reinforcing steel, two-way slabs are divided into column and middle strips. The column strips have more reinforcement to act in concert with the beams, while the middle strips have less reinforcement because they function primarily as a slab.

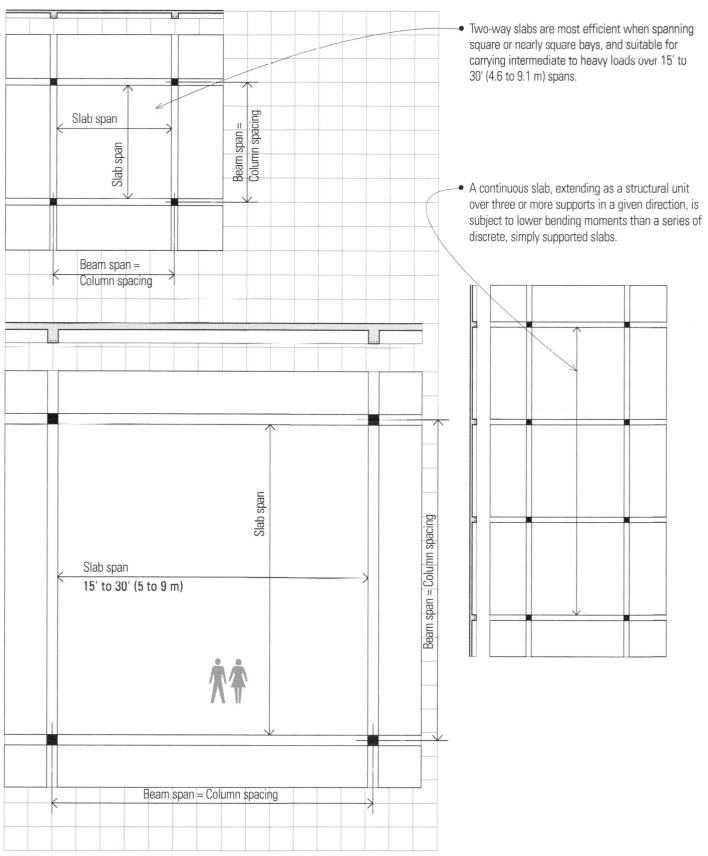

Slab span

Slab span

Beam span = Column spacing

Beam span = Column spacing

Slab span

Slab span
15' to 30' (5 to 9 m)

Beam span = Column spacing

Beam span = Column spacing

• Two-way slabs are most efficient when spanning square or nearly square bays, and suitable for carrying intermediate to heavy loads over 15' to 30' (4.6 to 9.1 m) spans.

• A continuous slab, extending as a structural unit over three or more supports in a given direction, is subject to lower bending moments than a series of discrete, simply supported slabs.

• Grid is based on a 3-foot (915) square.

### Waffle Slabs

Waffle slabs are two-way concrete slabs reinforced by ribs in two directions. They are able to carry heavier loads and span longer distances than flat slabs.

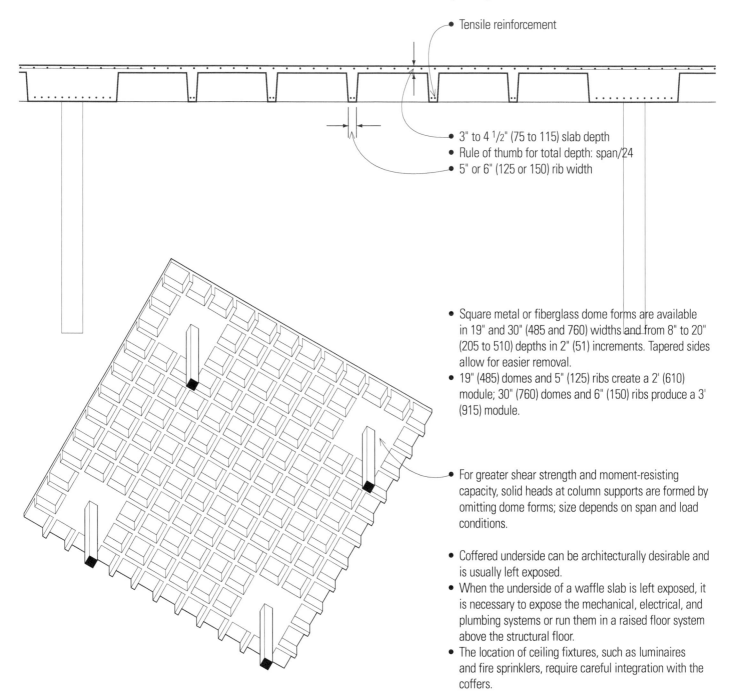

- Tensile reinforcement

- 3" to 4 1/2" (75 to 115) slab depth
- Rule of thumb for total depth: span/24
- 5" or 6" (125 or 150) rib width

- Square metal or fiberglass dome forms are available in 19" and 30" (485 and 760) widths and from 8" to 20" (205 to 510) depths in 2" (51) increments. Tapered sides allow for easier removal.
- 19" (485) domes and 5" (125) ribs create a 2' (610) module; 30" (760) domes and 6" (150) ribs produce a 3' (915) module.

- For greater shear strength and moment-resisting capacity, solid heads at column supports are formed by omitting dome forms; size depends on span and load conditions.

- Coffered underside can be architecturally desirable and is usually left exposed.
- When the underside of a waffle slab is left exposed, it is necessary to expose the mechanical, electrical, and plumbing systems or run them in a raised floor system above the structural floor.
- The location of ceiling fixtures, such as luminaires and fire sprinklers, require careful integration with the coffers.

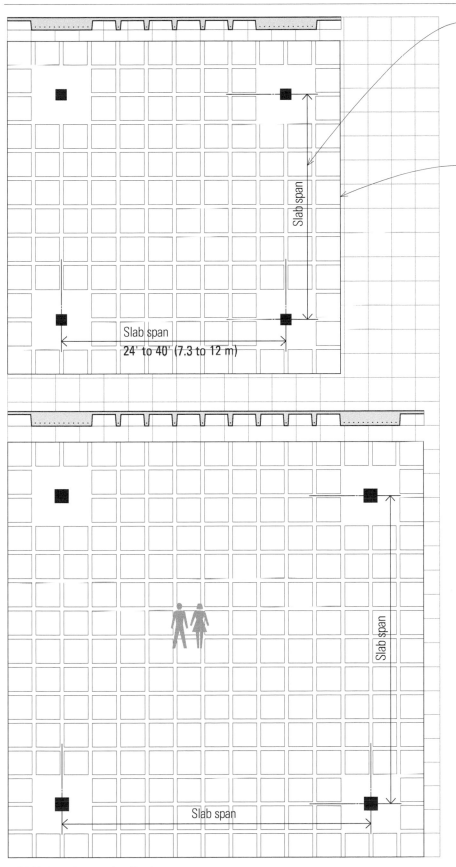

- Grid is based on a 3-foot (915) square.

- Ribbed construction produces a relatively light concrete system for spans of 24' to 40' (7.3 to 12.2 m); longer spans up to 60' (18 m) are possible with post-tensioning.

- For maximum efficiency, bays should be square or nearly as square as possible.
- Waffle slabs can be efficiently cantilevered in two directions up to a third of the main span. When no cantilever is present, a perimeter slab band is formed by omitting dome forms.

- The modular nature of the dome system encourages the use of a structural grid with regular, repetitive dimensions and geometry.

Slab span
24' to 40' (7.3 to 12 m)

Slab span

Slab span

Slab span

## Precast Concrete Slabs

Precast concrete slabs are one-way spanning units that may be supported by site-cast concrete, precast concrete, or masonry bearing walls, or by steel, site-cast concrete, or precast concrete frames. The precast units are manufactured with normal-density or structural lightweight concrete and prestressed for greater structural efficiency, which results in less depth, reduced weight, and longer spans.

The units are cast and steam-cured in a plant off-site, transported to the construction site, and set in place as rigid components with cranes. The size and proportion of the units may be limited by the means of transportation. Fabrication in a factory environment enables the units to have a consistent quality of strength, durability, and finish, and eliminates the need for on-site formwork.

- A 2" to 3 1/2" (51 to 90) concrete topping reinforced with steel fabric or reinforcing bars bonds with the precast units to form a composite structural unit.
- The topping also conceals any surface irregularities, increases the fire-resistance rating of the slab, and accommodates underfloor conduit for wiring.

- Grout key

- If the floor is to serve as a horizontal diaphragm and transfer lateral forces to shear walls, steel reinforcement must tie the precast slab units to each other over their supports and at their end bearings.

- Because moment-resistant joints are difficult to create, lateral stability must be provided by shear walls or cross bracing.

- Small openings in precast slabs may be cut in the field.
- Narrow openings parallel to slab span are preferred. Engineering analysis is required for wide openings.

- The inherent fire resistance and quality finish allows the underside of precast slabs to be caulked, painted, and exposed as a finish ceiling; a ceiling finish may also be applied to or be suspended from the slab units.
- When the undersides of the slab units are exposed as a finished ceiling, mechanical, plumbing, and electrical are also exposed.
- Precast slabs exposed as a finish ceiling may require noise-abatement treatment.

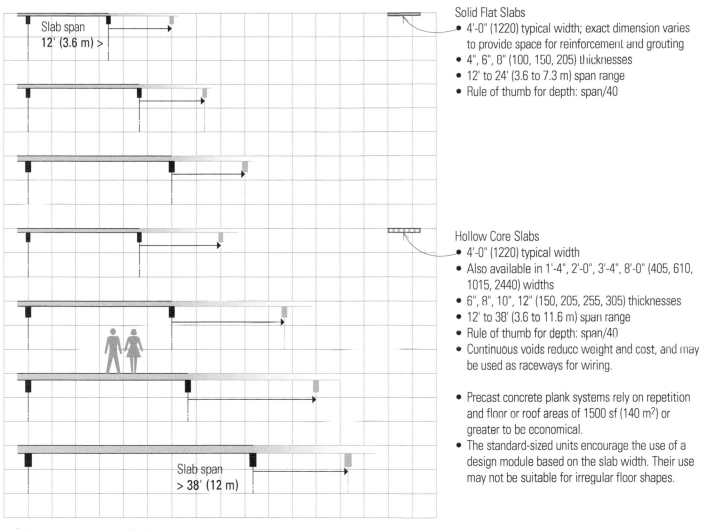

**Solid Flat Slabs**
- 4'-0" (1220) typical width; exact dimension varies to provide space for reinforcement and grouting
- 4", 6", 8" (100, 150, 205) thicknesses
- 12' to 24' (3.6 to 7.3 m) span range
- Rule of thumb for depth: span/40

**Hollow Core Slabs**
- 4'-0" (1220) typical width
- Also available in 1'-4", 2'-0", 3'-4", 8'-0" (405, 610, 1015, 2440) widths
- 6", 8", 10", 12" (150, 205, 255, 305) thicknesses
- 12' to 38' (3.6 to 11.6 m) span range
- Rule of thumb for depth: span/40
- Continuous voids reduce weight and cost, and may be used as raceways for wiring.

- Precast concrete plank systems rely on repetition and floor or roof areas of 1500 sf (140 m²) or greater to be economical.
- The standard-sized units encourage the use of a design module based on the slab width. Their use may not be suitable for irregular floor shapes.

Slab span 12' (3.6 m) >

Slab span > 38' (12 m)

- Grid is based on a 3-foot (915) square.

- Rule of thumb for estimating beam depth: span/16, including the slab depth, in 2" (51) increments
- ³/4" (19) bevel or chamfer
- Beam width is ¹/3 to ¹/2 of beam depth in 2" or 3" (50 or 75) multiples.
- Beam width should be equal to or greater than width of supporting column.

### Structural Steel Framing

Structural steel girders, beams, trusses, and columns are used to construct a skeleton frame for structures ranging in size from one-story buildings to skyscrapers. Because structural steel is difficult to work on-site, it is normally cut, shaped, and drilled in a fabrication shop according to design specifications; this can result in relatively fast, precise construction of a structural frame.

Structural steel may be left exposed in unprotected noncombustible construction, but because steel can lose strength rapidly in a fire, fire-rated assemblies or coatings are required to qualify as fire-resistive construction. In exposed conditions, corrosion resistance is also required.

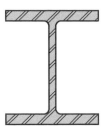

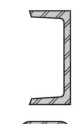

### Steel Beams and Girders

- More structurally efficient wide-flange (W) shapes have largely superseded the classic I-beam (S) shapes. Beams may also be in the form of channel (C) sections, structural tubing, or composite sections.
- Connections usually use transitional elements, such as steel angles, tees, or plates. The actual connections may be riveted but are more often bolted or welded.

- Typical span range for steel beams is 20' to 40' (6 to 12 m); above 32' (10 m), however, open-web steel joists become an economical alternative due to their reduced weight.
- Rules of thumb for estimating beam depth:
  Steel beams: span/20
  Steel girders: span/15
- Beam width: 1/3 to 1/2 of beam depth

- The general objective is to use the lightest steel section that will resist bending and shear forces within allowable limits of stress and without excessive deflection for the intended use.
- In addition to material costs, the labor costs required for erection must also be considered.

- Floor or roof deck may consist of:
  - Metal decking
  - Precast concrete slabs
  - Structural wood panels or planking, requiring a nailable top chord or nailer.

- Beams or open-web joists supporting the floor or roof deck are spaced 4' to 16' (1.2 to 4.9 m) o.c., depending on the magnitude of the applied load and spanning capability of the deck.

- Resistance to lateral wind or earthquake forces requires the use of shear walls, diagonal bracing, or rigid framing with moment-resisting connections.

- K series joists have webs consisting of a single bent bar, running in a zigzag pattern between the upper and lower chords.
- 8" to 30" (205 to 760) depths

- LH (long-span) series joists and DLH (deep long-span) series joists have heavier web and chord members for increased loads and spans.
- LH series joist depths: 18" to 48" (455 to 1220)
- DLH series joist depths: 52" to 72" (1320 to 1830)

- Span range or open-web steel joists: 12' to 60' (3.6 to 18 m)
- Rule of thumb for estimating open-web joist depth: span/24

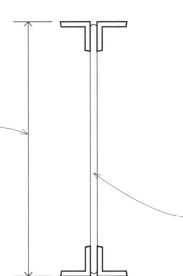

### Open-Web Steel Joists

Open-web joists are lightweight, shop-fabricated steel members having a trussed web. They provide an economical alternative to steel beams for light to moderate distributed loads, especially for spans greater than 32' (10 m).

- The framing works most efficiently when the joists carry uniformly distributed loads. If properly engineered, concentrated loads may bear over the panel points of the joists.

- Open webs permit the passage of mechanical services.
- Ceiling may be attached to bottom chords or be suspended if additional space for services is required; ceiling may also be omitted to expose joists and floor deck.

- 2' to 10' (0.6 to 3 m) spacing; 4' to 8' (1.2 to 2.4 m) spacing common in large buildings
- Horizontal or diagonal bridging is required to prevent lateral movement of joist chords.
- Bridging is spaced from 10' to 20' (3 to 6 m) o.c., depending on joist span and chord size.

- Fire-resistance rating of the joist structure depends on the fire rating of the floor and ceiling assemblies.

- Limited overhangs are possible by extending the top chords.

- Open-web steel joists may be supported by steel beams or joist girders, which are heavier versions of open-web joists, or by bearing walls of masonry, reinforced concrete, or light-gauge steel framing.

### One-Way Beam System

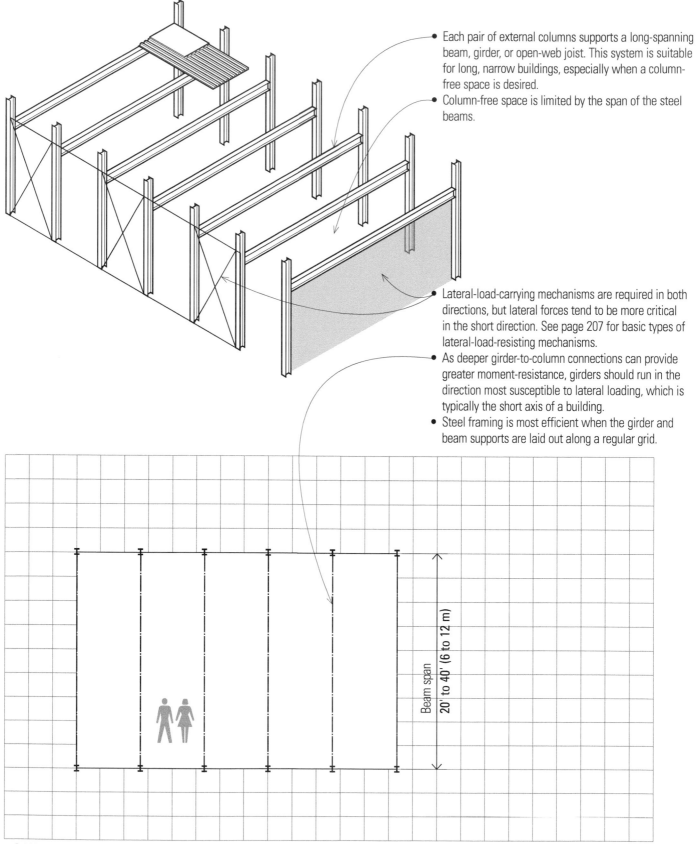

- Each pair of external columns supports a long-spanning beam, girder, or open-web joist. This system is suitable for long, narrow buildings, especially when a column-free space is desired.
- Column-free space is limited by the span of the steel beams.

- Lateral-load-carrying mechanisms are required in both directions, but lateral forces tend to be more critical in the short direction. See page 207 for basic types of lateral-load-resisting mechanisms.
- As deeper girder-to-column connections can provide greater moment-resistance, girders should run in the direction most susceptible to lateral loading, which is typically the short axis of a building.
- Steel framing is most efficient when the girder and beam supports are laid out along a regular grid.

Beam span 20' to 40' (6 to 12 m)

- Grid is based on a 3-foot (915) square.

## Beam-and-Girder System

- Economical spans for primary beams or girders range from 20' to 40' (6 to 12 m).
- Economical spans for secondary beams range from 22' to 60' (7 to 20 m).
- Both primary and secondary beams may consist of structural steel sections for spans up to 32' (10 m). For greater spans, open-web joists or truss girders are more economical.

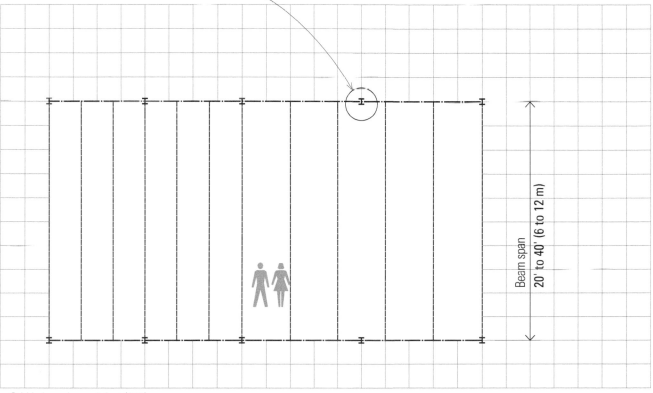

- Steel decking with concrete slab
- Beams
- Girder

- Steel framing should use rectangular bay units, with comparatively lightly loaded secondary beams having longer spans than the more heavily loaded primary beams or girders.

- Staggering the secondary beams provides space for vertical chases alongside each column.

- Framing beams into girders minimizes floor depth; some mechanical services can pass through holes cut into the beam webs, but large lines may have to be accommodated in a suspended ceiling space below.
- Having beams bearing on and continuing over girders increases floor depth considerably but provides more space for mechanical services.

Beam span 20' to 40' (6 to 12 m)

- Grid is based on a 3-foot (915) square.

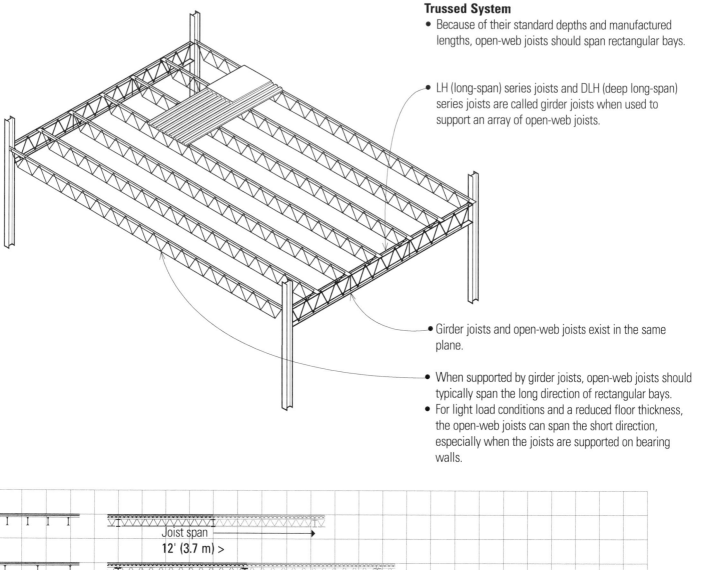

### Trussed System

- Because of their standard depths and manufactured lengths, open-web joists should span rectangular bays.

- LH (long-span) series joists and DLH (deep long-span) series joists are called girder joists when used to support an array of open-web joists.

- Girder joists and open-web joists exist in the same plane.

- When supported by girder joists, open-web joists should typically span the long direction of rectangular bays.
- For light load conditions and a reduced floor thickness, the open-web joists can span the short direction, especially when the joists are supported on bearing walls.

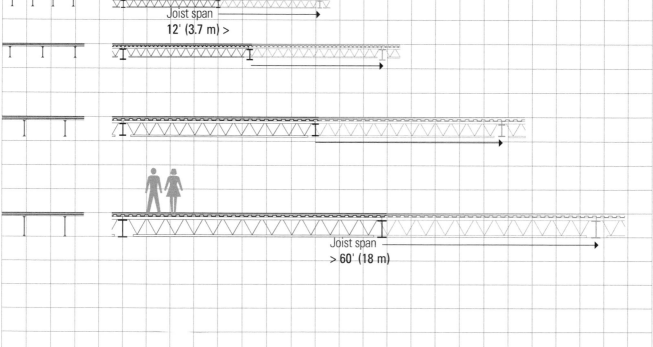

Joist span
12' (3.7 m) >

Joist span
> 60' (18 m)

- Grid is based on a 3-foot (915) square.

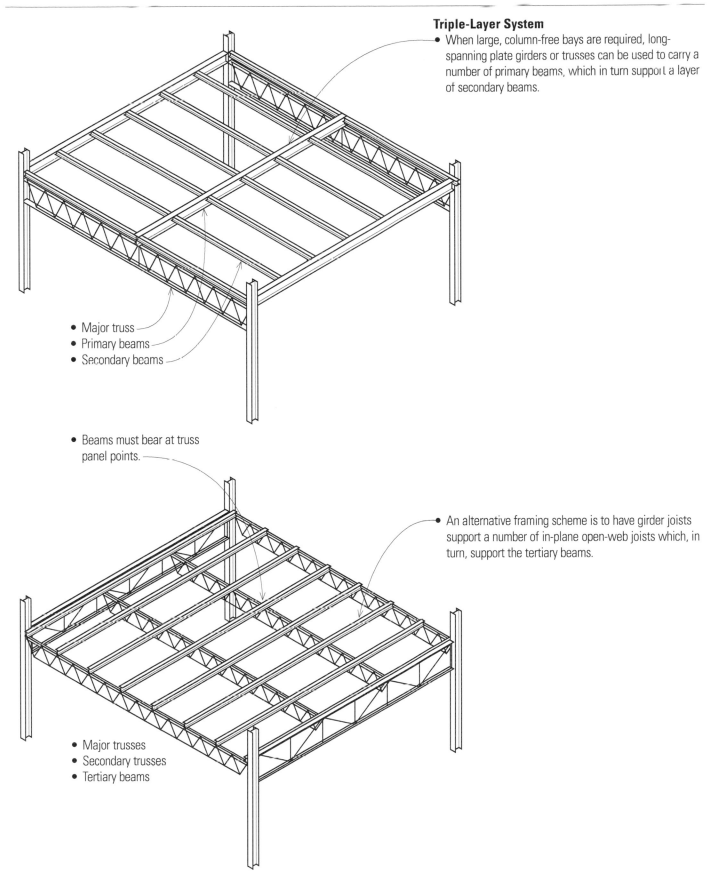

**Triple-Layer System**
- When large, column-free bays are required, long-spanning plate girders or trusses can be used to carry a number of primary beams, which in turn support a layer of secondary beams.

- Major truss
- Primary beams
- Secondary beams

- Beams must bear at truss panel points.

- An alternative framing scheme is to have girder joists support a number of in-plane open-web joists which, in turn, support the tertiary beams.

- Major trusses
- Secondary trusses
- Tertiary beams

## Metal Decking

Metal decking is corrugated to increase its stiffness and spanning capability. The floor deck serves as a working platform during construction and as formwork for a site-cast concrete slab.

- Form decking serves as permanent formwork for a reinforced concrete slab until the slab can support itself and its live load.

- Concrete slab

- Composite decking is available in 1 1/2", 2", and 3" (38, 51, and 75) depths.
- Total slab depth ranges from 4" to 8" (100 to 205).

- Steel beam or open-web joist supports

- Composite decking serves as tensile reinforcement for the concrete slab to which it is bonded with embossed rib patterns. Composite action between the concrete slab and the floor beams or joists can be achieved by welding shear studs through the decking to the supporting beam below.

- Similar to composite decking is cellular decking, which is manufactured by welding a corrugated sheet to a flat steel sheet, forming a series of spaces or raceways for electrical and communications wiring; special cutouts are available for floor outlets. The decking may serve as an acoustic ceiling when the perforated cells are filled with glass fiber.

- The decking panels are secured with puddle-welds or shear studs welded through the decking to the supporting steel joists or beams.
- The panels are fastened to each other along their sides with screws or welds.
- If the deck is to serve as a structural diaphragm and transfer lateral loads to shear walls, its entire perimeter must be welded to steel supports. In addition, more stringent requirements for support and side lap fastening may apply.
- In roof applications, rigid insulation can be placed directly over the steel deck in place of the concrete topping.

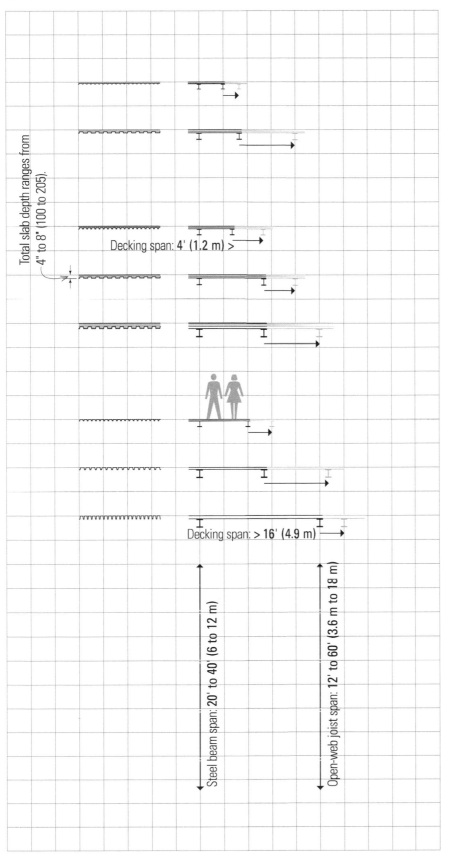

Total slab depth ranges from 4" to 8" (100 to 205).

Decking span: 4' (1.2 m) >

Decking span: > 16' (4.9 m) →

Steel beam span: 20' to 40' (6 to 12 m)

Open-web joist span: 12' to 60' (3.6 m to 18 m)

## Form Decking

- 1" (25) spanning 3' to 5' (915 to 1525)

- 2" (51) spanning 5' to 12' (1525 to 3660)

## Composite Decking

- 1 1/2" (38) + concrete, spanning 4' to 8' (1220 to 2440)

- 2" (51) + concrete, spanning 8' to 12' (2440 to 3660)

- 3" (75) + concrete, spanning 8' to 15' (2440 to 4570)

## Roof Decking

- 1 1/2" (38) spanning 6' to 12' (1830 to 3660)

- 2" (51) spanning 6' to 12' (1830 to 3660)

- 3" (75) spanning 10' to 16' (3050 to 4875)

- Rule of thumb for overall depth of metal decking: span/35

- Grid is based on a 3-foot (915) square.

## Light-Gauge Steel Joists

Light-gauge steel joists are manufactured by cold-forming sheet or strip steel. The resulting steel joists are lighter, more dimensionally stable, and can span longer distances than their wood counterparts but conduct more heat and require more energy to process and manufacture. The cold-formed steel joists can be easily cut and assembled with simple tools into a floor structure that is lightweight, noncombustible, and dampproof. As in wood light frame construction, the framing contains cavities for utilities and thermal insulation and accepts a wide range of finishes.

- Light-gauge steel joists are noncombustible and may be used in Type I and Type II construction.
- Light-gauge steel joists are laid out in and assembled in a manner similar to wood joist framing.
- Connections are made with self-drilling, self-tapping screws inserted with an electric or pneumatic tool, or with pneumatically driven pins.

- Strap bridging prevents the rotation or lateral displacement of the joists; space 5' to 8' (1.5 to 2.4 m) o.c., depending on joist span.

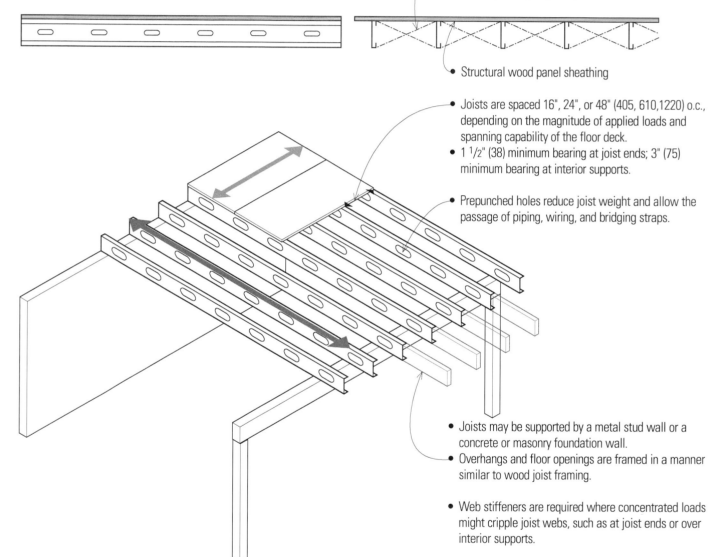

- Structural wood panel sheathing

- Joists are spaced 16", 24", or 48" (405, 610,1220) o.c., depending on the magnitude of applied loads and spanning capability of the floor deck.
- 1 1/2" (38) minimum bearing at joist ends; 3" (75) minimum bearing at interior supports.

- Prepunched holes reduce joist weight and allow the passage of piping, wiring, and bridging straps.

- Joists may be supported by a metal stud wall or a concrete or masonry foundation wall.
- Overhangs and floor openings are framed in a manner similar to wood joist framing.

- Web stiffeners are required where concentrated loads might cripple joist webs, such as at joist ends or over interior supports.

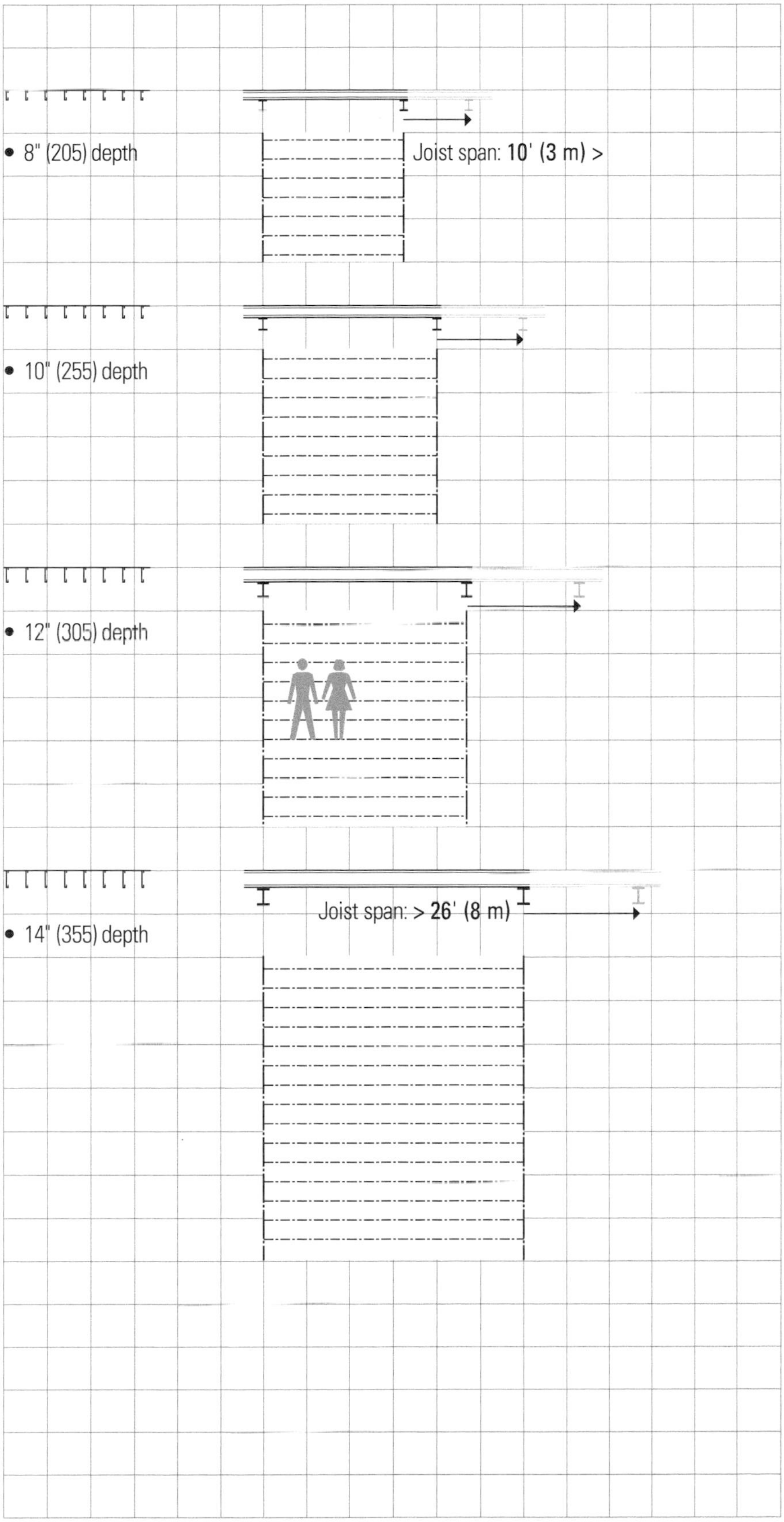

- 8" (205) depth

Joist span: **10'** (3 m) >

- 10" (255) depth

- 12" (305) depth

- 14" (355) depth

Joist span: > **26'** (8 m)

- Nominal depths: 6", 8", 10", 12", 14" (150, 205, 255, 305, 355)
- Flange widths: 1 $1/2$", 1 $3/4$", 2", 2 $1/2$" (38, 45, 51, 64)
- Gauges: 14 through 22

- Rule of thumb for estimating joist depth: span/20

- Grid is based on a 3-foot (915) square.

### Wood Construction

There are two distinctly different wood construction systems in current use—heavy timber framing and light wood framing. Heavy timber framing uses large, thick members such as beams and columns that have a substantially higher fire-rating than unprotected steel. Due to the scarcity of large sawn logs, most timber frames are currently composed of glue-laminated timber and parallel strand lumber rather than solid wood. Architecturally, timber framing is often left exposed for its aesthetic quality.

Light wood framing uses relatively small, closely spaced members to form assemblies that perform as structural units. The light wood members are highly flammable and must rely on finish surfacing materials for the required fire-resistance rating. The susceptibility of light wood framing to decay and insect infestation requires adequate separation from the ground, appropriate use of pressure-treated lumber, and ventilation to control condensation in enclosed spaces.

Because moment-resistant joints are difficult to achieve in wood construction, both light- and heavy-framed structures must be stabilized with either shear walls or diagonal bracing to resist lateral forces.

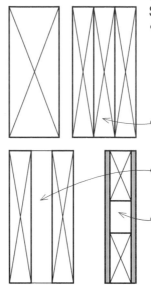

### Wood Beams
#### Solid Sawn Lumber

- In the selection of a wood beam the following should be considered: lumber species, structural grade, modulus of elasticity, allowable bending and shear stress values, and the minimum deflection permitted for the intended use. In addition, attention should be paid to the precise loading conditions and the types of connections used.
- Built-up beams can be equal in strength to the sum of the strengths of the individual pieces if none of the laminations are spliced.
- Spaced beams are blocked and securely nailed at frequent intervals to enable the individual members to act as an integral unit.
- Box beams are made by gluing two or more plywood or OSB webs to sawn or LVL flanges. They can be engineered to span up to 90 feet (27 m).

### Glue-Laminated Timber

- Glue-laminated timber is made by laminating stress-grade lumber with adhesive under controlled conditions, usually with the grain of all plies being parallel. The advantages of glued-laminated timber over solid-sawn lumber are generally higher allowable unit stresses, improved appearance, and availability of various sectional shapes. Glue-laminated timbers may be end-joined with scarf or finger joints to any desired length, or edge-glued for greater width or depth.

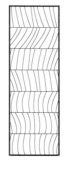

### Parallel Strand Lumber

- Parallel strand lumber (PSL) is produced by bonding long, narrow wood strands together under heat and pressure using a waterproof adhesive. It is a proprietary product marketed under the trademark Parallam, used as beams and columns in post-and-beam construction and for beams, headers, and lintels in light frame construction.

### Laminated Veneer Lumber

- Laminated veneer lumber (LVL) is manufactured by bonding layers of wood veneers together under heat and pressure using a waterproof adhesive. Having the grain of all veneers run in the same longitudinal direction results in a product that is strong when edge loaded as a beam or face loaded as a plank. Laminated veneer lumber is marketed under various brand names, such as Microlam, and used as headers and beams or as flanges for prefabricated wood I-joists.

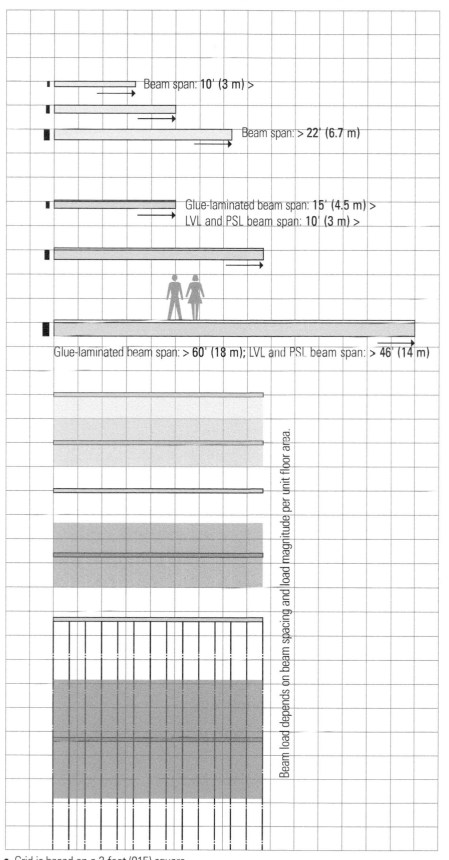

## Solid Wood Beams

- Available in 2" (51) nominal increments from 4x8 to 6x12; actual dimensions are $^3/_4$" (19) less in depth and $^1/_2$" (13) less in width than nominal.

- Rule of thumb for estimating the depth of solid wood beams: span/15
- Beam width = $^1/_3$ to $^1/_2$ of beam depth

## Glue-Laminated Timber

- Beam widths: 3 $^1/_8$", 5 $^1/_8$", 6 $^3/_4$", 8 $^3/_4$", and 10 $^3/_4$" (80, 130, 170, 220, and 275)
- Beam depth is in multiples of 1 $^3/_8$" or 1 $^1/_2$" (35 or 38) laminations up to 75" (19 050). Curved members can be laminated in $^3/_4$" (19) laminations to create tighter curvature.

## Parallel Strand Lumber

- Beam widths: 3 $^1/_2$", 5 $^1/_4$", and 7" (90, 135, and 180)
- Beam depths: 9 $^1/_2$", 11 $^7/_8$", 14", 16", and 18" (240, 300, 355, 410, and 460)

## Laminated Veneer Lumber

- 1 $^3/_4$" (45) beam width; can be laminated for greater widths.
- 5 $^1/_2$", 7 $^1/_4$", 9 $^1/_4$", 11 $^1/_4$", 11 $^7/_8$", 14", 16", 18", and 20" (140, 185, 235, 285, 300, 355, 405, 455, and 510) beam depths

- Rule of thumb for estimating the depth of manufactured beams: span/20
- Beam spans are only estimates. Any accurate calculation of beam size must take into account the tributary load area for a beam, based on its spacing and the magnitude of load being carried.

- Beam width should be $^1/_4$ to $^1/_3$ of beam depth
- Because of transport limitations, the maximum standard length for manufactured beams is 60' (18 m).

Labels within figure:

Beam span: **10'** (3 m) >

Beam span: > **22'** (6.7 m)

Glue-laminated beam span: **15'** (4.5 m) >
LVL and PSL beam span: **10'** (3 m) >

Glue-laminated beam span: > **60'** (18 m); LVL and PSL beam span: > **46'** (14 m)

Beam load depends on beam spacing and load magnitude per unit floor area.

- Grid is based on a 3-foot (915) square.

## Plank-and-Beam Systems

Wood plank-and-beam spanning systems are typically used with a supporting grid of columns to form a skeleton frame structure. Using larger but fewer structural members that can span greater distances translates into potential savings in material and labor costs.

- Plank-and-beam framing is most effective when supporting moderate, evenly distributed loads; concentrated loads may require additional framing.
- When this structural system is left exposed, as is often the case, careful attention must be paid to the species and grade of wood used, the detailing of joints, especially at beam-to-beam and beam-to-post connections, and the quality of workmanship.

Plank-and-beam framing may qualify as heavy timber construction if the structure is supported by noncombustible, fire-resistive exterior walls and the members and decking meet the minimum size requirements specified in the building code. Disadvantages of the plank-and-beam floor system include its susceptibility to impact sound transmission, and its inherent lack of concealed spaces for thermal insulation, piping, wiring, and ductwork.

- Wood beams may be supported by:
  - Timber, steel, or concrete columns
  - Timber or steel girders
  - Concrete or masonry bearing walls
- Bearing area should be sufficient to ensure the allowable compressive stresses of the beam and bearing material are not exceeded.

- Span of decking

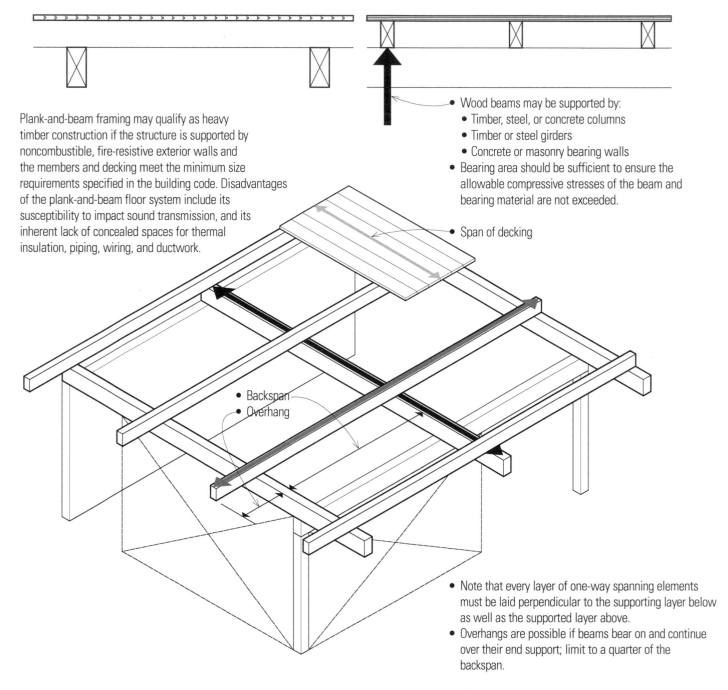

- Backspan
- Overhang

- Note that every layer of one-way spanning elements must be laid perpendicular to the supporting layer below as well as the supported layer above.
- Overhangs are possible if beams bear on and continue over their end support; limit to a quarter of the backspan.

- Diagonal bracing or shear walls are required to provide lateral stability. It is not possible to develop moment-resistant connections in timber post-and-beam framing.

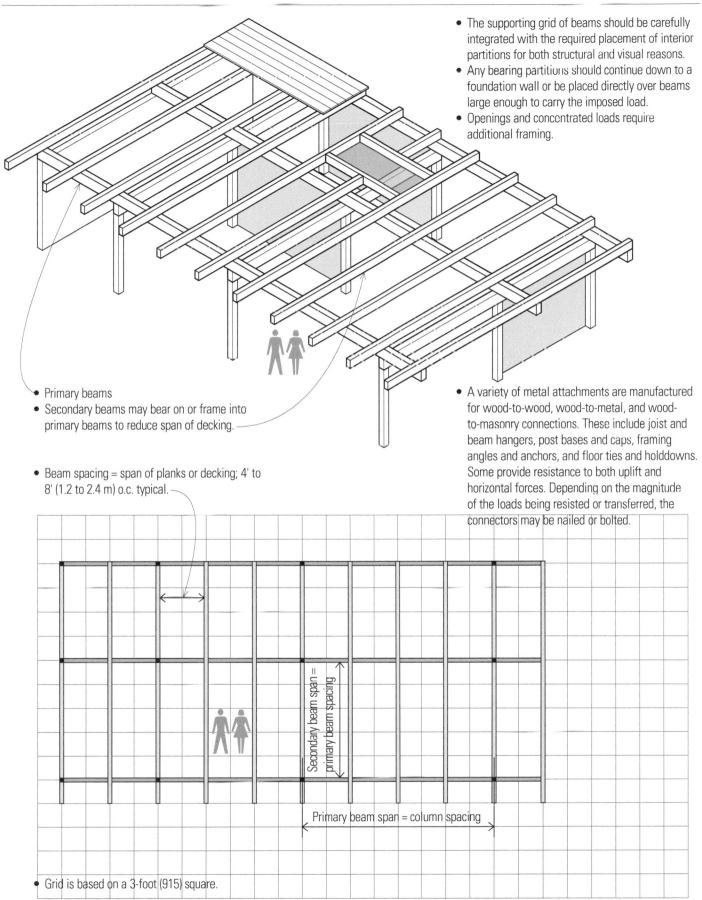

- The supporting grid of beams should be carefully integrated with the required placement of interior partitions for both structural and visual reasons.
- Any bearing partitions should continue down to a foundation wall or be placed directly over beams large enough to carry the imposed load.
- Openings and concentrated loads require additional framing.

- Primary beams
- Secondary beams may bear on or frame into primary beams to reduce span of decking.

- Beam spacing = span of planks or decking; 4' to 8' (1.2 to 2.4 m) o.c. typical.

- A variety of metal attachments are manufactured for wood-to-wood, wood-to-metal, and wood-to-masonry connections. These include joist and beam hangers, post bases and caps, framing angles and anchors, and floor ties and holddowns. Some provide resistance to both uplift and horizontal forces. Depending on the magnitude of the loads being resisted or transferred, the connectors may be nailed or bolted.

Secondary beam span = primary beam spacing

Primary beam span = column spacing

- Grid is based on a 3-foot (915) square.

## Wood Decking

Wood decking is typically used with plank-and-beam systems but can also form the surface layer of steel frame construction. The underside of the decking may be left exposed as a finished ceiling surface.

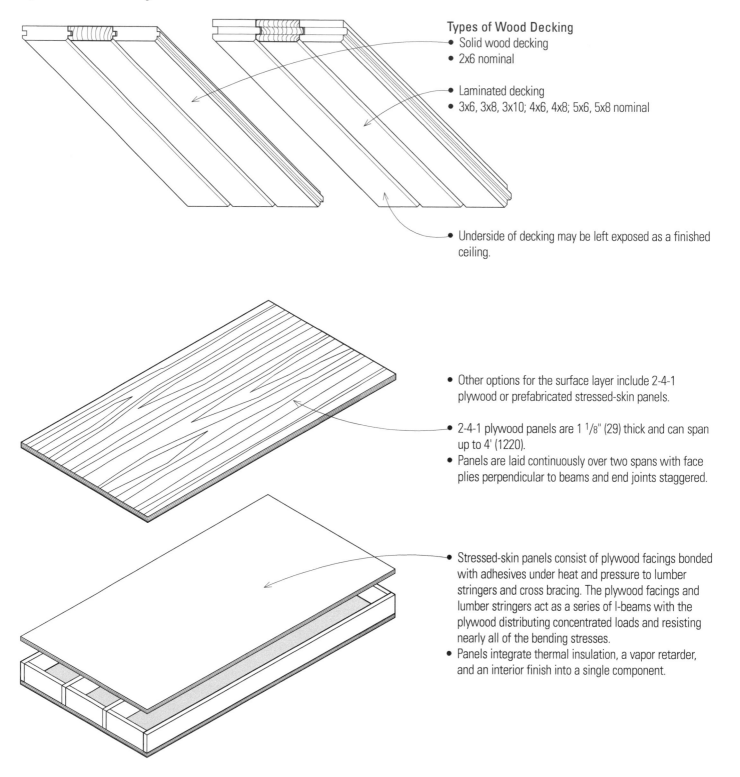

Types of Wood Decking
- Solid wood decking
- 2x6 nominal

- Laminated decking
- 3x6, 3x8, 3x10; 4x6, 4x8; 5x6, 5x8 nominal

- Underside of decking may be left exposed as a finished ceiling.

- Other options for the surface layer include 2-4-1 plywood or prefabricated stressed-skin panels.

- 2-4-1 plywood panels are 1 1/8" (29) thick and can span up to 4' (1220).
- Panels are laid continuously over two spans with face plies perpendicular to beams and end joints staggered.

- Stressed-skin panels consist of plywood facings bonded with adhesives under heat and pressure to lumber stringers and cross bracing. The plywood facings and lumber stringers act as a series of I-beams with the plywood distributing concentrated loads and resisting nearly all of the bending stresses.
- Panels integrate thermal insulation, a vapor retarder, and an interior finish into a single component.

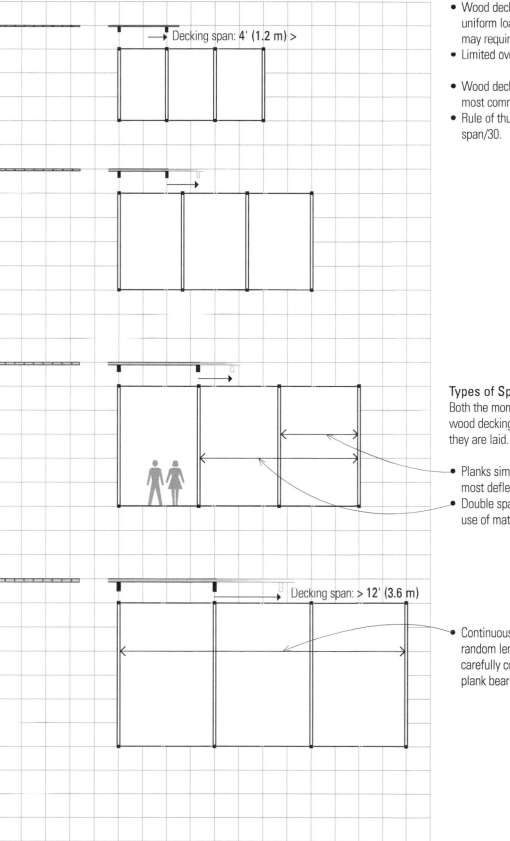

- Wood decking is most effective in supporting uniform loads. Openings and concentrated loads may require additional framing.
- Limited overhangs are possible.

- Wood decking can span up to 12' (3.6 m), but the most common span range is 4' to 8' (1.2 to 2.4 m).
- Rule of thumb for estimating depth of decking: span/30.

Decking span: 4' (1.2 m) >

### Types of Spans
Both the moment-resisting capacity and deflection of wood decking are affected by the manner in which they are laid.

- Planks simply supported at each end have the most deflection for a given load.
- Double spans offer the most efficient structural use of material of a given length.

Decking span: > 12' (3.6 m)

- Continuous spans over four or more supports use random lengths and reduce waste. Layout must be carefully controlled with offset end joints and each plank bearing on at least one support.

- Grid is based on a 3-foot (915) square.

## Wood Joists

The term joist refers to any of various spanning members designed for closely spaced, multiple member spanning assemblies. The close spacing of joists results in a relatively small tributary load area for each member and a distributed load pattern on the supporting beam or wall.

- Joists are spaced 12", 16", or 24" ( 305, 405, or 610) o.c., depending on the anticipated magnitude of applied load and spanning capability of the subflooring or sheathing.

- Joists are designed for uniform loads and are more efficient if they are cross-braced or bridged to allow them to transfer and share point loads.

Wood joists are an essential subsystem of light wood frame construction. The dimension lumber used for joists is easily worked and can be quickly assembled on-site with simple tools. Together with wood panel sheathing or subflooring, the wood joists form a level working platform for construction. If properly engineered, the resulting floor structure can serve as a structural diaphragm to transfer lateral loads to shear walls.

- Cavities can accommodate piping, wiring, and thermal insulation.
- A ceiling may be applied directly to joists, or be suspended to lower ceiling area or conceal mechanical runs perpendicular to joists.
- Because wood light framing is combustible, it must rely on finish flooring and ceiling materials for its fire-resistance rating.
- Joist ends require lateral support.

- Subflooring ties and stabilizes the joists to prevent twisting and buckling. This layer typically consists of plywood although other nonveneer panel materials, such as oriented strand board (OSB), waferboard, and particleboard, can be used if manufactured according to approved standards. Panels are $7/16$" to 1" (11 to 25) thick capable of 16", 20", and 24" (405, 600, and 610) spans.

- 1 $1/2$" (38) minimum bearing on wood or metal
- 3" (75) minimum bearing on concrete or masonry

- Joists may bear on and overhang the supporting beam or wall.
- For a reduced construction depth, the joists may frame into the supporting beams using prefabricated joist hangers.

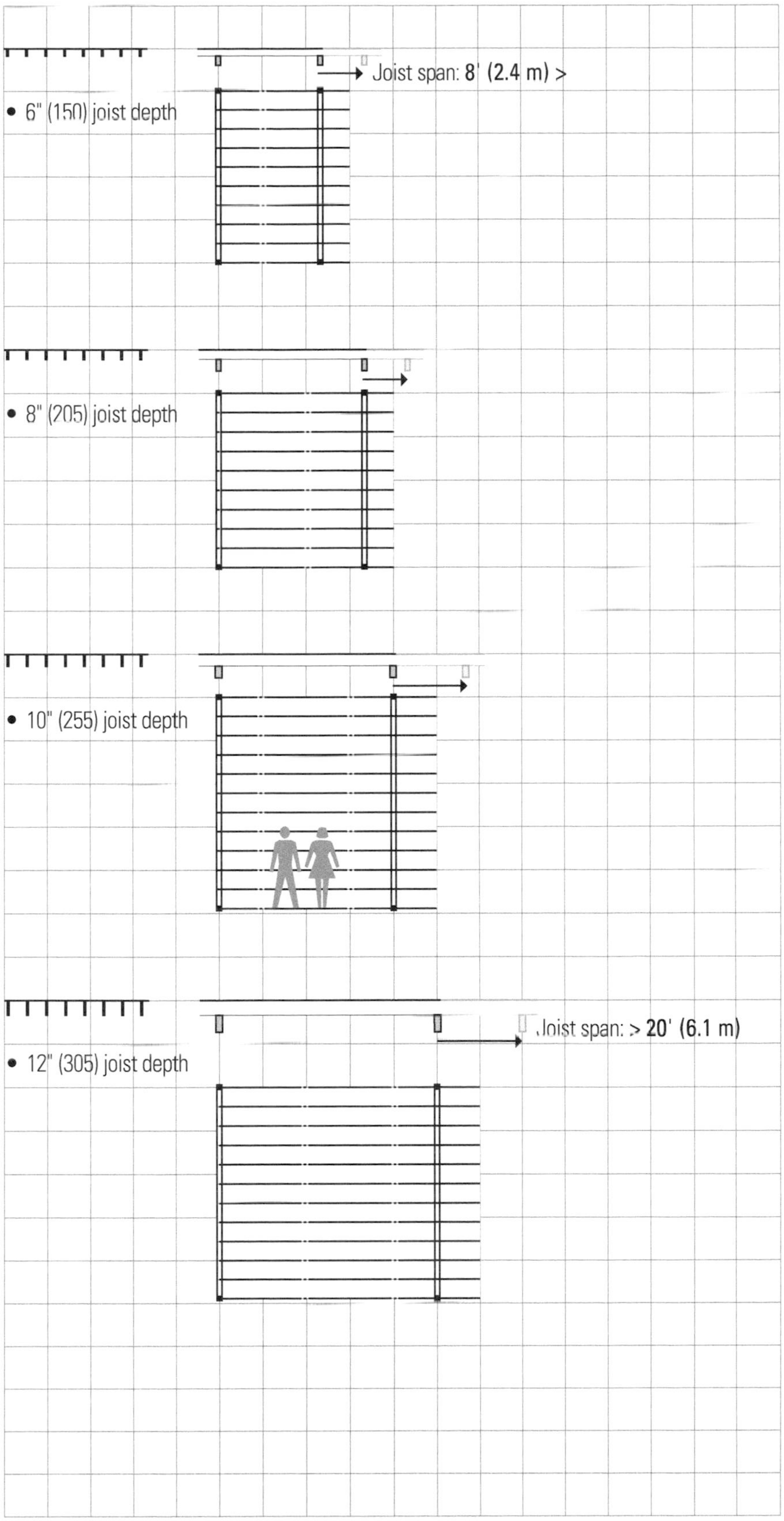

- 6" (150) joist depth

→ Joist span: **8'** **(2.4 m)** >

- 8" (205) joist depth

- 10" (255) joist depth

Joist span: **> 20'** **(6.1 m)**

- 12" (305) joist depth

- Grid is based on a 3-foot (915) square.

- Wood joist framing is highly flexible and well suited for irregular layouts due to the workability of the material.

- Wood joist sizes: 2x6, 2x8, 2x10, and 2x12 nominal
- Dressed sizes of joists:
  Subtract $1/2$" (13) from nominal dimensions of 2" to 6" (51 to 150);
  Subtract $3/4$" (19) from nominal dimensions greater than 6" (150).

- Span ranges for wood joists:
  2x6    up to 10' (3 m)
  2x8    8'–12' (2.4–3.6 m)
  2x10   10'–14' (3–4.3 m)
  2x12   12'–20' (3.6–6.1 m)
- Rule of thumb for estimating joist depth: span/16

- Solid wood joists are available in lengths up to 20' (6 m).

- The stiffness of the joist framing under stress is often more critical than its strength as the joist members approach the limit of their span range.

- If the overall construction depth is acceptable, deeper joists spaced farther apart are more desirable for stiffness than shallow joists spaced more closely together.

## Prefabricated Joists and Trusses

Prefabricated, pre-engineered wood joists and trusses are increasingly used in the place of dimension lumber to frame floors and roofs because they are generally lighter and more dimensionally stable than sawn lumber, are manufactured in greater depths and lengths, and can span longer distances. While the precise form of a prefabricated floor joist or truss varies with the manufacturer, the way they are laid out to frame a floor is similar in principle to conventional wood joist framing. They are most appropriate for long spans and simple floor plans; complex floor layouts may be difficult to frame.

## I-Joists

- I-joists are manufactured with sawn or laminated veneer lumber flanges along the top and bottom edges of a single plywood or oriented strand board (OSB) web.
- 10" to 16" (255 to 405) nominal depths
- Depths up to 24" (610) are available for commercial construction.

- 3 1/2" (90) minimum bearing

- Double joists provide support for parallel bearing partitions.
- Bracing is necessary to provide lateral support perpendicular to the plane of prefabricated wood trusses.

## Wood Trussed Joists

- Two 2x4 or 2x6 chords w/ 1" (25.4), 1 1/4" (32), up to 2" (51) ø steel webs
- Up to 42" (1065) nominal depths

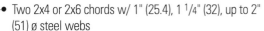
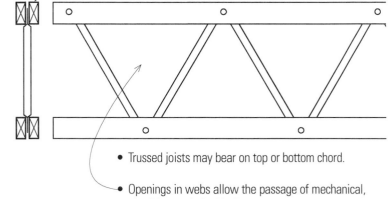

- Trussed joists may bear on top or bottom chord.

- Openings in webs allow the passage of mechanical, plumbing, and electrical runs.

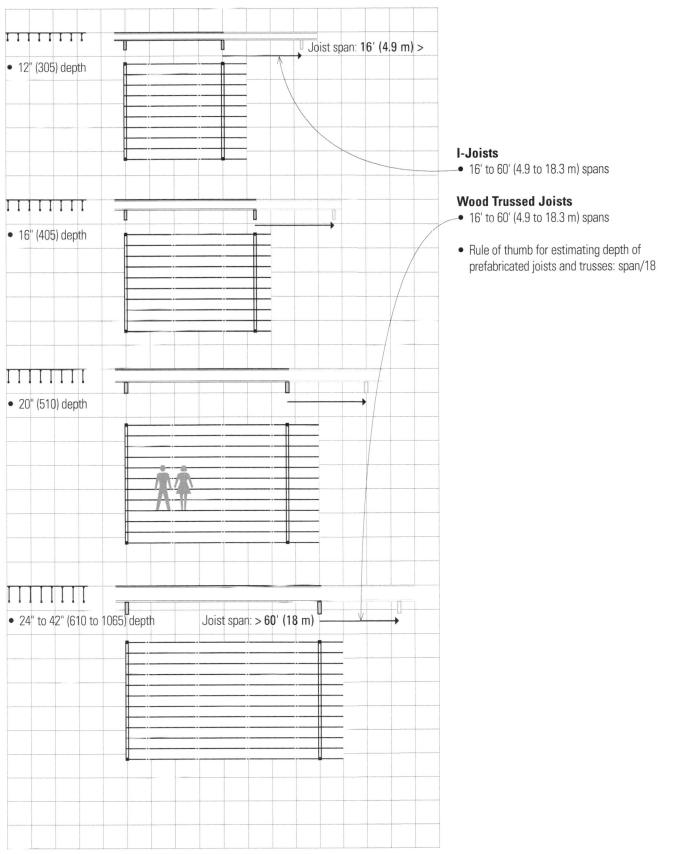

- 12" (305) depth

Joist span: **16' (4.9 m)** >

- 16" (405) depth

- 20" (510) depth

- 24" to 42" (610 to 1065) depth    Joist span: **> 60' (18 m)**

### I-Joists
- 16' to 60' (4.9 to 18.3 m) spans

### Wood Trussed Joists
- 16' to 60' (4.9 to 18.3 m) spans

- Rule of thumb for estimating depth of prefabricated joists and trusses: span/18

- Grid is based on a 3-foot (915) square.

## Cantilevers

A cantilever is a beam, girder, truss, or other rigid structural framework that is securely fixed at one end and free at the other end. The fixed end of a cantilever resists loads transversely and rotationally while the other end is free to deflect and rotate. Pure cantilever beams exhibit a single downward curvature when loaded from above. The top surface of the beam will be stressed in tension while the bottom fibers are subjected to compressive stresses. Cantilever beams tend to have very large deflections and the critical bending moment develops at the support.

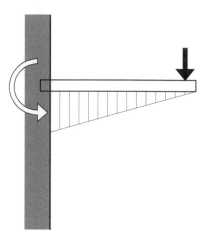

## Overhanging Beams

An overhanging beam is formed by extending one or both ends of a simple beam. Cantilever action results from the beam extension, which has the positive effect of counteracting the deflection present in the interior span. Overhanging beams exhibit multiple curvatures, unlike a simple cantilever beam. Tensile and compressive stresses reverse along the beam's length corresponding to the deflected shape.

- Assuming a uniformly distributed load, the projection of a single overhanging beam for which the moment over the support is equal and opposite to the moment at midspan is approximately 3/8 of the span.

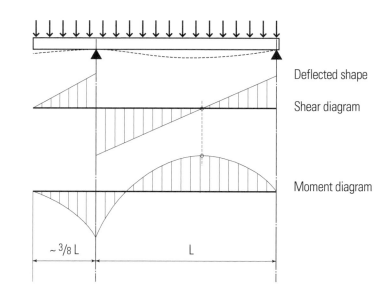

Deflected shape

Shear diagram

Moment diagram

- Assuming a uniformly distributed load, the projections of a double overhanging beam for which the moments over the supports are equal and opposite to the moment at midspan are approximately 1/3 of the span.

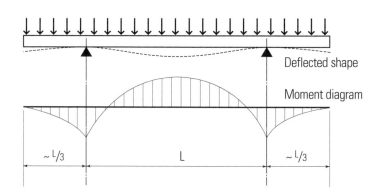

Deflected shape

Moment diagram

**Cantilevered Buildings**

Cantilevered and overhanging structures are commonly used to form a range of building components, from balconies and roof eaves to the larger-scale structures of stadium roofs. Even large portions of buildings can cantilever or overhang beyond the line of vertical column or wall supports.

The major horizontal structural elements for larger building cantilevers or overhangs may be wall beams, Vierendeel frames, or trusses, often one or more stories in depth. These horizontal structures, in turn, are supported by one or more cores, which typically contain the vertical transport and supply systems. Parallel steel trusses overhanging a concrete core appear to be the most common strategy applied in many contemporary buildings.

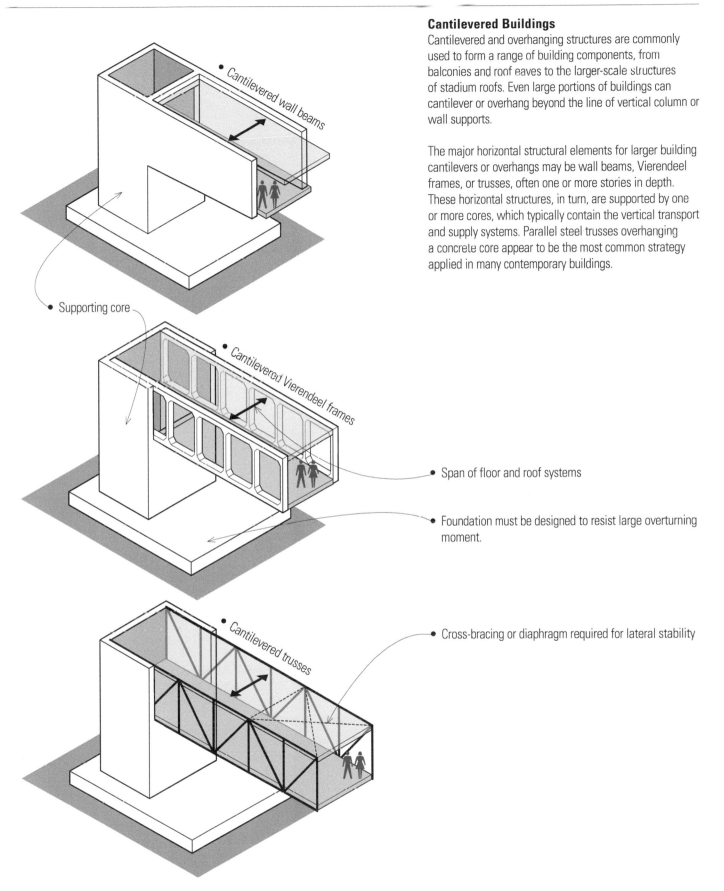

Cantilevered wall beams

Supporting core

Cantilevered Vierendeel frames

Span of floor and roof systems

Foundation must be designed to resist large overturning moment.

Cross-bracing or diaphragm required for lateral stability

Cantilevered trusses

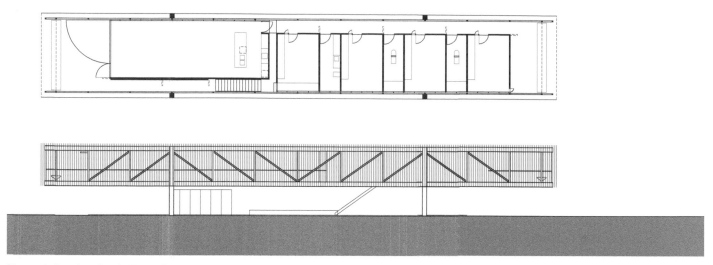

Plan and elevation: Beach House, St. Andrews Beach, Victoria, Australia, 2003–2006, Sean Godsell Architects

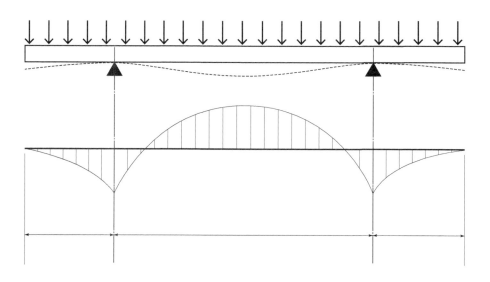

St. Andrew's Beach House exemplifies a double overhanging beam formed by extending both ends of a simple beam. In this case, a pair of full-length, story-high trusses, linked by the floor and roof framing, defines and raises the volume of the main living level above the ground for better views and to provide space below for cars and storage. The cantilever action results from the extension of the trusses beyond their column supports, which has the positive effect of counteracting the deflection present in the interior span.

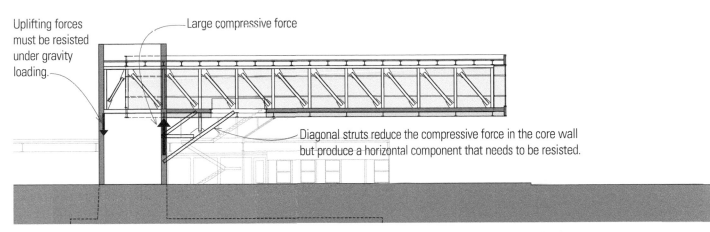

Uplifting forces must be resisted under gravity loading.

Large compressive force

Diagonal struts reduce the compressive force in the core wall but produce a horizontal component that needs to be resisted.

Diagram and section: Lamar Construction Corporate Headquarters, Grand Rapids, Michigan, 2006–2007, Integrated Architecture

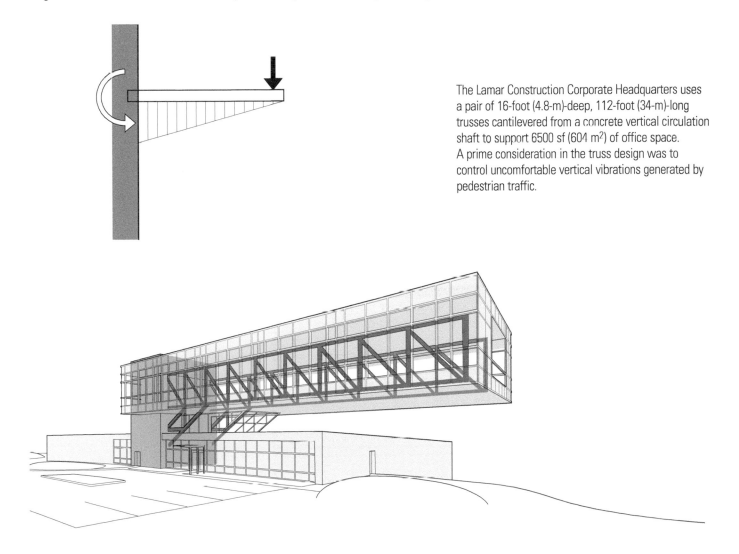

The Lamar Construction Corporate Headquarters uses a pair of 16-foot (4.8-m)-deep, 112-foot (34-m)-long trusses cantilevered from a concrete vertical circulation shaft to support 6500 sf (604 m²) of office space. A prime consideration in the truss design was to control uncomfortable vertical vibrations generated by pedestrian traffic.

One-way spanning systems are most efficient when spanning regular, rectangular bays. In the case of two-way systems, the structural bays should not only be regular but also as nearly square as possible. Using regular bays also allows the use of repetitive members of identical cross section and length, which results in an economy of scale. However, programmatic requirements, contextual constraints, or aesthetic initiatives can often suggest the development of structural bays that are neither rectangular nor geometrically regular.

Whatever the reason for their being, irregularly shaped bays do not often exist in isolation. They often are formed along the periphery of a more regular grid or pattern of supports and spanning elements. Nevertheless, irregularly shaped bays will nearly always result in some structural inefficiency, as the spanning members must be designed for the longest span in each layer even though the lengths of each spanning member may vary.

Presented here are alternative ways of structuring and framing irregularly shaped bays.

- Concrete slabs can be shaped in an irregular fashion as long as the length of the cantilevers are within the capability of the reinforced slab or beams.

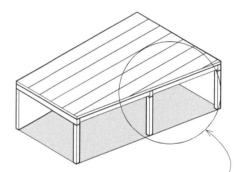

- When structural panels or decking span in the direction of the irregularity, it can be difficult to shape or trim the planar material at the acute angle created. It is also necessary to add support for the free edges of the cut panels.

- One-way spanning elements, such as structural decking or joists, should typically span counter to the irregular edge of a bay.

- When primary beams or girders span counter to an irregular edge, the surface layer of panels or decking can also span in the same direction if a supporting layer of joists is introduced.

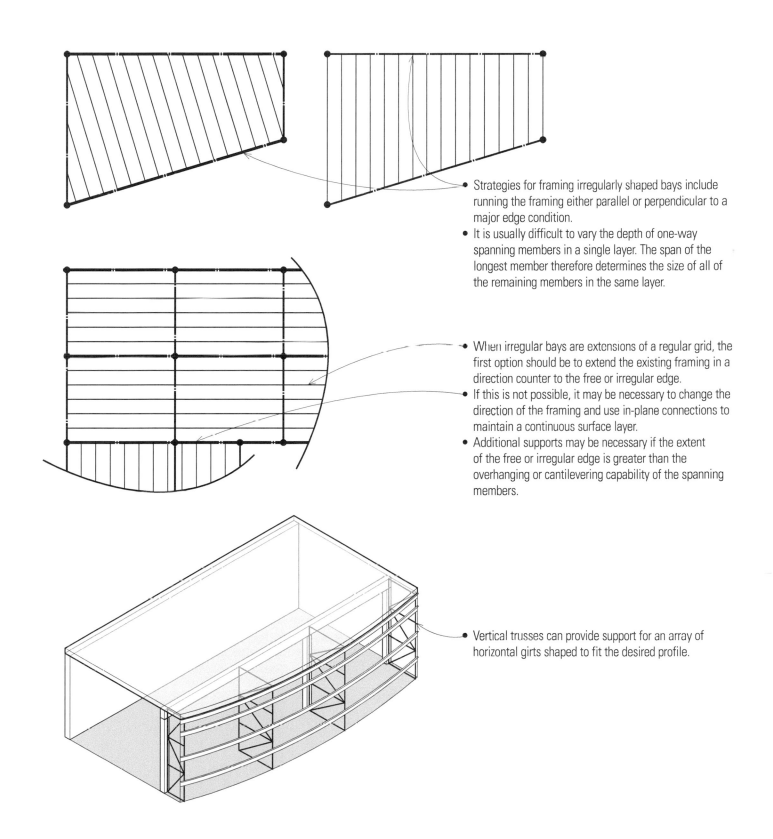

Strategies for framing irregularly shaped bays include running the framing either parallel or perpendicular to a major edge condition.

It is usually difficult to vary the depth of one-way spanning members in a single layer. The span of the longest member therefore determines the size of all of the remaining members in the same layer.

When irregular bays are extensions of a regular grid, the first option should be to extend the existing framing in a direction counter to the free or irregular edge.

If this is not possible, it may be necessary to change the direction of the framing and use in-plane connections to maintain a continuous surface layer.

Additional supports may be necessary if the extent of the free or irregular edge is greater than the overhanging or cantilevering capability of the spanning members.

Vertical trusses can provide support for an array of horizontal girts shaped to fit the desired profile.

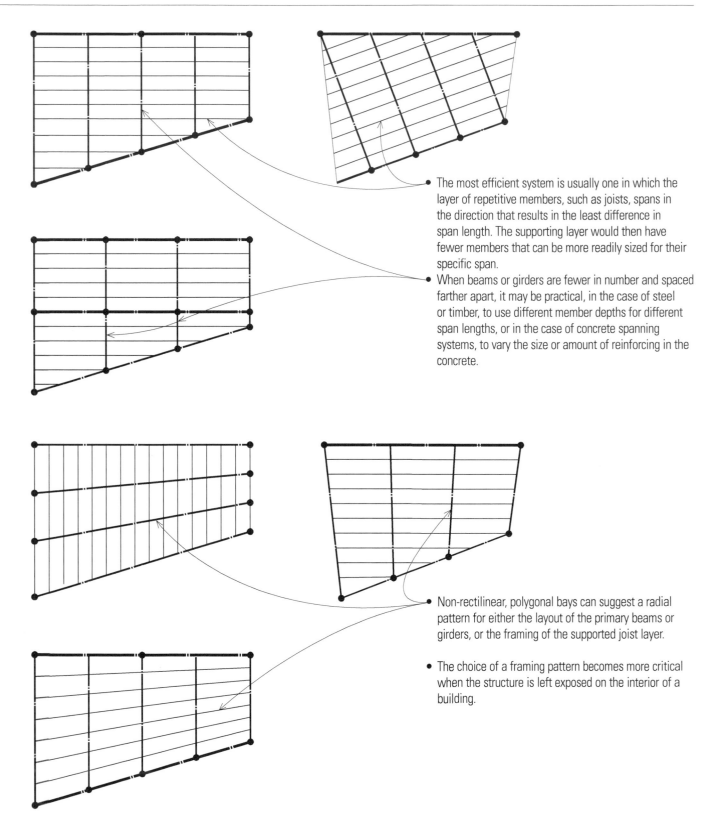

The most efficient system is usually one in which the layer of repetitive members, such as joists, spans in the direction that results in the least difference in span length. The supporting layer would then have fewer members that can be more readily sized for their specific span.

When beams or girders are fewer in number and spaced farther apart, it may be practical, in the case of steel or timber, to use different member depths for different span lengths, or in the case of concrete spanning systems, to vary the size or amount of reinforcing in the concrete.

Non-rectilinear, polygonal bays can suggest a radial pattern for either the layout of the primary beams or girders, or the framing of the supported joist layer.

- The choice of a framing pattern becomes more critical when the structure is left exposed on the interior of a building.

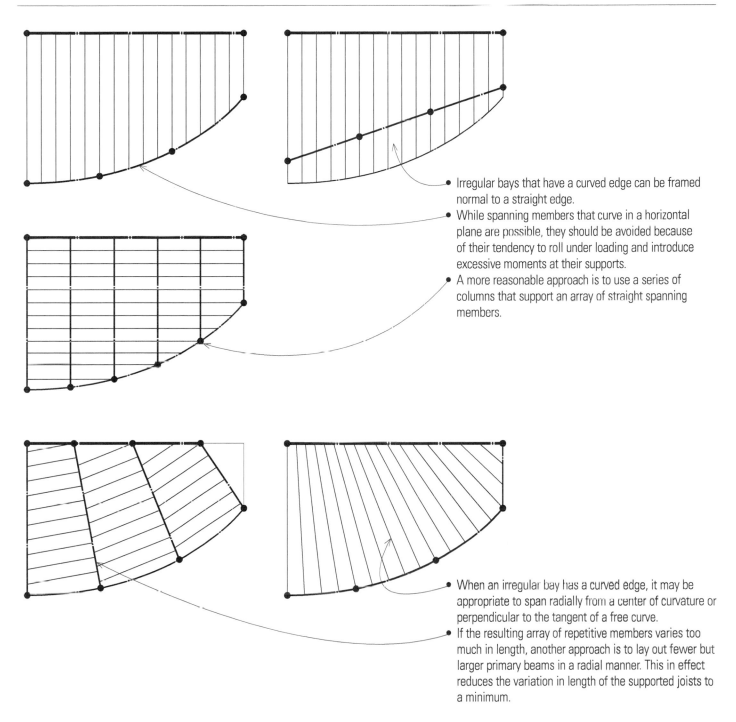

- Irregular bays that have a curved edge can be framed normal to a straight edge.
- While spanning members that curve in a horizontal plane are possible, they should be avoided because of their tendency to roll under loading and introduce excessive moments at their supports.
- A more reasonable approach is to use a series of columns that support an array of straight spanning members.

- When an irregular bay has a curved edge, it may be appropriate to span radially from a center of curvature or perpendicular to the tangent of a free curve.
- If the resulting array of repetitive members varies too much in length, another approach is to lay out fewer but larger primary beams in a radial manner. This in effect reduces the variation in length of the supported joists to a minimum.

Structuring and framing edge and corner bays present challenges that have ramifications on the design of the exterior facades of buildings. For example, curtain walls rely on the concrete or steel structural frame of a building for their support. How a curtain wall turns a corner—that is, whether it remains the same or changes appearance as it wraps around from one side of a building to another—is often influenced by how the edge and corners bays are structured and framed. Because one-way framing systems are directional, it can be difficult for adjacent facades to be treated in the same manner. One advantage of two-way systems is that adjacent facades can be treated in the same manner structurally.

Another impact is the extent to which edge and corner bays extend beyond the perimeter supports to create floor or roof overhangs. This is especially important if the intent is to have a curtain wall float free of the edge of the structural framework.

One distinction between wood or timber framing and steel or concrete structures is in how overhangs are implemented in each system. Because timber connections cannot be made moment-resistant, overhangs in timber framing require the overhanging joists or beams and the supporting beam or girder to be in separate layers. In both steel and concrete construction, it is possible to place both the overhanging elements and their supports in the same layer.

### Concrete

Reinforced or cast-in-place post-tensioned concrete systems inherently provide moment-resistance at intersections where columns, beams, and slabs meet. These intersections are capable of resisting cantilever bending moments in two directions.

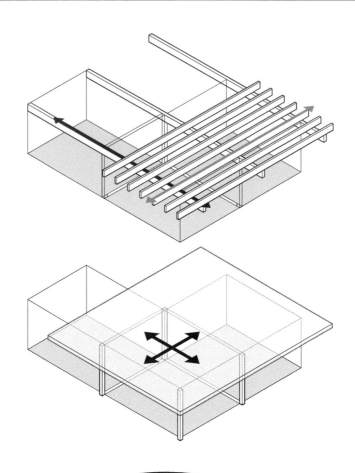

- Flat slabs and plates are both two-way systems that are capable of extending beyond the edge and corner columns in two directions.
- One-way and two-way slab-and-beam systems use in-plane framing of the beams that span in the two principal directions to minimize the overall construction depth.

- The extent of overhangs is generally a fraction of the bay dimension. An overhang dimension that is equal to or greater than the backspan would result in an extremely large bending moment at the column support and necessitate a very deep beam depth.

**Steel**
Overhangs in steel structures may be framed in-plane with moment connections or bear on and continue over the end supporting beam or girder. In either case, the directionality of the one-way framing system will likely be evident in adjacent facades, certainly at the detail level if not visually in the finished building.

- Steel column-beam connections can be made moment-resistant by bolting or welding the beam flanges to the column.
- Rigid steel connections can be used to extend in-plane girder and beam members beyond the edge and corner columns.

- Having a layer of secondary beams or joists bear on and continue over the supporting girder can create a double overhang without the need for moment connections.
- Another method for extending steel framing in two directions at a corner while minimizing the construction depth and the need for moment connections is to extend in-plane girders to pick up fascia beams, which in turn carry the outer range of joists.

- Double overhanging steel framing can also be supported by diagonal knee braces at the corner columns. This added support provides another vertical support component, thus negating the requirement for moment connections at the column intersections.

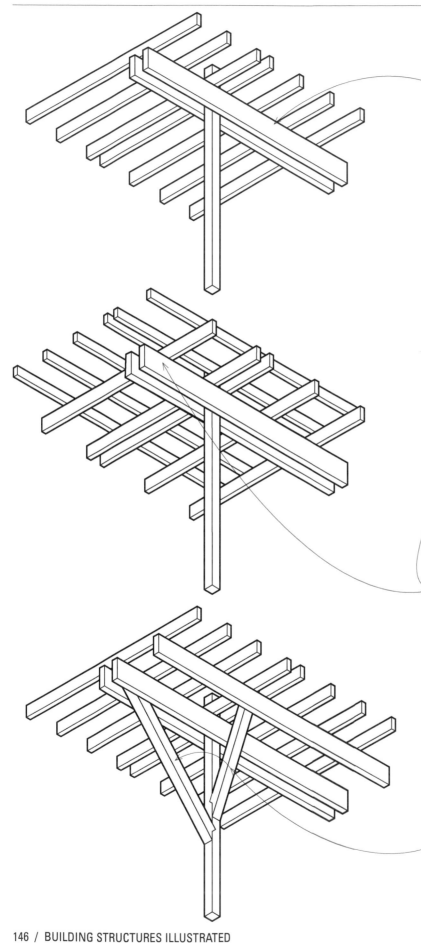

### Timber

The directionality of one-way systems is most clearly expressed in wood framing systems.

- It is virtually impossible to develop moment-resisting connections in timber construction. To achieve a double overhang at a corner requires the supported layer of framing to change direction, bear on and continue over the supporting beams or girders.

- Exterior columns are generally smaller in size and responsible for smaller tributary areas than interior columns. By cantilevering beams and joists at the corners, the corner columns will support loads more equivalent to the interior columns and can be designed to be approximately of equal size.

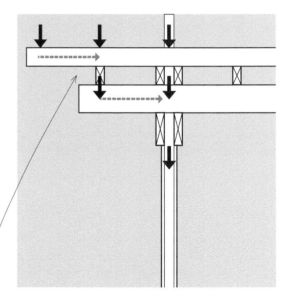

- Bracketing is a method for increasing the extent of overhangs for a roof or floor framing system when the depth of the bending member is limited. It takes advantage of the overhang reducing the moment in the backspan and is most efficient when the two bending members are connected beyond the support—ideally at the location of maximum moment. The concentrated load created by a bracket tends to make the lower member more sensitive to shear failure because of its high load and short span.

In traditional Chinese construction, bracketing has been used to increase the area of support afforded by a post or column and reduce the effective span of a beam. See page 5.

- Diagonal bracing can help support and extend the length of an overhanging beam at a corner or edge column.

# 4
# Vertical Dimensions

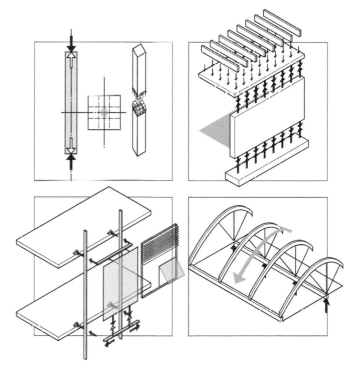

## VERTICAL DIMENSIONS

This chapter addresses the vertical dimensions of building structures—the vertical supports for horizontal spanning systems and the vertical systems of enclosure that provide shelter and protection from the climatic elements and aid in controlling the flow of air, heat, and sound into and through the interior spaces of a building.

The pattern of horizontal spanning systems must, of course, be intimately related to the pattern of vertical supports, be they an array of columns and beams, a parallel series of bearing walls, or a combination of both. The pattern of these vertical supports should, in turn, be coordinated with the desired form and layout of the interior spaces of a building. Both columns and walls have a greater presence in our visual field than horizontal planes and are therefore more instrumental in defining a discrete volume of space and providing a sense of enclosure and privacy for those within it. In addition, they serve to separate one space from another and establish a common boundary between the interior and exterior environments.

The reason roof structures are included in this chapter rather than the previous chapter is that, while roof structures necessarily are inherently spanning systems, they have a vertical aspect that must be considered in terms of the impact they might have on the external form of buildings as well as the shaping of interior space.

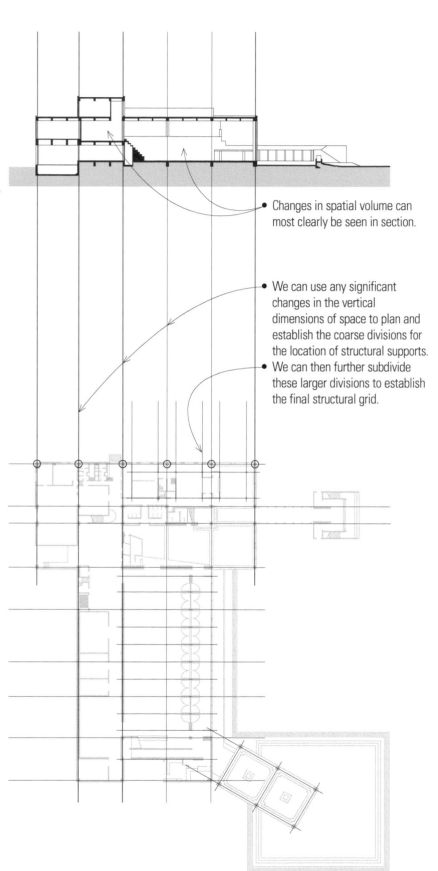

- Changes in spatial volume can most clearly be seen in section.

- We can use any significant changes in the vertical dimensions of space to plan and establish the coarse divisions for the location of structural supports.
- We can then further subdivide these larger divisions to establish the final structural grid.

- During the design process, we use plans, sections, and elevations to establish two-dimensional planar fields on which we are able to study formal patterns and scale relationships in a composition, as well as impose an intellectual order on a design. Any single multiview drawing, whether it be a plan, a section, or an elevation, can only reveal partial information about a three-dimensional idea, structure, or construction. There is an inherent ambiguity of depth as the third dimension is flattened in these views. We therefore require a series of distinct but related views to fully describe the three-dimensional nature of a form, structure, or composition.

## Building Scale

We can categorize the vertical scale of buildings into low-rise, mid-rise, and high-rise structures. Low-rise structures generally have one, two, or three stories and no elevator; mid-rise structures have a moderately large number of stories, usually five to ten floors, and are equipped with elevators; and high-rise structures have a comparatively large number of stories and must be equipped with elevators. It is useful to think in these categories when selecting and designing a structural system because the scale of a building is directly related to the type of construction required and the uses or occupancies allowed by the building code.

The vertical scale of a building also influences the selection and design of a structural system. For low-rise and short-span structures constructed of relatively heavy materials, such as concrete, masonry, or steel, the primary determinant of the structural form is typically the magnitude of the live load. For long-span structures constructed of similar materials, the dead load of the structure may be the principal factor in establishing the structural strategy. As buildings become taller, however, not only do gravity loads accumulate over a large number of stories but lateral wind and seismic forces become critical issues to address in the development of the overall structural system.

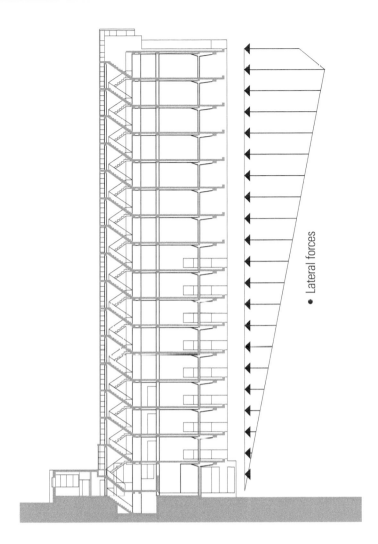

• Lateral forces

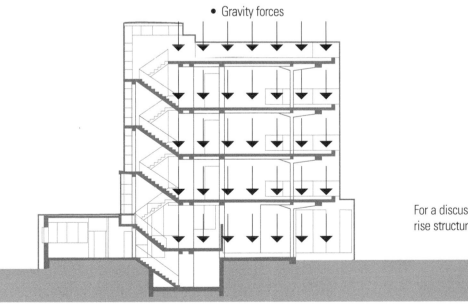

• Gravity forces

For a discussion of lateral forces, see Chapter 5; for high-rise structures, see Chapter 7.

## Human Scale

Of a room's three dimensions, its height has a greater effect on its scale than either its width or length. While the walls of the room provide enclosure, the height of the ceiling plane overhead determines its qualities of shelter and intimacy. Raising the ceiling height of a space will be more noticeable and affect its scale more than increasing its width by a similar amount. While a modest room with a normal ceiling height might feel comfortable to most people, a large assembly space with a similar ceiling height would likely feel oppressive. Columns and bearing walls must be of sufficient height to establish the desired scale of a building story or a single space within the building. As their unsupported height increases, columns and bearing walls must necessarily become thicker to maintain their stability.

- The scale of interior spaces is largely determined by the ratio of their height to their horizontal dimensions of width and length.

## Exterior Walls

Walls are the vertical constructions that enclose, separate, and protect the interior spaces of buildings. They may be loadbearing structures of homogeneous or composite construction designed to support imposed loads from floors and roofs, or consist of a framework of columns and beams with nonstructural panels attached to or filling in between them. The interior walls or partitions, which subdivide the space within a building, may be either structural or nonloadbearing. Their construction should be able to support the desired finish materials, provide the required degree of acoustical separation, and accommodate when necessary the distribution and outlets of mechanical and electrical services.

Openings for doors and windows must be constructed so that any vertical loads from above are distributed around the openings and not transferred to the door and window units themselves. Their size and location are determined by the requirements for natural light, ventilation, view, and physical access, as well as the constraints of the structural system and modular wall materials.

- Exterior walls contribute to the visual character of a building, whether they have the weight and opacity of loadbearing walls or the lightness or the transparency of nonbearing curtain walls supported by a structural framework of columns and beams.

### Roof Structures

The principal sheltering element of a building is its roof structure. It not only shields the interior spaces of a building from sun, rain, and snow, but it also has a major impact on the overall form of a building and the shaping of its spaces. The form and geometry of the roof structure, in turn, is established by the manner in which it spans across space to bear on its supports and slopes to shed rain and melting snow. As a design element, the roof plane is significant because of the impact it can have on the form and silhouette of a building within its setting.

The roof plane can be hidden from view by the exterior walls of a building or merge with the walls to emphasize the volume of the building mass. It can be expressed as a single sheltering form that encompasses a variety of spaces beneath its canopy, or comprise a number of hats that articulate a series of spaces within a single building.

A roof plane can extend outward to form overhangs that shield door and window openings from sun or rain, or continue downward further still to relate itself more closely to the ground plane. In warm climates, it can be elevated to allow cooling breezes to flow across and through the interior spaces of a building.

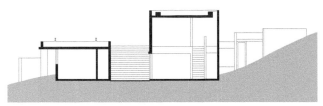

Koshino House, Ashiya, Hyogo Prefecture, Japan
Tadao Ando, 1979–1984.

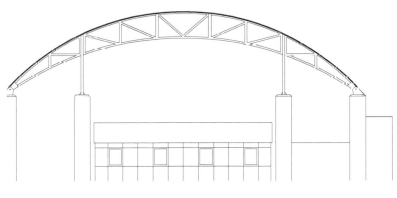

Menara Mesiniaga (Top Floor), Subang Jaya, Selangor, Malaysia
Ken Yeang, 1989–1992

Barnes House, Nanaimo, British Columbia
Patkau Architects, 1991–1993.

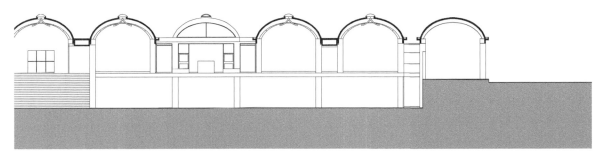

Kimball Art Museum, Fort Worth, Texas, USA, Louis Kahn, 1966–1972.

## VERTICAL SUPPORTS

Throughout history, developments in building materials and construction technology have resulted in the transformation of vertical supports for buildings, from bearing walls of stacked stones to masonry walls penetrated with linteled or arched openings, from post-and-beam frames of timber to rigid frames of reinforced concrete and steel.

Because exterior walls serve as a protective shield against the weather for the interior spaces of a building, their construction should control the passage of heat, infiltrating air, sound, moisture, and water vapor. The exterior skin, which may be either applied to or integral with the wall structure, should be durable and resistant to the weathering effects of sun, wind, and rain. Building codes specify the fire-resistance rating of exterior walls, loadbearing walls, and interior partitions. In addition to supporting vertical loads, exterior wall constructions must be able to withstand horizontal wind loading. If rigid enough, they can serve as shear walls and transfer lateral wind and seismic forces to the ground foundation.

Columns and walls have a greater presence in our visual field than horizontal planes and are therefore more instrumental in defining a discrete volume of space and providing a sense of enclosure and privacy for those within it. For example, a structural frame of timber, steel, or concrete columns and beams would give us the opportunity to establish relationships with adjacent spaces on all four sides of the volume. To provide enclosure, we could use any number of nonloadbearing panel or wall systems that would be tied to the structural frame and designed to withstand wind, shear, and other lateral forces.

If a pair of parallel bearing walls of masonry or concrete were used instead of the structural frame, then the volume would take on a directional quality and be oriented toward the open ends of the space. Any openings in the bearing walls would have to be limited in size and location so as not to weaken the walls' structural integrity. If all four sides of the volume were enclosed by bearing walls, the space would become introverted and rely entirely on openings to establish relationships with adjacent spaces.

In all three cases, the spanning system required to provide overhead shelter could be flat or sloped in any number of ways, further modifying the spatial and formal qualities of the volume.

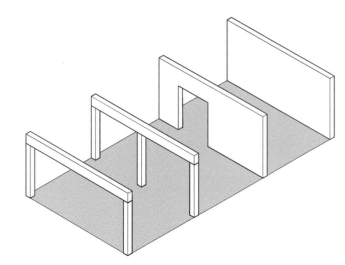

- Transformation from bearing walls capable of carrying imposed floor and roof loads to a structural framework of columns and beams.

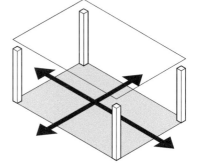
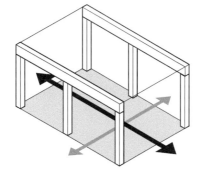

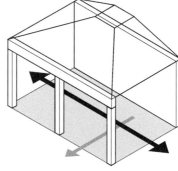
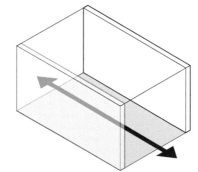

- Also influencing the physical qualities of a space is the ceiling plane, which is out of our reach and almost always a purely visual event. It can express the form of an overhead floor or roof structure as it spans the space between its supports, or be suspended as a detached lining to alter the scale of a space or to define spatial zones within a room.

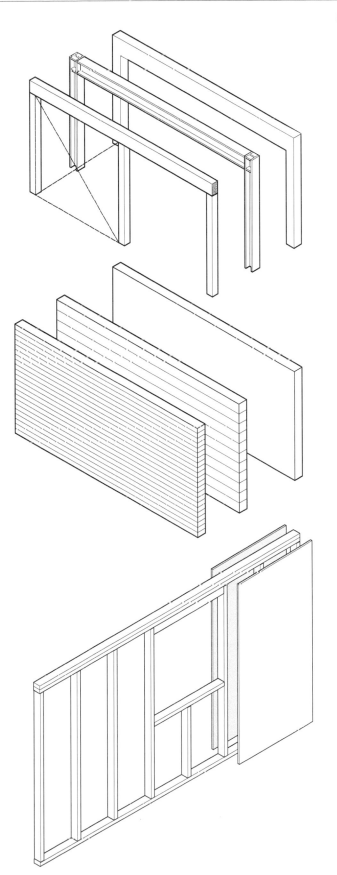

## Structural Frames

- Concrete frames are typically rigid frames and qualify as noncombustible, fire-resistive construction.
- Noncombustible steel frames may use moment connections and require fireproofing to qualify as fire-resistive construction.
- Timber frames require diagonal bracing or shear planes for lateral stability. They may qualify as heavy timber construction if used with noncombustible, fire-resistive exterior walls and the members meet the minimum size requirements specified in the building code.
- Steel and concrete frames are able to span greater distances and carry heavier loads than timber structures.
- Structural frames can support and accept a variety of nonbearing or curtain-wall systems.
- The detailing of connections is critical for structural and visual reasons when the frame is left exposed.

## Concrete and Masonry Bearing Walls

- Concrete and masonry walls qualify as noncombustible construction and rely on their mass for their load-carrying capability.
- While strong in compression, concrete and masonry require reinforcing to handle tensile stresses.
- Height-to-width ratio, provisions for lateral stability, and proper placement of expansion joints are critical factors in wall design and construction.
- Wall surfaces may be left exposed.

## Metal and Wood Stud Walls

- Studs of cold-formed metal or wood are normally spaced @ 16" or 24" (406 or 610) o.c.; this spacing is related to the width and length of common sheathing materials.
- Studs carry vertical loads while sheathing or diagonal bracing stiffens the plane of the wall.
- Cavities in the wall frame can accommodate thermal insulation, vapor retarders, and mechanical distribution and outlets of mechanical and electrical services.
- Stud framing can accept a variety of interior and exterior wall finishes; some finishes require a nail-base sheathing.
- The finish materials determine the fire-resistance rating of the wall assembly.
- Stud wall frames may be assembled on-site or panelized off-site.
- Stud walls are flexible in form due to the workability of relatively small pieces and the various means of fastening available.

### Tributary Loads

Determining the tributary area for loads on vertical supports must take into account the layout of the structural grid and the type and pattern of horizontal spanning systems being supported. Bearing walls and columns are designed to collect gravity loads from trusses, girders, beams, and slabs and redirect these loads vertically down to the foundation. Braced frames, rigid frames, and shear walls may also induce lateral loads on bearing walls and columns, which have to be redirected downward in a vertical direction.

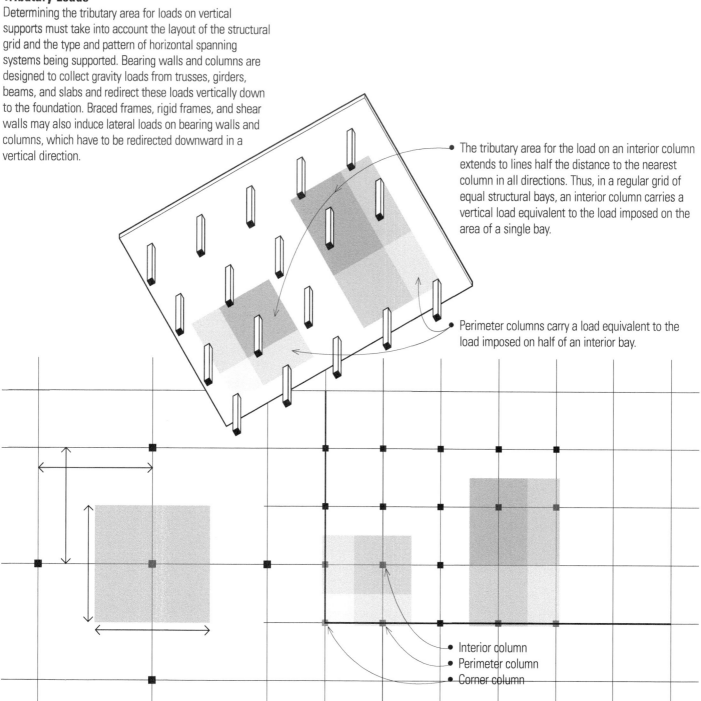

- The tributary area for the load on an interior column extends to lines half the distance to the nearest column in all directions. Thus, in a regular grid of equal structural bays, an interior column carries a vertical load equivalent to the load imposed on the area of a single bay.

- Perimeter columns carry a load equivalent to the load imposed on half of an interior bay.

- Interior column
- Perimeter column
- Corner column

- The tributary area of the gravity load on a particular bearing wall or column is determined by the distance from the bearing wall or column to adjacent vertical supports, which is equivalent to the length of the span of the floor or roof structure being carried.

- Omitting a column from the grid essentially transfers the load it would have carried to adjacent columns. This also results in a doubling of the floor or roof span and deeper spanning members.
- Columns located at outside corners carry the equivalent of one-fourth of the load of an interior bay.

## Load Accumulation

Columns redirect the gravity loads collected from beams and girders as vertical concentrated loads. In multistory buildings these gravity loads accumulate and increase as they are directed downward along bearing walls and columns through successive floors from the roof through to the foundation.

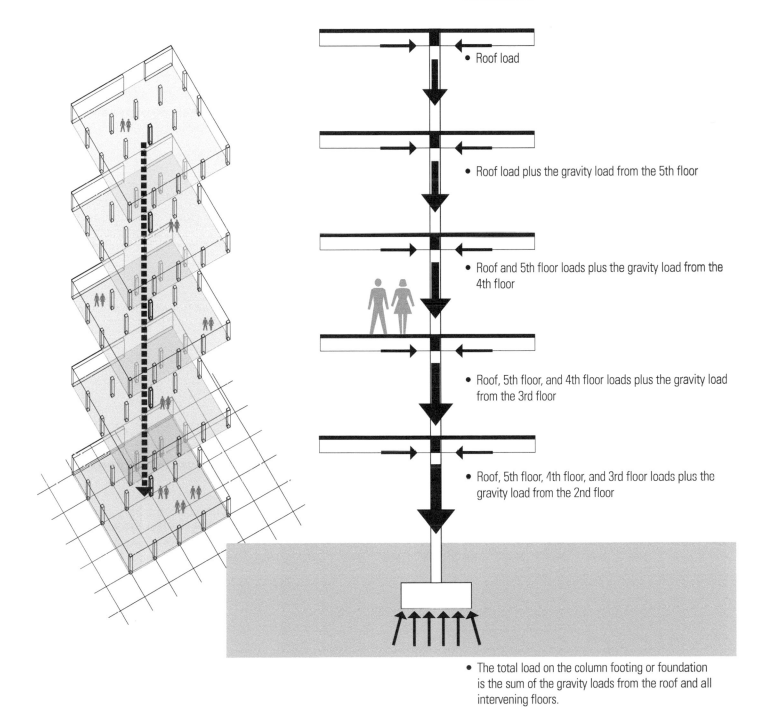

- Roof load

- Roof load plus the gravity load from the 5th floor

- Roof and 5th floor loads plus the gravity load from the 4th floor

- Roof, 5th floor, and 4th floor loads plus the gravity load from the 3rd floor

- Roof, 5th floor, 4th floor, and 3rd floor loads plus the gravity load from the 2nd floor

- The total load on the column footing or foundation is the sum of the gravity loads from the roof and all intervening floors.

### Vertical Continuity

The most efficient path for gravity loads is directly downward through vertically aligned columns and bearing walls to the foundation. This means that the same grid should control the placement of vertical supports for all of the floor structures as well as the roof structure of a building. Any deviation in the path of a vertical load requires that the load be redirected horizontally through a transfer beam or truss to alternative vertical supports, resulting in an increased load and depth for the spanning member.

While a regular grid of vertically aligned supports is always desirable, a design program may call for a spatial volume much larger than can be accommodated by the normal grid spacing. Illustrated on this and the facing page are several options for accommodating exceptionally large spaces within a building.

- Transfer beams or trusses are often required to accommodate spaces that require exceptional volume or larger clear spans within a more regular bay spacing.

- Transfer beams should have as short a span as possible.
- A concentrated load applied close to the end support of a transfer beam generates extremely high shear forces.

- At abrupt breaks in the sectional profile of a building, it is usually best to support the horizontal spanning system with a bearing wall or a series of columns along the plane of the break.

- Locating the large space outside the main volume of the building allows for the development of a structural scheme appropriate to the special conditions of the space. Deeper beams or trusses are required to accommodate the longer roof span, but the span is not subject to floor loads from above.

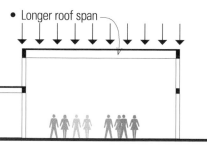

- Longer roof span

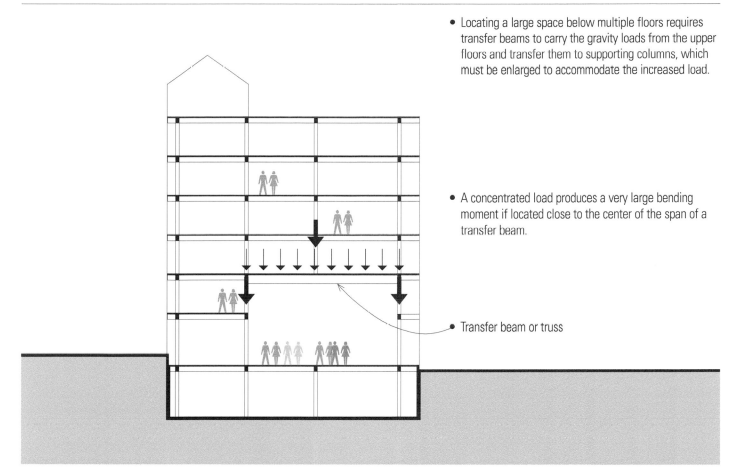

- Locating a large space below multiple floors requires transfer beams to carry the gravity loads from the upper floors and transfer them to supporting columns, which must be enlarged to accommodate the increased load.

- A concentrated load produces a very large bending moment if located close to the center of the span of a transfer beam.

- Transfer beam or truss

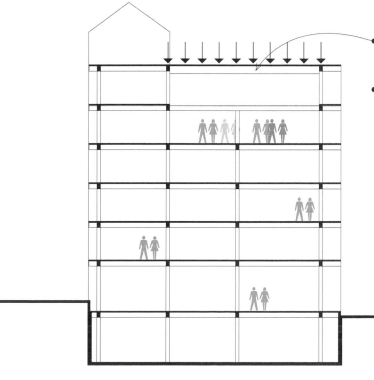

- Longer roof span

- When a large space is located at the top floor of a building, the longer span only carries uniform roof loads, and a transfer beam is not necessary. The roof beams, however, will be considerably deeper due to their longer spans. As larger spaces often involve greater occupancy, the strategy of locating high-occupancy spaces high in buildings may create additional difficulties in meeting the egress requirements.

Columns are rigid, relatively slender structural members designed primarily to support axial compressive loads applied to the ends of the members. Relatively short, thick columns are subject to failure by crushing rather than by buckling. Failure occurs when the direct stress from an axial load exceeds the compressive strength of the material available in the cross section. An eccentric load, however, can produce bending and result in an uneven stress distribution in the section.

Long, slender columns are subject to failure by buckling rather than by crushing. As opposed to bending, buckling is the sudden lateral or torsional instability of a slender structural member induced by the action of an axial load before the elastic limit of the material is reached. Under a buckling load, a column begins to deflect laterally and cannot generate the internal forces necessary to restore its original linear condition. Any additional loading would cause the column to deflect further until collapse occurs in bending. The higher the slenderness ratio of a column, the lower is the critical stress that will cause it to buckle. A primary objective in the design of a column is to reduce its slenderness ratio by shortening its effective length or maximizing the radius of gyration of its cross section.

Intermediate columns have a mode of failure between that of a short column and a long column, often partly inelastic by crushing and partly elastic by buckling.

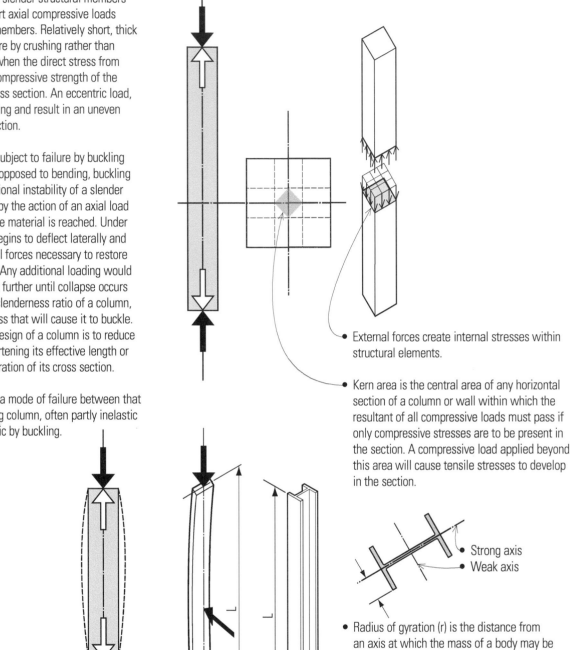

- External forces create internal stresses within structural elements.

- Kern area is the central area of any horizontal section of a column or wall within which the resultant of all compressive loads must pass if only compressive stresses are to be present in the section. A compressive load applied beyond this area will cause tensile stresses to develop in the section.

Strong axis
Weak axis

- Radius of gyration (r) is the distance from an axis at which the mass of a body may be assumed to be concentrated. For a column section, the radius of gyration is equal to the square root of the quotient of the moment of inertia and the area.
- The slenderness ratio of a column is the ratio of its effective length (L) to its least radius of gyration.

- For asymmetrical column sections, buckling will tend to occur about the weaker axis or in the direction of the least dimension.

- Short columns fail by crushing.
- Slender columns fail by buckling.

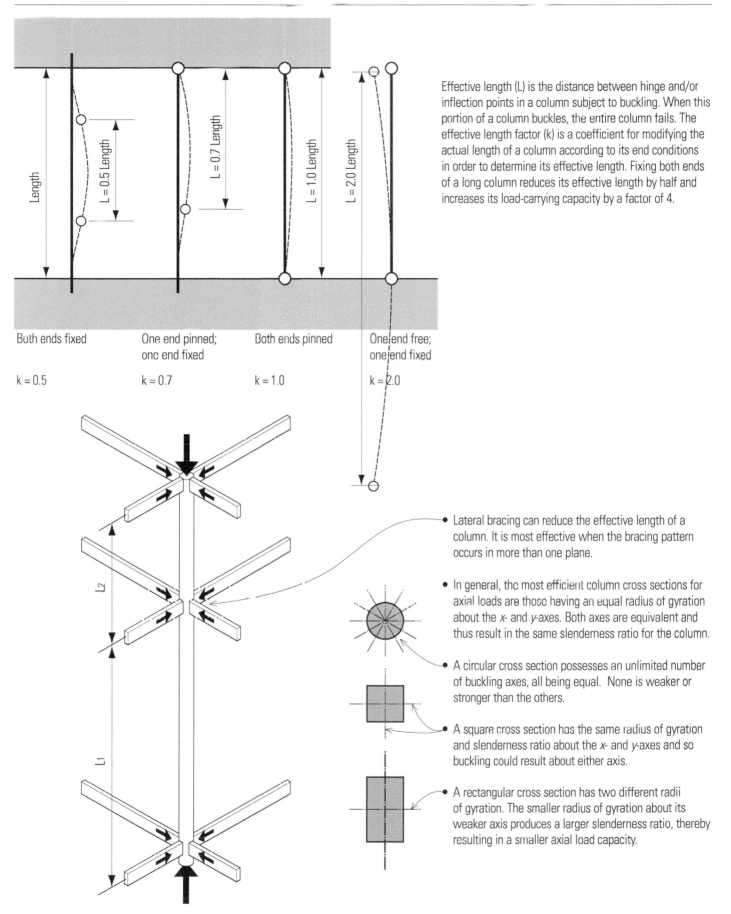

Both ends fixed

k = 0.5

One end pinned;
one end fixed

k = 0.7

Both ends pinned

k = 1.0

One end free;
one end fixed

k = 2.0

Effective length (L) is the distance between hinge and/or inflection points in a column subject to buckling. When this portion of a column buckles, the entire column fails. The effective length factor (k) is a coefficient for modifying the actual length of a column according to its end conditions in order to determine its effective length. Fixing both ends of a long column reduces its effective length by half and increases its load-carrying capacity by a factor of 4.

- Lateral bracing can reduce the effective length of a column. It is most effective when the bracing pattern occurs in more than one plane.

- In general, the most efficient column cross sections for axial loads are those having an equal radius of gyration about the x- and y-axes. Both axes are equivalent and thus result in the same slenderness ratio for the column.

- A circular cross section possesses an unlimited number of buckling axes, all being equal. None is weaker or stronger than the others.

- A square cross section has the same radius of gyration and slenderness ratio about the x- and y-axes and so buckling could result about either axis.

- A rectangular cross section has two different radii of gyration. The smaller radius of gyration about its weaker axis produces a larger slenderness ratio, thereby resulting in a smaller axial load capacity.

### Inclined Columns

Columns may be inclined to transfer otherwise misaligned concentrated loads. An important secondary effect of inclining a column is the introduction of a horizontal component of the axial load into the supporting beam, floor slab, or footing, which must be incorporated into the design of these elements.

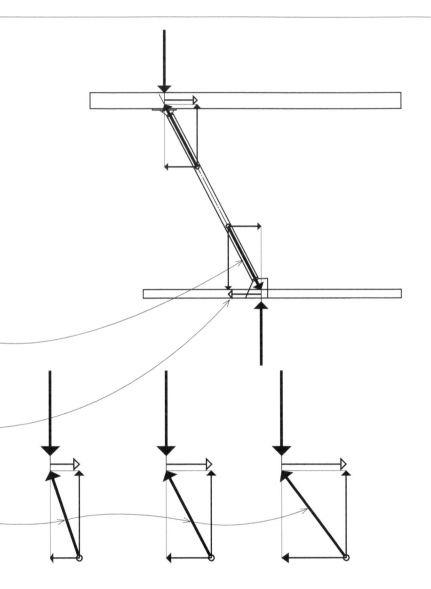

- Inclined columns can be designed as vertical columns while taking into account the additional moments resulting from the column's self weight and the additional shear forces due to its inclination.
- Only the vertical component of the strut's reaction can resist the gravity load.

- As a vertical gravity load is redirected along the axis of an inclined column strut, the axial reaction of the strut has both a vertical and a horizontal component. Thus, a strut must be larger in cross section than an equivalent vertical column as the axial load will always be larger than its vertical component.
- The axial load on the strut will also have a horizontal component that must be resisted by the structure. The magnitude of this horizontal component is directly affected by the inclination of the strut.

- The more inclined a strut, the greater is the horizontal component of its axial load.

### Struts

While inclined columns that carry gravity loads are often referred to as struts, struts can refer to any inclined member subjected to compressive or tensile loads along its length, such as a component connected at its ends to other members of a trussed framework to maintain the rigidity of the structure. Struts fail primarily due to elastic buckling but are capable of resisting tension as well.

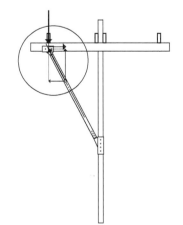

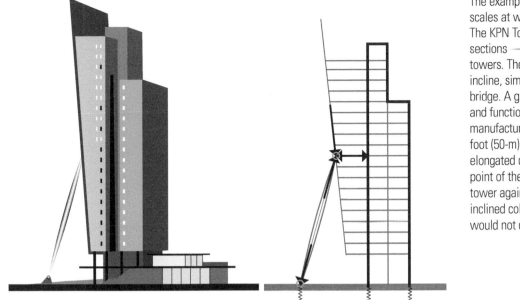

The examples on this page illustrate the various scales at which inclined columns can be used. The KPN Telecom Building is composed of three sections —a central vertical core and two adjacent towers. The second tallest section has a 5.9° incline, similar to the cables of the nearby Erasmus bridge. A glass curtain wall covers the inclined face and functions as a billboard using 896 specially manufactured lights. A distinctive feature is a 164-foot (50-m) inclined steel column, shaped like an elongated cigar, which is attached to the center point of the facade to assist in stabilizing the tower against lateral forces. If for some reason the inclined column were to be damaged, the building would not collapse.

Schematic exterior view and diagrammatic section: KPN Telecom Building, Rotterdam, Netherlands, 1997–2000, Renzo Piano

Centra at Metropark employs an asymmetrical tree column and full floor-to-ceiling trusses, 20 feet (6 m) deep and spanning 120 feet (36 m), to support a large overhang of the fourth floor. The fourth floor is suspended from the roof structure, enabling a rectangular opening in the center to be created to allow light to enter the plaza area below. The tree column was prefabricated in four sections out of thick steel plates, which were then welded together on site and injected with concrete.

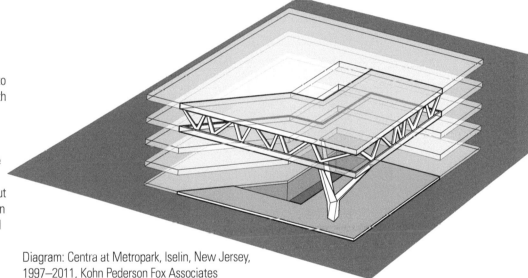

Diagram: Centra at Metropark, Iselin, New Jersey, 1997–2011, Kohn Pederson Fox Associates

The roof of the Angus Glen Community Center and Library relies on a primary truss that spans the length of the swimming pool. Designed as a tension arch constructed of hollow tubular steel members without diagonals, the truss supports major glue-laminated beams and decking. Inclined columns support the truss only at its ends; there are no interior columns to create physical barriers in the space. Inclined trussed columns are also used to support the exterior ends of the glue-laminated beams.

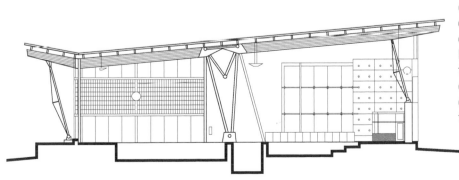

Section: Angus Glen Community Center and Library, Markham, Ontario, Canada, 2004, Perkins + Will

# COLUMNS

Concrete columns are designed to act together with vertical and lateral reinforcement in resisting applied forces.

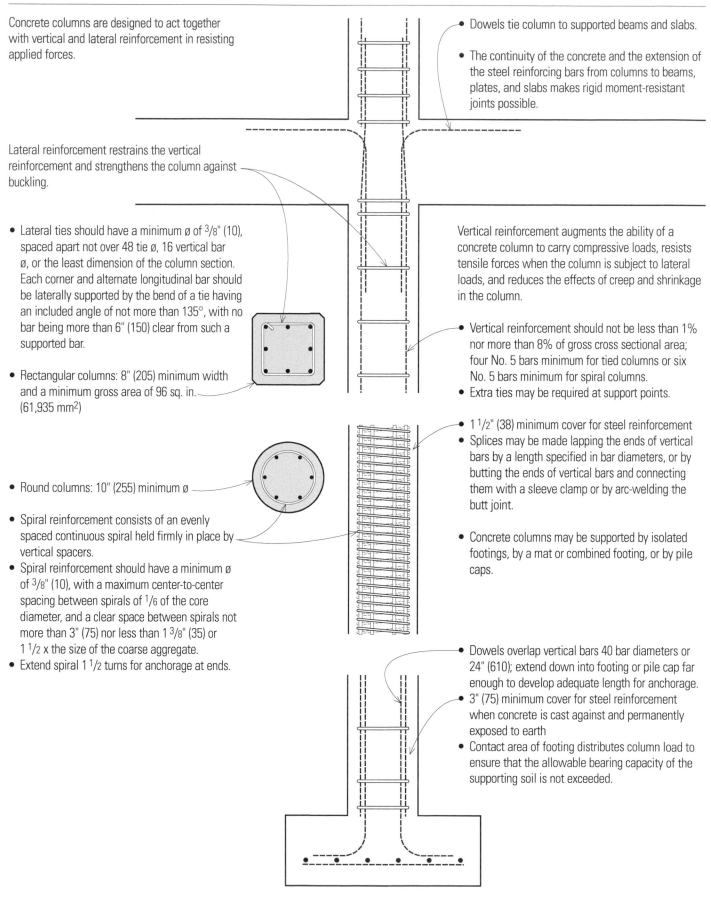

- Dowels tie column to supported beams and slabs.

- The continuity of the concrete and the extension of the steel reinforcing bars from columns to beams, plates, and slabs makes rigid moment-resistant joints possible.

Lateral reinforcement restrains the vertical reinforcement and strengthens the column against buckling.

- Lateral ties should have a minimum ø of $^3/_8$" (10), spaced apart not over 48 tie ø, 16 vertical bar ø, or the least dimension of the column section. Each corner and alternate longitudinal bar should be laterally supported by the bend of a tie having an included angle of not more than 135°, with no bar being more than 6" (150) clear from such a supported bar.

- Rectangular columns: 8" (205) minimum width and a minimum gross area of 96 sq. in. (61,935 mm²)

Vertical reinforcement augments the ability of a concrete column to carry compressive loads, resists tensile forces when the column is subject to lateral loads, and reduces the effects of creep and shrinkage in the column.

- Vertical reinforcement should not be less than 1% nor more than 8% of gross cross sectional area; four No. 5 bars minimum for tied columns or six No. 5 bars minimum for spiral columns.
- Extra ties may be required at support points.

- Round columns: 10" (255) minimum ø

- Spiral reinforcement consists of an evenly spaced continuous spiral held firmly in place by vertical spacers.
- Spiral reinforcement should have a minimum ø of $^3/_8$" (10), with a maximum center-to-center spacing between spirals of $^1/_6$ of the core diameter, and a clear space between spirals not more than 3" (75) nor less than 1 $^3/_8$" (35) or 1 $^1/_2$ x the size of the coarse aggregate.
- Extend spiral 1 $^1/_2$ turns for anchorage at ends.

- 1 $^1/_2$" (38) minimum cover for steel reinforcement
- Splices may be made lapping the ends of vertical bars by a length specified in bar diameters, or by butting the ends of vertical bars and connecting them with a sleeve clamp or by arc-welding the butt joint.

- Concrete columns may be supported by isolated footings, by a mat or combined footing, or by pile caps.

- Dowels overlap vertical bars 40 bar diameters or 24" (610); extend down into footing or pile cap far enough to develop adequate length for anchorage.
- 3" (75) minimum cover for steel reinforcement when concrete is cast against and permanently exposed to earth
- Contact area of footing distributes column load to ensure that the allowable bearing capacity of the supporting soil is not exceeded.

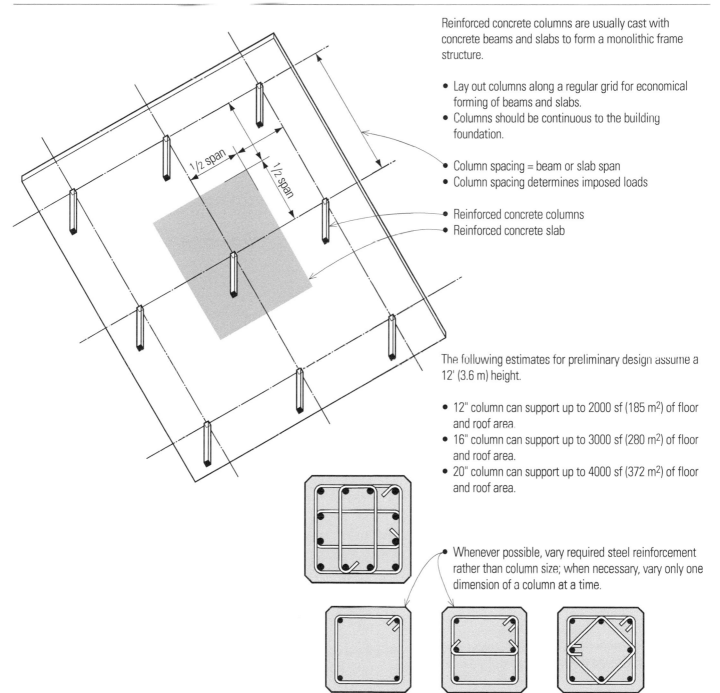

Reinforced concrete columns are usually cast with concrete beams and slabs to form a monolithic frame structure.

- Lay out columns along a regular grid for economical forming of beams and slabs.
- Columns should be continuous to the building foundation.

- Column spacing = beam or slab span
- Column spacing determines imposed loads

- Reinforced concrete columns
- Reinforced concrete slab

The following estimates for preliminary design assume a 12' (3.6 m) height.

- 12" column can support up to 2000 sf (185 m²) of floor and roof area.
- 16" column can support up to 3000 sf (280 m²) of floor and roof area.
- 20" column can support up to 4000 sf (372 m²) of floor and roof area.

- Whenever possible, vary required steel reinforcement rather than column size; when necessary, vary only one dimension of a column at a time.

- With the aid of a variety of steel connectors, reinforced concrete columns can also support a grid of timber or steel beams.

The most frequently used steel section for columns is the wide-flange (W) shape. It is suitable for connections to beams in two directions, and all of its surfaces are accessible for making bolted or welded connections. Other steel shapes used for columns are round pipes and square or rectangular tubing. Column sections may also be fabricated from a number of shapes or plates to fit the desired end use of a column.

- Compound columns are structural steel columns encased in concrete at least 2 1/2" (64 mm) thick, reinforced with wire mesh.

- Composite columns are structural steel sections thoroughly encased in concrete reinforced with both vertical and spiral reinforcement.

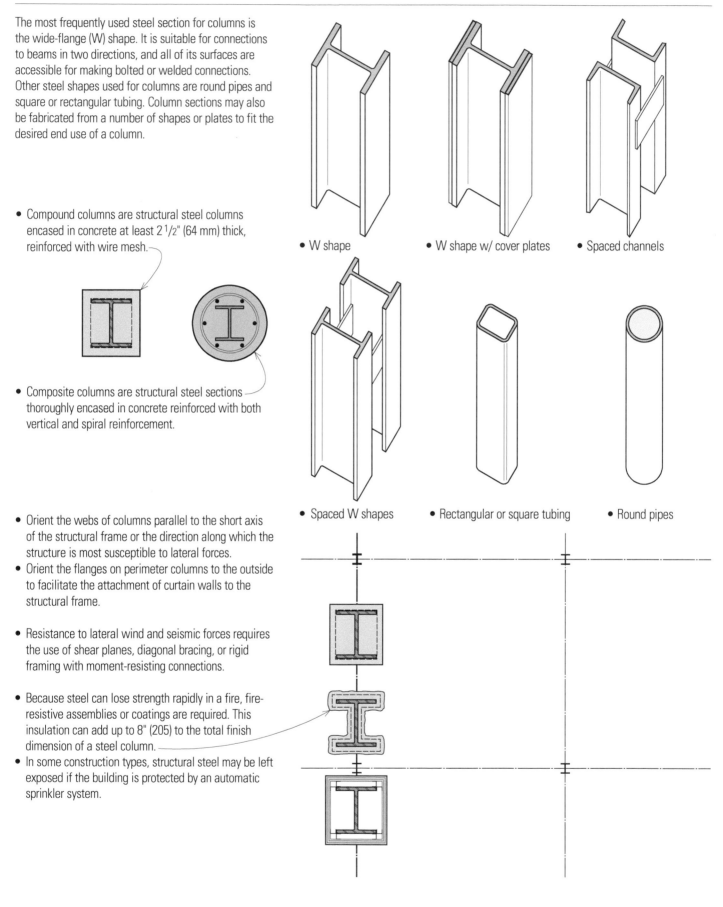

- W shape
- W shape w/ cover plates
- Spaced channels

- Spaced W shapes
- Rectangular or square tubing
- Round pipes

- Orient the webs of columns parallel to the short axis of the structural frame or the direction along which the structure is most susceptible to lateral forces.
- Orient the flanges on perimeter columns to the outside to facilitate the attachment of curtain walls to the structural frame.

- Resistance to lateral wind and seismic forces requires the use of shear planes, diagonal bracing, or rigid framing with moment-resisting connections.

- Because steel can lose strength rapidly in a fire, fire-resistive assemblies or coatings are required. This insulation can add up to 8" (205) to the total finish dimension of a steel column.
- In some construction types, structural steel may be left exposed if the building is protected by an automatic sprinkler system.

The allowable load on a steel column depends on its cross sectional area and its slenderness ratio (L/r), where (L) is the unsupported length of the column in inches and (r) is the least radius of gyration for the cross section of the column.

The following estimating guidelines for steel columns assumes an effective length of 12' (3.7 m).

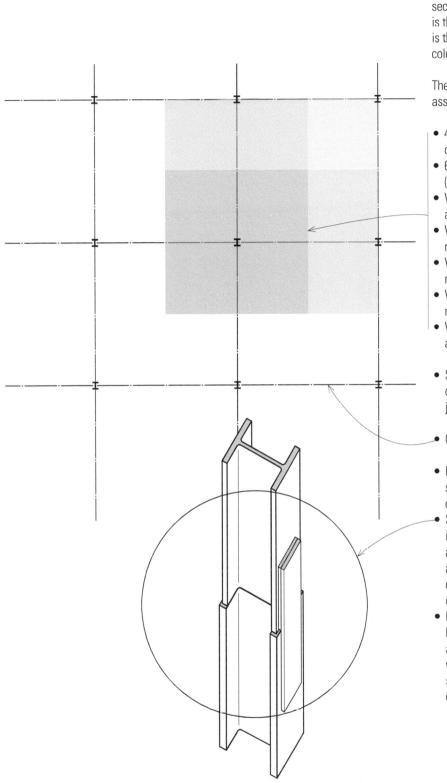

- 4x4 steel tube column may support up to 750 sf (70 m²) of floor and roof area.
- 6x6 steel tube column may support up to 2400 sf (223 m²) of floor and roof area.
- W6x6 may support up to 750 sf (70 m²) of floor and roof area.
- W8x8 may support up to 3000 sf (279 m²) of floor and roof area.
- W10x10 may support up to 4500 sf (418 m²) of floor and roof area.
- W12x12 may support up to 6000 sf (557 m²) of floor and roof area.
- W14x14 may support up to 12,000 sf (1115 m²) of floor and roof area.

- Steel framing is most efficient when columns are laid out to support a regular grid of girders, beams, and joists.

- Column spacing = beam span

- Increased sizes or weights are required for columns supporting heavy loads, rising to greater heights, or contributing to the lateral stability of a structure.
- Steel columns can be strengthened without increasing its size either by using higher strength steel or by using a thicker, heavier section. When the size of vertically aligned columns must change from one floor to the next, columns within the interior are centered on each other on successive floors.
- Because the perimeter structure of a building will often bear the additional weight of exterior cladding and also be involved in the lateral bracing for the building, we can assume, for preliminary design purposes, the same size requirements for both interior and perimeter columns.

### Wood Columns

Wood columns may be solid, built-up, or spaced. In selecting a wood column, the following should be considered: lumber species; structural grade; modulus of elasticity; and allowable compressive, bending, and shear stress values permitted for the intended use. In addition, attention should be paid to the precise loading conditions and the types of connections used. The lack of old-growth lumber has reduced the availability of the higher structural grades of solid lumber, placing greater reliance on manufactured glue-laminated and parallel-strand-laminated (PSL) lumber for larger member sizes and higher structural grades.

Wood columns and posts are loaded axially in compression. Failure can result from crushing of the wood fibers if the maximum unit stress exceeds the allowable unit stress in compression parallel to the grain. The load capacity of a column is also determined by its slenderness ratio. As the slenderness ratio of a column increases, a column can fail from buckling.

- $L/d < 50$ for solid or built-up columns
- $L/d < 80$ for individual member of a spaced column

- $L$ = unsupported length in inches
- $d$ = the least dimension of the compression member in inches

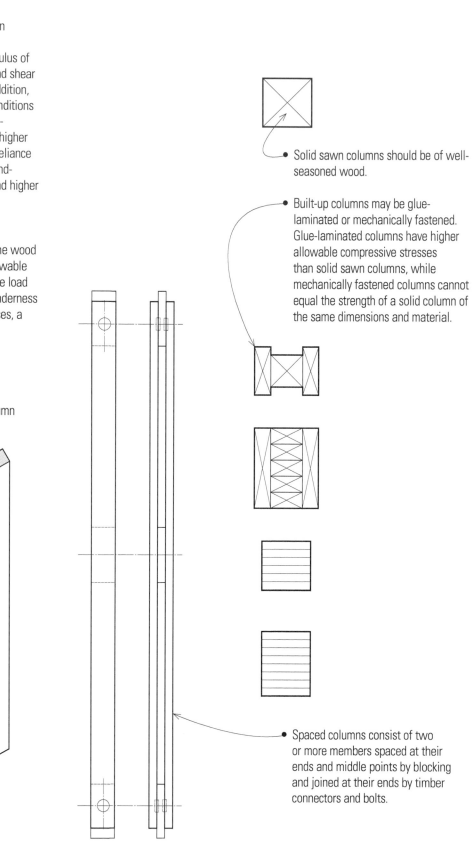

- Solid sawn columns should be of well-seasoned wood.

- Built-up columns may be glue-laminated or mechanically fastened. Glue-laminated columns have higher allowable compressive stresses than solid sawn columns, while mechanically fastened columns cannot equal the strength of a solid column of the same dimensions and material.

- Spaced columns consist of two or more members spaced at their ends and middle points by blocking and joined at their ends by timber connectors and bolts.

The following are estimating guidelines for wood columns.

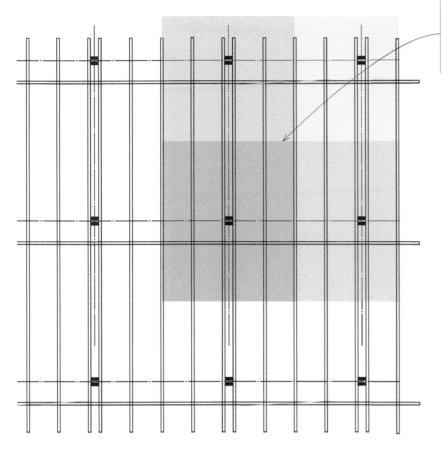

- 6x6 may support up to 500 sf (46 m²) of floor and roof area.
- 8x8 may support up to 1000 sf (93 m²) of floor and roof area.
- 10x10 may support up to 2500 sf (232 m²) of floor and roof area.

- Columns are assumed to have an unsupported height of 12' (3.6 m).
- Increased sizes are required for columns supporting heavy loads, rising to greater heights, or resisting lateral forces.
- In addition to selecting a larger cross section, the capacity of a wood column can be increased by using a species with a greater modulus of elasticity or allowable stress in compression parallel to the wood grain.

**Timber Connectors**

If there is insufficient surface contact area to accommodate the required number of bolts, timber connectors can be used. Timber connectors are metal rings, plates, or grids for transferring shear between the faces of two timber members, used with a single bolt that serves to restrain and clamp the assembly together. Timber connectors are more efficient than bolts or lag screws used alone because they enlarge the area of wood over which a load is distributed and develop lower stresses.

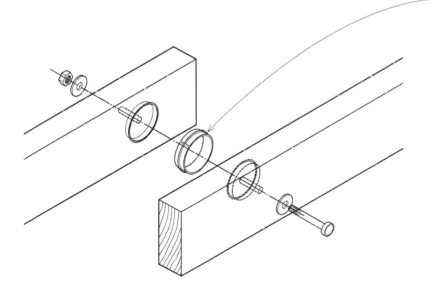

- Split-ring connectors consist of a metal ring inserted into corresponding grooves cut into the faces of the joining members and held in place by a single bolt. The tongue-and-groove split in the ring permits it to deform slightly under loading and maintain bearing at all surfaces, while the beveled cross section eases insertion and ensures a tight-fitting joint after the ring is fully seated in the grooves.

- Available in 2 1/2" and 4" (64 and 100) diameters
- 3 5/8" (90) minimum face width for 2 1/2" (64) split rings; 5 1/2" (140) minimum for 4" (100) split rings
- 1/2" (13) ø bolt for 2 1/2" (64) split rings; 3/4" (19) ø for 4" (100) split rings

- Shear plates consist of a round plate of malleable iron inserted into a corresponding groove, flush with the face of a timber, and held in place by a single bolt. Shear plates are used in back-to-back pairs to develop shear resistance in demountable wood-to-wood connections, or singly in a wood-to-metal connection.

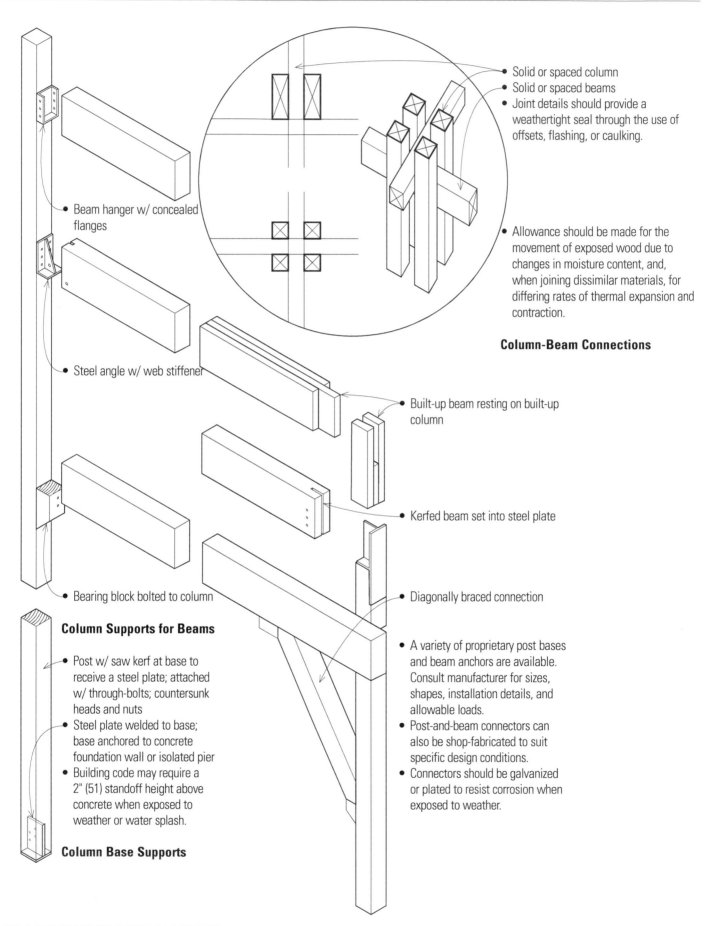

• Solid or spaced column
• Solid or spaced beams
• Joint details should provide a weathertight seal through the use of offsets, flashing, or caulking.

• Allowance should be made for the movement of exposed wood due to changes in moisture content, and, when joining dissimilar materials, for differing rates of thermal expansion and contraction.

**Column-Beam Connections**

• Beam hanger w/ concealed flanges

• Steel angle w/ web stiffener

• Built-up beam resting on built-up column

• Kerfed beam set into steel plate

• Bearing block bolted to column

**Column Supports for Beams**

• Post w/ saw kerf at base to receive a steel plate; attached w/ through-bolts; countersunk heads and nuts
• Steel plate welded to base; base anchored to concrete foundation wall or isolated pier
• Building code may require a 2" (51) standoff height above concrete when exposed to weather or water splash.

**Column Base Supports**

• Diagonally braced connection

• A variety of proprietary post bases and beam anchors are available. Consult manufacturer for sizes, shapes, installation details, and allowable loads.
• Post-and-beam connectors can also be shop-fabricated to suit specific design conditions.
• Connectors should be galvanized or plated to resist corrosion when exposed to weather.

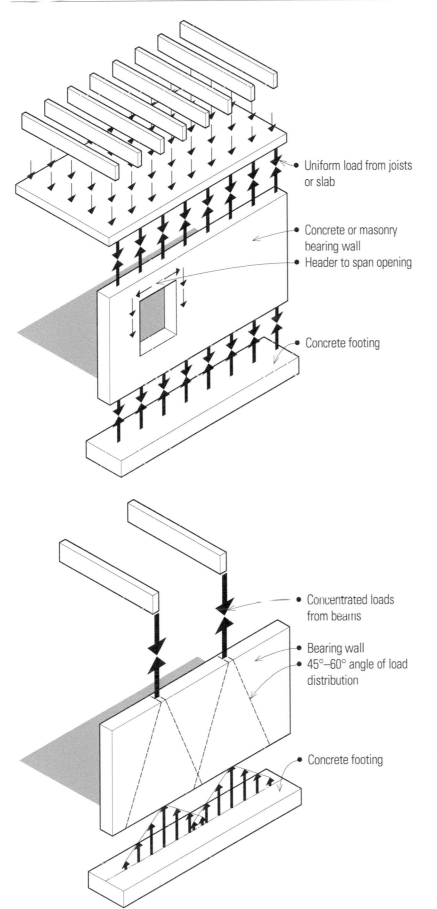

- Uniform load from joists or slab

- Concrete or masonry bearing wall
- Header to span opening

- Concrete footing

- Concentrated loads from beams

- Bearing wall
- 45°–60° angle of load distribution

- Concrete footing

## Bearing Walls

A bearing wall is any wall construction capable of supporting an imposed load, as from a floor or roof of a building, and transmitting the compressive forces through the plane of the wall down to the foundation. Bearing wall systems can be constructed of masonry, cast-in-place concrete, site-cast tilt-up concrete, or wood or metal studs.

Bearing walls should be continuous from floor to floor and be aligned vertically from the roof to the foundation. Because of this continuity, bearing walls can act as shear walls and provide lateral resistance against earthquake or wind forces acting parallel to the plane of the walls. However, due to their relative thinness, bearing walls are unable to provide significant shear resistance to lateral forces acting perpendicular to their plane.

In addition to resisting the crushing or buckling from gravity loads, exterior bearing walls are subject to bending from horizontal wind loads. These forces are transferred to horizontal roof and floor planes and then to lateral force-resisting elements acting perpendicular to the bearing walls.

- Concrete slabs and roof or floor joists impose a uniformly distributed load along the top of a bearing wall. If there are no openings to disrupt the load path from the top of the wall, a uniform load will result on the top of the footing.
- Vertical loads must be redirected to either side of openings through the use of header beams in light-frame construction; arches or lintels in masonry construction; or additional reinforcing steel in concrete construction.

- Concentrated loads develop at the top of a wall when the columns or beams they support are spaced at wide intervals. Depending on the wall material, the concentrated load is distributed along an angle of 45° to 60° as it moves down the wall. The resulting footing load will be nonuniform, with the largest forces directly under the applied load.

- Building codes specify the required fire-resistance of exterior walls based on location, type of construction, and occupancy. Often walls meeting these requirements are also appropriate as bearing walls.

## Concrete Walls

Concrete walls may be precast, either on-site or off-site; more often, they are cast in place. The advantage of precast walls is in the high quality of concrete finishes that can be achieved and the fact that they can be prestressed. Typically, precast panels are used when the concrete wall will provide the finish wall surfaces. Precast wall panels are particularly appropriate for low-rise buildings that are not subject to high lateral loads.

- Site-cast concrete walls may be used as the primary vertical loadbearing elements of a structure or in conjunction with steel or concrete frames.
- The high fire resistance of concrete makes it an ideal material for enclosing building cores and shafts, and for serving as shear walls.

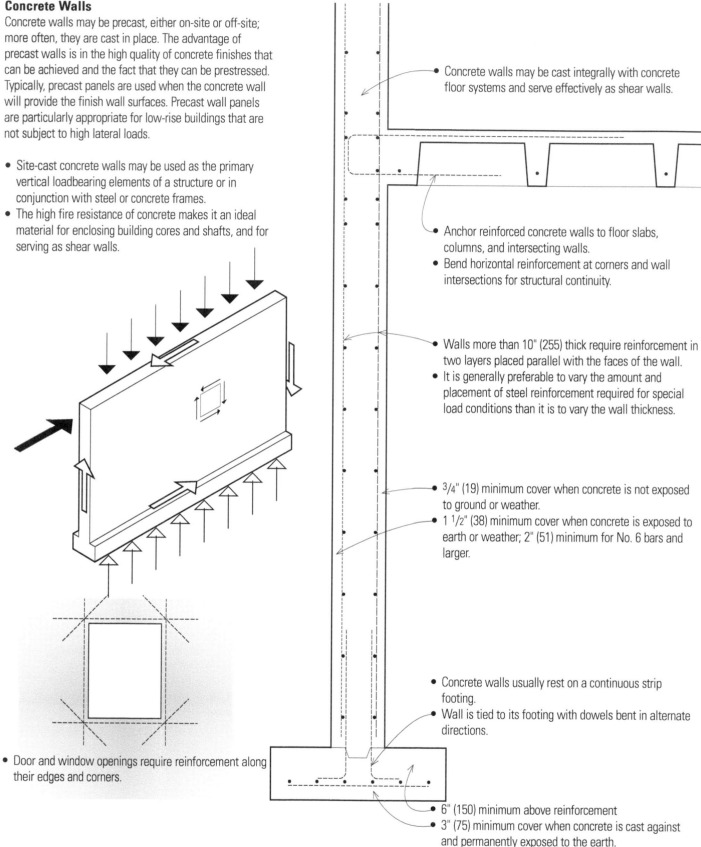

- Door and window openings require reinforcement along their edges and corners.

- Concrete walls may be cast integrally with concrete floor systems and serve effectively as shear walls.

- Anchor reinforced concrete walls to floor slabs, columns, and intersecting walls.
- Bend horizontal reinforcement at corners and wall intersections for structural continuity.

- Walls more than 10" (255) thick require reinforcement in two layers placed parallel with the faces of the wall.
- It is generally preferable to vary the amount and placement of steel reinforcement required for special load conditions than it is to vary the wall thickness.

- 3/4" (19) minimum cover when concrete is not exposed to ground or weather.
- 1 1/2" (38) minimum cover when concrete is exposed to earth or weather; 2" (51) minimum for No. 6 bars and larger.

- Concrete walls usually rest on a continuous strip footing.
- Wall is tied to its footing with dowels bent in alternate directions.

- 6" (150) minimum above reinforcement
- 3" (75) minimum cover when concrete is cast against and permanently exposed to the earth.

With the possible exception of multistory buildings, the bearing capacity of reinforced concrete walls typically will not be the critical factor in determining the thickness of the wall. Concrete walls must be supported laterally at regular intervals, both vertically and along their length. Intersecting floors or roofs stabilize the height of concrete walls while perpendicular walls or pilasters stabilize their length.

Minimum Wall Thicknesses:
- 6" (150) minimum for bearing walls or 1/25 of the unsupported height or length between stiffening elements
- 4" (100) minimum for nonbearing walls or 1/36 of unsupported height or length
- 8" (205) minimum for basement, foundation, fire, or party walls

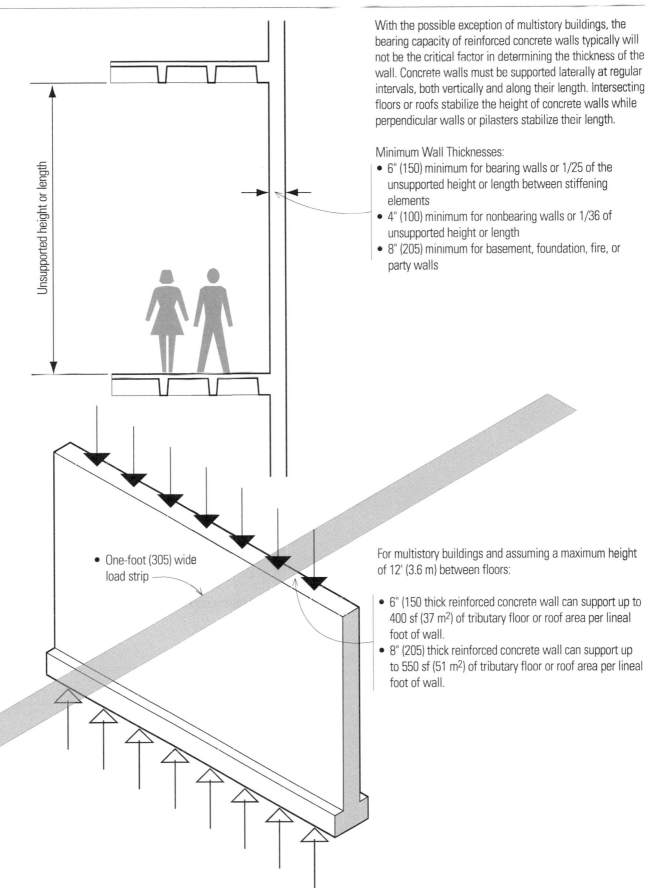

Unsupported height or length

- One-foot (305) wide load strip

For multistory buildings and assuming a maximum height of 12' (3.6 m) between floors:

- 6" (150 thick reinforced concrete wall can support up to 400 sf (37 m²) of tributary floor or roof area per lineal foot of wall.
- 8" (205) thick reinforced concrete wall can support up to 550 sf (51 m²) of tributary floor or roof area per lineal foot of wall.

### Masonry Walls

Masonry construction refers to building with units of various natural or manufactured products, such as stone, brick, or concrete block, usually with the use of mortar as a bonding agent to form walls that are durable, fire-resistant, and structurally efficient in compression. The most common structural masonry units are precast concrete masonry units (CMU) or concrete block. Because concrete block is more economical and easily reinforced, it has generally replaced fired clay brick and tile for bearing walls. Brick and clay tile are used primarily for their appearance as a finished surface, typically as a veneer on light frame or concrete block bearing walls.

Masonry bearing walls may be constructed as solid walls, cavity walls, or veneered walls. While they can be constructed without reinforcing, masonry bearing walls should be reinforced in seismic zones by embedding steel reinforcing bars placed in thickened joints or cavities with a fluid grout mix of portland cement, aggregate, and water for greater strength in carrying vertical loads and increased resistance to buckling and lateral forces. It is essential that a strong bond develop between the reinforcing steel, grout, and masonry units.

- Standard CMU blocks have two or three cores and nominal dimensions of 8" x 8" x 16" (7 5/8" x 7 5/8" x 15 5/8" actual; 205 x 205 x 405).
- 6", 10" and 12" (150, 255 and 305) nominal widths are also available.

- Mortar is a plastic mixture of cement or lime, or a combination of both, with sand and water, used as a bonding agent in masonry construction. Mortar joints vary in thickness from 1/4" to 1/2" (6 to 13) but are typically 3/8" (10) thick.

- Exterior masonry walls must be weather-resistant and control heat flow.
- Water penetration must be controlled through the use of tooled joints, cavity spaces, flashing, and caulking.
- Cavity walls are preferred for their increased resistance to water penetration and improved thermal performance.

- 8" (205) minimum nominal thickness for:
  Masonry bearing walls
  Masonry shear walls
  Masonry parapets.

- 6" (150) minimum nominal thickness for reinforced masonry bearing walls; masonry walls relied upon for resistance to lateral loading are limited to 35' (10 m) in height.

- Modular dimensions

- Grouted masonry walls have all interior joints and cavities filled entirely with grout as the work progresses. The grout used to consolidate the adjoining materials into a solid mass is a fluid Portland cement mortar that will flow easily without segregation of the ingredients.
- Horizontal joint reinforcement
- Steel reinforcement
- Reinforcement continues down to a reinforced concrete footing.

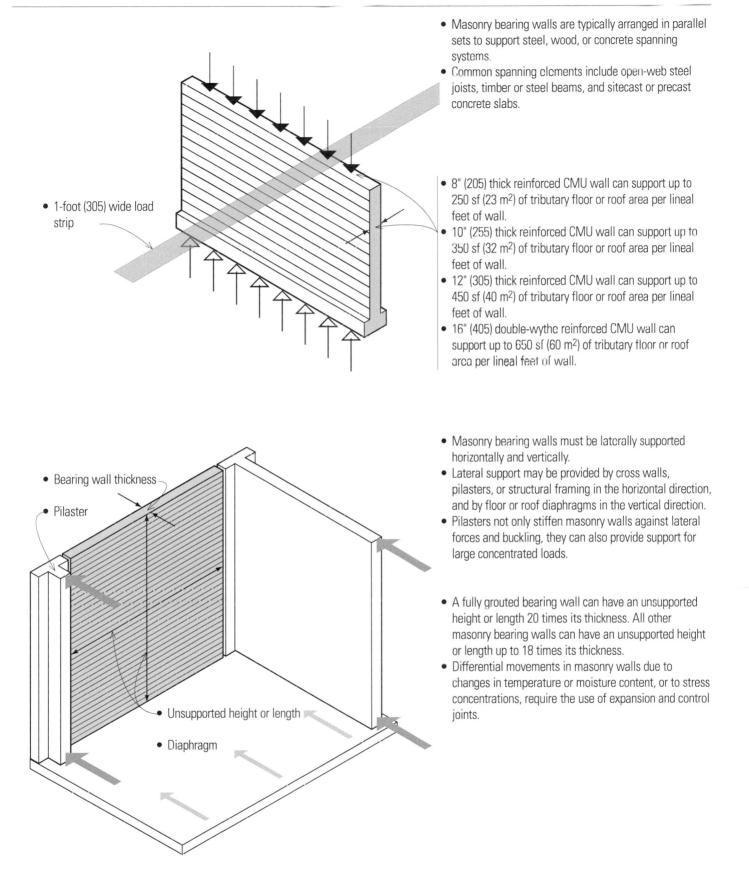

- Masonry bearing walls are typically arranged in parallel sets to support steel, wood, or concrete spanning systems.
- Common spanning elements include open-web steel joists, timber or steel beams, and sitecast or precast concrete slabs.

- 1-foot (305) wide load strip

- 8" (205) thick reinforced CMU wall can support up to 250 sf (23 m²) of tributary floor or roof area per lineal feet of wall.
- 10" (255) thick reinforced CMU wall can support up to 350 sf (32 m²) of tributary floor or roof area per lineal feet of wall.
- 12" (305) thick reinforced CMU wall can support up to 450 sf (40 m²) of tributary floor or roof area per lineal feet of wall.
- 16" (405) double-wythe reinforced CMU wall can support up to 650 sf (60 m²) of tributary floor or roof area per lineal feet of wall.

- Bearing wall thickness
- Pilaster

- Masonry bearing walls must be laterally supported horizontally and vertically.
- Lateral support may be provided by cross walls, pilasters, or structural framing in the horizontal direction, and by floor or roof diaphragms in the vertical direction.
- Pilasters not only stiffen masonry walls against lateral forces and buckling, they can also provide support for large concentrated loads.

- Unsupported height or length

- Diaphragm

- A fully grouted bearing wall can have an unsupported height or length 20 times its thickness. All other masonry bearing walls can have an unsupported height or length up to 18 times its thickness.
- Differential movements in masonry walls due to changes in temperature or moisture content, or to stress concentrations, require the use of expansion and control joints.

### Stud-Framed Walls

Light frame walls are constructed of light-gauge metal or wood studs that are typically spaced 12", 16", or 24" (305, 405, or 610) on center, depending on the desired wall height and the size and spanning capability of common sheathing and surfacing materials. Light frame construction is typically used for bearing walls in low-rise structures that take advantage of the lightweight components and ease of assembly. The system is particularly well suited for buildings that are irregular in form or layout.

Light-gauge metal studs are manufactured by cold-forming sheet or strip steel. The cold-formed metal studs can be easily cut and assembled with simple tools into a wall structure that is lightweight, noncombustible, and dampproof. Metal stud walls may be used as nonloadbearing partitions or as bearing walls supporting light-gauge steel joists. Unlike wood light framing, metal light framing can be used for fabricating partitions in noncombustible construction. However, the fire-resistance rating of both wood and metal light frame wall assemblies is based on the fire resistance of the surfacing materials.

Both metal and wood stud walls can be idealized as monolithic walls when loaded uniformly from above. The studs carry the vertical and horizontal bending loads while the sheathing stiffens the plane of the wall and distributes both horizontal and vertical loads between individual studs. Any opening in the wall framing requires the use of header beams that redirect the loads to either side of the openings. Concentrated loads from the header reactions must be supported by a build-up of studs resembling a column.

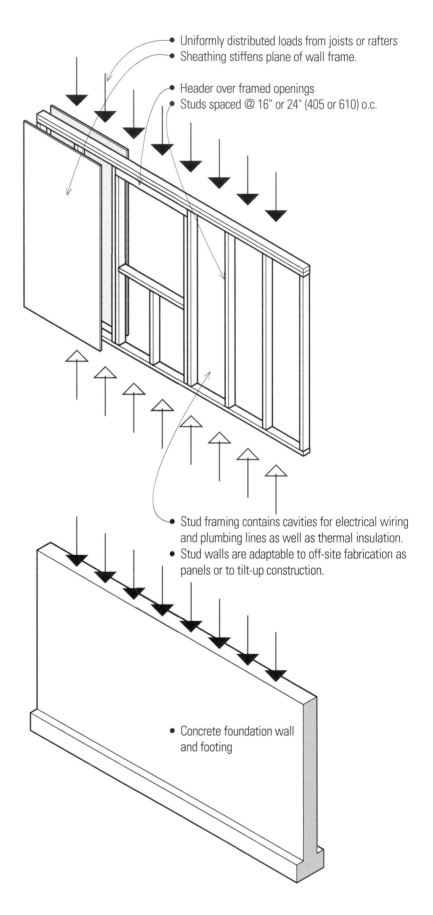

- Uniformly distributed loads from joists or rafters
- Sheathing stiffens plane of wall frame.

- Header over framed openings
- Studs spaced @ 16" or 24" (405 or 610) o.c.

- Stud framing contains cavities for electrical wiring and plumbing lines as well as thermal insulation.
- Stud walls are adaptable to off-site fabrication as panels or to tilt-up construction.

- Concrete foundation wall and footing

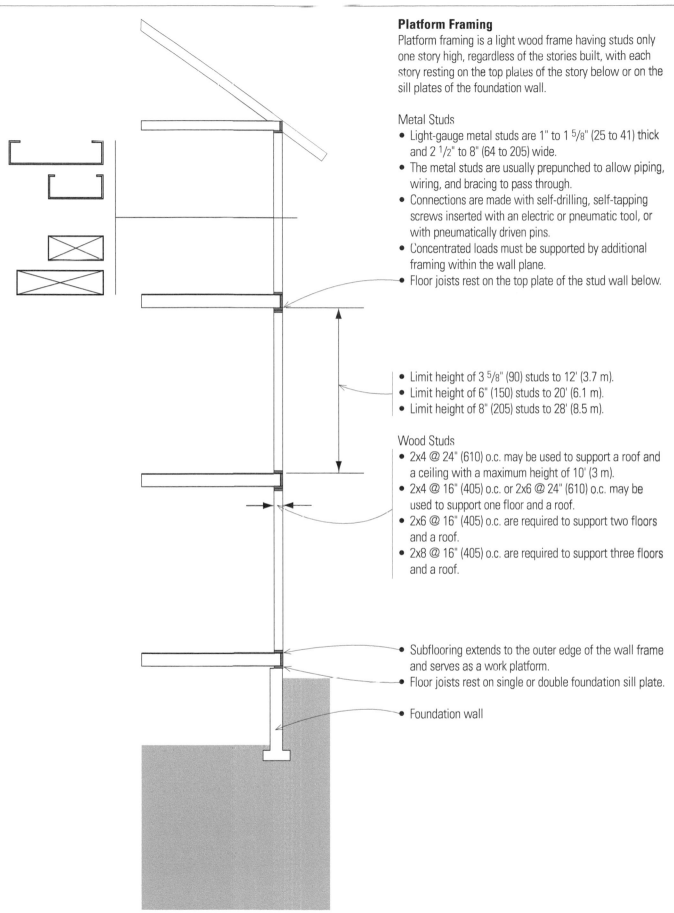

### Platform Framing

Platform framing is a light wood frame having studs only one story high, regardless of the stories built, with each story resting on the top plates of the story below or on the sill plates of the foundation wall.

Metal Studs

- Light-gauge metal studs are 1" to 1 5/8" (25 to 41) thick and 2 1/2" to 8" (64 to 205) wide.
- The metal studs are usually prepunched to allow piping, wiring, and bracing to pass through.
- Connections are made with self-drilling, self-tapping screws inserted with an electric or pneumatic tool, or with pneumatically driven pins.
- Concentrated loads must be supported by additional framing within the wall plane.
- Floor joists rest on the top plate of the stud wall below.

- Limit height of 3 5/8" (90) studs to 12' (3.7 m).
- Limit height of 6" (150) studs to 20' (6.1 m).
- Limit height of 8" (205) studs to 28' (8.5 m).

Wood Studs

- 2x4 @ 24" (610) o.c. may be used to support a roof and a ceiling with a maximum height of 10' (3 m).
- 2x4 @ 16" (405) o.c. or 2x6 @ 24" (610) o.c. may be used to support one floor and a roof.
- 2x6 @ 16" (405) o.c. are required to support two floors and a roof.
- 2x8 @ 16" (405) o.c. are required to support three floors and a roof.

- Subflooring extends to the outer edge of the wall frame and serves as a work platform.
- Floor joists rest on single or double foundation sill plate.

- Foundation wall

### Curtain Walls

Curtain walls are exterior walls supported wholly by the steel or concrete structural frame of a building and carrying no loads other than their own weight and lateral loads. A curtain wall cannot contribute to the stability of the structure.

A curtain wall may consist of metal framing holding either vision glass or opaque spandrel units, or of thin veneer panels of precast concrete, cut stone, masonry, or metal. The wall units may be one, two, or three stories in height, and may be preglazed or glazed after installation. Panel systems offer controlled shop assembly and rapid erection, but are bulky to ship and handle.

While simple in theory, curtain wall construction is complex and requires careful development, testing, and erection. Close coordination is also required between the architect, structural engineer, contractor, and a fabricator who is experienced in curtain wall construction.

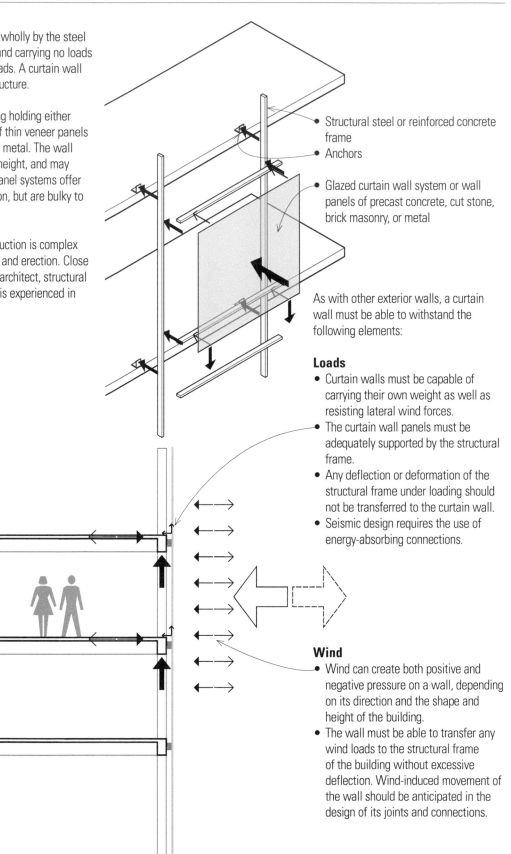

- Structural steel or reinforced concrete frame
- Anchors

- Glazed curtain wall system or wall panels of precast concrete, cut stone, brick masonry, or metal

As with other exterior walls, a curtain wall must be able to withstand the following elements:

#### Loads

- Curtain walls must be capable of carrying their own weight as well as resisting lateral wind forces.
- The curtain wall panels must be adequately supported by the structural frame.
- Any deflection or deformation of the structural frame under loading should not be transferred to the curtain wall.
- Seismic design requires the use of energy-absorbing connections.

#### Wind

- Wind can create both positive and negative pressure on a wall, depending on its direction and the shape and height of the building.
- The wall must be able to transfer any wind loads to the structural frame of the building without excessive deflection. Wind-induced movement of the wall should be anticipated in the design of its joints and connections.

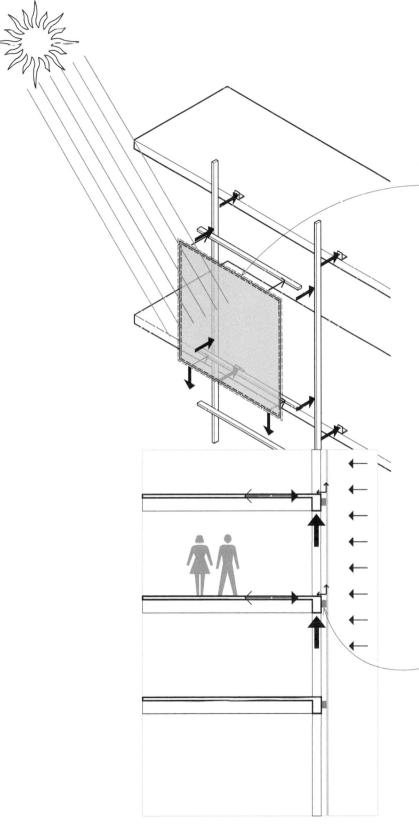

### Sun
- Brightness and glare should be controlled with shading devices or the use of reflective or tinted glass.
- The ultraviolet rays of the sun can also cause deterioration of joint and glazing materials and fading of interior furnishings.

### Temperature
- Daily and seasonal variations in temperature cause expansion and contraction of the materials comprising a wall assembly, especially metals. Allowance must be made for differential movement caused by the variable thermal expansion and contraction of different materials.
- Joints and sealants must be able to withstand the movement caused by thermal stresses.
- Heat flow through glazed curtain walls should be controlled by using insulating glass, insulating opaque panels, and by incorporating thermal breaks into metal frames.
- Thermal insulation of veneer panels may also be incorporated into the wall units, attached to their backsides, or provided with a backup wall constructed on site.

### Water
- Rain can collect on the wall surface and be wind-driven under pressure through the smallest openings.
- Water vapor that condenses and collects within the wall must be drained to the outside.
- Pressure-equalized design principles become critical in the detailing of curtain walls, especially in larger and taller buildings, where the pressure differential between the outside atmosphere and an interior environment can cause rainwater to migrate through even the smallest openings in wall joints.

### Fire
- A noncombustible material, sometimes referred to as safing, must be installed to prevent the spread of fire at each floor within column covers and between the wall panels and the slab edge or spandrel beam.
- The building code also specifies the fire-resistance requirements for the structural frame and the curtain wall panels themselves.

The curtain wall assembly must incorporate members that span either horizontally between columns or vertically between floors. While spanning horizontally from column to column is possible, the spans dictated by the column spacing of the structural frame are usually much greater than the floor-to-floor heights. For this reason, curtain wall systems typically span vertically from floor to floor and are suspended from steel or concrete spandrel beams or from the edge of cantilevered concrete slabs.

The primary spanning members of a curtain wall assembly may be aluminum extrusions, smaller steel channels and angles, or light-gauge metal framing. In panelized curtain walls, the spanning members form the strong-back that allows that panel to be handled as a unit.

If desired, secondary framing perpendicular to the primary spanning members can subdivide the module of the curtain wall design into smaller parts and incorporate a variety of devices that serve varying functions, such as opaque, insulated panels, operable windows for natural ventilation, and louvers or other sunscreening devices.

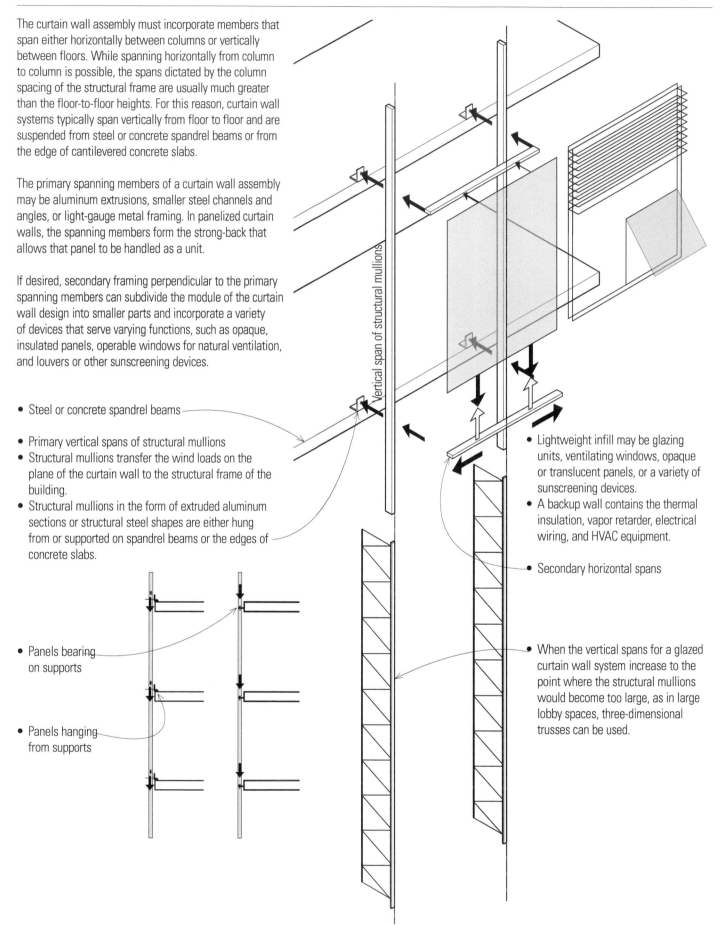

Vertical span of structural mullions

- Steel or concrete spandrel beams

- Primary vertical spans of structural mullions
- Structural mullions transfer the wind loads on the plane of the curtain wall to the structural frame of the building.
- Structural mullions in the form of extruded aluminum sections or structural steel shapes are either hung from or supported on spandrel beams or the edges of concrete slabs.

- Panels bearing on supports

- Panels hanging from supports

- Lightweight infill may be glazing units, ventilating windows, opaque or translucent panels, or a variety of sunscreening devices.
- A backup wall contains the thermal insulation, vapor retarder, electrical wiring, and HVAC equipment.

- Secondary horizontal spans

- When the vertical spans for a glazed curtain wall system increase to the point where the structural mullions would become too large, as in large lobby spaces, three-dimensional trusses can be used.

There are a variety of metal devices that may be used to secure a curtain wall to the structural frame of a building. Some connections are fixed to resist loads applied from any direction. Others are designed to resist only lateral wind loads. These joints typically permit adjustment in three dimensions in order to allow for discrepancies between the dimensions of the curtain wall units and the structural frame, as well as to accommodate the differential movement when the structural frame deflects under loading or when the curtain wall reacts to thermal stresses and changes in temperature.

Shim plates and angles with slotted holes allow adjustments to be made in one direction; a combination of angles and plates allows adjustments to be made in three dimensions. After final adjustments are made, the connections can be permanently secured by welding if a fixed connection is required.

### Structural Steel Frame

• For accessibility, top anchorages are best.

• Angle clip shimmed and bolted or welded to flange of spandrel beam or to steel angle cast into its edge of concrete slab

• A wedge-shaped slot receives a wedge-shaped nut that provides for both vertical adjustment and a positive connection.

### Reinforced Concrete Frame

• Angle cast into slab edge of concrete slab

• Connections must be able to accommodate discrepancies between the rough dimensions of the structural frame and the finish dimensions of the curtain wall assembly.

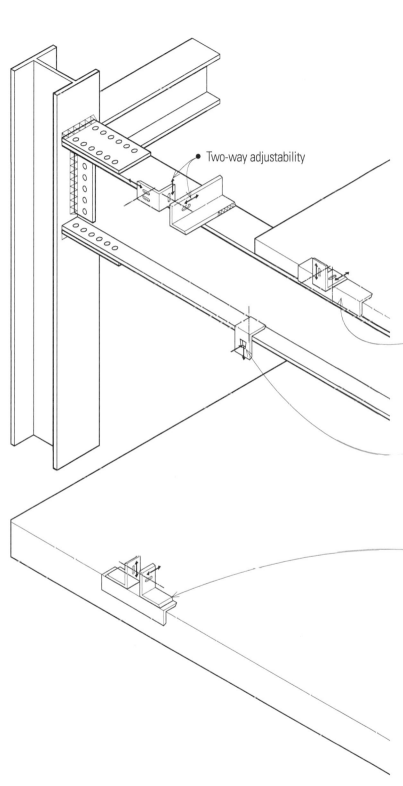

Two-way adjustability

### Relation of Curtain Wall to Structural Frame

The ability to separate the weather enclosure of the curtain wall from the structural function of the building frame leads to an important design decision—determining the position of the curtain wall in relation to the structural frame.

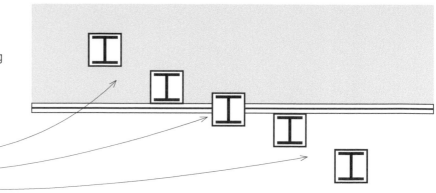

A curtain wall assembly can be related to the structural frame of a building in three fundamental ways:
• Behind the plane of the structural frame
• Within the plane of the structural frame
• In front of the plane of the structural frame

### Curtain Walls in Front of the Structural Frame

The most common arrangement is to position the curtain wall assembly in front of the structural frame. Setting the plane of the curtain wall in this relation to the building structure allows the design of the exterior cladding to either emphasize the grid of the structural frame or offer a counterpoint to the pattern of columns and beams or slabs.

• The curtain wall is able to form a continuous weather barrier without any structural penetrations.
• Although the cumulative effects of thermal movement may be greater in the exterior curtain wall, the movement may be easier to accommodate because it is not constrained by the structural frame.

• The space within the depth of the column structure can be used for vertical services.

• Structural steel members exposed on the interior of the building require fire-resistive assemblies or coatings.

• Columns and diagonal bracing are exposed within the interior spaces of the building.

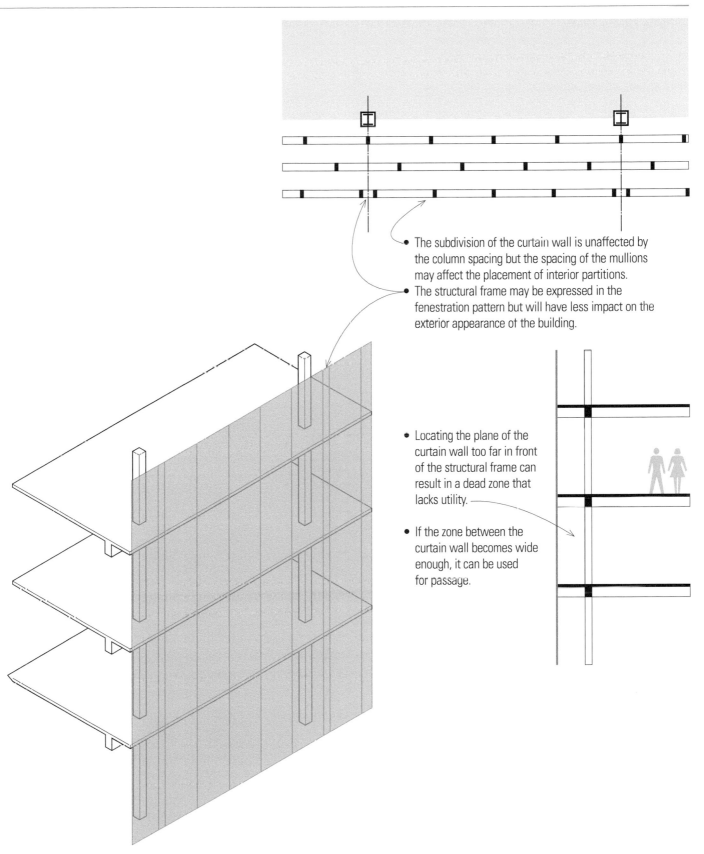

- The subdivision of the curtain wall is unaffected by the column spacing but the spacing of the mullions may affect the placement of interior partitions.
- The structural frame may be expressed in the fenestration pattern but will have less impact on the exterior appearance of the building.

- Locating the plane of the curtain wall too far in front of the structural frame can result in a dead zone that lacks utility.

- If the zone between the curtain wall becomes wide enough, it can be used for passage.

### In-Plane Curtain Walls

Positioning the curtain wall panels or assemblies within the plane of the structural frame will express the scale, proportions, and visual weight of the column-and-beam frame in the building facade.

- The exposed columns and beams or slab edges may require weather-resistant cladding that incorporates a thermal barrier.

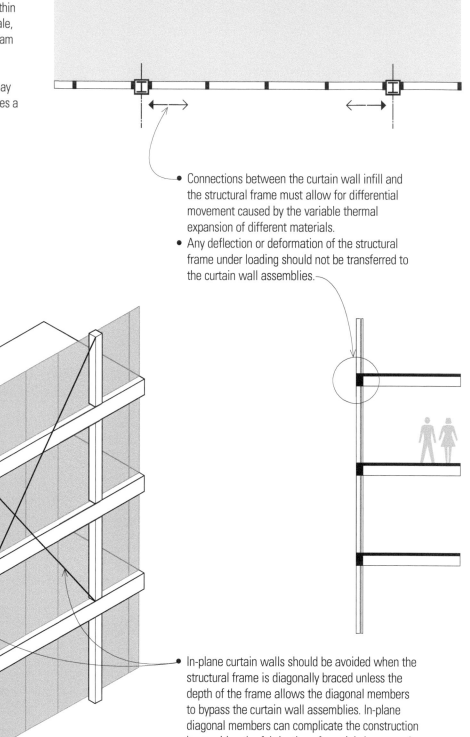

- Connections between the curtain wall infill and the structural frame must allow for differential movement caused by the variable thermal expansion of different materials.
- Any deflection or deformation of the structural frame under loading should not be transferred to the curtain wall assemblies.

- In-plane curtain walls should be avoided when the structural frame is diagonally braced unless the depth of the frame allows the diagonal members to bypass the curtain wall assemblies. In-plane diagonal members can complicate the construction by requiring the fabrication of special shapes and connections.

## Curtain Walls Behind the Structural Frame

When the curtain wall is positioned behind the structural frame, the design of the structural frame becomes the major expressive feature of the exterior facade.

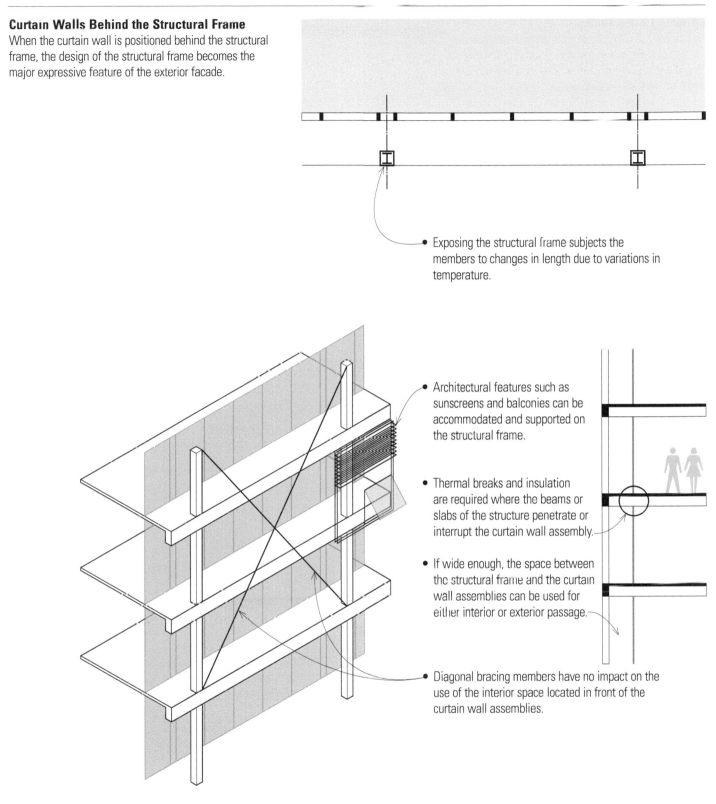

- Exposing the structural frame subjects the members to changes in length due to variations in temperature.

- Architectural features such as sunscreens and balconies can be accommodated and supported on the structural frame.

- Thermal breaks and insulation are required where the beams or slabs of the structure penetrate or interrupt the curtain wall assembly.

- If wide enough, the space between the structural frame and the curtain wall assemblies can be used for either interior or exterior passage.

- Diagonal bracing members have no impact on the use of the interior space located in front of the curtain wall assemblies.

## Structural Glass Facades

Curtain walls and structural glass facades are closely related but differ in their manner of support. Typically, curtain walls span from floor to floor, attached to and supported by the primary structure of a building. Aluminum extrusions are generally used as part of a framework that secures some type of panel material—glazing, composite metal, stone, or terra cotta.

Structural glass facades have emerged over the past several decades as a means of providing maximum transparency in buildings. Structural glass facades integrate structure and cladding and can be used in long-span applications. The structural systems used to support the glazing are exposed and distinct from the building's primary structure. Structural glass facades are generally categorized by the nature of the underlying support structure.

- Strong-back system: The system consists of structural sections capable of accommodating the required span using vertical and/or horizontal components. Sometimes, horizontal beams, either straight or curved, are suspended from overhead cables and fixed to the anchoring building structure at their ends.

- Glass fin systems: Glass fin-supported facades date back to the 1950s and represent a special case of glass technology that does not rely on a metal supporting structure except for hardware and splice plates. The glass fins are set perpendicular to the glass facade to provide lateral support and perform in a similar manner to strong-back structural members. A recent development uses multi-ply laminates of heat-treated glass beams as major structural elements.

- Planar truss system: Various configurations and types of planar trusses may be used to support the glass facades. The most commonly used truss is oriented vertically with its depth perpendicular to the plane of the glazing. Trusses are usually positioned at some regular interval, generally along a gridline of the building or a subdivision of the grid module. While trusses are most often vertical in elevation or linear in plan, they can also be sloped inward or outward and follow a curved geometry in plan. Trusses may be placed either on the exterior or interior side of the facade. The truss system will often incorporate bracing spreaders with diagonal tension counters for lateral stability.

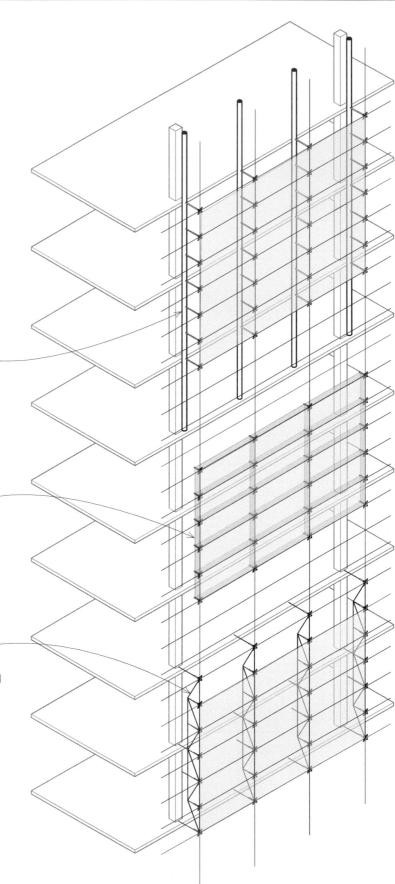

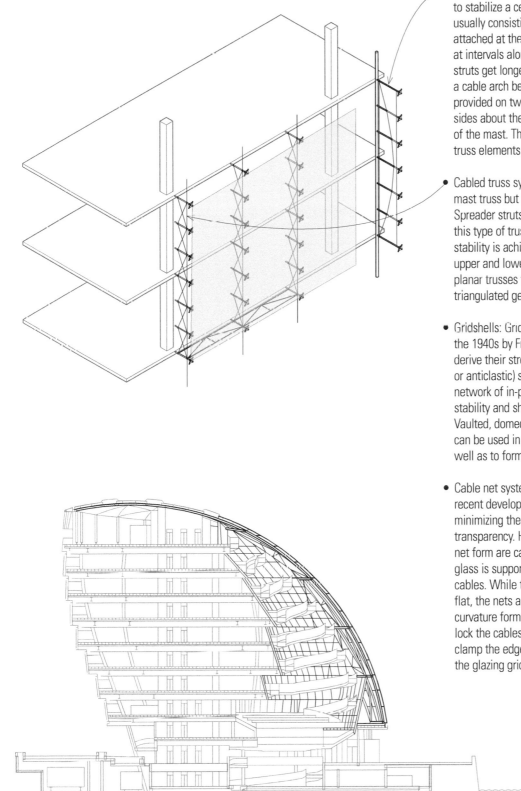

- Mast truss system: A mast truss uses tension elements to stabilize a central compression member (mast), usually consisting of a pipe or tube section. Cables are attached at the mast ends with spreader struts secured at intervals along the length of the mast. These spreader struts get longer toward the center of the mast, forming a cable arch between the mast ends. Cable arches provided on two sides or radially spaced on three or four sides about the mast can increase the buckling capacity of the mast. This system relies on pretensioning of the truss elements to provide stability.

- Cabled truss systems: A cabled truss is similar to the mast truss but has no primary compression member. Spreader struts are the only compression elements in this type of truss. Without a main compression element, stability is achieved by tensioning the cables to the upper and lower boundary structure, unlike conventional planar trusses that achieve stability through their triangulated geometry.

- Gridshells: Gridshells, a structural type pioneered in the 1940s by Frei Otto, are form-active structures that derive their strength from double-curved (synclastic or anticlastic) surface geometry. The system uses a network of in-plane prestressed cables to provide stability and shear resistance to the thin shell grid. Vaulted, domed, and other double-curved configurations can be used in vertical and overhead applications as well as to form complete building enclosures.

- Cable net systems: Cable nets represent one of the most recent developments in structural glass technology, minimizing the visible structural system and maximizing transparency. Horizontal and vertical cables yielding a net form are capable of spanning in two directions. The glass is supported by the net geometry of pretensioned cables. While the design of a cable net system can be flat, the nets are more often tensioned into double-curvature forms. Dual-function clamping components lock the cables together at their intersections as well as clamp the edges or corners of adjacent glass panes on the glazing grid.

Section: London City Hall, London, England, 1998–2003, Foster + Partners

### Diagrids

A diagrid refers to a structure of intersecting members that
form a diagonal grid, connected at specially jointed nodes
to create an integral network across a building surface
capable of resisting lateral forces as well as gravity
loads. This exoskeletal framework allows for the possible
reduction of the number of internal supports, saving on
space and building materials and providing for greater
flexibility in interior layouts. Horizontal rings that tie all of
the triangulated pieces together into a three-dimensional
framework are necessary to provide buckling resistance to
the exoskeletal grid.

- A diagrid pairs the structure of a continuous rigid
  shell, which resists loads in any direction, with
  the constructability afforded by the use of discrete
  elements.
- Each diagonal can be viewed as providing a continuous
  load path to the ground. The number of possible load
  paths results in a high degree of redundancy.

- See also the discussion of diagrids and their application
  in stabilizing high-rise structures on pages 297–301.

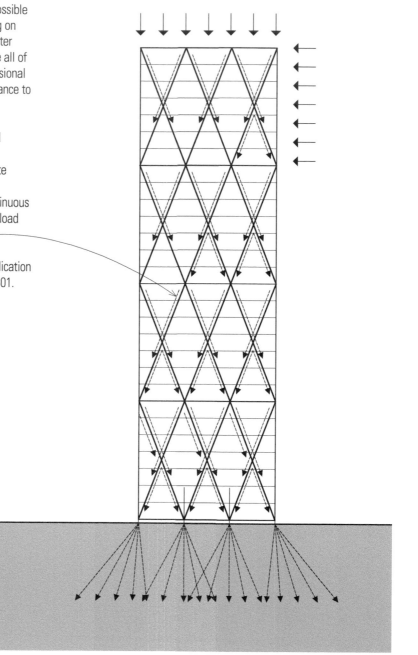

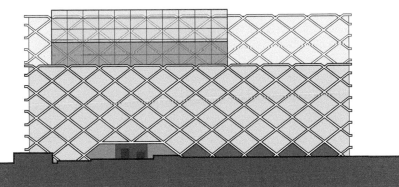

Elevation: One Shelley Street, Sydney, Australia, 2009, Fitzpatrick + Partners

The One Shelley Street project uses a structural diagrid system to create a visually unique exterior. Because the diagrid is positioned on the outside of and very close to the glass facade, close monitoring, management, and coordination during fabrication and installation was required.

Unlike the geometric regularity of One Shelley Street's diagrid, the concrete diagrid used in TOD's Omotesando Building is based on a pattern of overlapping tree silhouettes that mimic the branch structure of nearby elm trees. Similar to the growth pattern of trees, the diagrid members get thinner and more numerous with a higher ratio of openings as you move up higher in the building. The resulting structure supports floor slabs spanning 32 to 50 feet (10 to 15 meters) without any internal columns. To minimize sway during an earthquake, the structure rests on a shock-absorbing foundation.

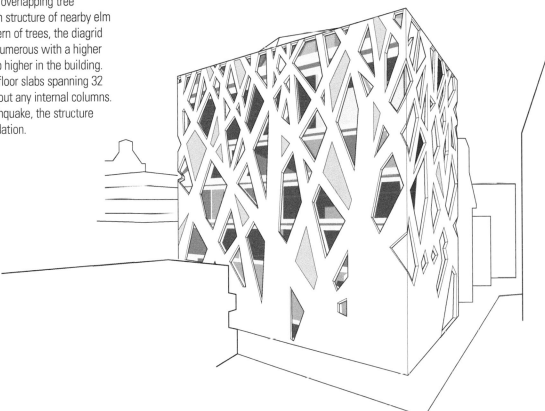

Exterior view: TOD's Omotesando Building, Tokyo, Japan, 2002–2004, Toyo Ito and Associates

# ROOF STRUCTURES

Roof structures, like floor structures, are horizontal spanning systems. However, while floor structures provide flat and level platforms for the support of our activities and furnishings, roof structures have a vertical aspect that can dramatically impact the exterior form of a building as well as the quality of the spatial volumes beneath their canopy. A roof structure may be flat or pitched, gabled or hipped, broad and sheltering, or rhythmically articulated. It may be exposed with edges flush with or overhanging the exterior walls, or it may be concealed from view, hidden behind a parapet. If its underside remains exposed, the roof also transmits its form to the upper boundaries of the interior spaces below.

Because the roof system functions as the primary sheltering element for the interior spaces of a building, its form and slope must be compatible with the type of roofing—shingles, tiles, or a continuous membrane—used to shed rainwater and melting snow to a system of drains, gutters, and downspouts. The construction of a roof should also control the passage of moisture vapor, the infiltration of air, and the flow of heat and solar radiation. Depending on the type of construction required by the building code, the roof structure and assembly may have to resist the spread of fire.

Like floor systems, a roof must be structured to span across space and carry its own weight as well as the weight of any attached equipment and accumulated rain and snow. Flat roofs used as decks are also subject to live occupancy loads. In addition to these gravity loads, the planes of the roof may be required to resist lateral wind and seismic forces, as well as uplifting wind forces, and transfer these forces to the supporting structure.

Because the gravity loads for a building originate with the roof system, its structural layout must correspond to that of the column and bearing wall systems through which its loads are transferred down to the foundation system. This pattern of roof supports and the extent of the roof spans, in turn, influences the layout of interior spaces and the type of ceiling that the roof structure may support. Long roof spans would open up a more flexible interior space while shorter roof spans might suggest more precisely defined spaces.

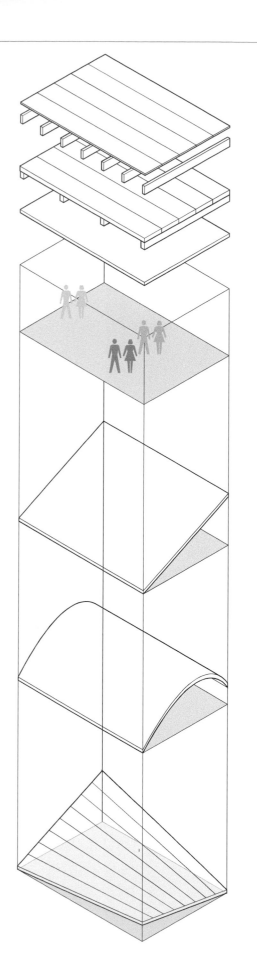

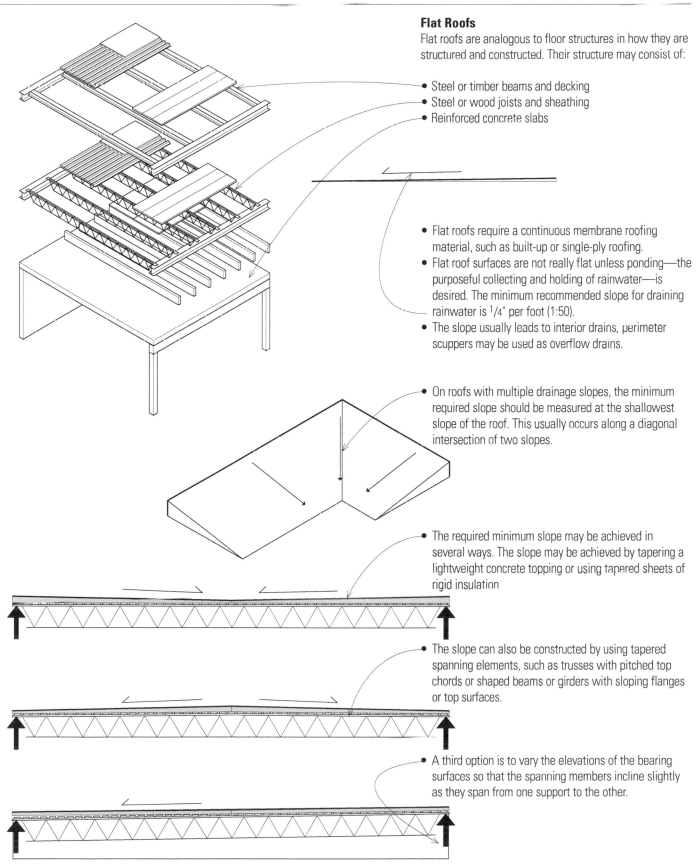

## Flat Roofs

Flat roofs are analogous to floor structures in how they are structured and constructed. Their structure may consist of:

- Steel or timber beams and decking
- Steel or wood joists and sheathing
- Reinforced concrete slabs

- Flat roofs require a continuous membrane roofing material, such as built-up or single-ply roofing.
- Flat roof surfaces are not really flat unless ponding—the purposeful collecting and holding of rainwater—is desired. The minimum recommended slope for draining rainwater is $1/4$" per foot (1:50).
- The slope usually leads to interior drains; perimeter scuppers may be used as overflow drains.

- On roofs with multiple drainage slopes, the minimum required slope should be measured at the shallowest slope of the roof. This usually occurs along a diagonal intersection of two slopes.

- The required minimum slope may be achieved in several ways. The slope may be achieved by tapering a lightweight concrete topping or using tapered sheets of rigid insulation.

- The slope can also be constructed by using tapered spanning elements, such as trusses with pitched top chords or shaped beams or girders with sloping flanges or top surfaces.

- A third option is to vary the elevations of the bearing surfaces so that the spanning members incline slightly as they span from one support to the other.

## Sloping Roofs

The roof slope affects the choice of roofing material, the requirements for underlayment and eave flashing, and design wind loads. Some roofing materials are suitable for low-slope roofs; others must be laid over roof surfaces with steeper pitches to shed rainwater properly.

- Sloping roofs shed rainwater more easily to eave gutters more easily than flat roofs.

- Minimum roof slopes for various roofing materials:

- 4:12      Slate shingles
            Wood shakes

- 3:12      Metal interlocking roof panels
            Metal roof shingles
            Wood shingles

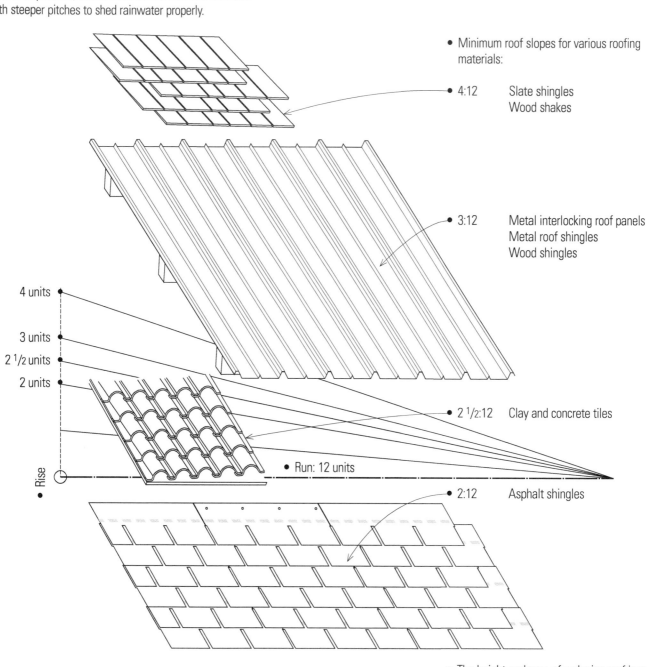

4 units

3 units

2 1/2 units

2 units

- 2 1/2:12      Clay and concrete tiles

Rise

Run: 12 units

- 2:12      Asphalt shingles

- The height and area of a sloping roof increase with its horizontal dimensions.
- The space under a high-slope roof may be usable.
- The ceiling may be hung from the roof structure or have its own separate structural system.

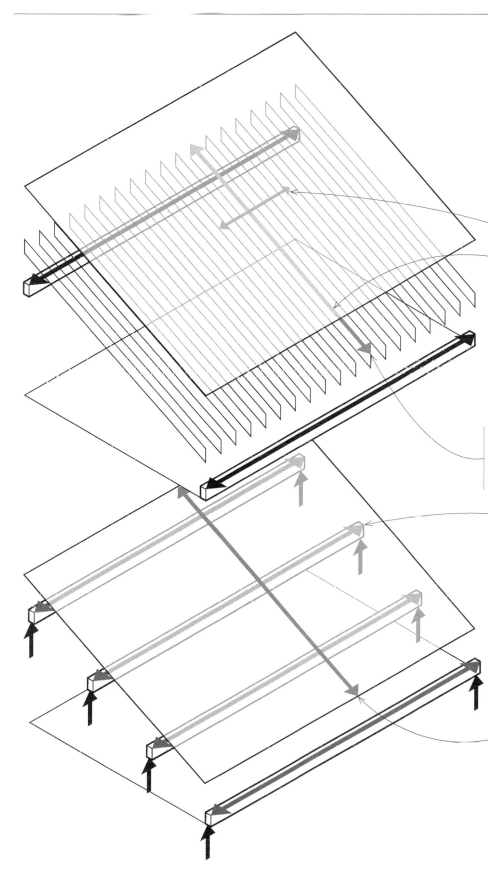

As with floor structures, the nature of the roofing material and the manner in which it is laid to shed rainwater determines the pattern of the secondary supports, which in turn dictates the direction and spacing of the primary spanning members of the roof structure. Understanding these relationships aids in developing the framing pattern for a roof structure.

- Roofing shingles, tiles, or panels may require either solid or spaced sheathing.
- Sheathing spans across the roof slope.

- Sheathing supports span down the roof slope.
- Depth and spanning capability of sheathing determines the spacing of its supports.

- The least complicated method for framing a sloped roof plane uses relatively small, closely spaced rafters that span down the slope and support solid or spaced sheathing.

Wood Rafter Span Ranges:
- 2x6    can span up to 10' (3.0 m);
- 2x8    can span up to 14' (4.3 m);
- 2x10   can span up to 16' (4.9 m);
- 2x12   can span up to 22' (6.7 m).

- Primary roof beams can span either across or down the roof slope.
- Roof beams spanning down the roof slope can support structural decking or panels.
- Depth and spanning capability of the structural decking or panels determines the spacing of the roof beams.
- Note that the spanning direction of the roof beams is perpendicular to that of the structural panels or decking.

- Depth and spanning capability of the purlins determines the spacing of the roof beams.

# ROOF STRUCTURES

There are alternative ways in which to frame steel and timber roof structures, depending on the direction and spacing of the roof beams, the elements used to span the beam spacing, and the overall depth of the construction assembly.

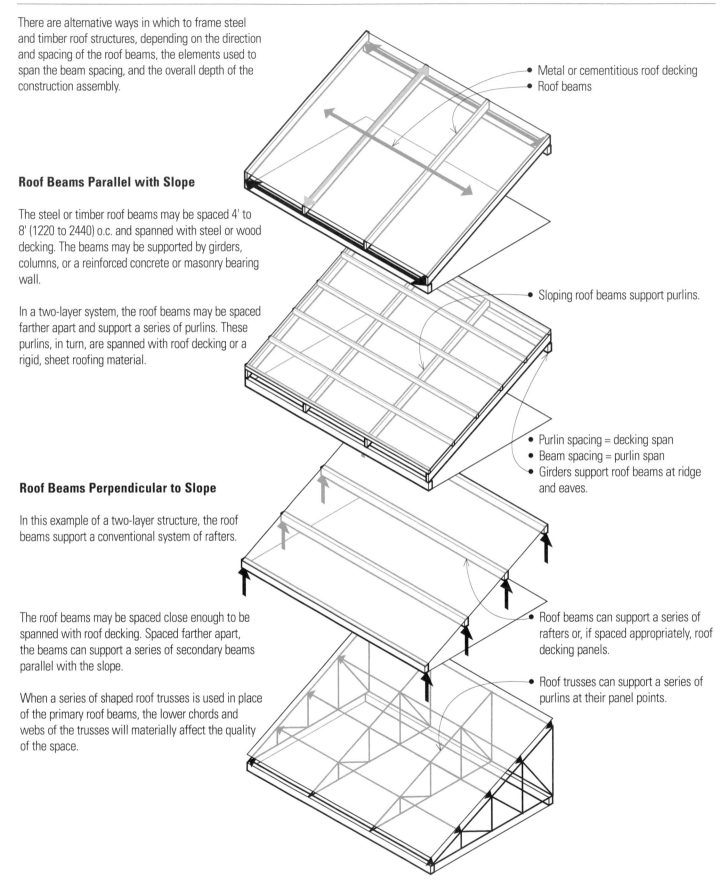

• Metal or cementitious roof decking
• Roof beams

## Roof Beams Parallel with Slope

The steel or timber roof beams may be spaced 4' to 8' (1220 to 2440) o.c. and spanned with steel or wood decking. The beams may be supported by girders, columns, or a reinforced concrete or masonry bearing wall.

In a two-layer system, the roof beams may be spaced farther apart and support a series of purlins. These purlins, in turn, are spanned with roof decking or a rigid, sheet roofing material.

• Sloping roof beams support purlins.

• Purlin spacing = decking span
• Beam spacing = purlin span
• Girders support roof beams at ridge and eaves.

## Roof Beams Perpendicular to Slope

In this example of a two-layer structure, the roof beams support a conventional system of rafters.

The roof beams may be spaced close enough to be spanned with roof decking. Spaced farther apart, the beams can support a series of secondary beams parallel with the slope.

When a series of shaped roof trusses is used in place of the primary roof beams, the lower chords and webs of the trusses will materially affect the quality of the space.

• Roof beams can support a series of rafters or, if spaced appropriately, roof decking panels.

• Roof trusses can support a series of purlins at their panel points.

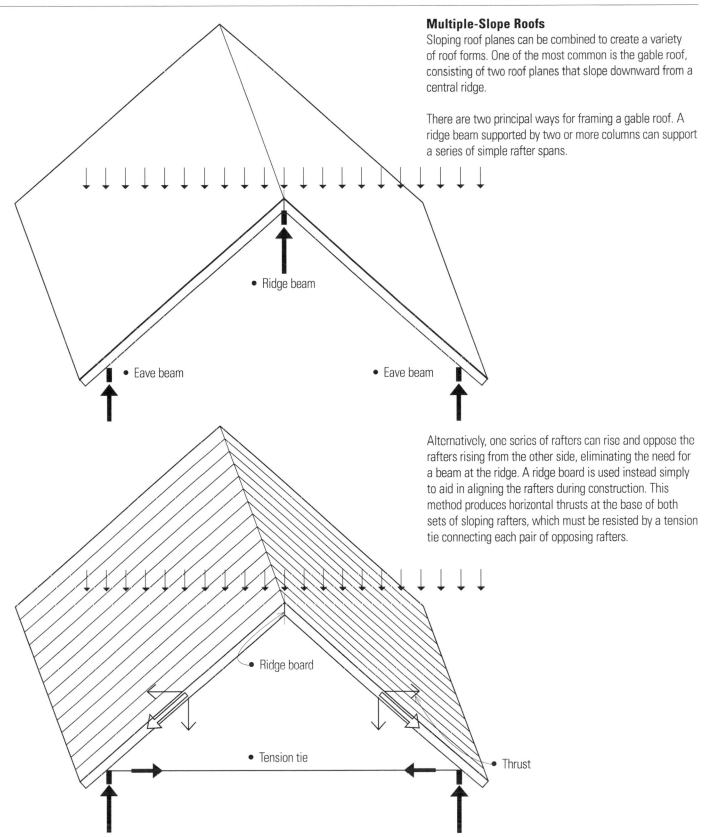

**Multiple-Slope Roofs**

Sloping roof planes can be combined to create a variety of roof forms. One of the most common is the gable roof, consisting of two roof planes that slope downward from a central ridge.

There are two principal ways for framing a gable roof. A ridge beam supported by two or more columns can support a series of simple rafter spans.

• Ridge beam

• Eave beam          • Eave beam

Alternatively, one series of rafters can rise and oppose the rafters rising from the other side, eliminating the need for a beam at the ridge. A ridge board is used instead simply to aid in aligning the rafters during construction. This method produces horizontal thrusts at the base of both sets of sloping rafters, which must be resisted by a tension tie connecting each pair of opposing rafters.

• Ridge board

• Tension tie          • Thrust

## ROOF STRUCTURES

It is useful to think of any roof composition as a number of sloping planes that meet or intersect at either ridges, hips, or valleys, keeping in mind the resulting drainage pattern for shedding rainwater and melting snow. Ridges, hips, and valleys all represent breaks in a roof plane that require a line of support, which may be in the form of a beam or truss supported by columns or bearing walls.

The spanning elements of hip roofs, domes, and similar roof forms can oppose and buttress each other at their peak. To counteract the horizontal thrust that results at their base supports, however, tension ties or rings, or a series of linked horizontal beams are required.

- Ridges are the lines of intersection formed where two sloping planes of a roof meet at the top.

- Hips are the inclined projecting angles formed by the junction of two adjacent sloping sides of a roof.
- Valleys are the internal angles formed at the intersection of two inclined roof surfaces and toward which rainwater flows.

- A break in the roof plane that ends within a space requires a ridge or valley beam supported by columns or a bearing wall.
- An alternative would be to have a shaped girder or truss span the space and support the ridge or valley beam as a concentrated load.

- A break in the roof plane that extends across a space can be supported by a clear-spanning beam or truss supported at the ends by perimeter columns or bearing walls. For example, a series of deep trusses can clear-span the width of a space to create a sawtooth roof.

## Vaulted Roofs

Curved roof surfaces may be structured by using spanning elements, such as built-up or custom-rolled steel beams, glue-laminated timber beams, or trusses that are shaped to match the desired profile of the form or space.

- Concrete slabs can also be formed to the desired curvature and extruded in the longitudinal direction. For example, a barrel shell can be extruded to behave as a deep beam with a curved section spanning in the longitudinal direction. If the barrel shell is relatively short, however, it exhibits archlike action and tie rods or transverse rigid frames are required to counteract the outward thrusts of the arching action.

- Shaped concrete members may be cast in place, but this would be economical only in situations where the spans are large and repetition minimal. For repetitive elements, precast concrete members are more economical. A shaped structural element is most efficient when its profile reflects the moment diagram for its span. For example, a section should be deeper where the bending moment is greater.

- When framing a curved roof with one-way spanning elements, the same considerations regarding roofing material and the direction of primary and secondary spans apply as they do for flat and sloping roofs.

# ROOF STRUCTURES

As the scale of a structure increases, interior lines of support may become necessary to keep the roof spans within reasonable limits. Whenever possible, these lines of support should reinforce the spatial quality of the volumes being developed by the roof form. Where interior supports would interfere with the functioning of a space and clear spans are desirable, as in sports arenas and concert halls, long-spanning roof structures become necessary. For more information on long-span structures, see Chapter 6.

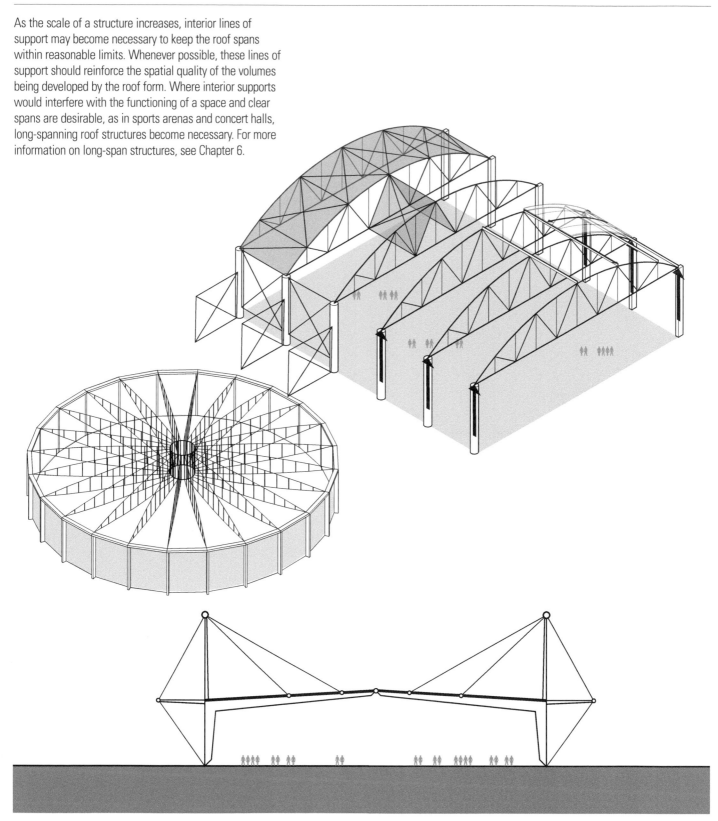

# 5
# Lateral Stability

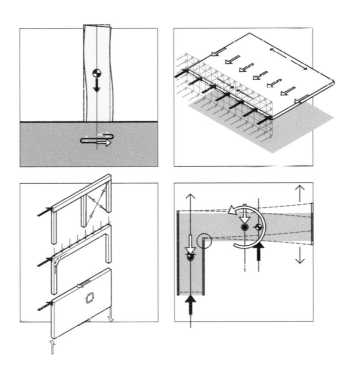

# LATERAL STABILITY

When we consider a building's structural system, we typically think first of how its vertical supports and horizontal spanning assemblies are designed to carry the dead and live loads imposed by the weight of its construction and occupancy. Just as critical to the building's stability, however, is its resistance to a combination of environmental conditions, such as wind, earthquake, earth pressure, and temperature, which can destabilize its gravity load-carrying elements. Of these, the forces exerted on a structure by wind and earthquakes are of primary concern in this chapter. Wind and earthquakes subject a structure to dynamic loading, often with rapid changes in magnitude and point of application. Under a dynamic load, a structure develops inertial forces in relation to its mass, and its maximum deformation does not necessarily correspond to the maximum magnitude of the applied force. Despite their dynamic nature, wind and earthquake loads are often treated as equivalent static loads acting in a lateral manner.

## Wind

Wind loads result from the forces exerted by the kinetic energy of a moving mass of air, which can produce a combination of direct pressure, negative pressure or suction, and drag forces on buildings and other obstacles in its path. Wind forces are typically assumed to be applied normal, or perpendicular, to the affected surfaces of a building.

## Earthquakes

Seismic forces result from the vibratory ground motions of an earthquake, which can cause a building's base to move suddenly and induce shaking of the structure in all directions simultaneously. While seismic ground motions are three-dimensional in nature and have horizontal, vertical, and rotational components, the horizontal component is considered to be the most important in structural design. During an earthquake, the mass of a building's structure develops an inertial force as it tries to resist the horizontal ground acceleration. The result is a shear force between the ground and the building's mass, which is distributed to each floor or diaphragm above the base.

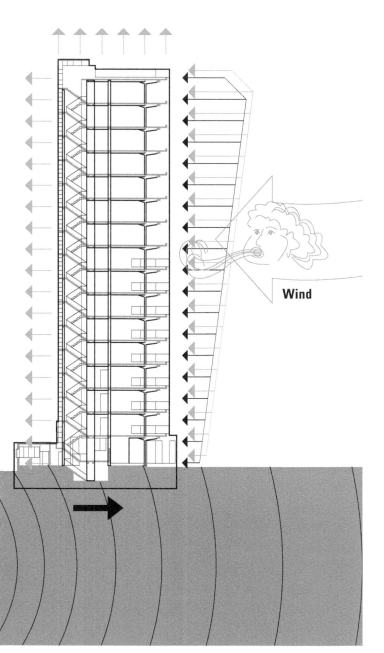

**Wind**

**Earthquake**

All buildings are subject to lateral loading from wind and earthquakes. The structural systems of tall or slender buildings, however, tend to be dominated by the need to resist lateral forces, which can impose large bending moments on and cause lateral displacement of their vertical members.

The structural design of buildings having a low aspect ratio, on the other hand, is predominantly governed by vertical gravity loads. Lateral loads due to wind and earthquakes have a relatively small effect on the sizing of members, but they cannot be ignored.

Also, while both wind and earthquakes exert lateral loads on all buildings, they differ in how the lateral forces are applied. Perhaps the most significant of these differences is the inertial nature of seismic forces, which causes the applied forces to increase with the weight of a building. Weight is therefore a major liability in seismic design. In responding to wind forces, however, a building can use its weight to advantage to resist sliding and overturning.

Likewise, a relatively stiff building subjected to wind forces responds favorably because its amplitude of vibration is small. However, a seismically loaded building tends to exhibit a better response if its structure is flexible, enabling it to dissipate some of the kinetic energy and moderate the resulting stresses through movement.

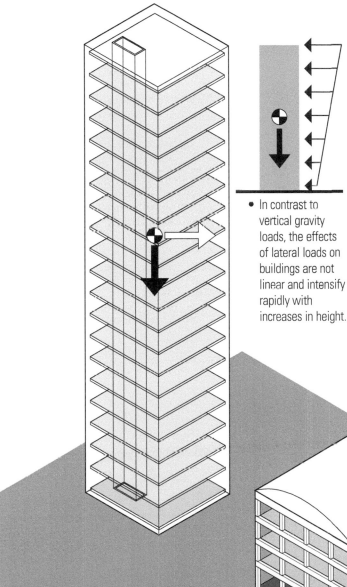

- In contrast to vertical gravity loads, the effects of lateral loads on buildings are not linear and intensify rapidly with increases in height.

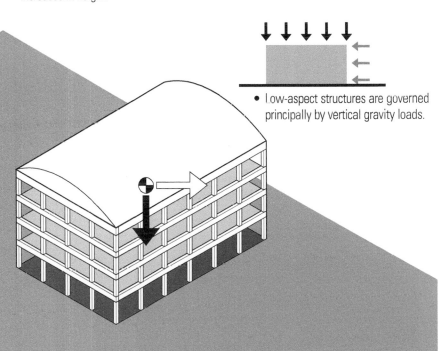

- Low-aspect structures are governed principally by vertical gravity loads.

# WIND

Wind is a moving mass of air. Buildings and other structures represent obstacles that deflect or impede the wind, converting the kinetic energy of the moving air mass into the potential energy of pressure.

Wind pressure increases as a function of wind velocity. The average mean wind velocity for any particular area, measured over a long period of time, generally increases with height. The rate of increase of the mean velocity is also a function of the ground roughness and the interference offered by surrounding objects that include other buildings, vegetation, and land forms.

The primary effect of wind on buildings are the lateral forces it places on the entire structure and, in particular, on the exterior cladding. The net effect is a combination of direct pressure, negative pressure or suction, and drag forces. Wind pressure can also cause a building structure to slide as well as overturn.

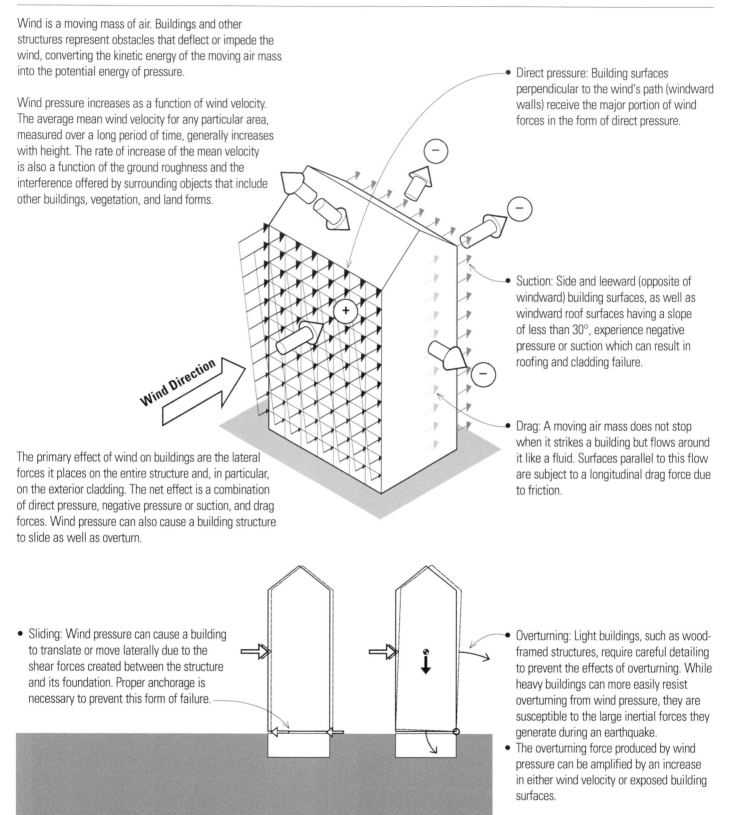

- Direct pressure: Building surfaces perpendicular to the wind's path (windward walls) receive the major portion of wind forces in the form of direct pressure.

- Suction: Side and leeward (opposite of windward) building surfaces, as well as windward roof surfaces having a slope of less than 30°, experience negative pressure or suction which can result in roofing and cladding failure.

- Drag: A moving air mass does not stop when it strikes a building but flows around it like a fluid. Surfaces parallel to this flow are subject to a longitudinal drag force due to friction.

- Sliding: Wind pressure can cause a building to translate or move laterally due to the shear forces created between the structure and its foundation. Proper anchorage is necessary to prevent this form of failure.

- Overturning: Light buildings, such as wood-framed structures, require careful detailing to prevent the effects of overturning. While heavy buildings can more easily resist overturning from wind pressure, they are susceptible to the large inertial forces they generate during an earthquake.
- The overturning force produced by wind pressure can be amplified by an increase in either wind velocity or exposed building surfaces.

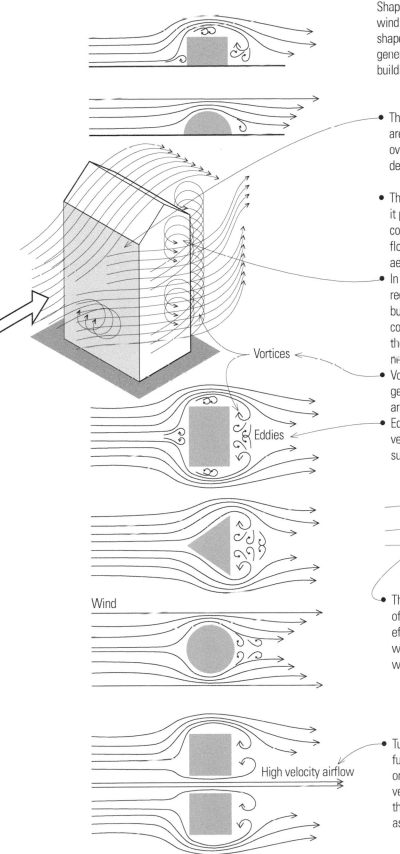

Shape and form can increase or decrease the effects of wind pressure on a building. For example, aerodynamically shaped buildings, such as rounded or curved forms, generally result in lower wind resistance than rectangular buildings with flat surfaces.

- The larger the exposed surfaces of rectangular forms are, the greater the effect of the wind pressure on the overall building shear and the overturning moment developed at the building's base.

- The flow of a moving air mass increases in velocity as it passes by buildings and other obstructions. Sharp corners and edges that compress the air particles in the flow increase this effect more than rounded or more aerodynamic edges.

- In any turbulent airflow, positive wind pressures are recorded as long as the air is in contact with the building's surface. When the building face is too sharply convex or the airflow is too rapid, the air mass will leave the surface of the building and create dead air zones of negative pressure.

- Vortices and eddies are the circular air currents generated by turbulent winds in these low-pressure areas.

- Eddies are slow moving while vortices are higher velocity air currents that create circular updrafts and suction streams adjacent to the building.

Vortices

Eddies

Wind

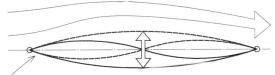

- The presence of turbulence can exacerbate the effects of wind on a building. One example is the harmonic effects that can cause unacceptable movement or flutter when the fundamental period of vibration caused by the wind coincides with the natural period of the structure.

High velocity airflow

- Turbulence often develops as the moving air mass is funneled through a narrow space between two buildings or through arcades in buildings. The corresponding wind velocity in this space often exceeds the wind velocity of the major airflow. This type of turbulence is referred to as the Venturi effect.

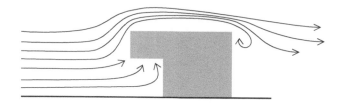

- Buildings with open sides or configurations with recesses or hollows that capture the wind are subject to larger design wind pressures.

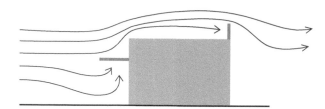

- Building projections, such as parapets, balconies, canopies, and overhangs, are subject to increased localized pressures from moving air masses.

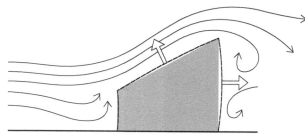

- Wind pressure can subject very tall walls and long spanning rafters to large bending moments and deflection.

Wind can produce dynamic loading on tall, slender structures that exceeds typical design levels. The efficient design of structural systems and cladding for tall buildings requires knowledge of how wind forces impact their slender forms. Structural designers use wind tunnel tests and computer modeling to determine the overall base shear, overturning moment, as well as the floor-by-floor distribution of wind pressure on a structure, and to gather information about how the building's motion might affect occupants' comfort.

- Tall, slender buildings with a high aspect (height-to-base width) ratio experience larger horizontal deflections at their tops and are more susceptible to overturning moments.

- Short-term gust velocities can also produce dynamic wind pressures that create additional displacement. For tall, slender buildings, this gust action may dominate and produce a dynamic movement called gust buffeting, which results in oscillation of the slender structure.

- Building forms that taper expose less surface area to the wind as they rise, which helps counteract the increasing wind velocities and pressures experienced higher up.

- For more information on tall building structures, see Chapter 7.

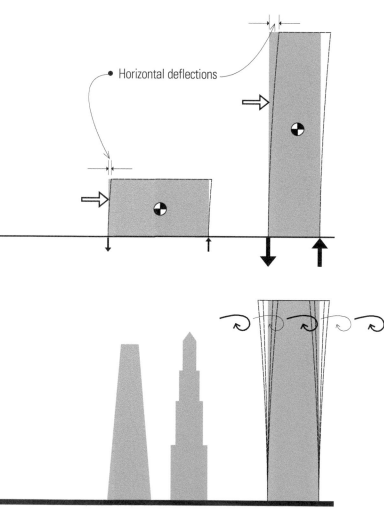

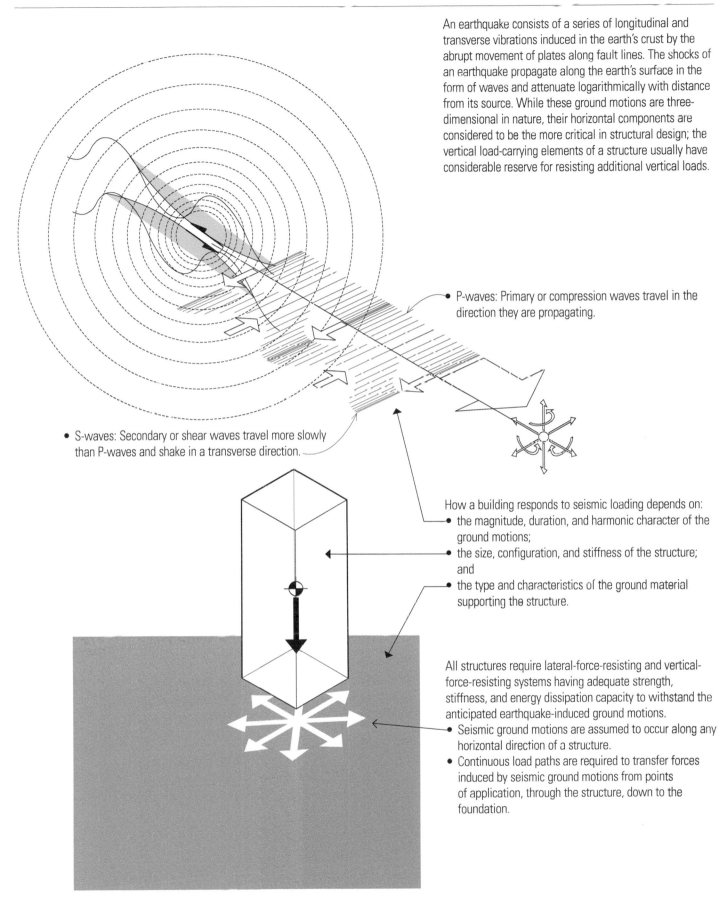

An earthquake consists of a series of longitudinal and transverse vibrations induced in the earth's crust by the abrupt movement of plates along fault lines. The shocks of an earthquake propagate along the earth's surface in the form of waves and attenuate logarithmically with distance from its source. While these ground motions are three-dimensional in nature, their horizontal components are considered to be the more critical in structural design; the vertical load-carrying elements of a structure usually have considerable reserve for resisting additional vertical loads.

- P-waves: Primary or compression waves travel in the direction they are propagating.

- S-waves: Secondary or shear waves travel more slowly than P-waves and shake in a transverse direction.

How a building responds to seismic loading depends on:
- the magnitude, duration, and harmonic character of the ground motions;
- the size, configuration, and stiffness of the structure; and
- the type and characteristics of the ground material supporting the structure.

All structures require lateral-force-resisting and vertical-force-resisting systems having adequate strength, stiffness, and energy dissipation capacity to withstand the anticipated earthquake-induced ground motions.
- Seismic ground motions are assumed to occur along any horizontal direction of a structure.
- Continuous load paths are required to transfer forces induced by seismic ground motions from points of application, through the structure, down to the foundation.

The overall tendency of a building subjected to an earthquake is to vibrate as the ground shakes. Seismically induced shaking affects a building in three primary ways: inertial force, overturning, and fundamental period of vibration.

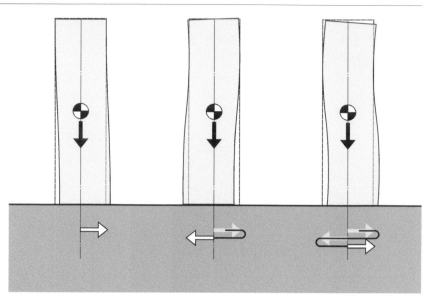

## Inertial Force

- The first response of a building during an earthquake is to not move at all due to the inertia of its mass. Almost instantaneously, however, the ground acceleration causes the building to move at the base, inducing a lateral load on the building and a shear force at the base (seismic base shear). The inertial force in the building opposes the base shear but both forces reverse directions as the building vibrates back and forth.

- From Newton's second law, the inertial force is equal to the product of mass and acceleration.

- Inertial forces can be lessened by reducing the building's mass. Therefore, lightweight construction is advantageous in seismic design. Light buildings, such as wood-frame houses, generally perform well in earthquakes, while heavy masonry structures are susceptible to significant damage.

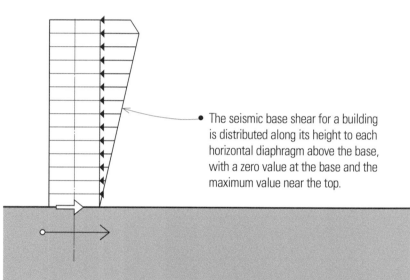

- Seismic base shear is the minimum design value for the total lateral seismic force on a structure assumed to act in any horizontal direction.

- For regular structures, low irregular structures, and structures at low seismic risk, seismic base shear is computed by multiplying the total dead load of the structure by a number of coefficients to reflect the character and intensity of the ground motions in the seismic zone, the soil profile type underlying the foundation, the type of occupancy, the distribution of the mass and stiffness of the structure, and the fundamental period—the time required for one complete oscillation—of the structure.

- A more complex dynamic analysis is required for high-rise structures, structures with irregular shapes or framing systems, or for structures built on soft or plastic soils susceptible to failure or collapse under seismic loading.

- The seismic base shear for a building is distributed along its height to each horizontal diaphragm above the base, with a zero value at the base and the maximum value near the top.

## Overturning Moment

- Any lateral load applied at a distance above grade generates an overturning moment at the base of a structure. For equilibrium, the overturning moment must be counterbalanced by an external restoring moment and an internal resisting moment provided by forces developed in column members and shear walls.

- Engineers and designers who have studied the performance of buildings in earthquakes conclude that a building's configuration and proportions have a major influence on how seismic forces work their way through the structure to its foundation. The ideal building configuration for resisting earthquake forces is a symmetrical form in both plan and elevation. See pages 220–223.

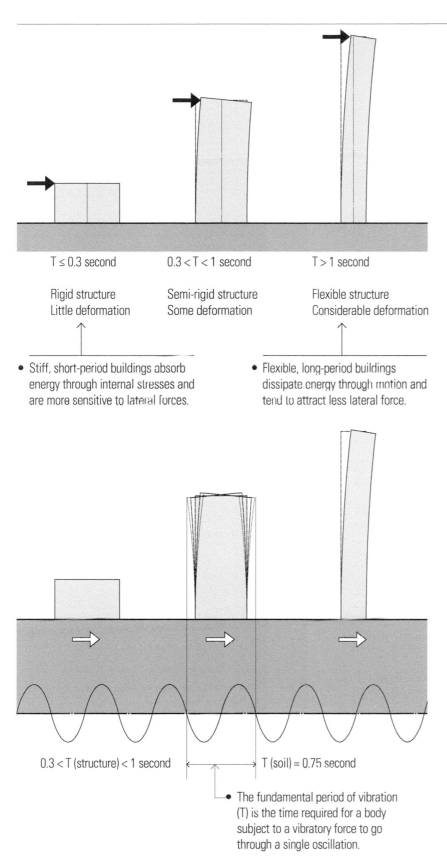

T ≤ 0.3 second  |  0.3 < T < 1 second  |  T > 1 second

Rigid structure | Semi-rigid structure | Flexible structure
Little deformation | Some deformation | Considerable deformation

- Stiff, short-period buildings absorb energy through internal stresses and are more sensitive to lateral forces.

- Flexible, long-period buildings dissipate energy through motion and tend to attract less lateral force.

0.3 < T (structure) < 1 second  ⟷  T (soil) = 0.75 second

- The fundamental period of vibration (T) is the time required for a body subject to a vibratory force to go through a single oscillation.

## Fundamental Period of Vibration

The natural or fundamental period of a structure (T) varies according to its height above the base and its dimension parallel to the direction of applied forces. Relatively stiff structures oscillate rapidly and have short periods while more flexible structures oscillate more slowly and have longer periods.

As seismic vibrations propagate through the ground material underlying a building structure, they may be either amplified or attenuated, depending on the fundamental period of the material. The fundamental period of ground material varies from approximately 0.40 seconds for hard soil or rock up to 1.5 seconds for soft soil. Very soft soil may have periods of up to 2 seconds. Earthquake shaking tends to be greater in a building situated on soft ground than in one built over hard ground. If the soil's period falls within the range of the building's period, it is possible for this correspondence to create a condition of resonance.

Any amplification in building vibration is undesirable. A structural design should ensure that the building period does not coincide with the period of the supporting soil. Short, stiff (short-period) buildings sited on soft (long-period) ground would be appropriate as well as tall buildings (long-period) built on hard, stiff (short-period) soil.

Damping, ductility, and strength-stiffness are three characteristics that can help a structure resist and dissipate the effects of seismically-induced motion.

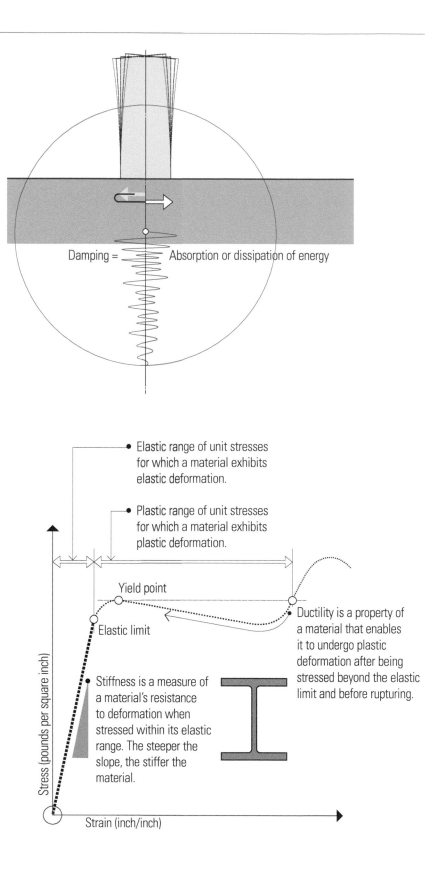

## Damping

Damping refers to any of several means of absorbing or dissipating energy to progressively diminish successive oscillations or waves of a vibrating structure. For specific types of damping mechanisms, see pages 302–304. In addition to these damping methods, a building's non-structural elements, connections, construction materials, and design assumptions can provide damping characteristics that greatly reduce the magnitude of the building's vibration or swaying during an earthquake.

Damping = Absorption or dissipation of energy

## Ductility

Ductility is the ability of a structural member to deform several times the design deformation at its flexural yield capacity, which allows excessive loads to be distributed to other structural members or to other parts of the same member. Ductility is an important source of reserve strength in buildings that allow materials like steel to distort considerably without breaking, and in doing so, to dissipate the energy of the earthquake.

## Strength & Stiffness

Strength is the ability of a structural member to resist a given load without exceeding the safe stress of the material. Stiffness, on the other hand, is a measure of the structural member's ability to control deformation and limit the amount of its movement under loading. Limiting movement in this way helps to minimize the detrimental effects on the non-structural components of a building, such as cladding, partitions, hung ceilings and furnishings, as well as on the comfort of the building's occupants.

Elastic range of unit stresses for which a material exhibits elastic deformation.

Plastic range of unit stresses for which a material exhibits plastic deformation.

Yield point

Elastic limit

Ductility is a property of a material that enables it to undergo plastic deformation after being stressed beyond the elastic limit and before rupturing.

Stiffness is a measure of a material's resistance to deformation when stressed within its elastic range. The steeper the slope, the stiffer the material.

Stress (pounds per square inch)

Strain (inch/inch)

In general, there are three basic mechanisms commonly used, alone or in combination, for assuring the lateral stability of a building. They are braced frames, moment frames, and shear walls. Note that all of these lateral-force-resisting mechanisms are only effective against in-plane lateral forces. They cannot be expected to resist lateral forces perpendicular to their planes.

The primary horizontal mechanism used to distribute lateral forces to vertical resisting elements is the diaphragm.

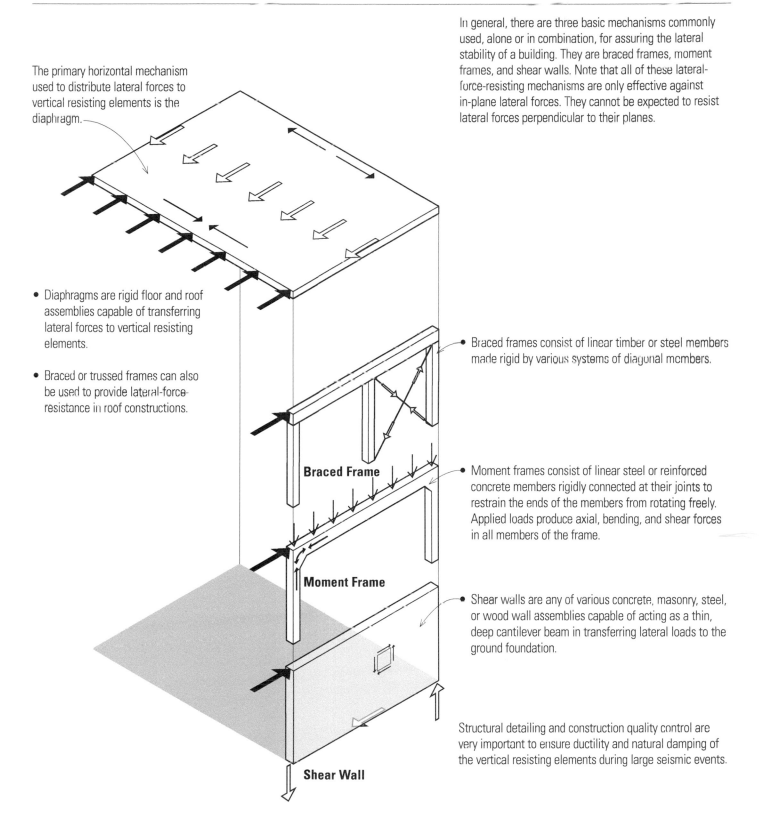

**Braced Frame**

**Moment Frame**

**Shear Wall**

- Diaphragms are rigid floor and roof assemblies capable of transferring lateral forces to vertical resisting elements.

- Braced or trussed frames can also be used to provide lateral-force-resistance in roof constructions.

- Braced frames consist of linear timber or steel members made rigid by various systems of diagonal members.

- Moment frames consist of linear steel or reinforced concrete members rigidly connected at their joints to restrain the ends of the members from rotating freely. Applied loads produce axial, bending, and shear forces in all members of the frame.

- Shear walls are any of various concrete, masonry, steel, or wood wall assemblies capable of acting as a thin, deep cantilever beam in transferring lateral loads to the ground foundation.

Structural detailing and construction quality control are very important to ensure ductility and natural damping of the vertical resisting elements during large seismic events.

### Braced Frames

Braced frames consist of column-and-beam frames made rigid with a system of diagonal members that create stable triangular configurations. Examples of the great variety of bracing systems in use are:

• Knee bracing
• Diagonal bracing
• Cross bracing
• V-bracing
• K-bracing
• Eccentric bracing
• Lattice bracing

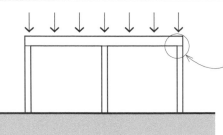

• A typical column-and-beam frame is assumed to be joined with pin or hinged connections, which can potentially resist applied vertical loads.

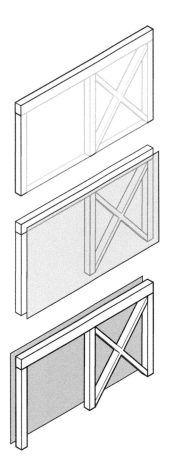

• The four-hinged quadrilateral is inherently unstable, however, and would be unable to resist a laterally applied load.

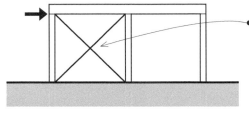

• The addition of a diagonal bracing system would provide the requisite lateral stability for the frame.

• Knee braces provide lateral resistance by developing relatively rigid joints at the beam-column connections through triangulation. Knee braces, which are relatively small in size, must be used in pairs to be able to resist lateral forces from either direction.

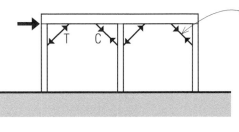

• Single diagonal braces must be able to handle both tension and compression. The size of a single diagonal brace is determined more by its resistance to buckling under compression, which, in turn, is related to its unsupported length.

Braced frames may be located internally within a building to brace a core or a major supporting plane, or be placed in the plane of the exterior walls. They may be concealed in walls or partitions or be exposed to view, in which case it establishes a strong structural expression.

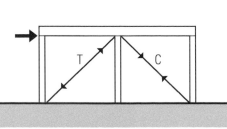

• The relative magnitude of the horizontal and vertical components in a diagonal brace result from the slope of the brace. The more vertical the diagonal brace, the stronger it will need to be to resist the same lateral load.

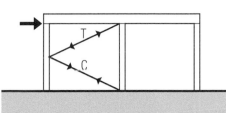

- K-bracing consists of a pair of diagonal braces that meet near the midpoint of a vertical frame member. Each diagonal brace can be subject to either tension or compression, depending on the direction of the lateral force acting on the frame.

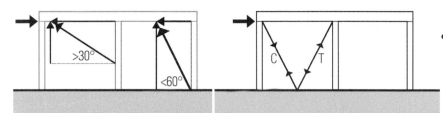

- The relative magnitude of the horizontal and vertical components in a diagonal brace result from the slope of the brace. The more vertical the diagonal brace, the stronger it will need to be to resist the same lateral load.

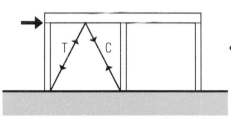

- V-bracing consists of a pair of diagonal braces that meet near the midpoint of a horizontal frame member. As with K-bracing, each of the diagonals can be subject to either tension or compression, depending on the direction of the lateral force.

- Chevron bracing is similar to V-bracing but its orientation allows for passage through the space below the inverted V.

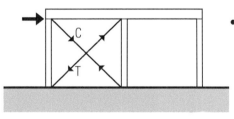

- X-bracing consists of a pair of diagonals. As in the previous examples, each of the diagonals can be subject to either tension or compression, depending on the direction of the lateral force. A certain degree of redundancy is achieved if each diagonal alone is capable of stabilizing the frame.

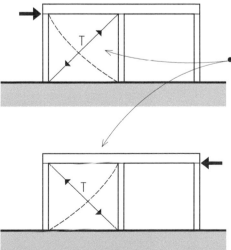

- Diagonal tension-counter systems consist of cables or rods that work primarily in tension. A pair of cables or rods is always necessary to stabilize the frame against lateral forces from either direction. For each force direction, one cable or rod will operate effectively in tension while the other becomes slack and is assumed to carry no load.

### Eccentric Bracing

Eccentrically braced frames combine the strength and stiffness of braced frames with the inelastic (plastic) behavior and energy dissipation characteristic of moment frames. They incorporate diagonal braces that connect at separate points to beam or girder members, forming short link-beams between the braces and column members or between two opposing braces. The link-beams act as fuses to limit large forces from being exerted on and overstressing other elements in the frame.

The expected magnitude of seismic loads and the conservative nature of building codes make it necessary to assume some yielding of a structure during large earthquakes. However, in zones of high seismic risk, such as California, designing a building to remain entirely elastic during a large earthquake would be cost-prohibitive. Because steel frames have the ductility to dissipate large amounts of seismic energy and maintain stability even under large inelastic deformations, eccentrically braced steel frames are commonly used in seismic regions. They also provide the necessary stiffness to reduce drift produced by wind loads.

Link-beam

Eccentric braces

Plastic hinges

Column

- The short link-beams absorb energy from seismic activity through plastic deformation prior to deformations of other members.
- Eccentrically braced frames may also be designed to control frame deformations and minimize damage to architectural elements during cyclical seismic loading.

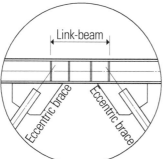

Link-beam

Eccentric brace

Link-beam

Eccentric brace

- Steel is the ideal material for eccentrically braced frames because of its ductility—the capacity to deform without fractures—combined with its high strength.

- Eccentrically braced frames are generally placed in the exterior wall planes of a structure but are also sometimes used to brace steel-framed cores.

Link-beam

Column

Stiffeners

Eccentric brace

Eccentric Brace-to-Beam Connection

- Eccentrically braced frames are useful when doorways and corridors are located in braced bays.

## Multi-Bay Arrangements

The amount of lateral bracing provided in multi-bay arrangements is a function of the lateral forces present; not all bays of a multi-bay arrangement need necessarily be braced.

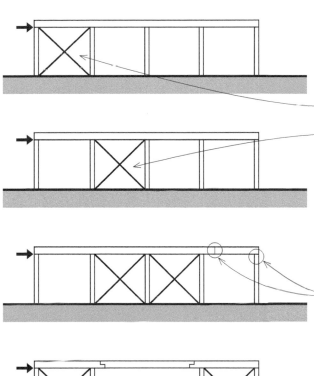

- A general rule-of-thumb is to brace every third or fourth bay as a minimum.
- An interior bay can be laterally braced to provide stability for the other bays.

- As more bays are braced, the member sizes of the bracing decrease and the lateral stiffness of the frame improves, resulting in less lateral displacement.

- Two internal bays can be braced to provide the exterior bays with lateral stability.
- The beam member of the multi-bay frame need not be continuous. For example, these pin connections would not adversely affect the lateral stability of the frame.

- Two exterior bays can be braced to provide an interior, column-free bay with lateral stability. The two overhanging beams support a simple beam.

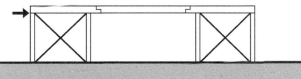

- When the bay proportions would cause a single diagonal brace to be too steep or too flat, consider other forms of bracing to ensure effective bracing action.

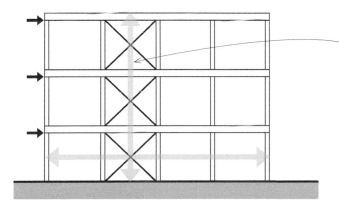

- While not every bay in a single story need be braced, it is critical that all levels in multistory buildings be braced. In this case, the diagonally braced bays act as a vertical truss.

- Note that in each of these illustrations, moment frames or shear walls may also be used in place of the braced frames shown.

### Moment Frames

Moment frames, also known as moment-resisting frames, consist of floor or roof spanning members in plane with, and connected to, column members with rigid or semi-rigid joints. The strength and stiffness of a frame is proportional to the beam and column sizes, and inversely proportional to the column's unsupported height and spacing. Moment frames require considerably larger beams and columns, especially at the lower levels of tall structures.

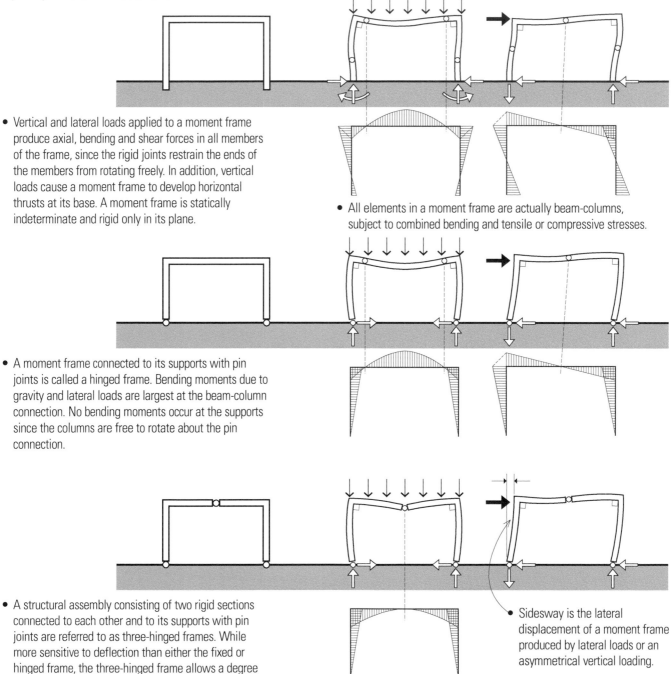

- Vertical and lateral loads applied to a moment frame produce axial, bending and shear forces in all members of the frame, since the rigid joints restrain the ends of the members from rotating freely. In addition, vertical loads cause a moment frame to develop horizontal thrusts at its base. A moment frame is statically indeterminate and rigid only in its plane.

- All elements in a moment frame are actually beam-columns, subject to combined bending and tensile or compressive stresses.

- A moment frame connected to its supports with pin joints is called a hinged frame. Bending moments due to gravity and lateral loads are largest at the beam-column connection. No bending moments occur at the supports since the columns are free to rotate about the pin connection.

- A structural assembly consisting of two rigid sections connected to each other and to its supports with pin joints are referred to as three-hinged frames. While more sensitive to deflection than either the fixed or hinged frame, the three-hinged frame allows a degree of prefabrication with a relatively simple field-pin connection.

- Sidesway is the lateral displacement of a moment frame produced by lateral loads or an asymmetrical vertical loading.

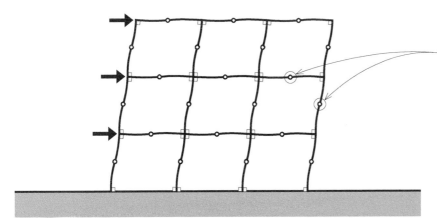

- Multistory moment frames develop inflection points (internal hinge points) when loaded laterally. These theoretical hinges, where no moment occurs, help in determining locations for joints for steel construction and reinforcing strategy in cast concrete.

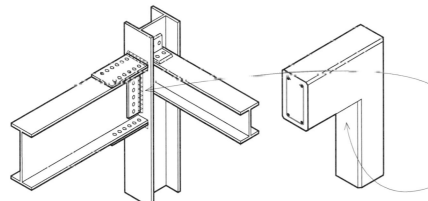

- Moment frames requiring moment-resisting capability are generally constructed of structural steel or reinforced concrete. The detailing of the beam-column connection is very important to assure rigidity of the joint.
- Structural steel beams and columns may be connected to develop moment-resisting action by means of welding, high-strength bolting, or a combination of the two. Steel moment-resisting frames provide a ductile system for resisting seismic forces after the elastic capacity of the system is exceeded.
- Reinforced-concrete moment frames may consist of beams and columns, flat slabs and columns, or slabs with bearing walls. The inherent continuity that occurs in the monolithic casting of concrete provides a naturally occurring moment-resistant connection and thus enables members to have cantilevers with very simple detailing of the reinforcing steel.

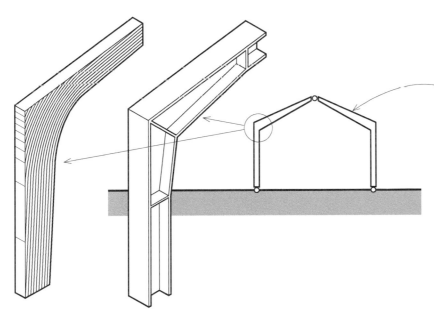

- Three-hinged frames can be constructed with sloped sections for roofs. Its basic structural response is similar to its flat-roof cousin. The shaping of the members is often an indication of the relative magnitude of the bending moment, especially at the beam-column junction. Member cross-sections are reduced at the pin joints since the bending moments there are essentially zero.
- In addition to structural steel, laminated timber can be used in fabricating the sections for three-hinged frames. Additional material is provided at the beam-column intersection for resisting the larger bending moments.

## Shear Walls

Shear walls are rigid vertical planes that are relatively thin and long. A shear wall may be considered analogous to a cantilever beam standing on end in a vertical plane and resisting the concentrated shear load delivered from the floor or roof diaphragm above.

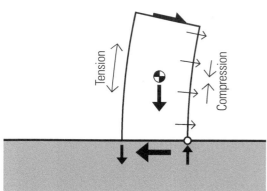

The shear wall is placed in equilibrium by the dead-load weight of the wall and the resisting couple created by the tension and compression at the wall edges or corners.

Shear walls may be constructed of:

- Cast-in-place, reinforced concrete
- Precast concrete
- Reinforced masonry
- Light-frame stud construction sheathed with structural wood panels, such as plywood, oriented-strand board (OSB), or diagonal board sheathing.

There are generally very few openings or penetrations in shear walls. If a shear wall does have regular penetrations, its structural action is intermediate between that of a shear wall and a moment-resisting frame.

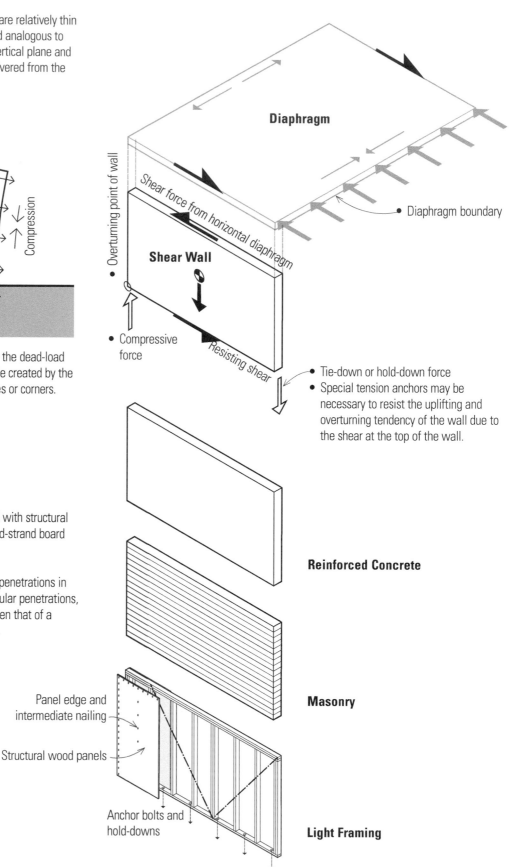

Diaphragm

Diaphragm boundary

Overturning point of wall

Shear force from horizontal diaphragm

Shear Wall

Compressive force

Resisting shear

- Tie-down or hold-down force
- Special tension anchors may be necessary to resist the uplifting and overturning tendency of the wall due to the shear at the top of the wall.

**Reinforced Concrete**

**Masonry**

Panel edge and intermediate nailing

Structural wood panels

Anchor bolts and hold-downs

**Light Framing**

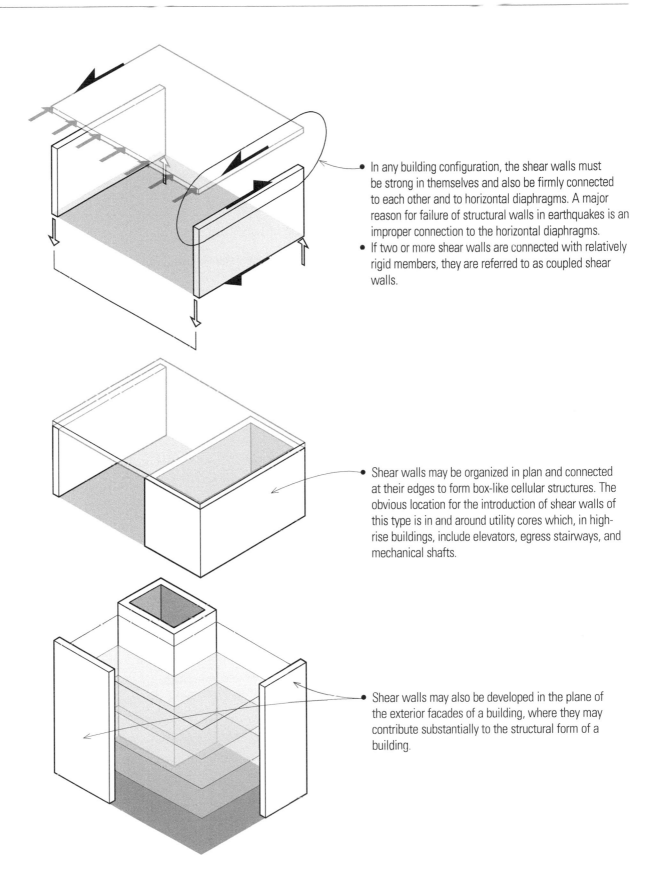

- In any building configuration, the shear walls must be strong in themselves and also be firmly connected to each other and to horizontal diaphragms. A major reason for failure of structural walls in earthquakes is an improper connection to the horizontal diaphragms.
- If two or more shear walls are connected with relatively rigid members, they are referred to as coupled shear walls.

- Shear walls may be organized in plan and connected at their edges to form box-like cellular structures. The obvious location for the introduction of shear walls of this type is in and around utility cores which, in high-rise buildings, include elevators, egress stairways, and mechanical shafts.

- Shear walls may also be developed in the plane of the exterior facades of a building, where they may contribute substantially to the structural form of a building.

### Diaphragms

To resist lateral forces, buildings must be composed of both vertical and horizontal resisting elements. Vertical elements used to transfer lateral forces to the ground are braced frames, moment frames, and shear walls. The principal horizontal elements used to distribute lateral forces to these vertical resisting elements are diaphragms and horizontal bracing.

Diaphragms are typically floor and roof constructions that have the capacity to transfer lateral wind and seismic forces to vertical resisting elements. Using the steel beam as an analogy, diaphragms act as flat beams where the diaphragm itself acts as the web of the beam and its edges act as flanges. Although diaphragms are usually horizontal, they can be curved or sloped, as is frequently the case in constructing roofs.

Structural diaphragms generally have tremendous strength and stiffness in their plane. Even when floors or roofs are somewhat flexible to walk on, they are extremely stiff in their own plane. This inherent stiffness and strength allows them to tie columns and walls at each level together and to provide lateral resistance to those elements that require bracing.

Diaphragms may be classified as either rigid or flexible. This distinction is important because it significantly affects how lateral loads are distributed from the diaphragm to the vertical resisting elements. The load distribution from rigid diaphragms to the vertical resisting elements is related to the stiffness of those vertical elements. Torsional effects can occur for rigid diaphragms that are connected to non-symmetrically arranged vertical resisting elements. Concrete slabs, metal decking with concrete fill, and some heavy-gauge steel decking are considered to be rigid diaphragms.

If a diaphragm is flexible, the in-plane deflections may be large and the load distribution to the vertical resisting elements is determined by the contributing load area of the diaphragm. Wood sheathing and light-gauge steel decking without a concrete fill are examples of flexible diaphragms.

Penetrations may critically weaken roof and floor diaphragms based on their size and location. The tension and compression that results along the leading and trailing edges of the diaphragm would increase as the diaphragm depth decreased. Careful detailing is required where stress concentrations occur at the reentrant corners.

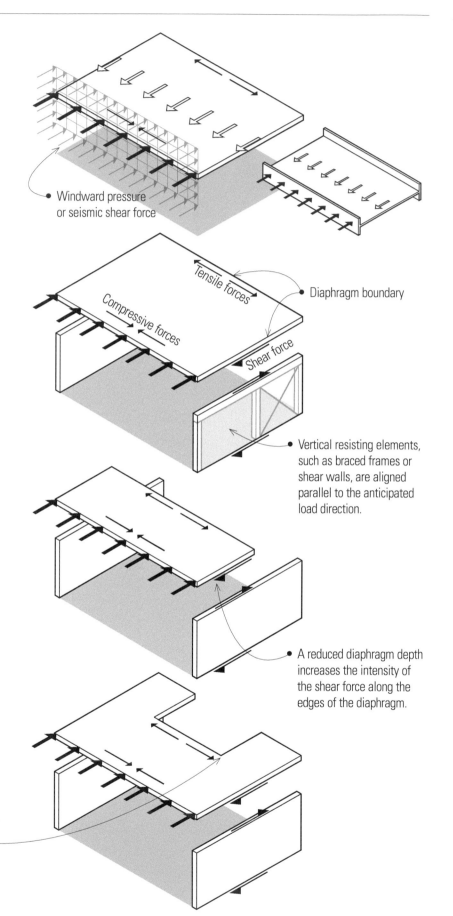

• Windward pressure or seismic shear force

Tensile forces

Compressive forces

• Diaphragm boundary

Shear force

• Vertical resisting elements, such as braced frames or shear walls, are aligned parallel to the anticipated load direction.

• A reduced diaphragm depth increases the intensity of the shear force along the edges of the diaphragm.

Floor and roof diaphragms may be constructed of wood, metal, or concrete assemblies.

### Light Framing with Sheathing

- In light frame construction, diaphragms consist of structural wood panels, such as plywood, laid as sheathing over wood or light-gauge steel framing. The sheathing acts as the shear web while the boundary elements of the floor or roof framing resists tension and compression like flanges on a steel beam.

- The shear strength of the diaphragm depends on the layout and edge nailing of the panels as well as the chord strength of the framing.

### Metal Decking

- Metal decking with a concrete fill can serve effectively as diaphragms. The concrete provides the stiffness while the metal decking and any steel reinforcement in the concrete contribute the tensile strength. A key requirement is the proper interconnection of all elements.

- Metal roof decking without a concrete fill can serve as a diaphragm but it is considerably more flexible and weaker than decking with a concrete fill.

### Concrete Slabs

- Cast-in-place reinforced concrete slabs act as the shear web of diaphragms, with chords and collectors being accommodated by adding reinforcing steel in the beams or the slab as appropriate. The continuous reinforcement inherent in monolithic concrete roof and floor systems provides an effective structural tie across the building.

- When concrete slabs serve as diaphragms in steel-framed buildings, proper bonding or attachment of the slabs to the steel framing must be provided to stabilize the compression flange of the steel beam as well as to facilitate the transfer of diaphragm forces to the steel frame. This generally requires encasing the steel beams with concrete or providing welded stud connectors on the top flanges of the steel beams.

- Precast concrete floor and roof systems offer more of a challenge in providing a sound structural diaphragm. When diaphragm stresses are large, a cast-in-place topping slab may be placed over the precast elements. Without a topping slab, the precast concrete elements must be interconnected with adequate fasteners to transmit the shear, tensile, and compressive forces along the boundaries of the precast elements. These fasteners generally consist of welded steel plates or bars between inserts in adjacent panels.

# LATERAL-FORCE-RESISTING SYSTEMS

Buildings are three-dimensional structures, not simply a collection of two-dimensional planes. Their geometric stability relies on a three-dimensional composition of horizontal diaphragms and vertical resisting elements arranged and interconnected to work together in resisting lateral forces assumed to come from any horizontal direction. For example, as a building shakes during an earthquake, the inertial forces generated must be transmitted through the structure to the foundation via a three-dimensional lateral-force-resisting system.

Understanding how lateral-force-resisting systems operate is important in architectural design because they can significantly impact the shape and form of a building. Decisions about the type and location of the lateral-force-resisting elements to be used directly affect the organizational plan of the building and ultimately its final appearance.

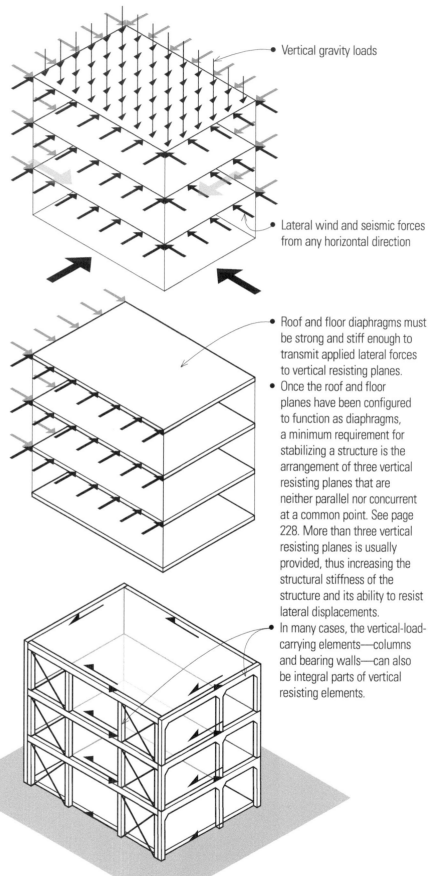

- Vertical gravity loads

- Lateral wind and seismic forces from any horizontal direction

- Roof and floor diaphragms must be strong and stiff enough to transmit applied lateral forces to vertical resisting planes.

- Once the roof and floor planes have been configured to function as diaphragms, a minimum requirement for stabilizing a structure is the arrangement of three vertical resisting planes that are neither parallel nor concurrent at a common point. See page 228. More than three vertical resisting planes is usually provided, thus increasing the structural stiffness of the structure and its ability to resist lateral displacements.

- In many cases, the vertical-load-carrying elements—columns and bearing walls—can also be integral parts of vertical resisting elements.

- The lateral resisting planes may be a combination of braced frames, moment frames, or shear walls. For example, shear walls may resist lateral forces in one direction while braced frames serve a similar function in another direction. See a comparison of these vertical resisting elements on the facing page.

Lateral-force-resistance in the vertical planes of a building may be provided by braced frames, moment frames, or shear walls, used singly or in combination. These vertical resisting mechanisms, however, are not equivalent in terms of stiffness and efficiency. In some cases, only a limited portion of a structural frame need be stabilized. To the left is illustrated the relative lengths required to brace a five-bay frame by the various types of vertical resisting mechanisms.

### Braced Frames

- Braced frames have high strength and stiffness and are more effective than moment frames in resisting racking deformation.
- Braced frames use less material and employ simpler connections than moment frames.
- Lower floor-to-floor heights are possible with braced frames than with moment frames.
- Braced frames can become an important visual component of a building's design. On the other hand, braced frames can interfere with access between adjacent spaces.

### Moment Frames

- Moment frames offer the most flexibility for visual and physical access between adjacent spaces.
- Moment frames have good ductility if their connections are properly detailed.
- Moment frames are less efficient than braced frames and shear walls.
- Moment frames require more material and labor to assemble than braced frames.
- Large deflections during an earthquake can damage non-structural elements of a building.

### Shear Walls

- Reinforced concrete or masonry walls are effective in absorbing energy if firmly tied to floor and roof diaphragms.
- Shear walls must be well proportioned to avoid excessive lateral deflection and high shear stresses.
- Avoid high aspect (height-to-width) ratios.

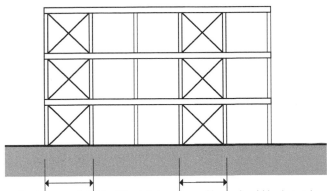

- A minimum of 25% of the total number of bays should be braced.

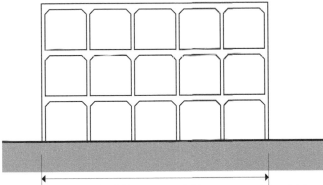

- The entire frame should incorporate rigid, moment-resisting joints.

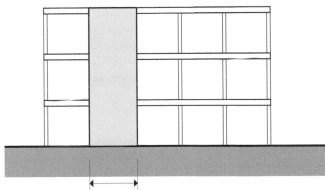

- Shear walls should occupy a minimum of 20% to 25% of the total number of bays.

### Building Configuration

Building configuration refers to the three-dimensional composition of lateral-force-resisting mechanisms in a structure. Decisions concerning the location and arrangement of these mechanisms—as well as their size and shape—can have a significant influence on the performance of a structure, especially when subjected to seismic forces during an earthquake.

### Regular Configurations

Building codes base seismic forces on the assumption of a regular configuration of resisting systems providing a balanced response to an equally balanced distribution of lateral forces. In addition, regular configurations are generally characterized by symmetrical plans, short spans, redundancy, equal floor heights, uniform sections and elevations, balanced resistance, maximum torsional resistance, and direct load paths.

Irregular configurations, such as discontinuous diaphragms or L- or T-shaped buildings, can develop severe stress concentrations and a twisting motion (torsion) that is very difficult to resist. See page 226.

- It should be remembered that vertical resisting elements—braced frames, moment frames, and shear walls—are only effective against lateral forces parallel to or in their plane.

- A minimum of three vertical resisting planes working in conjunction with roof and floor diaphragms must be present to resist gravity loads and lateral forces from two orthogonal directions.

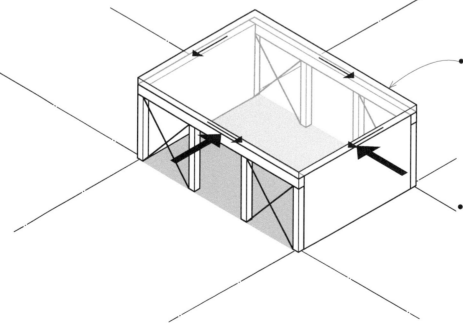

- A preferable solution is to have two vertical resisting planes parallel to one another and a reasonable distance apart providing lateral resistance in one direction, and another perpendicular pair resisting lateral forces in the other. Such an arrangement would result in smaller, lighter lateral resisting elements.

- In the early stages of a design project, it is more important to determine the three-dimensional pattern of lateral resisting elements—and its potential impact on the spatial organization and formal composition—rather than identify the specific types of lateral resisting elements to be used.

The arrangement of vertical resisting planes in relation to one another is crucial to the ability of a building structure to resist lateral loads from multiple directions. Balanced and symmetrical layouts of lateral-force-resisting elements are always preferable to avoid the torsional effects that occur when the centers of building mass and resistance are not concurrent.

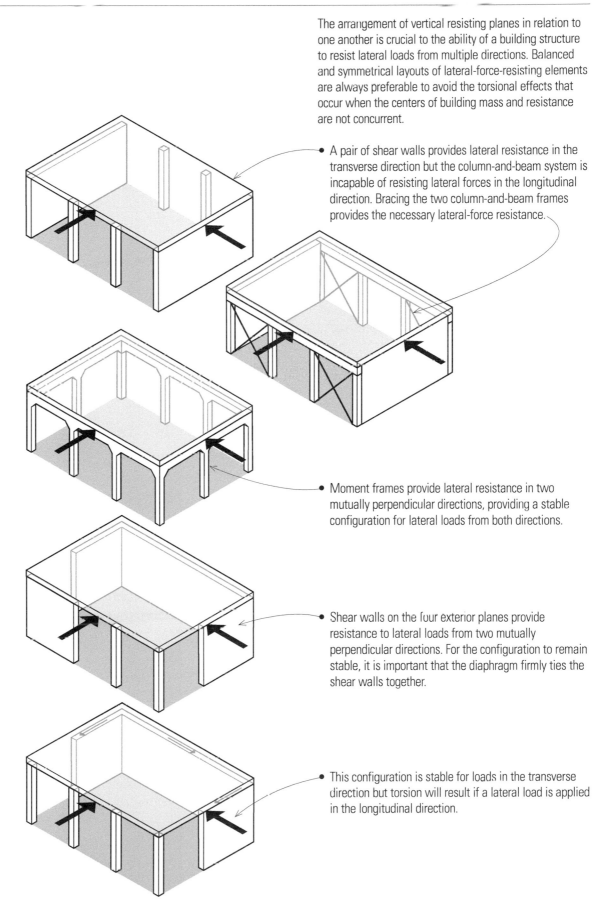

• A pair of shear walls provides lateral resistance in the transverse direction but the column-and-beam system is incapable of resisting lateral forces in the longitudinal direction. Bracing the two column-and-beam frames provides the necessary lateral-force resistance.

• Moment frames provide lateral resistance in two mutually perpendicular directions, providing a stable configuration for lateral loads from both directions.

• Shear walls on the four exterior planes provide resistance to lateral loads from two mutually perpendicular directions. For the configuration to remain stable, it is important that the diaphragm firmly ties the shear walls together.

• This configuration is stable for loads in the transverse direction but torsion will result if a lateral load is applied in the longitudinal direction.

# LATERAL-FORCE-RESISTING SYSTEMS

The preceding page illustrated stable configurations of relatively small-scale structures. In larger buildings, it is even more critical that lateral resisting elements be located strategically to resist lateral loads from any horizontal direction and to minimize the potential of torsional moments and displacements. For multistory buildings with square or rectangular grids, the vertical resisting elements are ideally placed in mutually perpendicular planes throughout the structure and are continuous from floor to floor.

How the vertical resisting elements are dispersed affects the effectiveness of a lateral-force-resisting strategy. The more concentrated the lateral resisting elements are in a building, the stronger and stiffer they must be. Conversely, the more dispersed and balanced the arrangement of lateral resisting elements, the less stiff each lateral resisting element can be.

Also critical to the performance of a lateral strategy that consists of dispersed resisting elements is the degree to which they are tied together by diaphragms so that they work in unison rather than individually. In the case where the lateral resisting elements are concentrated, for example, the horizontal diaphragms must be able to transfer lateral forces from the exterior surfaces to these internal resisting elements.

In multistory buildings the service cores housing elevators, stairways, and mechanical shafts can be constructed with shear walls or braced frames. These core walls can be viewed as resisting lateral forces from each of the planar directions or they can be viewed as forming a three-dimensional structural tube able to stabilize and stiffen the building structure against lateral loads. Because core shafts are normally rectangular or circular in cross section, their tubular action offers an efficient means for resisting moments and shear from all directions. A combination of structural cores and lateral resisting planes can offer excellent resistance to lateral forces when placed strategically and connected to one another by horizontal diaphragms at each floor level.

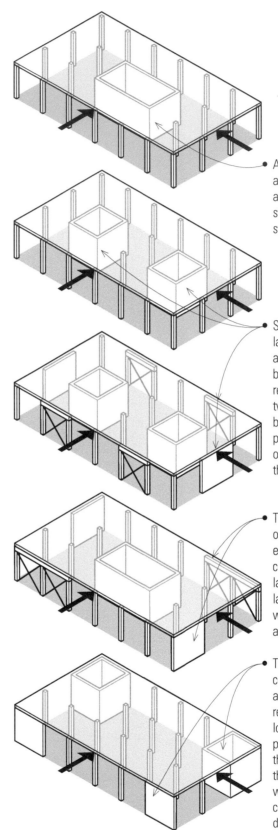

A single, centered core providing all of the lateral resistance for a structure would need to be stronger and stiffer than twin symmetrically placed cores.

Symmetrically placed exterior lateral resisting elements as well as two interior cores provide better dispersion and balanced resistance to lateral forces from two directions. Shear walls can be employed to resist in one principal direction while braced or moment frames are used in the perpendicular direction.

The asymmetrical placement of the exterior lateral resisting elements results in an irregular configuration. However, the layout remains effective against lateral loads from two directions with the interior core providing additional lateral capacity.

This is another irregular configuration due to the asymmetrical layout of lateral resisting elements about the longitudinal axis. The core walls provide lateral resistance in the transverse direction while the exterior lateral resisting walls work in tandem with the core walls in the longitudinal direction.

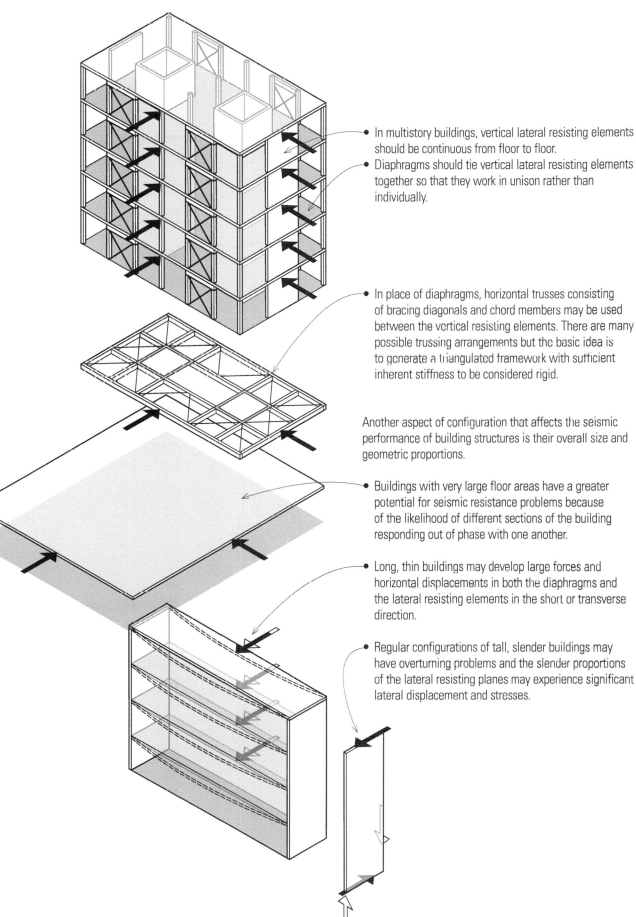

- In multistory buildings, vertical lateral resisting elements should be continuous from floor to floor.
- Diaphragms should tie vertical lateral resisting elements together so that they work in unison rather than individually.

- In place of diaphragms, horizontal trusses consisting of bracing diagonals and chord members may be used between the vertical resisting elements. There are many possible trussing arrangements but the basic idea is to generate a triangulated framework with sufficient inherent stiffness to be considered rigid.

Another aspect of configuration that affects the seismic performance of building structures is their overall size and geometric proportions.

- Buildings with very large floor areas have a greater potential for seismic resistance problems because of the likelihood of different sections of the building responding out of phase with one another.

- Long, thin buildings may develop large forces and horizontal displacements in both the diaphragms and the lateral resisting elements in the short or transverse direction.

- Regular configurations of tall, slender buildings may have overturning problems and the slender proportions of the lateral resisting planes may experience significant lateral displacement and stresses.

### Irregular Configurations

It is inconceivable that all buildings will have regular configurations. Irregularities in plan and section often result from programmatic and contextual requirements, concerns, or desires. Unbalanced building layouts, however, can impact the stability of the structure under lateral loading and especially its susceptibility to damage in an earthquake. In the context of seismic design, irregular configurations vary both in importance and the extent to which a particular irregularity exists. When irregularities cannot be avoided, the designer should be aware of the possible seismic consequences and carefully detail the building structure in a way to ensure its proper performance.

### Horizontal Irregularities

Horizontal irregularities include those arising from plan configurations, such as torsional irregularity, reentrant corners, nonparallel systems, diaphragm discontinuities, and out-of-plane offsets.

### Torsional Irregularity

Variations in the perimeter strength and stiffness of a structure can produce an eccentricity or separation between its center of mass (the centroid of the lateral force) and its center of rigidity or resistance (the center of stiffness of the lateral-force-resisting elements of the system). The result is a horizontal twisting or torsion of the building, which can result in overstressing of structural elements and stress concentrations at certain locations, most often at reentrant corners. To avoid destructive torsional effects, structures should be arranged and braced symmetrically with centers of mass and rigidity as coincident as possible.

When a building plan is not symmetrical, the lateral-force-resisting system must be adjusted so that its center of stiffness or rigidity is proximate to the center of mass. If this is not possible, then the structure must be designed specifically to counter the torsional effects of the asymmetrical layout. An example would be distributing the bracing elements with stiffnesses that correspond to the distribution of the mass.

- Horizontal torsion results from a lateral force acting on a structure having noncoincident centers of mass and rigidity.

- Torsional irregularity is considered to exist when the maximum story drift at one end of a structure is 120% to 140% greater than the average of the story drifts at the two ends of the structure.

- Locating a shear wall, braced frame, or moment frame at the open end would rebalance the centers of mass and rigidity and make them very nearly concurrent.

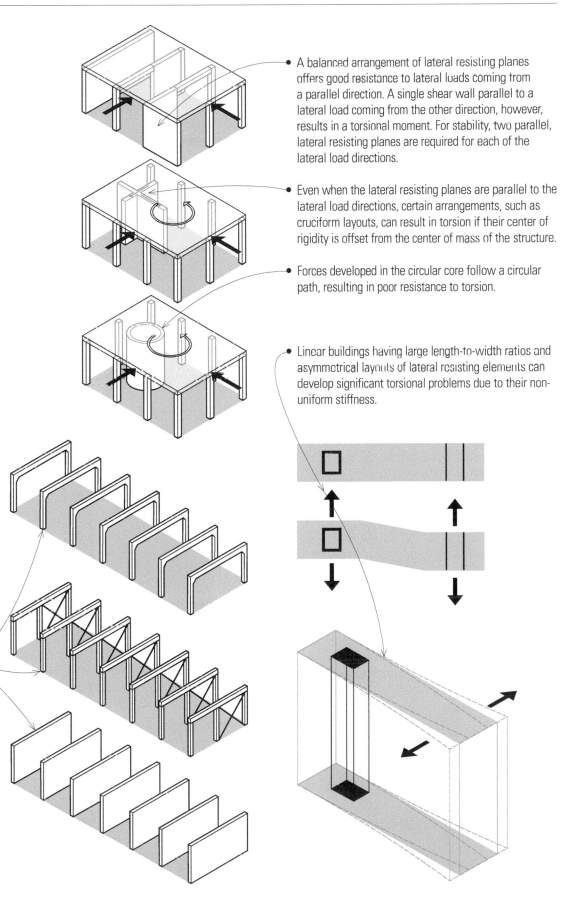

- A balanced arrangement of lateral resisting planes offers good resistance to lateral loads coming from a parallel direction. A single shear wall parallel to a lateral load coming from the other direction, however, results in a torsional moment. For stability, two parallel, lateral resisting planes are required for each of the lateral load directions.

- Even when the lateral resisting planes are parallel to the lateral load directions, certain arrangements, such as cruciform layouts, can result in torsion if their center of rigidity is offset from the center of mass of the structure.

- Forces developed in the circular core follow a circular path, resulting in poor resistance to torsion.

- Linear buildings having large length-to-width ratios and asymmetrical layouts of lateral resisting elements can develop significant torsional problems due to their non-uniform stiffness.

- Because transverse lateral loads tend to be more critical than those in the longitudinal direction, the more efficient type of lateral-load-resisting mechanisms are used in the short direction.

### Reentrant Corners

L-, T-, U-, and H-shaped buildings, as well as cruciform plan organizations, are problematic because areas of large stress concentration can develop at the reentrant corners—interior corners where building projections are greater than 15% of the plan dimension in a given direction.

These building shapes tend to have differences in rigidity among the parts, which tends to produce differential motions between different portions of the structure, resulting in localized stress concentrations at the reentrant corners.

Stress concentrations and torsional effects at reentrant corners are interrelated. The centers of mass and rigidity of these configurations cannot geometrically coincide for all possible directions of seismic forces, thus resulting in torsion.

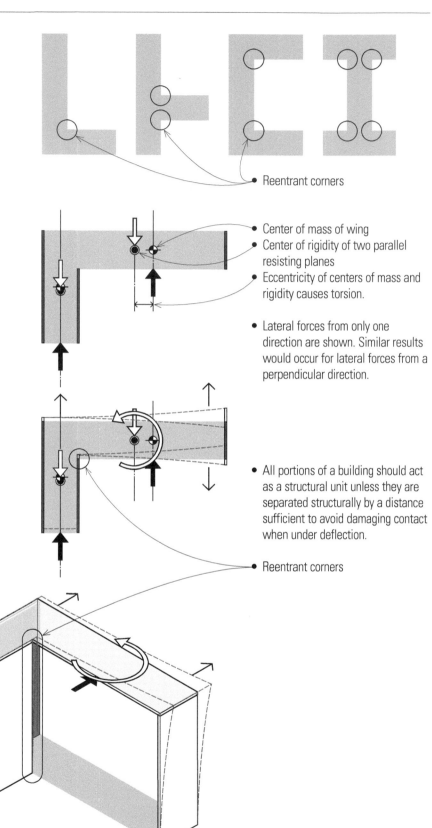

- Reentrant corners

- Center of mass of wing
- Center of rigidity of two parallel resisting planes
- Eccentricity of centers of mass and rigidity causes torsion.

- Lateral forces from only one direction are shown. Similar results would occur for lateral forces from a perpendicular direction.

- All portions of a building should act as a structural unit unless they are separated structurally by a distance sufficient to avoid damaging contact when under deflection.

- Reentrant corners

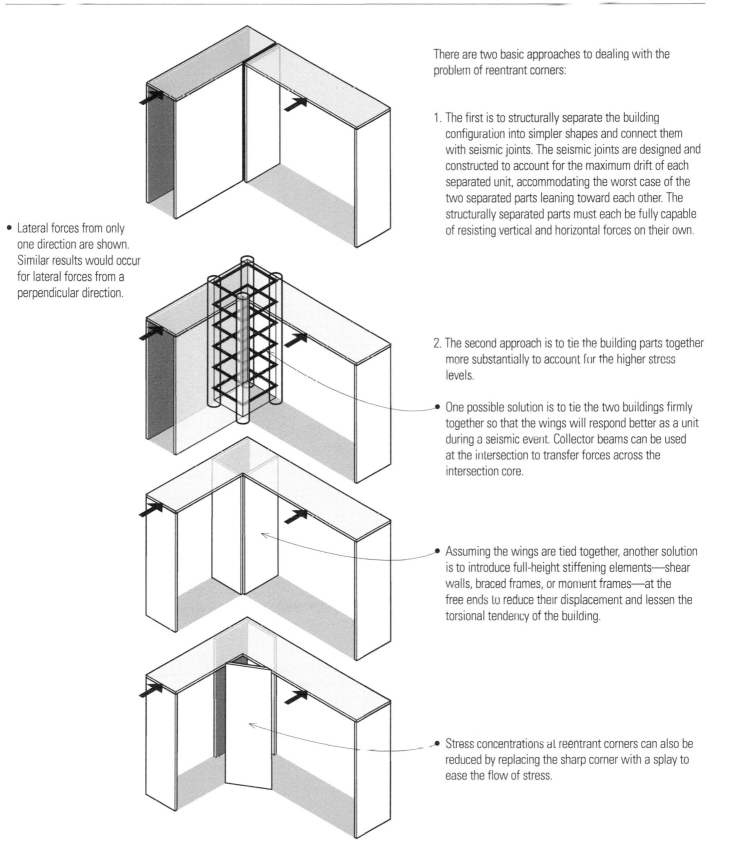

There are two basic approaches to dealing with the problem of reentrant corners:

1. The first is to structurally separate the building configuration into simpler shapes and connect them with seismic joints. The seismic joints are designed and constructed to account for the maximum drift of each separated unit, accommodating the worst case of the two separated parts leaning toward each other. The structurally separated parts must each be fully capable of resisting vertical and horizontal forces on their own.

• Lateral forces from only one direction are shown. Similar results would occur for lateral forces from a perpendicular direction.

2. The second approach is to tie the building parts together more substantially to account for the higher stress levels.

• One possible solution is to tie the two buildings firmly together so that the wings will respond better as a unit during a seismic event. Collector beams can be used at the intersection to transfer forces across the intersection core.

• Assuming the wings are tied together, another solution is to introduce full-height stiffening elements—shear walls, braced frames, or moment frames—at the free ends to reduce their displacement and lessen the torsional tendency of the building.

• Stress concentrations at reentrant corners can also be reduced by replacing the sharp corner with a splay to ease the flow of stress.

### Nonparallel Systems

Nonparallel systems are structural layouts in which the vertical lateral-force-resisting elements are neither parallel nor symmetrical about the major orthogonal axes of the structure. The nonparallel resisting planes would not be able to resist the torsion resulting from the lateral load and the resisting shear forces in the wall planes parallel to the load.

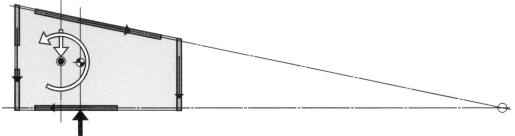

### Diaphragm Discontinuities

Diaphragms having significant variations in stiffness from one story to the next—as well as those incorporating large cutouts or open areas—represent another type of plan irregularity. These discontinuities affect how effectively the diaphragms are able to distribute lateral forces to vertical elements of the lateral-force-resisting system.

### Out-of-Plane Offsets

Out-of-plane offsets are discontinuities in the path of vertical elements of the lateral-force-resisting system. Forces acting on a structure should flow with as much directness as possible along a continuous path from one structural element to the next and eventually be resolved through the foundation system to the supporting ground. When a vertical element of the lateral-force-resisting system is discontinuous, a horizontal diaphragm must be able to redistribute the horizontal shear forces to a vertical resisting element in the same or another plane.

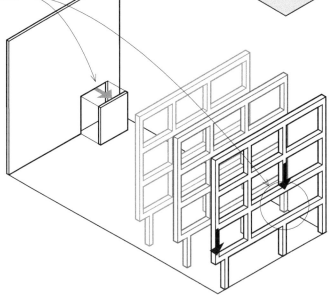

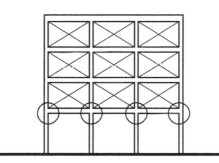

## Vertical Irregularities

Vertical irregularities arise from sectional configurations, such as soft stories, weak stories, geometric irregularities, in-plane discontinuities, and irregularities in mass or weight.

## Soft Stories

Soft stories have a lateral stiffness significantly less than that in the story above. A soft story can occur at any level but since seismic forces accumulate toward the base, the discontinuity in stiffness tends to be greatest between the first and second floor of a building. The reduced stiffness produces large deformations in the soft-story columns and generally results in a shear failure at the beam-column connection.

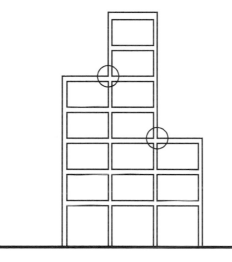

## Weak Stories

Weak stories are caused by the lateral strength of one story being significantly less than that in the story above. When shear walls do not line up in plan from one story to the next, the lateral forces are unable to flow directly downward through the walls from the roof to the foundation. An altered load path will redirect the lateral forces in an attempt to bypass the discontinuity, resulting in critical overstresses at locations of discontinuity. The discontinuous shear wall condition represents a special case of the soft first-story problem.

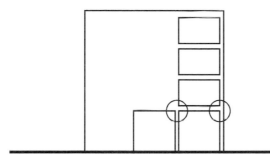

## Geometric Irregularities

Geometric irregularities are caused by a horizontal dimension of the lateral-force-resisting system being significantly greater than that of an adjacent story. This vertical irregularity can cause the various parts of a building to have different and very complex responses. Special attention needs to be paid at the points of connection where changes in elevation occur.

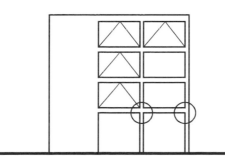

## In-Plane Discontinuities

In-plane discontinuities create variations in stiffness in vertical lateral-force-resisting elements. Variations in stiffness should normally increase from the roof down to the base of a building. Seismic forces accumulate at each successive lower diaphragm level and become critical at the second floor level. Any reduction of lateral bracing at this level can result in large lateral deformations of the first-floor columns and very high shear stresses in the shear wall and columns.

### Weight or Mass Irregularity

Weight or mass irregularity is caused by the mass of a story being significantly heavier than the mass of an adjacent story. Similar to the soft-story irregularity, the change in stiffness will result in a redistribution of loads that may cause stress concentrations at the beam-column joints and larger column displacements in the columns below.

- Swimming pools, green roofs requiring substantial amounts of soil, and heavy roofing materials constitute large masses at the roof diaphragm level, which translate into large horizontal inertial forces during a seismic event. In response, it will be necessary to provide a more substantial vertical lateral-force-resisting system to handle the increased load. Either structural member sizes will have to be increased or bay spacing will have to be decreased to handle the larger forces.

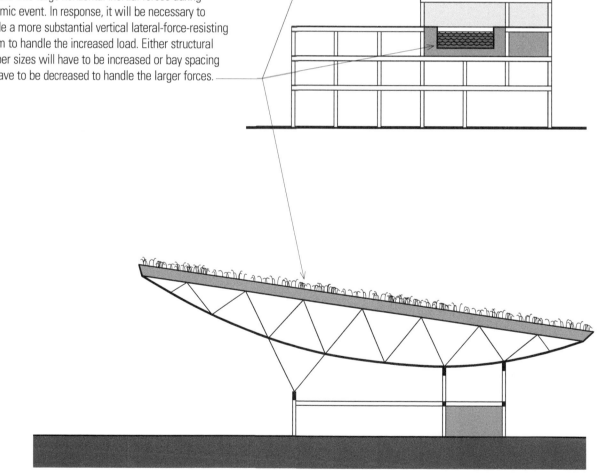

### Horizontal Braced Framing

Occasionally, when the roof or floor sheathing is too light or flexible and unable to sustain diaphragm forces, the horizontal framework must be designed to incorporate bracing similar to that of braced wall frames. In steel-framed buildings, particularly industrial or warehouse structures with long-span trusses, the roof diaphragm is provided by diagonal steel bracing and struts. The most important consideration is to provide a complete load path from the lateral forces to the vertical resisting elements.

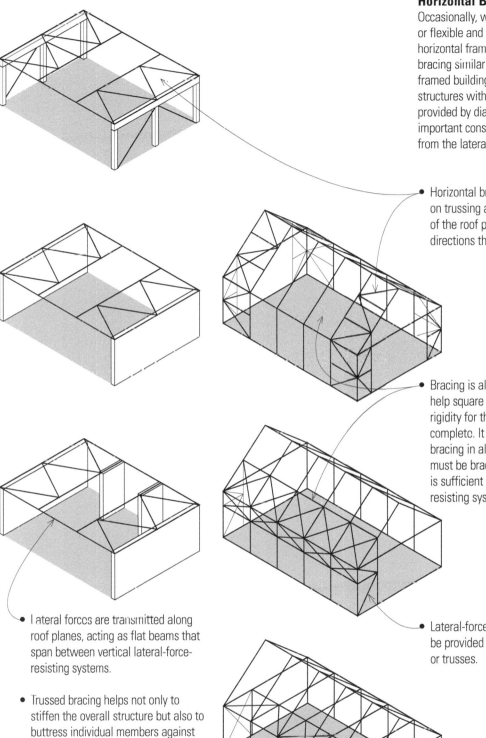

- Horizontal bracing, often called wind bracing, depends on trussing action and can effectively resist the racking of the roof plane, especially for loads coming from directions that are neither longitudinal nor transverse.

- Bracing is also useful during the construction stage to help square the plan dimensions as well as provide rigidity for the structure before the roof diaphragm is complete. It is generally not necessary to provide wind bracing in all bays of a roof plane. Only enough bays must be braced to ensure that the horizontal framework is sufficient to transfer the lateral loads to the vertical resisting system.

- Lateral forces are transmitted along roof planes, acting as flat beams that span between vertical lateral-force-resisting systems.

- Trussed bracing helps not only to stiffen the overall structure but also to buttress individual members against buckling.

- Lateral-force resistance in the transverse direction must be provided in the form of tension counters, stiff panels, or trusses.

### Base Isolation

Base isolation is a strategy involving the separation or isolation of the building from its foundation in such a way that it can absorb the shock of an earthquake. As the ground moves, the building moves at a lower frequency because the isolators dissipate a large part of the shock. In this approach, the building structure is decoupled from the horizontal components of the earthquake ground motion by interposing a layer with low horizontal stiffness between the structure and foundation, thereby reducing the resulting inertia force the structure must resist.

Currently, the most commonly used base isolator consists of alternating layers of natural rubber or neoprene and steel bonded together, with a cylinder of pure lead tightly inserted through the middle. The rubber layers allow the isolator to easily displace horizontally, reducing the seismic loads experienced by the building and its occupants. They also act as a spring, returning the building to its original position once the shaking has stopped. The vulcanization bonding of rubber sheets to thin steel reinforcing plates allows the flexibility to occur in the horizontal direction but remain very stiff in the vertical direction. Vertical loads are transmitted to the structure relatively unchanged.

Base isolation systems are generally suitable for stiff buildings up to about seven stories in height; taller buildings would be subject to overturning, which base isolation systems cannot mitigate. Recently, however, taller buildings have benefited from base isolation. Buildings normally require the isolated period to be 2.5 to 3 times that of the typical non-isolated building.

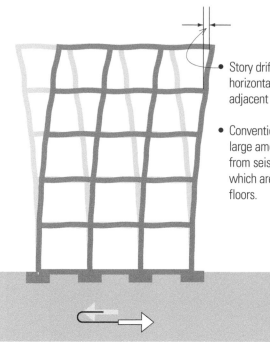

- Story drift refers to the relative horizontal displacement between adjacent floors of a building.

- Conventional structures are subject to large amounts of drift and deformation from seismic ground accelerations, which are amplified at the upper floors.

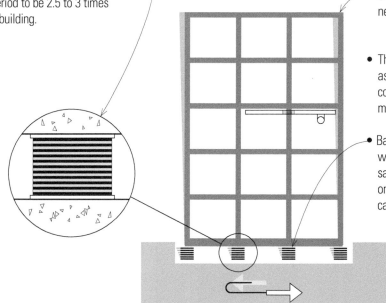

- Small structural deflection with negligible story drift

- The building must be designed to act as a rigid unit and have flexible utility connections to accommodate the movement.

- Base isolation bearings should, within reason, be located at the same elevation. Stepped footings on hillsides or sloping sites are poor candidates for base isolation.

### Detailing of Building Components

Building codes generally contain requirements for the design and detailing of the components making up the seismic-force-resisting systems of a building, such as diaphragms and shear walls, as well as addressing the problems associated with irregular building configurations. Among the details to be considered are:

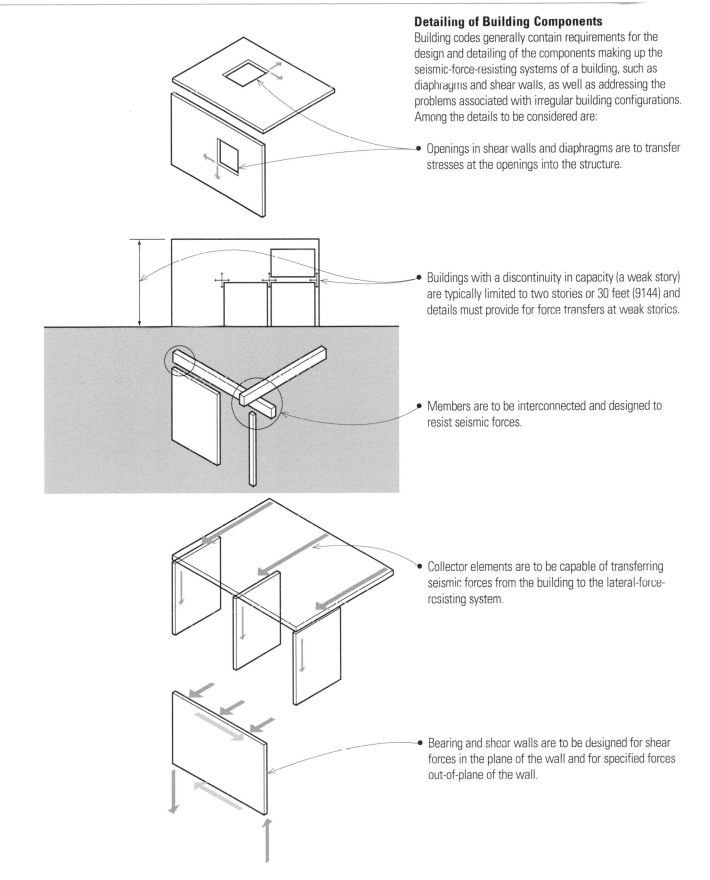

- Openings in shear walls and diaphragms are to transfer stresses at the openings into the structure.

- Buildings with a discontinuity in capacity (a weak story) are typically limited to two stories or 30 feet (9144) and details must provide for force transfers at weak stories.

- Members are to be interconnected and designed to resist seismic forces.

- Collector elements are to be capable of transferring seismic forces from the building to the lateral-force-resisting system.

- Bearing and shear walls are to be designed for shear forces in the plane of the wall and for specified forces out-of-plane of the wall.

The effects of gravity and lateral loading apply to all structures, no matter what their shape or geometry may wish to convey. Even freeform buildings that appear to have no regularity to their structure often have relatively regular framing systems beneath their surface, or they may incorporate a nonrectilinear structural geometry that is inherently stable. There are a number of ways one can structure nonrectilinear, irregular, organic forms. The important issue is that these apparently free forms should have an underlying geometric or structural basis, even if not apparent to the eye, and that this basis incorporate the requisite lateral-force-resisting strategies.

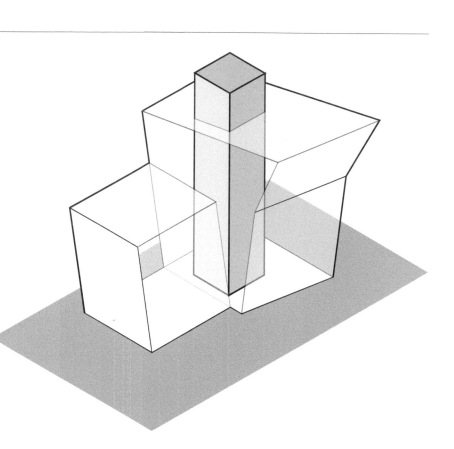

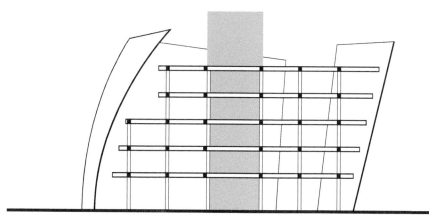

- Tertiary supporting elements such as vertical trussing to support a freeform facade from a regular, rectilinear structural frame
- Regularity of support spacing in one plan direction with a series of freeform moment frames defining the exterior form
- A composition of doubly curved surfaces that are, in fact, portions of regular geometric surfaces

# 6
# Long-Span Structures

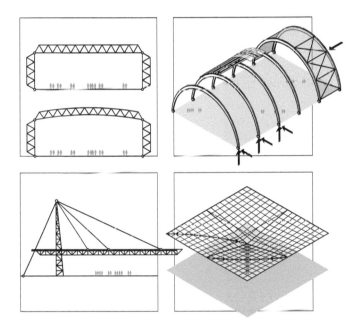

While span is a major problem in most large buildings, it dominates the design of auditoriums, exhibition halls, and similar facilities requiring a large expanse of column-free space. For buildings that have such requirements, designers and engineers have the task of selecting an appropriate structural system capable of resisting the large bending moments and deflections of long spans in as efficient a manner as possible without sacrificing safety.

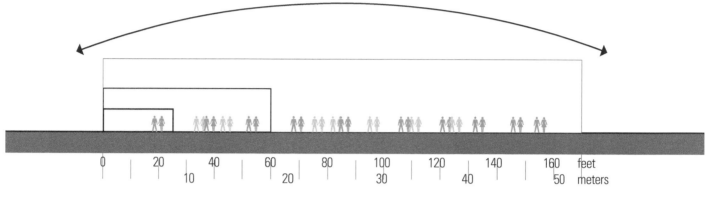

No specific definition exists for what constitutes a long-span structure. In this text, we are considering any span in excess of 60 feet (18 m) to be a long span. Long-span structures are used most often to shape and support the roofs of large, open floor spaces for a variety of building types, such as sports arenas, theaters, swimming centers, and airplane hangars. They can also be used to support the floors of buildings if a large space is embedded within a building structure.

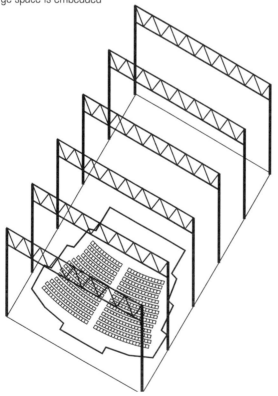

• Stadiums used for football, baseball, or soccer may be either open or enclosed. Some enclosed stadiums have roof systems that shelter 50,000 to 80,000 spectators and have spans in excess of 800 feet (244 m).

• The size and shape of sports arenas are related to that of the central floor space and the configuration and capacity of the spectator seating area. The shape of the roof may be circular, oval, square, or rectangular, with critical spans generally in the range of 150 to 300 feet (45.7 to 91 m) or more. Almost all modern venues are column-free for unobstructed viewing.

• Theaters and performance halls are generally smaller than sports arenas but still require long-span roof systems to achieve column-free spaces.

• Exhibition and convention halls generally include a large space reserved for exhibits or consumer shows with floor area requirements ranging from 25,000 sf to more than 300,000 sf (2323 to 27,870 m²). Columns are spaced as far apart as feasible to provide maximum flexibility in layout. Although a column spacing of 20 to 35 feet (6.1 to 10.7 m) is used quite frequently for standard types of occupancies, exhibition halls may have a column spacing in excess of 100 feet (30 m) or more.

• Other building types that typically use long-span systems include warehouses, industrial and manufacturing facilities, airport terminals and hangars, and large retail stores.

## Structural Issues

Scale plays a major role in the determination of structural form. For relatively small structures, such as a single-family residence or utility buildings, the structural requirements can be met through simple structural systems using a variety of materials. However, for very large structures, vertical gravity forces and lateral forces of wind and earthquakes often limit the structural materials that can be used, and the limitations of construction methods begin to dominate the concept of the structural system.

- Deflection is a major design determinant in the design of long-span structures. The depth and sizing of the elements in long-span members are often based on controlling deflection rather than bending stresses.

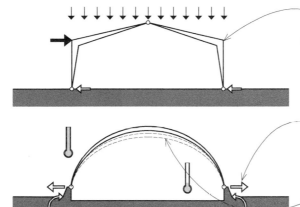

- Sections of long-span structures should be deepest where the bending moments are greatest.
- Some long-span structures, such as domes and cable systems, are effective in supporting distributed loads but are sensitive to concentrated loads from heavy equipment.

- The nature of some long-span structures, such as arches, vaults, and domes, develop thrust at their supports, which must be counteracted by tension ties or abutments.

- Long structural members are prone to significant changes in length due to thermal expansion and contraction, especially for exposed and open-air structures.
- Stabilizing long-span structures against lateral forces is especially critical because of the large occupancies they typically house.

- Long-span structures have little redundancy and are subject to catastrophic failure if a key element or elements fail. Columns, frames, and walls supporting long-span members have very large tributary loads, and little opportunity exists for a redistribution of these loads to other members if a localized failure occurs.
- Ponding is one of the most critical conditions in the design of long-span roofs. If a roof experiences deflection that prevents normal water runoff, additional water might collect in the middle of the span and cause even more deflection, which allows even more load to accumulate. This progressive cycle can continue until structural failure results. Roofs should be designed with sufficient slope or camber to ensure proper drainage or be designed to support maximum loads that include ponding.

## Design Issues

For economy and efficiency, long-span structures should be shaped according to an appropriate structural geometry. For example, their sections should be deepest where the largest bending moments occur and thinnest at pin joints where bending moments are at a minimum or nonexistent. The resulting profile can have a powerful impact on the exterior of a building, and in particular its roof profile, as well as on the form of the interior space they house.

The choice of an appropriate long-span structural system is a matter of the span range desired or required by the activities to be housed, the formal and spatial implications on the building design, and the economic factors related to material, fabrication, shipping, and erection. Any one of these factors may limit the possible choices of a long-span structure.

Another decision a designer faces is to what extent the long-span structure is expressed or even celebrated. Because of the large scale of long-span structures, it would be difficult to conceal their presence. Nevertheless, some long-span structures more clearly express how they soar across space while others are more muted in their structural role. Thus the decision can be made as to whether the building design exploits the structural mechanics of a long-span system or moderates its impact so that the focus is on the activities within a space.

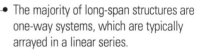

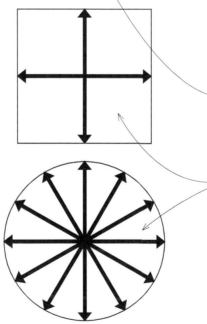

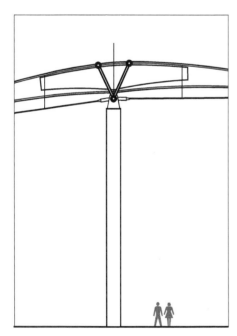

- Connection details in long-span structures can establish both visual interest and a sense of scale.

- The majority of long-span structures are one-way systems, which are typically arrayed in a linear series.
- The spanning capability of secondary elements determines the spacing of the primary long-span elements and their tributary load.
- Repetition of structural elements should be maximized for greater economy.
- In addition to lateral stability within the plane of long-span structures, resistance to lateral forces must be provided perpendicular to the spans.

- Two-way systems, such as space frames and dome structures, require a nearly square or circular pattern of supports.

- Building codes may allow, except in certain factory, hazardous, and mercantile occupancies, omitting the fire-resistance requirements of the roof structure if it is high enough above the occupied floor.

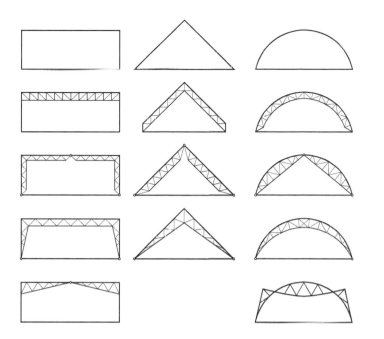

- Because the majority of long-span structures are one-way systems, their profile is an important design consideration.
- Flat beam and trussed structures permeate both exterior forms and interior spaces with a rectilinear geometry.
- Vaulted and domed structures give rise to convex exterior forms and concave interior spaces.
- Trussed, arched, and cable systems offer a variety of profiles. For example, illustrated here are a few of the many possible profiles for long-span trusses and trussed arches.

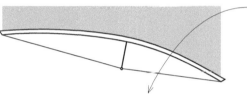

- Symmetrical long-span structures are always desirable for balanced load conditions, but asymmetrical profiles can be useful in relating a structure to its site and context or accommodating a specific program activity. In building concourses, for example, asymmetry can help to orient users as they travel along a path and aid in differentiating right from left.
- The ability of a long-span structure to vary heights can help to establish and identify smaller-scale places within a larger space.

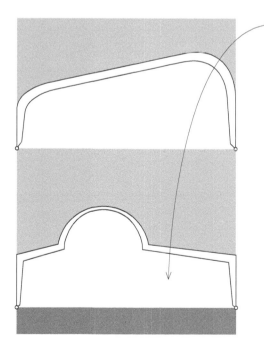

### Construction Issues

- Long-span members are difficult to ship and require significant space for storage at the construction site. The maximum length is typically 60 feet (18.3 m) for truck transport and approximately 80 feet (24.4 m) for rail transport. The depth of long-span beams and trusses can also cause problems in shipping. The maximum width for highway transport is about 14 feet (4.3 m).
- Because of transport limitations, field assembly is generally required for long-span members. The assembly of long-span members normally occurs on the ground, before they are hoisted into place with a crane. The total weight of each long-span member is therefore a major consideration when specifying the capacity of the crane at the site.

## ONE-WAY SYSTEMS

Listed on this and the facing page are span ranges for the basic types of long-span structures.

### Beams

- Timber     Laminated beams
- Steel     Wide-flange beams

           Plate girders

- Concrete     Precast tees

### Trusses

- Timber     Flat trusses

           Shaped trusses

- Steel     Flat trusses

           Shaped trusses

           Space trusses

### Arches

- Timber     Laminated arches
- Steel     Built-up arches
- Concrete     Formed arches

### Cable Structures

- Steel     Cable systems

### Plate Structures

- Timber     Folded plates
- Concrete     Folded plates

### Shell Structures

- Wood     Lamella vaults
- Concrete     Barrel shells

## TWO-WAY SYSTEMS

### Plate Structures

- Steel     Space frames
- Concrete     Waffle slabs

### Shell Structures

- Steel     Ribbed domes
- Concrete     Domes

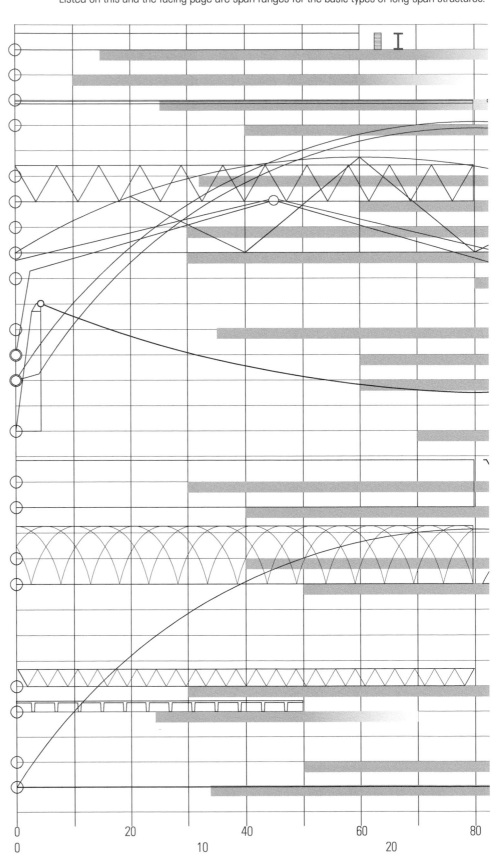

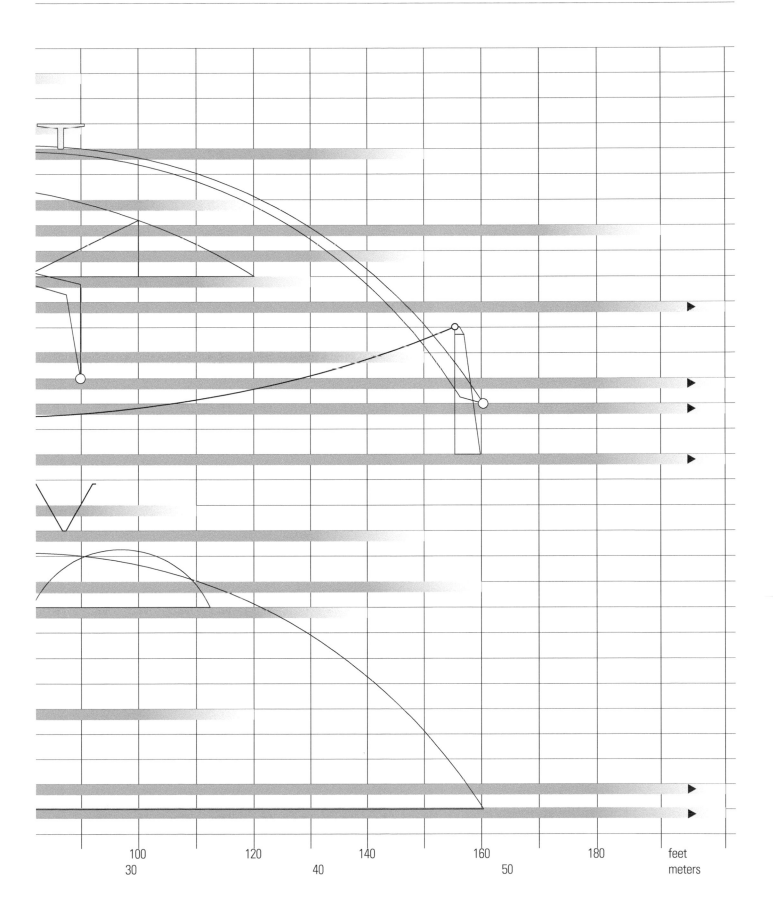

100          120          140          160          180          feet
30                        40                        50          meters

Flat beam structures are most appropriate when the minimum volume of space is required within the desired clear height. The achievable span is then directly related to the depth of the beams which, for normal loadings, would require a depth-to-span ratio of approximately 1:20 for glue-laminated beams and steel girders. Although solid web beam structures have a depth-to-span advantage, they have a high self-weight and do not easily accommodate mechanical services as do open-web or trussed beam structures.

## Glue-Laminated Beams

Solid-sawn timber beams are not available for long spans but glue-laminated (glulam) timber beams are capable of spanning up to 80 feet (24.4 m). Glulam beams have superior strength and can be manufactured with large cross sections and curved or tapered profiles.

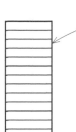

- Glulam beams have standard widths of 3 1/8", 5 1/8", 6 3/4", 8 3/4", and 10 3/4" (80, 130, 170, 220, and 275), but custom widths up to 14 1/4" (360 mm) are available on special order.
- Glulam beam depths range in multiples of 1 3/8" or 1 1/2" (35 or 38) laminations up to 75" (1905). Curved members can be laminated in 3/4" (19) laminations to create tighter curvature.

- Because of their length, long-span glulam beams require special transport from the fabricating facility to the job site.
- Various profiles are available to allow for roof drainage.
- The cross sectional size of long-spanning glulam beams is large enough to qualify their use in Type IV or "heavy timber" construction, which is roughly the equivalent of one-hour fire-resistive construction.

- Structural diaphragm or horizontal bracing
- Vertical lateral-force-resistance required in two primary directions.

- In long-span roof construction, glulam beams are most often used as the primary spanning members with lighter secondary joists or purlins spanning between them.

### Steel Beams

Wide-flange steel sections are capable of spanning up to 70 feet (21 m) with a depth of 44 inches (1120). Deeper sections for longer spans are possible by fabricating plate girders built up from steel plates and sections welded together to create the equivalent of a rolled beam.

Both plate girders and rolled wide-flange sections are not very efficient in long-span applications because the amount of material necessary to meet the bending and deflection requirements becomes excessive. It is often economical to vary the profile of the plate girder to provide the largest section for the maximum bending moment and reduce the section where the bending moment is low, thus reducing the beam's dead load by removing material where it is not necessary. Such tapered profiles are especially useful in accommodating the drainage of rainwater on roof structures.

### Concrete Beams

Conventional reinforced concrete members can be used to span long distances but in doing so, they become very large and bulky. Prestressing the concrete results in more efficient, smaller, and lighter cross sections that experience less cracking than standard reinforced concrete.

Concrete members may be prestressed by either pretensioning at a factory site or posttensioning at the construction site. Precast, pretensioned members require carefully planned handling and transport. An advantage of on-site posttensioning of a concrete beam or girder is the elimination of the transport of very long precast members to the job site.

Precast, prestressed concrete members come in standard shapes and dimensions. The two most commonly used shapes are the single-tee and double-tee. Double-tees are commonly used for spans up to 70 feet (21 m) while single-tees are used for spans up to 100 feet (30 m) or more. Special shapes are also possible but are only economical when there is enough repetition to justify the cost of the specialized forms necessary for their casting.

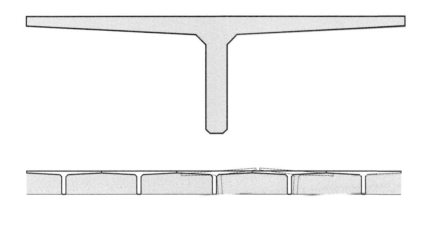

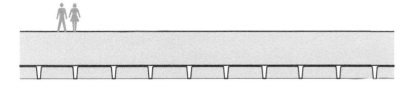

## Trussed Beams

A trussed beam is a continuous beam stiffened by a combination of compression struts and diagonal tension rods. The vertical struts provide intermediate support points for the beam member, reducing its bending moments, while the resulting trussing action increases the load-carrying capacity of the beam.

- Trussed beams are an efficient and relatively economical way of increasing the load and span capability of glue-laminated and rolled steel beams.
- The beam member may be flat for use in either floor or roof structures, while pitched and curved beam members can be used for better drainage on roof spans.

- Longer spans are possible when trussed beams are used in combination to form three-hinged arches. Because three-hinged arches (see page 256) develop horizontal thrust at each support, abutments or tension ties may be required for thrust resistance.

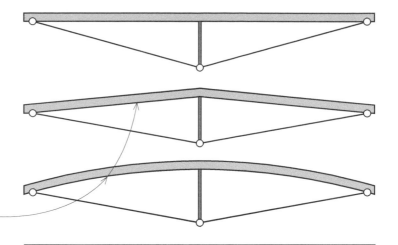

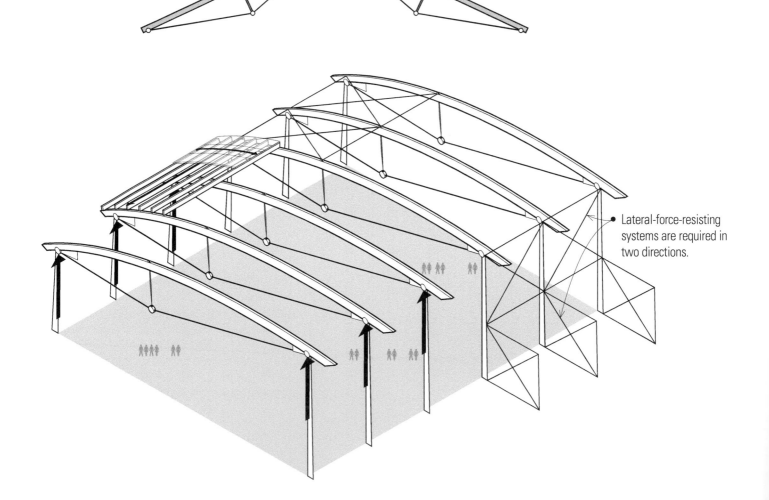

- Lateral-force-resisting systems are required in two directions.

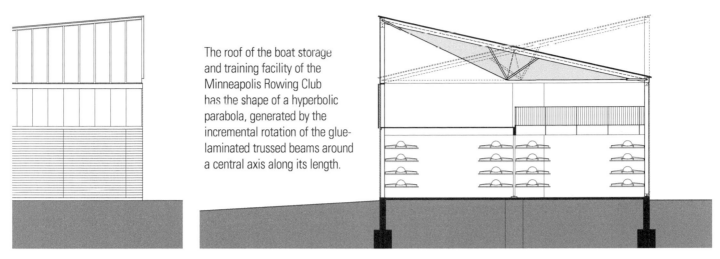

The roof of the boat storage and training facility of the Minneapolis Rowing Club has the shape of a hyperbolic parabola, generated by the incremental rotation of the glue-laminated trussed beams around a central axis along its length.

Partial elevation and section: Minneapolis Rowing Club, Minneapolis, Minnesota, 1999–2001, Vincent James Associates

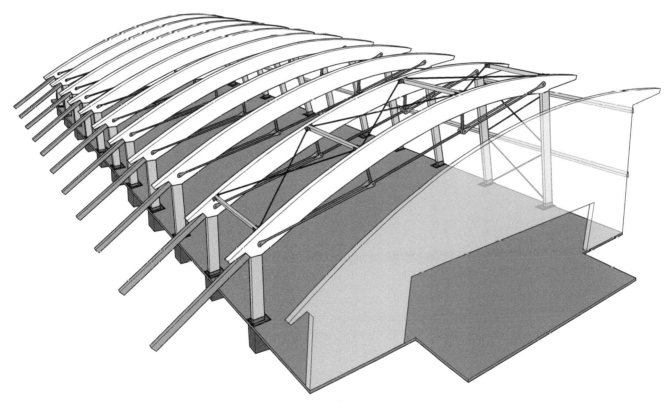

Schematic view: Banff Community Recreation Center, Banff, Alberta, Canada, 2011, GEC Architecture

The roof of the Banff Community Recreation Center is supported by glue-laminated trussed arches salvaged from the old curling rink. Salvaged glue-laminated members were also used for columns throughout the complex. All salvaged members were inventoried, inspected, and tested to modern standards to determine the suitability of the members for reuse. In some cases, members were cut to create two smaller members.

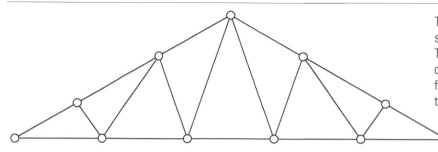

Trusses are pin-jointed and triangulated assemblies of simple struts stressed in either tension or compression. Truss bending moments are resolved into tension and compression forces in the bottom and top chords. Shear forces are resolved into tension and compression forces in the diagonal and vertical members.

- Flat trusses have parallel top and bottom chords. Flat trusses are generally not as efficient as pitched or bowstring trusses.

- Scissors trusses have tension members extending from the foot of each top chord to an intermediate point on the opposite top chord.

- Crescent trusses have both top and bottom chords curving upward from a common point at each side.

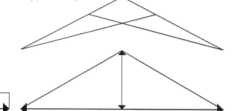

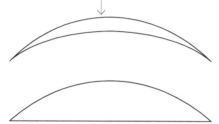

- Span range for flat trusses: up to 120' (37 m)
- Depth range for flat trusses: span/10 to span/15

- Span range for shaped trusses: up to 150' (46 m)
- Depth range for shaped trusses: span/6 to span/10

- Bowstring trusses have a curved top chord meeting a straight bottom chord at each end.

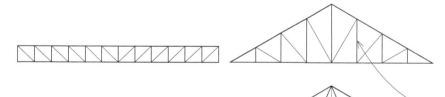

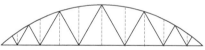

- Pratt trusses have vertical web members in compression and diagonal web members in tension. It is generally more efficient to use a truss type in which the longer web members are loaded in tension.

- Warren trusses have inclined web members forming a series of equilateral triangles. Vertical web members are sometimes introduced to reduce the panel lengths of the top chord, which is in compression.

- Howe trusses have vertical web members in tension and diagonal web members in compression.

- Belgian trusses have only inclined web members.
- Fink trusses are Belgian trusses having subdiagonals to reduce the length of compression web members toward the centerline of the span.

Trusses use material more economically and are more efficient in spanning long distances than solid beams but are relatively expensive to fabricate because of the number of connections and the complexity of the joints. They become more economical when spanning 100 feet (30 m) or more and when used as primary structural members supporting secondary trusses or beams.

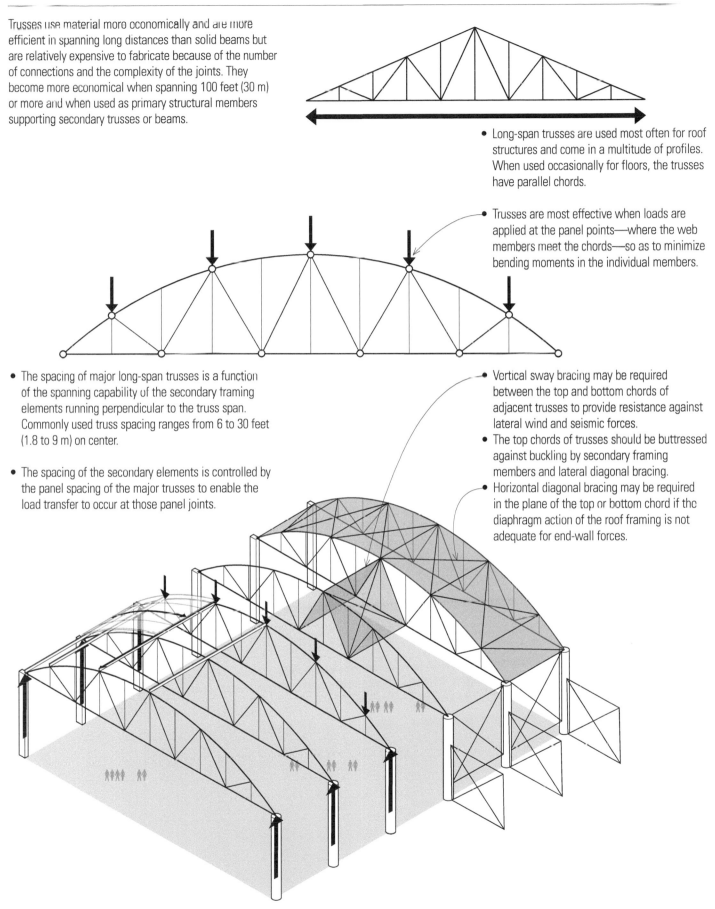

- Long-span trusses are used most often for roof structures and come in a multitude of profiles. When used occasionally for floors, the trusses have parallel chords.

- Trusses are most effective when loads are applied at the panel points—where the web members meet the chords—so as to minimize bending moments in the individual members.

- The spacing of major long-span trusses is a function of the spanning capability of the secondary framing elements running perpendicular to the truss span. Commonly used truss spacing ranges from 6 to 30 feet (1.8 to 9 m) on center.

- The spacing of the secondary elements is controlled by the panel spacing of the major trusses to enable the load transfer to occur at those panel joints.

- Vertical sway bracing may be required between the top and bottom chords of adjacent trusses to provide resistance against lateral wind and seismic forces.
- The top chords of trusses should be buttressed against buckling by secondary framing members and lateral diagonal bracing.
- Horizontal diagonal bracing may be required in the plane of the top or bottom chord if the diaphragm action of the roof framing is not adequate for end-wall forces.

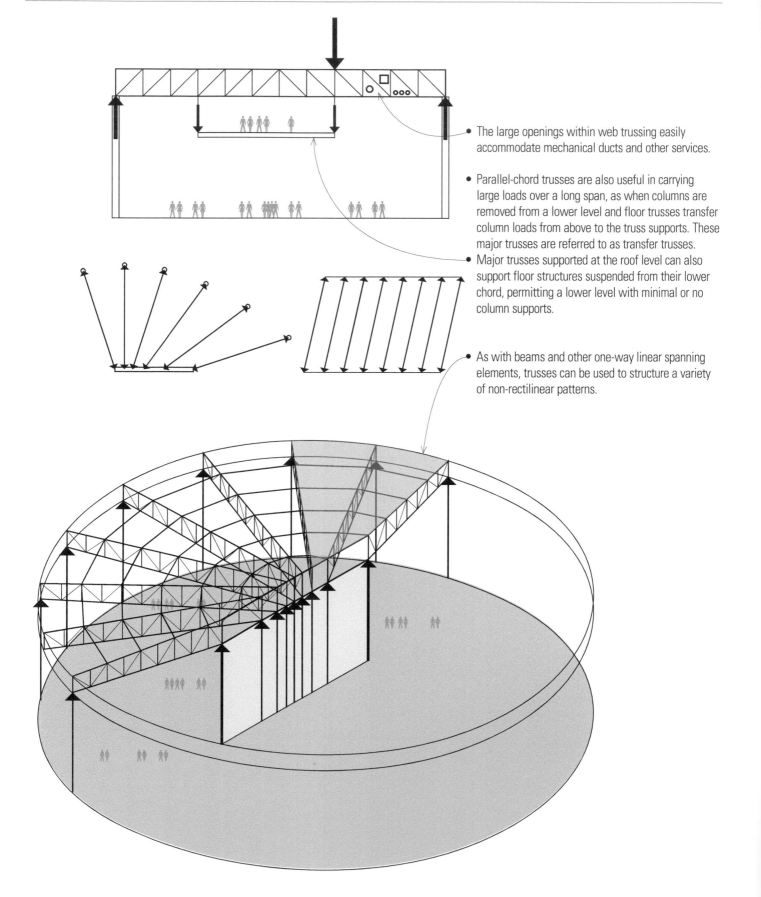

- The large openings within web trussing easily accommodate mechanical ducts and other services.

- Parallel-chord trusses are also useful in carrying large loads over a long span, as when columns are removed from a lower level and floor trusses transfer column loads from above to the truss supports. These major trusses are referred to as transfer trusses.

- Major trusses supported at the roof level can also support floor structures suspended from their lower chord, permitting a lower level with minimal or no column supports.

- As with beams and other one-way linear spanning elements, trusses can be used to structure a variety of non-rectilinear patterns.

Trusses are generally constructed out of timber, steel, and sometimes a combination of timber and steel. Due to its weight, concrete is seldom used for trusses. The decision to use timber or steel depends on the desired appearance, compatibility with the roof framing and roofing materials, and the required type of construction.

## Steel Trusses

Steel trusses are generally fabricated by welding or bolting structural angles and tees together to form the triangulated framework. Because of the slenderness of these truss members, connections usually require the use of steel gusset plates. Heavier steel trusses may utilize wide-flange shapes and structural tubing.

## Wood Trusses

In contrast to monoplanar trussed rafters, heavier wood trusses can be assembled by layering multiple members and joining them at the panel points with split-ring connectors. These wood trusses are capable of carrying greater loads than trussed rafters and are therefore spaced farther apart.

- To minimize secondary shear and bending stresses, the centroidal axes of truss members and the load at a joint should pass through a common node.
- Members are bolted or welded with gusset plate connectors.
- Any knee bracing should also connect to the top or bottom chord at a panel point.
- The cross sectional size of compression members, being governed by buckling, is larger than that of tension members, which is controlled by tensile stresses. It is better to place shorter truss members in compression and longer ones in tension.

- Solid wood members may be joined with steel plate connectors.
- Composite trusses have timber compression members and steel tension members.
- Member sizes and joint details are determined by engineering calculations based on truss type, load pattern, span, and grade and species of lumber used.

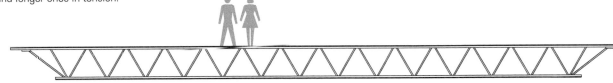

## Open-Web Joists

- Commercially manufactured open-web timber and steel joists are much lighter than regular trusses and are capable of spans up to 120 feet (37 m).
- Composite open-web joists have top and bottom wood chords and a web of diagonal steel tubing. Composite joists suitable for spans in excess of 60 feet (18.3 m) have depths from 32" to 46" (810 to 1170). Heavier weight composite joists range in depth from 36" to 60" (915 to 1525).

- The LH and DLH series of open-web steel joists are suitable for long-span applications. The LH series are suitable for the direct support of both floors and roof decks while the DLH series are suitable only for the direct support of roof decks.
- LH series joists have depths from 32" to 48" (810 to 1220) for spans in the 60- to 100-foot (18- to 30-m) range. The DLH-series ranges in depth from 52" to 72" (1320 to 1830) with spanning capabilities in the 60- to 140-foot (18.3- to 42.7-m) range.

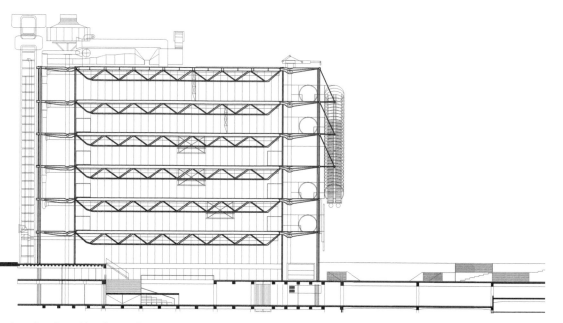

Partial plan and section: Pompidou Center, Paris, France, 1971–1977, Renzo Piano and Richard Rogers

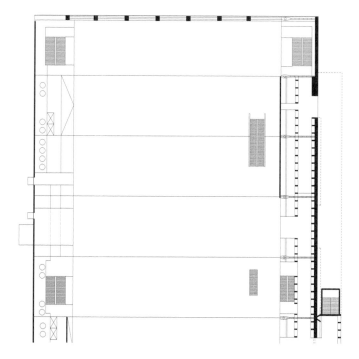

The major steel trusses of the Pompidou Center are spaced at 42-foot (12-m) intervals and span approximately 157 feet (48 m). On top of the supporting columns at each level are custom molded steel hangers, each measuring 26 feet (8 m) in length and weighing 20,000 pounds. Composite concrete and steel wide-flange beams span the major trusses.

The roof of the central space of the Phaeno Science Center (facing page) ⟶ is supported by a long-spanning space frame. The center's intricate forms were made possible by the use of advanced finite-element analysis modeling software developed by structural engineers Adams Kara Taylor. Complex forces within the entire structure were calculated and resolved as a single element, thus optimizing the integrity and material efficiency of the structure. If engineered in the traditional manner a few years ago, the structural systems would have been engineered separately, resulting in a significantly over-designed structure.

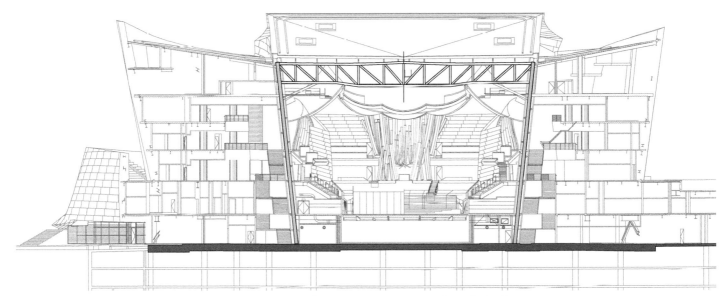

Section: Walt Disney Concert Hall, Los Angeles, California, 1991–2003, Frank Gehry/Gehry Partners

The Walt Disney Concert Hall is a complex steel framework of curves and shapes that required the use of a sophisticated software program developed for the French aerospace industry. The centerpiece of the building is the auditorium that is home to the Los Angeles Philharmonic and the Los Angeles Master Chorale. Long-span steel trusses span the large column-free space.

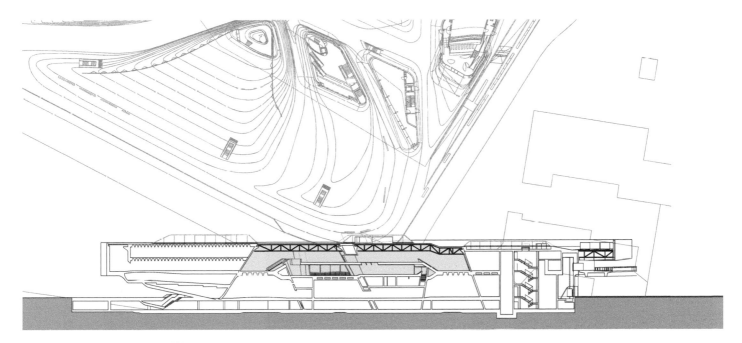

Section: Phaeno Science Center, Wolfsburg, Germany, 2005, Zaha Hadid Architects

## Space Trusses

A space truss is a one-way structure that can be visualized as two planar trusses meeting each other at the bottom chord with the top two chords being framed as a third truss. This three-dimensional truss is now capable of resisting vertical, horizontal, as well as torsional forces.

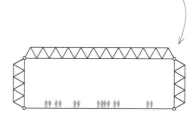

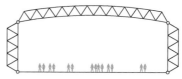

- Space trusses can be used to span long distances with a wide array of roof profiles. Bending moments and deflection can be effectively resisted by controlling the truss depth at critical points.

- The depth of space trusses fall in the range of span/5 to span/15, depending on the tributary load being carried and the magnitude of the deflection permitted for the long span.

- The spacing of space trusses depends on the spanning capability of secondary members. Loads from the secondary members should occur at panel joints to avoid inducing localized bending moments in the individual members.

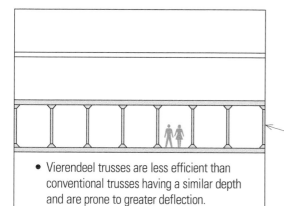

- Vierendeel trusses are less efficient than conventional trusses having a similar depth and are prone to greater deflection.
- Most Vierendeel trusses are a full story in height and the absence of diagonals allows them to be used in bays where circulation through the structure is necessary.

## Vierendeel Trusses

A Vierendeel truss has vertical web members rigidly connected to parallel top and bottom chords. Because it has no diagonals, it is not a true truss and behaves structurally as a rigid frame structure. The top chord resists compression forces while the bottom chord is stressed in tension, similar to a true truss. However, because no diagonals are present, the chords must also resist shear forces and bending moments develop at the joints between the chords and vertical web members.

The retractable roof of Safeco Field consists of three moveable panels covering an area of 9 acres when closed. The roof panels are supported by four space trusses that glide on 128 steel wheels powered by 96 ten-horsepower electric motors; a push of a button can close or open the roof in 10 to 20 minutes. For closing, roof panels 1 and 3, which span 631 feet (192 m) tuck inside panel 2, which spans 655 feet (200 m).

The roof was designed to support 80 to 90 psf or up to 7 feet (2.1 m) of snow and operate in sustained winds of up to 70 mph. The moveable trusses supporting the three roof panels have fixed moment connections on one side and pinned and dampened connections on the other side. This enables the roof to flex in high winds or during seismic events without overstressing truss components or carrying horizontal forces down to the runway tracks.

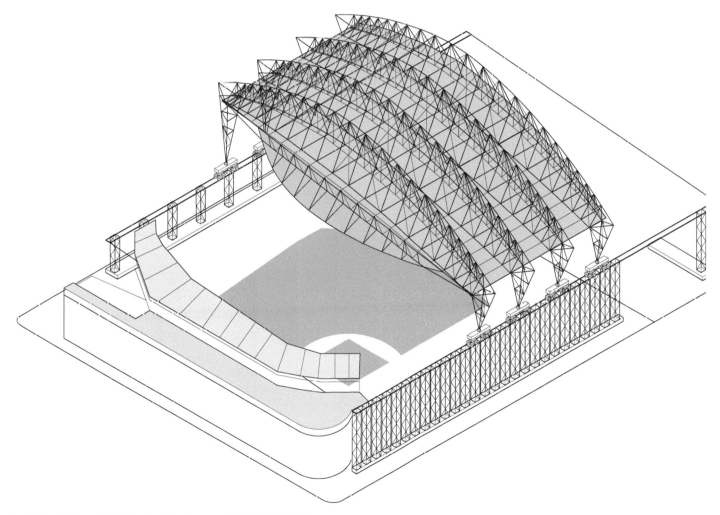

Aerial view: Safeco Field, Seattle, Washington, 1997–1999, NBBJ

Arches are designed to support vertical loads primarily by axial compression. They use their curvilinear form to transform the vertical forces of a supported load into inclined components and transmit them to abutments on either side of the archway.

## Fixed Arches

A fixed arch is designed as a continuous member, rigidly connected to both base supports. The arch must be designed to resist bending stresses throughout its length and at both of its supports. The shape of the fixed arch will generally exhibit a deeper section at the supports and a gradual decrease in the cross section at the crown. Fixed arches are generally constructed of reinforced, prestressed concrete or of steel sections.

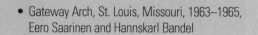

- Gateway Arch, St. Louis, Missouri, 1963–1965, Eero Saarinen and Hannskarl Bandel

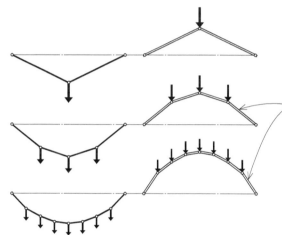

- While circular arches are generally easier to construct, funicular arches are subject to a minimum of bending stresses.
- A funicular arch is one that is shaped to develop only axial compression under a given loading. This shape may be found by inverting the funicular shape for a cable carrying a similar loading pattern.
- There is no single funicular shape for an arch since it may be subject to many possible load conditions. If the loading pattern for which a funicular arch is designed changes, it would be subject to bending.

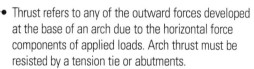

- Thrust refers to any of the outward forces developed at the base of an arch due to the horizontal force components of applied loads. Arch thrust must be resisted by a tension tie or abutments.
- The magnitude of the thrust produced is large for shallow (low rise-to-span ratio) arches and small for steep (high rise-to-span) arches.

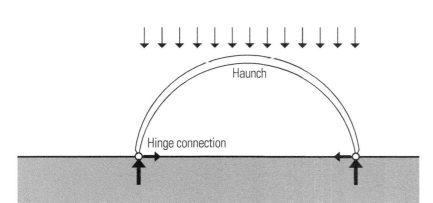

- Because the pinned connections develop no bending moments, they can usually be smaller in cross section and taper to the shoulder or haunch where the bending is largest and requires a larger section.
- Vertical loads are transferred to the members of a rigid frame through a combination of compression and bending, but because the frame develops a degree of arch action, horizontal thrust results at each base support. Specially designed abutments or tension ties are required for thrust resistance.

### Rigid Arches

Contemporary arches consist of curved rigid structures of timber, steel, or reinforced concrete capable of carrying some bending stresses. Their structural behavior resembles that of rigid or moment-resisting frames. The geometry of the curves that replace the straight segments of the gabled rigid frame affects not only the cost of construction but also the resulting stresses in the frame members since no single funicular arch shape is possible for all possible load conditions.

### Two-Hinged Arches

Two-hinged arches are designed as a continuous structure with pin connections at both base supports. The pin joints prevent high bending stresses from developing by allowing the frame to rotate as a unit when strained by support settlements, and to flex slightly when stressed by changes in temperature. They are generally designed to be thicker at the crown to allow the load path to vary while limiting the magnitude of the bending stresses and retaining an arch-like form. Glue-laminated timber, fabricated steel sections, wood and steel trusses, and concrete have all been used in the construction of two-hinged arches.

- The rigid arch is statically indeterminate and rigid only in its plane. A structural diaphragm or diagonal bracing is required to resist lateral forces in a perpendicular direction.

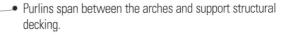

- Purlins span between the arches and support structural decking.
- Tension ties or abutments are required at the pin-connected base supports.

### Three-Hinged Arches

Three-hinged arches are structural assemblies of two rigid sections connected to each other at the crown and to the base supports with pin joints. While more sensitive to deflection than either fixed or two-hinged frames, three-hinged arches are least affected by support settlements and thermal stresses. An advantage of three-hinged arches over two-hinged arches is their ease of fabrication as two or more rigid parts, which can then be transported to the construction site to be joined and erected.

- Glue-laminated timber arches are capable of spanning from 100 to 250 feet (30 to 76 m) with a depth to span ratio of about span/40. Transportation from the fabrication site to the construction site may be the limiting factor.
- Steel arches are capable of spanning in excess of 500 feet (152 m), especially if a trussed-arch system is used. Their depth range varies from span/50 to span/100.
- Concrete arches can span up to 300 feet (91 m) and have a depth range of about span/50.

- Long-span arches behave like rigid frames and may have either arched or gabled profiles.
- Applied loads produce axial, bending, and shear forces in all members of a rigid frame because the use of moment-resisting joints restrain the ends of members from rotating freely.
- Vertical loads are transferred to the vertical members of a rigid frame through a combination of compression and bending, but because the frame develops a degree of arch action, horizontal thrust results at each base support. Specially designed abutments or tension ties are required for thrust resistance.

- Purlins span between the three-hinged arches and support structural decking.

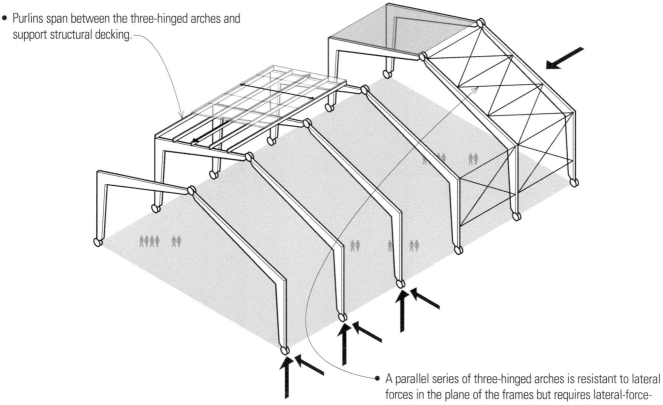

- A parallel series of three-hinged arches is resistant to lateral forces in the plane of the frames but requires lateral-force-resisting systems in the perpendicular direction.

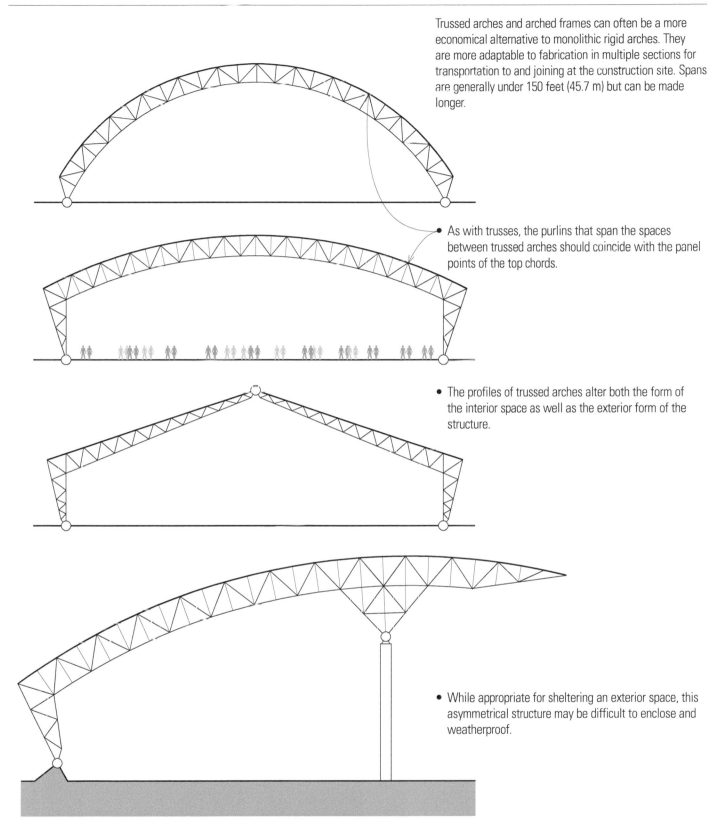

Trussed arches and arched frames can often be a more economical alternative to monolithic rigid arches. They are more adaptable to fabrication in multiple sections for transportation to and joining at the construction site. Spans are generally under 150 feet (45.7 m) but can be made longer.

• As with trusses, the purlins that span the spaces between trussed arches should coincide with the panel points of the top chords.

• The profiles of trussed arches alter both the form of the interior space as well as the exterior form of the structure.

• While appropriate for sheltering an exterior space, this asymmetrical structure may be difficult to enclose and weatherproof.

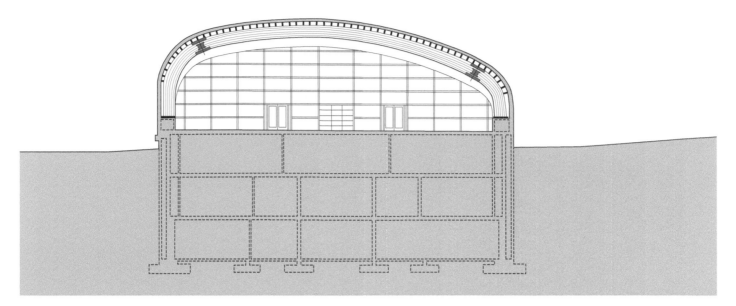

LeMay—America's Car Museum, Tacoma, Washington, 2012, Large Architecture, Engineer: Western Wood Structures

The arch-shaped glue-laminated members that form the soaring roof of America's Car Museum represent one of the world's largest wood moment-frame systems. The arched timbers vary in size to accommodate the asymmetrical roof taper at the front and rear of the structure. Because the roof curves in two directions, each of the 757 purlins were cut to unique dimensions.

Special steel connections were designed to provide ductility in the arch systems, allowing the steel to yield plastically during a seismic event. The aim was to prevent the glue-laminated members from failing in a brittle fashion.

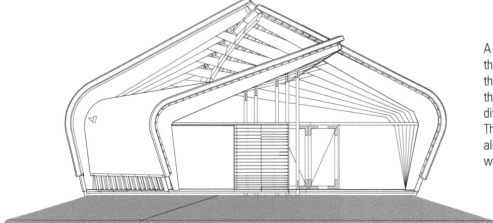

A limited budget led the architects to use three-hinged arched frames, patterned after those often used in local barn structures. All of the bents are identical but tilted at a slightly different angle relative to the ground plane. The resulting shifting and twisted roof surfaces almost meet along a fractured ridge line, which is glazed to admit indirect daylight.

Section: The Imagination Art Pavilion, Zeewolde, Netherlands, 2000, René van Zuuk

Aerial view and transverse section: Olympic Velodrome, Athens, Greece, 2004 (renovation of original 1991 structure), Santiago Calatrava

The roof structure of the Olympic Velodrome is composed of two massive tubular arches, each weighing 4000 tons, from which 40 transverse ribs are suspended. There are 23 unique ribs, each used twice in the symmetrical structure. The last three ribs at each end are supported by the rim tube. The doubled cables from the upper arch not only carry part of the roof load but also help stabilize the structure laterally through its triangulated geometry.

# CABLE STRUCTURES

Cable structures use the cable as the principal means of support. Because cables have high tensile strength but offer no resistance to compression or bending, they must be used purely in tension. When subject to concentrated loads, the shape of a cable consists of straight-line segments. Under a uniformly distributed load, it will take on the shape of an inverted arch.

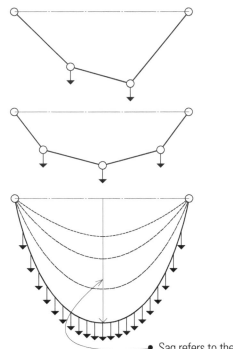

- A funicular shape is one that is assumed by a freely deforming cable in direct response to the magnitude and location of external forces. A cable always adapts its shape so that it is in pure tension under the action of an applied load.
- A catenary is the curve assumed by a perfectly flexible, uniform cable suspended freely from two points not in the same vertical line. For a load that is uniformly distributed in a horizontal projection, the curve approaches that of a parabola.

- Single-cable structures must be carefully designed for uplift due to wind gusts and turbulence. Flutter or vibration present serious concerns in relatively light tensile structures.

- Sag refers to the vertical distance from the supports to the lowest point of a cable structure. As the sag of a cable increases, the internal forces developed in the cable decrease. Cable structures generally have sag:span ratios between 1:8 and 1:10.

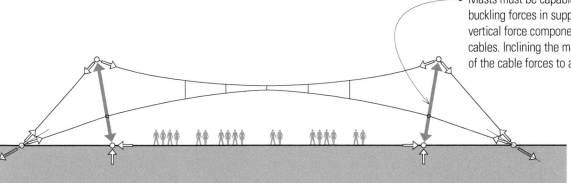

- Double-cable structures have upper and lower sets of cables of different curvatures, pretensioned by ties or compression struts to make the system more rigid and resistant to flutter.

- Guy cables absorb the horizontal component of thrust in a suspension or cable-stayed structure and transfer the force to a ground foundation.
- Rings or umbrellas distribute the cable forces to the mast.
- Masts must be capable of resisting compressive buckling forces in supporting the sum of the vertical force components in the primary and guy cables. Inclining the mast enables the resultant of the cable forces to act through its axis.

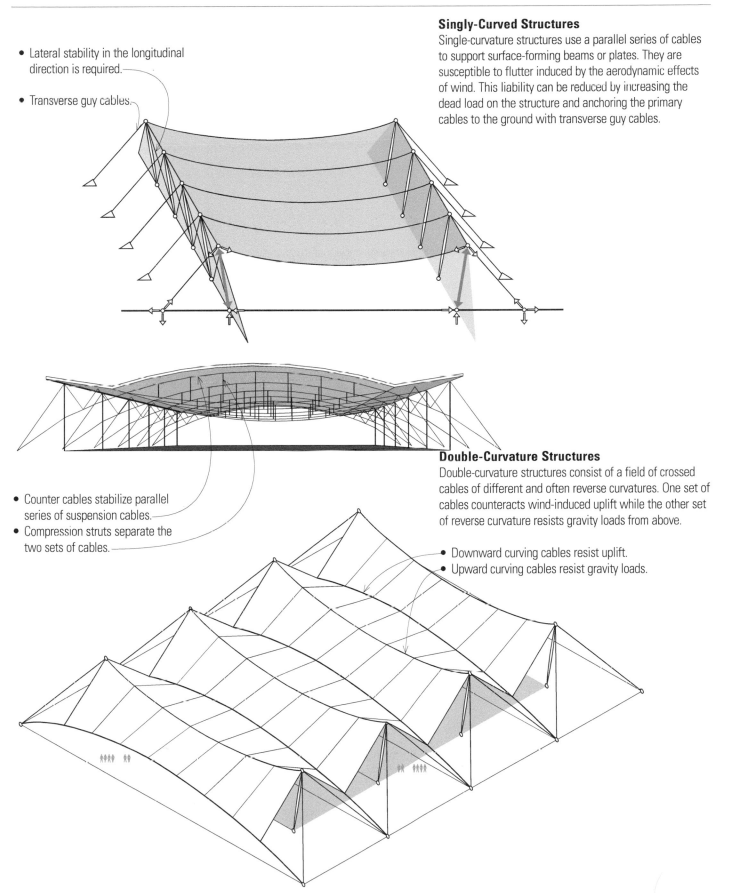

### Singly-Curved Structures

Single-curvature structures use a parallel series of cables to support surface-forming beams or plates. They are susceptible to flutter induced by the aerodynamic effects of wind. This liability can be reduced by increasing the dead load on the structure and anchoring the primary cables to the ground with transverse guy cables.

- Lateral stability in the longitudinal direction is required.
- Transverse guy cables.

- Counter cables stabilize parallel series of suspension cables.
- Compression struts separate the two sets of cables.

### Double-Curvature Structures

Double-curvature structures consist of a field of crossed cables of different and often reverse curvatures. One set of cables counteracts wind-induced uplift while the other set of reverse curvature resists gravity loads from above.

- Downward curving cables resist uplift.
- Upward curving cables resist gravity loads.

# CABLE STRUCTURES

Structural cables of high-strength steel can be stretched, crisscrossed, and combined with surfacing materials to achieve relatively lightweight, long-span roof structures. Illustrated on this page are three of the numerous cable structure configurations that are possible.

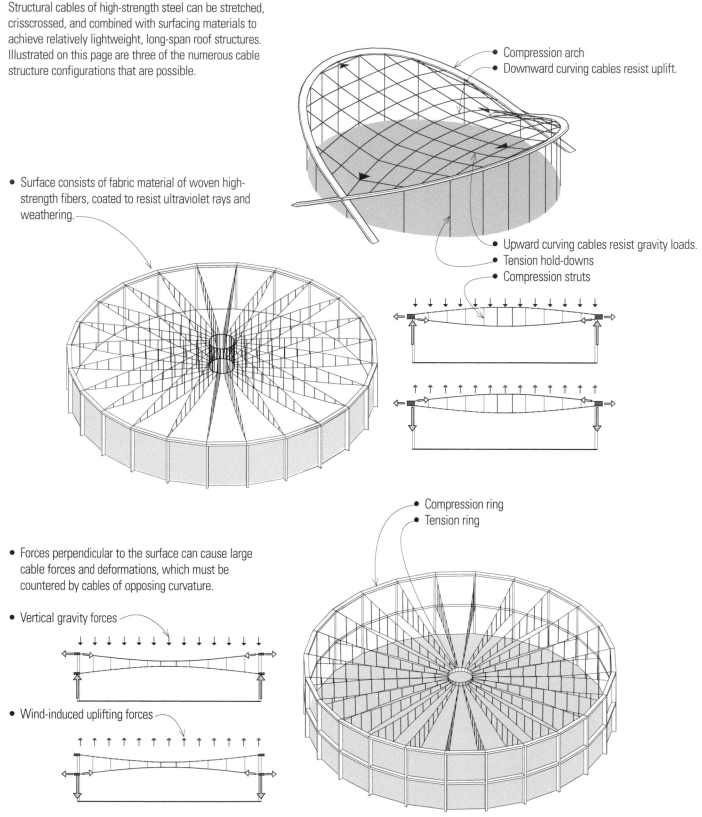

- Compression arch
- Downward curving cables resist uplift.

- Surface consists of fabric material of woven high-strength fibers, coated to resist ultraviolet rays and weathering.

- Upward curving cables resist gravity loads.
- Tension hold-downs
- Compression struts

- Compression ring
- Tension ring

- Forces perpendicular to the surface can cause large cable forces and deformations, which must be countered by cables of opposing curvature.

- Vertical gravity forces

- Wind-induced uplifting forces

- Ponding rainwater or drifting snow can cause localized or unbalanced loading on roof structure.

## Cable-Stayed Structures

Cable-stayed structures consist of towers or masts from which cables extend to support horizontally spanning members. The cables must have not only sufficient capacity to carry the dead load of a structure, but also enough reserve capacity to carry the live load as well. The supported structural surface must be sufficiently stiff to transfer or resist the lateral and torsional stresses induced by wind, unbalanced live loads, and the normal force created by the upward pull of the stays.

The cable stays are usually attached symmetrically to a single tower or mast with an equal number of stays on both sides so that the horizontal force component of the inclined cables will cancel each other out and minimize the moment at the top of the tower or mast.

There are two primary cable configurations: radial or fan patterns and parallel or harp systems. Radial systems attach the upper ends of the cable stays to a single point at the top of the tower, while parallel systems secure the upper ends of the cable stays to the mast at different heights. The radial system is usually preferred because the single point of attachment minimizes the bending moment in the tower.

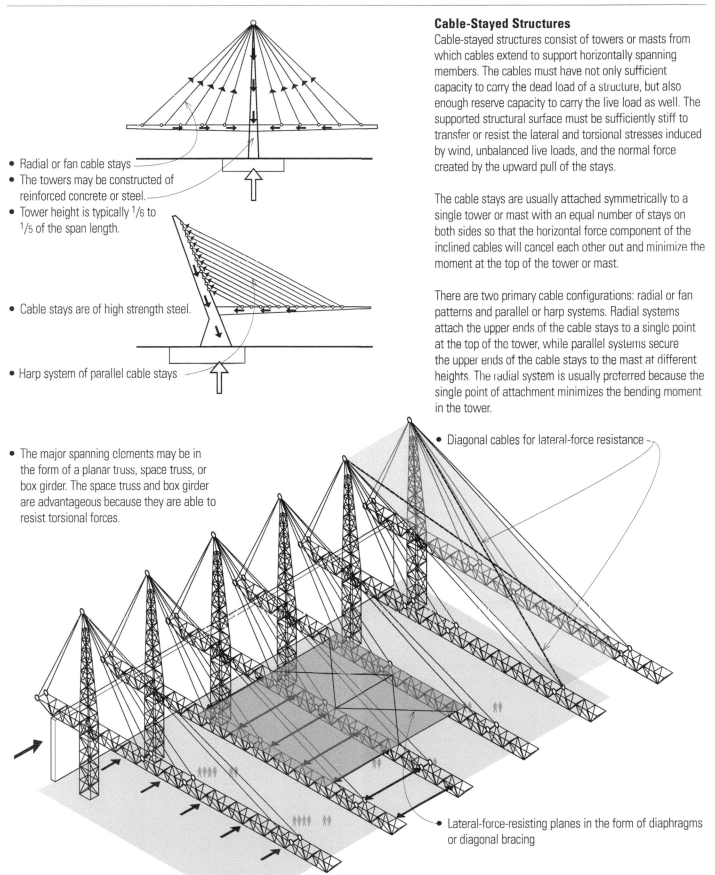

- Radial or fan cable stays
- The towers may be constructed of reinforced concrete or steel.
- Tower height is typically $1/6$ to $1/5$ of the span length.

- Cable stays are of high strength steel.

- Harp system of parallel cable stays

- The major spanning elements may be in the form of a planar truss, space truss, or box girder. The space truss and box girder are advantageous because they are able to resist torsional forces.

- Diagonal cables for lateral-force resistance

- Lateral-force-resisting planes in the form of diaphragms or diagonal bracing

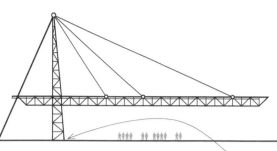

This cable-stayed structure supports a very large roof area with a minimal amount of supporting structure at the ground level. However, large uplifting wind forces may require a restraint system along the overhanging roof edge.

• Large gravity loads and possible overturning moments require a substantial foundation.

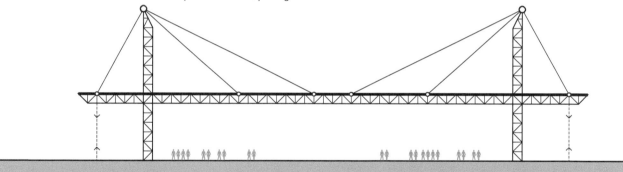

The cable-stayed structure defines large column-free spaces to either the side of the central support system. Tension members or hold-downs are required to resist uplifting wind forces.

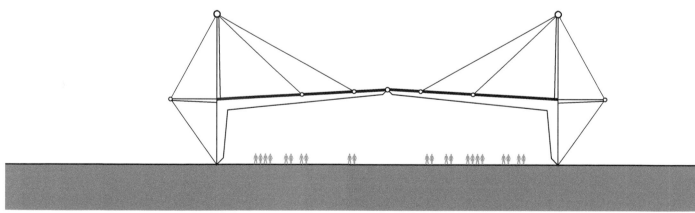

This cable-stayed system uses two of the structures in the top example to increase the coverage and provide a very large column-free space.

This concept uses a three-hinged frame whose horizontal span is increased through the use of the cable stays.

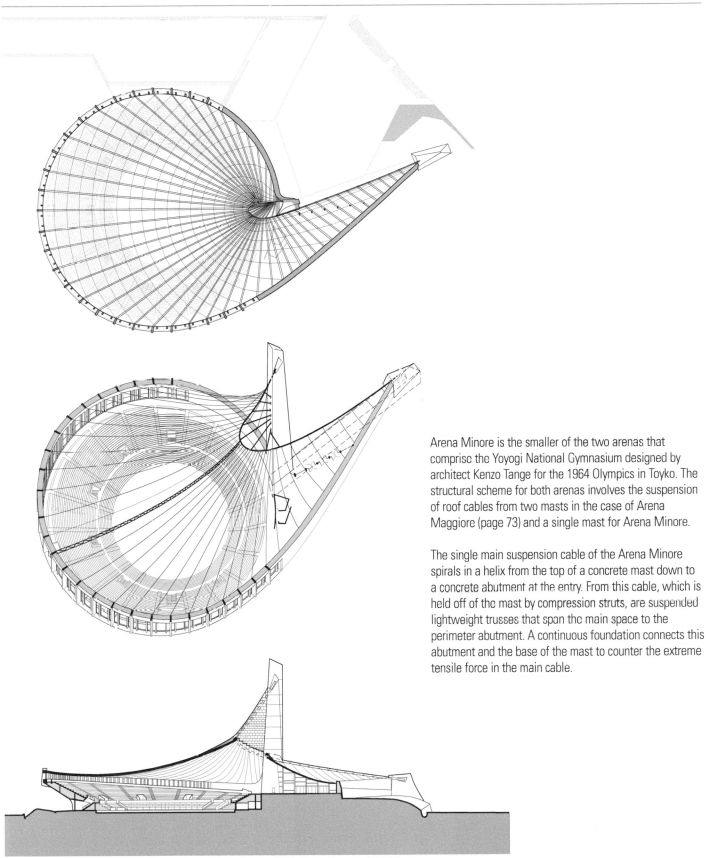

Arena Minore is the smaller of the two arenas that comprise the Yoyogi National Gymnasium designed by architect Kenzo Tange for the 1964 Olympics in Toyko. The structural scheme for both arenas involves the suspension of roof cables from two masts in the case of Arena Maggiore (page 73) and a single mast for Arena Minore.

The single main suspension cable of the Arena Minore spirals in a helix from the top of a concrete mast down to a concrete abutment at the entry. From this cable, which is held off of the mast by compression struts, are suspended lightweight trusses that span the main space to the perimeter abutment. A continuous foundation connects this abutment and the base of the mast to counter the extreme tensile force in the main cable.

Arena Minore, Yoyogi National Gymnasium, Tokyo, Japan, 1964, Kenzo Tange + URTEC

### Membrane Structures

Membrane structures consist of thin, flexible surfaces that carry loads primarily through the development of tensile stresses.

Tent structures are membrane structures prestressed by externally applied forces so that they are held completely taut under all anticipated load conditions. To avoid extremely high tensile forces, a membrane structure should have relatively sharp curvatures in opposite directions.

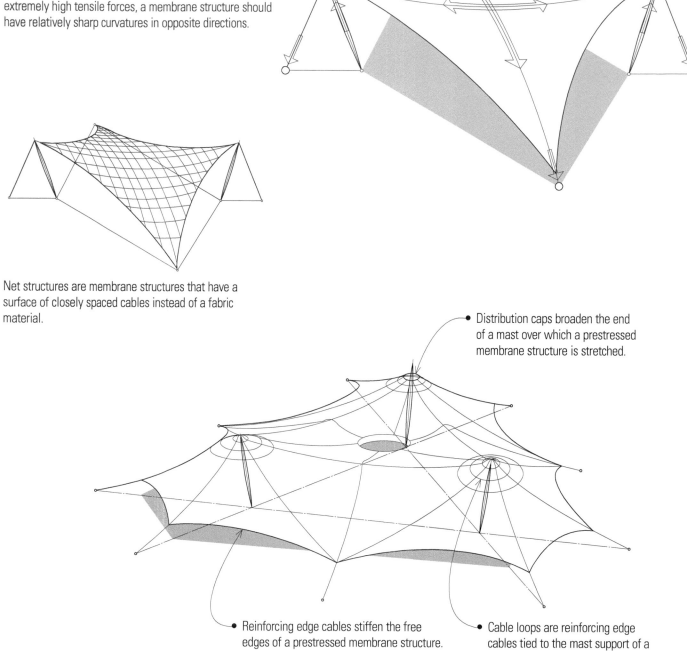

Net structures are membrane structures that have a surface of closely spaced cables instead of a fabric material.

• Distribution caps broaden the end of a mast over which a prestressed membrane structure is stretched.

• Reinforcing edge cables stiffen the free edges of a prestressed membrane structure.

• Cable loops are reinforcing edge cables tied to the mast support of a membrane structure.

Pneumatic structures are membrane structures that are placed in tension and stabilized by the pressure of compressed air.

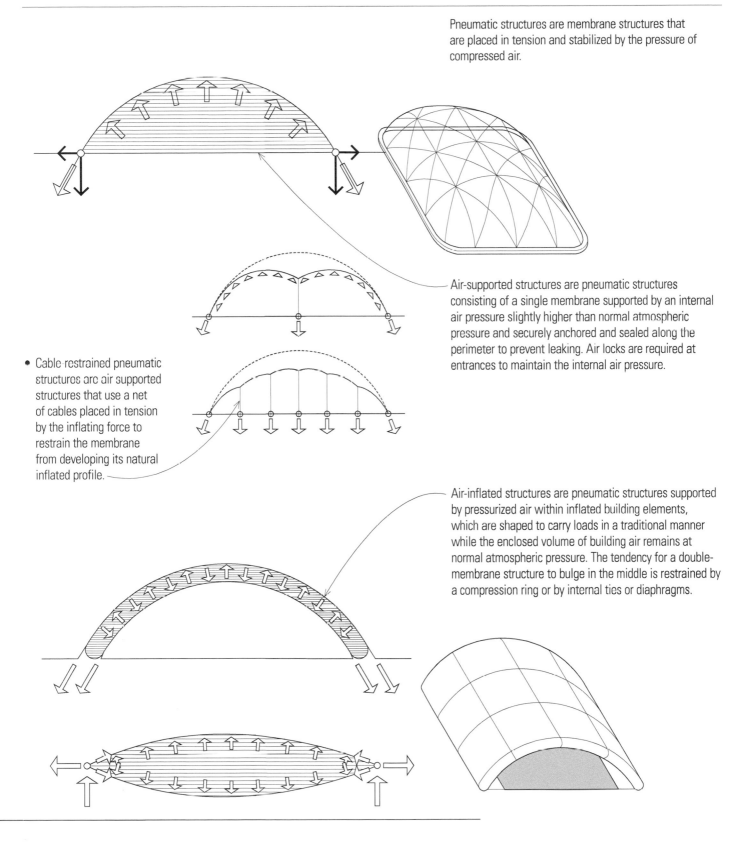

Air-supported structures are pneumatic structures consisting of a single membrane supported by an internal air pressure slightly higher than normal atmospheric pressure and securely anchored and sealed along the perimeter to prevent leaking. Air locks are required at entrances to maintain the internal air pressure.

• Cable-restrained pneumatic structures are air-supported structures that use a net of cables placed in tension by the inflating force to restrain the membrane from developing its natural inflated profile.

Air-inflated structures are pneumatic structures supported by pressurized air within inflated building elements, which are shaped to carry loads in a traditional manner while the enclosed volume of building air remains at normal atmospheric pressure. The tendency for a double-membrane structure to bulge in the middle is restrained by a compression ring or by internal ties or diaphragms.

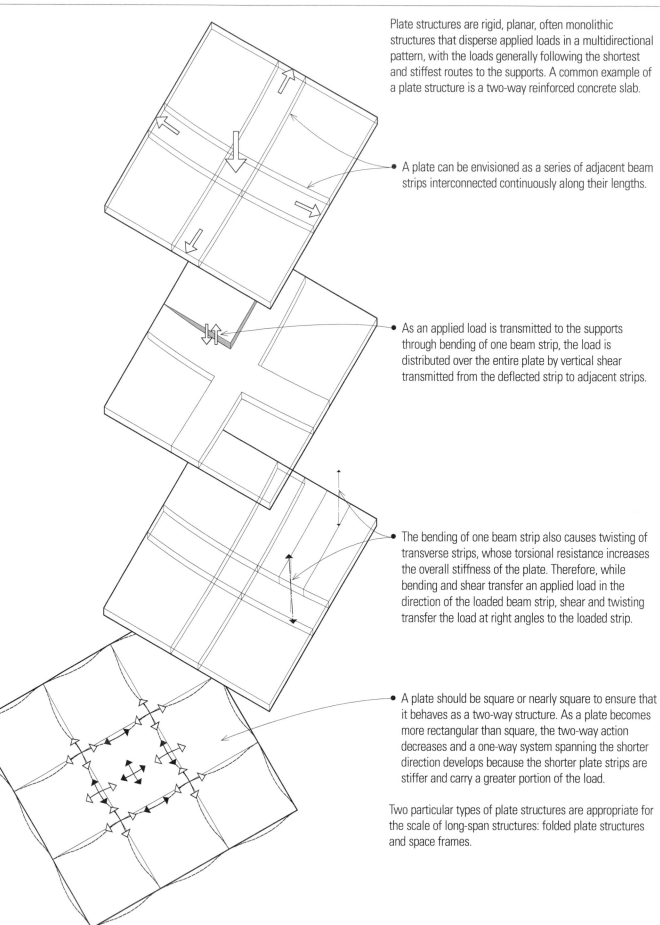

Plate structures are rigid, planar, often monolithic structures that disperse applied loads in a multidirectional pattern, with the loads generally following the shortest and stiffest routes to the supports. A common example of a plate structure is a two-way reinforced concrete slab.

• A plate can be envisioned as a series of adjacent beam strips interconnected continuously along their lengths.

• As an applied load is transmitted to the supports through bending of one beam strip, the load is distributed over the entire plate by vertical shear transmitted from the deflected strip to adjacent strips.

• The bending of one beam strip also causes twisting of transverse strips, whose torsional resistance increases the overall stiffness of the plate. Therefore, while bending and shear transfer an applied load in the direction of the loaded beam strip, shear and twisting transfer the load at right angles to the loaded strip.

• A plate should be square or nearly square to ensure that it behaves as a two-way structure. As a plate becomes more rectangular than square, the two-way action decreases and a one-way system spanning the shorter direction develops because the shorter plate strips are stiffer and carry a greater portion of the load.

Two particular types of plate structures are appropriate for the scale of long-span structures: folded plate structures and space frames.

## Folded Plate Structures

Folded plate structures are composed of thin, deep elements joined rigidly along their boundaries and forming sharp angles to brace each other against lateral buckling.

- Vertical diaphragms or rigid frames stiffen a folded plate against deformation of the fold profile. The resulting stiffness of the cross section enables a folded plate to span relatively long distances.

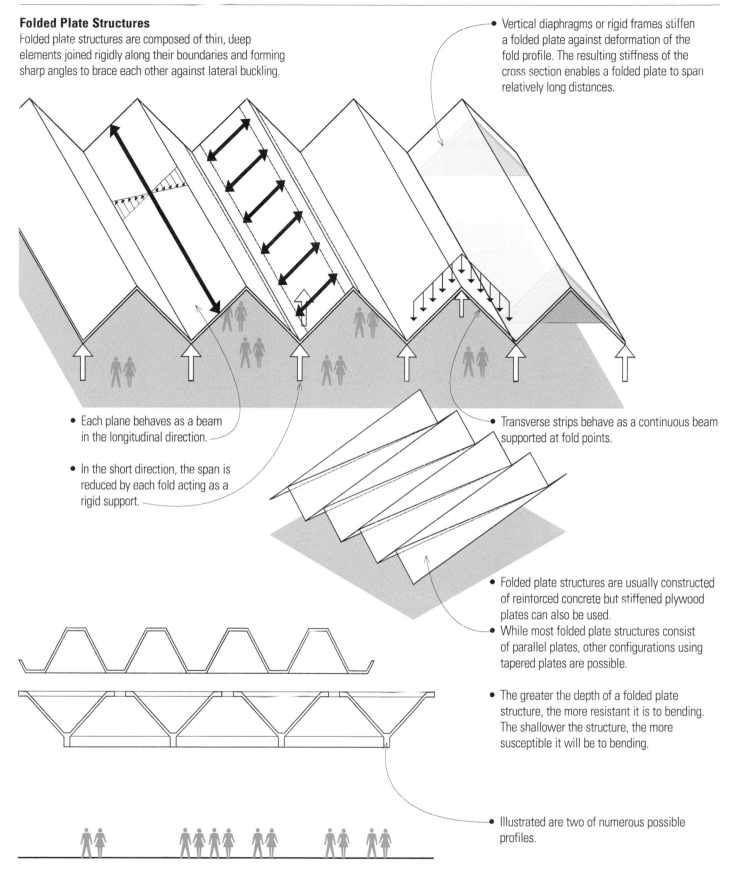

- Each plane behaves as a beam in the longitudinal direction.

- In the short direction, the span is reduced by each fold acting as a rigid support.

- Transverse strips behave as a continuous beam supported at fold points.

- Folded plate structures are usually constructed of reinforced concrete but stiffened plywood plates can also be used.
- While most folded plate structures consist of parallel plates, other configurations using tapered plates are possible.

- The greater the depth of a folded plate structure, the more resistant it is to bending. The shallower the structure, the more susceptible it will be to bending.

- Illustrated are two of numerous possible profiles.

- One of the simplest spatial units of a space frame is a square-based pyramid having five sides and five joints.
- Space frames may be constructed of structural steel pipe, tubing, channels, tees, or W-shapes.

- Members may be joined with welded, bolted, or threaded connectors.

### Space Frames

Space frames are three-dimensional structural frames based on the rigidity of the triangle and composed of linear elements subject only to axial tension or compression. The relatively lightweight, long-span structures are used primarily for roof construction and often at least partially glazed for natural daylighting. The constituent parts can be assembled on-site at the ground level and lifted or jacked into position; no large equipment is required for erection. As with plate structures, the supporting bay for a space frame should be square or nearly square to ensure that it acts as a two-way structure.

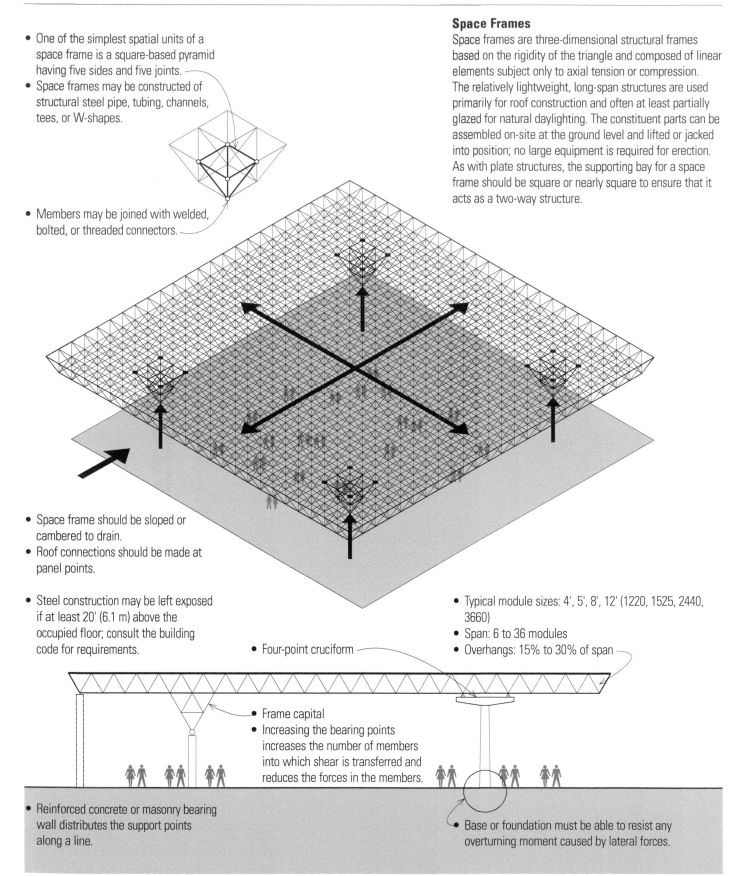

- Space frame should be sloped or cambered to drain.
- Roof connections should be made at panel points.

- Steel construction may be left exposed if at least 20' (6.1 m) above the occupied floor; consult the building code for requirements.

- Four-point cruciform

- Typical module sizes: 4', 5', 8', 12' (1220, 1525, 2440, 3660)
- Span: 6 to 36 modules
- Overhangs: 15% to 30% of span

- Frame capital
- Increasing the bearing points increases the number of members into which shear is transferred and reduces the forces in the members.

- Reinforced concrete or masonry bearing wall distributes the support points along a line.

- Base or foundation must be able to resist any overturning moment caused by lateral forces.

Shells are thin, curved plate structures typically constructed of reinforced concrete and used for the roofs of buildings. They are shaped to transmit applied forces by membrane stresses—the compressive, tensile, and shear stresses acting in the plane of their surfaces. A shell can sustain relatively large forces if uniformly applied. Because of its thinness, however, a shell has little bending resistance and is unsuitable for concentrated loads.

### Types of Shell Surfaces

- Translational surfaces are generated by sliding a plane curve along a straight line or over another plane curve.

- Barrel shells are cylindrical shell structures. If the length of a barrel shell is three or more times its transverse span, it behaves as a deep beam with a curved section spanning in the longitudinal direction.
- If it is relatively short, it exhibits archlike action. Tie rods or transverse rigid frames are required to counteract the outward thrusts of the arching action.

- Ruled surfaces are generated by the motion of a straight line. Because of its straight-line geometry, a ruled surface is generally easier to form and construct than a rotational or translational surface.

- A hyperbolic paraboloid or hypar is a surface generated by sliding a parabola with downward curvature along a parabola with upward curvature, or by sliding a straight line segment with its ends on two skew lines. It can be considered to be both a translational and a ruled surface.
- Saddle surfaces have an upward curvature in one direction and a downward curvature in the perpendicular direction. In a saddle-surfaced shell structure, regions of downward curvature exhibit archlike action, while regions of upward curvature behave as a cable structure. If the edges of the surface are not supported, beam behavior may also be present.

- Rotational surfaces are generated by rotating a plane curve about an axis. Spherical, elliptical, and parabolic dome surfaces are examples of rotational surfaces.

Any number of formal and spatial compositions
can be created by combining geometric surfaces.
For constructibility, the intersection of any two
shells should be coincident and continuous.

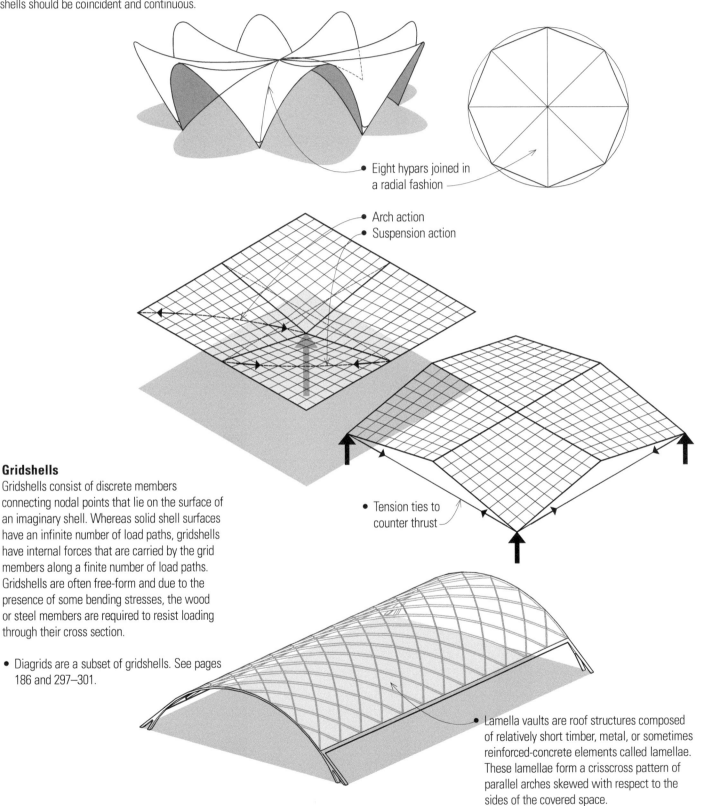

- Eight hypars joined in
  a radial fashion

- Arch action
- Suspension action

- Tension ties to
  counter thrust

## Gridshells

Gridshells consist of discrete members
connecting nodal points that lie on the surface of
an imaginary shell. Whereas solid shell surfaces
have an infinite number of load paths, gridshells
have internal forces that are carried by the grid
members along a finite number of load paths.
Gridshells are often free-form and due to the
presence of some bending stresses, the wood
or steel members are required to resist loading
through their cross section.

- Diagrids are a subset of gridshells. See pages
  186 and 297–301.

- Lamella vaults are roof structures composed
  of relatively short timber, metal, or sometimes
  reinforced-concrete elements called lamellae.
  These lamellae form a crisscross pattern of
  parallel arches skewed with respect to the
  sides of the covered space.

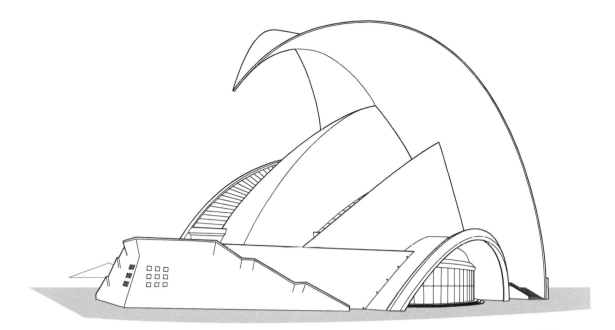

Tenerife Concert Hall is a reinforced concrete structure that houses a main auditorium that seats 1600 and a smaller chamber music hall that seats 400. The cantilevered roof shell, constructed from two intersecting cone segments and designed to be supported on only five points, soars to a height of 190 feet (58 m) over the main auditorium before curving downward to a point. The symmetrical inner shell of the concert hall, 165 feet (50 m) high, is a rotational body, generated by rotating a curve to describe an ellipse. A wedge of approximately 15° has been removed from the center of this body so that its two segments form a pronounced ridge like that of a folded plate. Wide arches spanning 165 feet (50 m) on each side serve as the artists' entrances.

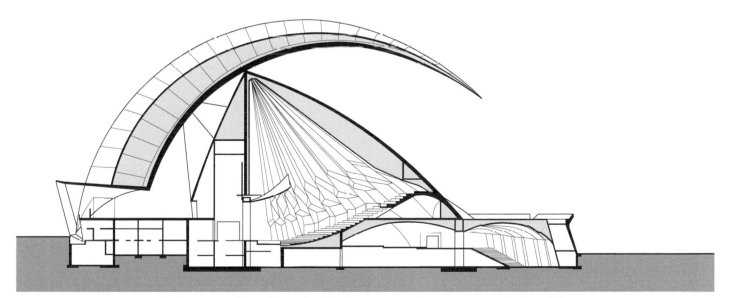

Exterior view and section: Tenerife Concert Hall, Santa Cruz de Tenerife, Canary Islands, Spain, 1997–2003, Santiago Calatrava

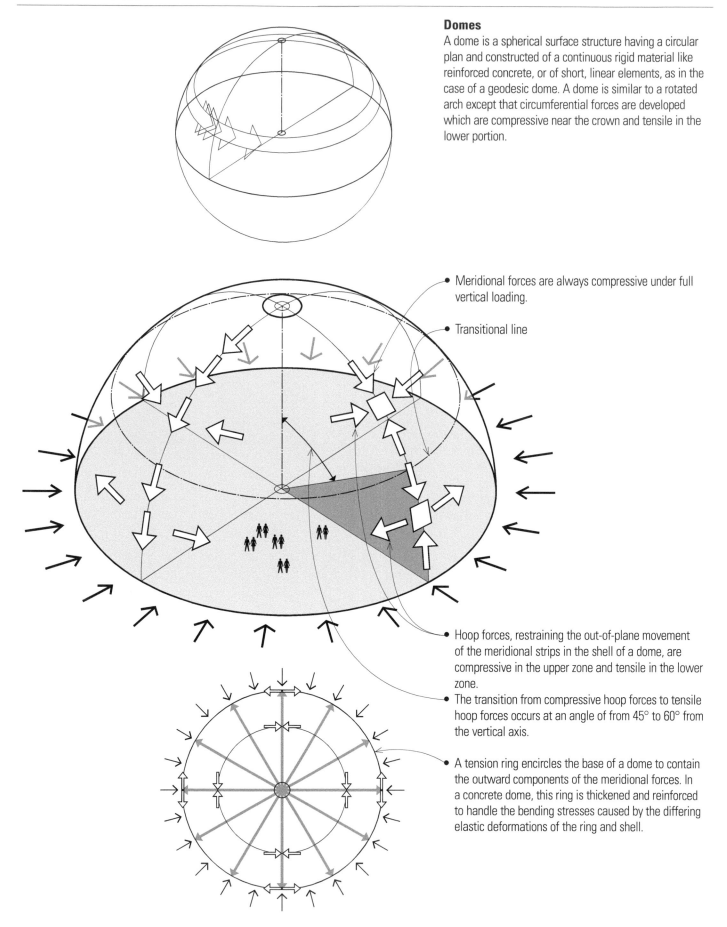

### Domes

A dome is a spherical surface structure having a circular plan and constructed of a continuous rigid material like reinforced concrete, or of short, linear elements, as in the case of a geodesic dome. A dome is similar to a rotated arch except that circumferential forces are developed which are compressive near the crown and tensile in the lower portion.

• Meridional forces are always compressive under full vertical loading.

• Transitional line

• Hoop forces, restraining the out-of-plane movement of the meridional strips in the shell of a dome, are compressive in the upper zone and tensile in the lower zone.

• The transition from compressive hoop forces to tensile hoop forces occurs at an angle of from 45° to 60° from the vertical axis.

• A tension ring encircles the base of a dome to contain the outward components of the meridional forces. In a concrete dome, this ring is thickened and reinforced to handle the bending stresses caused by the differing elastic deformations of the ring and shell.

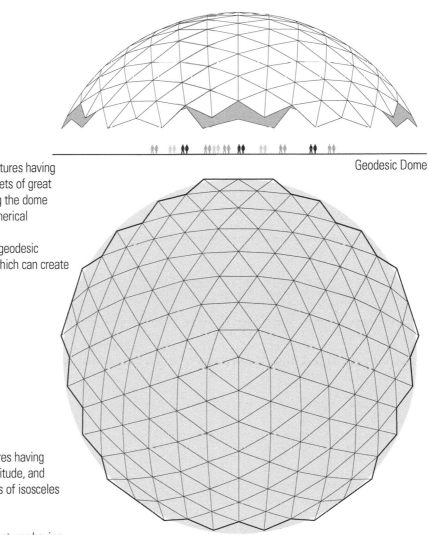

Geodesic Dome

- Geodesic domes are steel dome structures having members that follow three principal sets of great circles intersecting at 60°, subdividing the dome surface into a series of equilateral spherical triangles.

- Unlike lattice and Schwedler domes, geodesic domes have irregular base profiles, which can create difficult support conditions.

- Lattice domes are steel dome structures having members that follow the circles of latitude, and two sets of diagonals forming a series of isosceles triangles.

- Schwedler domes are steel dome structures having members that follow the lines of latitude and longitude, and a third set of diagonals completing the triangulation.

Lattice Dome

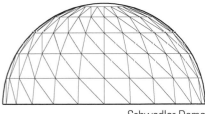

Schwedler Dome

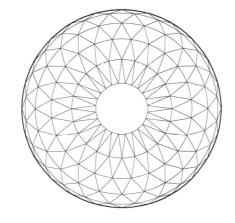

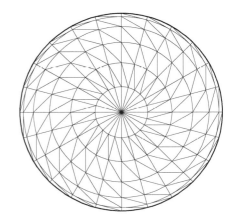

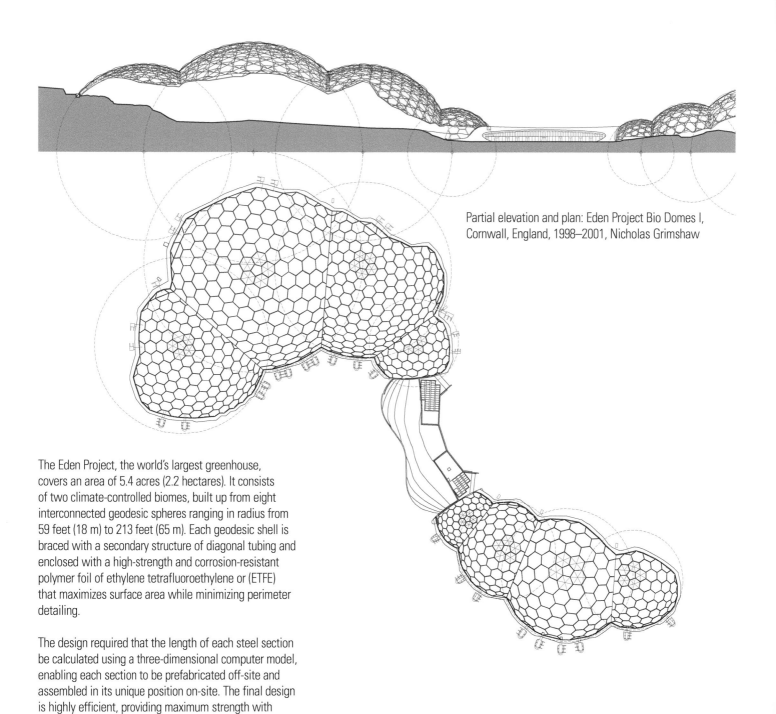

Partial elevation and plan: Eden Project Bio Domes I, Cornwall, England, 1998–2001, Nicholas Grimshaw

The Eden Project, the world's largest greenhouse, covers an area of 5.4 acres (2.2 hectares). It consists of two climate-controlled biomes, built up from eight interconnected geodesic spheres ranging in radius from 59 feet (18 m) to 213 feet (65 m). Each geodesic shell is braced with a secondary structure of diagonal tubing and enclosed with a high-strength and corrosion-resistant polymer foil of ethylene tetrafluoroethylene or (ETFE) that maximizes surface area while minimizing perimeter detailing.

The design required that the length of each steel section be calculated using a three-dimensional computer model, enabling each section to be prefabricated off-site and assembled in its unique position on-site. The final design is highly efficient, providing maximum strength with minimum steelwork and defining maximum volume with minimum surface area.

# 7
# High-Rise Structures

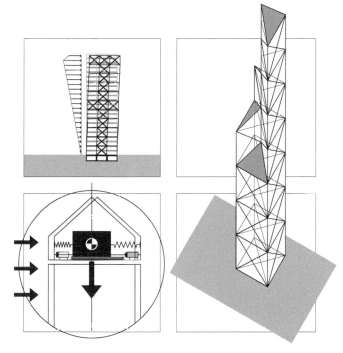

# HIGH-RISE STRUCTURES

Building engineers, architects, builders, inspectors, and related professions often define a high-rise as a building that is at least ten stories or more, or one that rises to a height of 100 feet (30 m) or more. Building codes may refer to a certain height above the lowest level of fire department vehicle access. The Council on Tall Buildings, however, defines a high-rise as follows:

A tall building is not defined by its height or number of stories. The important criterion is whether or not the design is influenced by some aspect of "tallness." It is a building in which "tallness" strongly influences planning, design and use. It is a building whose height creates different conditions in the design, construction, and operation from those that exist in "common" buildings of a certain region and period.

From this definition, we can see that a tall building is not just defined by its height alone but by its proportions.

The same basic principles of structural design apply to high-rise buildings as for any other type of construction. Individual members and the overall structure must be designed for adequate strength under gravity and lateral loads and there needs to be enough stiffness built into the structure to restrict deflections to acceptable levels. Nevertheless, the structural systems of high-rise buildings tend to be dominated by the need to resist lateral forces. The provisions for lateral force strength, drift control, dynamic behavior, and resistance to overturning overshadow the provisions for gravity load-carrying ability.

- The effects of lateral forces on a structure increase significantly with its height and slenderness.

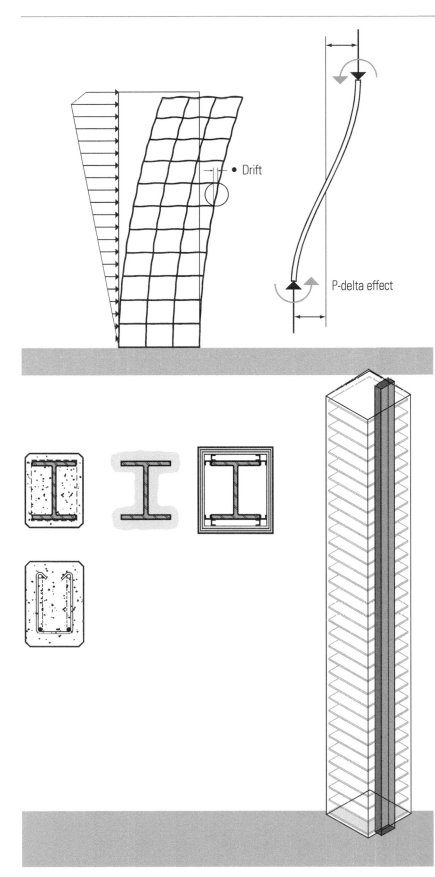

- Drift

P-delta effect

Lateral deflection or drift can become very large as the height of a building increases. Excessive deflections can cause elevators to become misaligned and occupants to have adverse reactions to the movement. The two primary causes of lateral deflections and vibrations are wind load and seismic forces. Another factor that cannot be ignored is the temperature differential, between the inside and outside, and between the sunny and shady sides of a building.

As tall structures are displaced from a true and plumb position, the weight of the structure, displaced from the neutral center position, contributes an additional overturning moment. The magnitude of this additional moment is commonly in the order of 10% of the moment creating the original displacement. This potentially serious phenomenon is known as the P-delta effect.

The construction materials for high-rise buildings are varied and are used most often in combination: structural steel, reinforced concrete, and prestressed concrete.

The quantity of structural material required per square foot of floor of a high-rise building exceeds the requirements for low- and medium-rise buildings. The vertical load carrying elements—columns, walls, and shafts—need strengthening over the entire height of the building and the quantity of materials required for lateral load resistance is even more significant.

Since the floor systems in high-rise buildings are typically repetitive in nature, the structural depth of the floor system can have a major impact on the building design. Saving a few inches per floor level can add up to an accumulation of many feet in the building. This will affect the cost of elevators, wall cladding, and other subsystems. Any weight added to the floor systems will also increase the size and cost of the foundation system.

To these supplemental costs must be added the increase in cost of the building services, primarily the vertical transportation system. The cost of the net usable floor area is further increased by the space required for the vertical transportation system, which increases with the height of the building. This increase in size of the vertical transportation core, however, can be used as an important part of the vertical and lateral load-carrying strategy.

## Gravity Loads

The vertical components carrying the vertical gravity loads of a high-rise structure, such as columns, core shafts, and bearing walls, need to be strengthened over the full height of the building due to the accumulating nature of the loads from the roof level down to the foundation. The quantity of structural materials therefore necessarily increases as the number of stories of a high-rise building increases.

The increase in weight for gravity loads is much greater for concrete than for steel-framed high-rise structures. This increase can be an advantage since the dead weight of the concrete structure assists in resisting the overturning effects of wind forces. On the other hand, the larger mass of a concrete building can be a liability during an earthquake, producing a greater overall lateral force during the seismic event.

In contrast to the vertical gravity-load-carrying elements, which need strengthening, the horizontal spanning floor and roof systems for high-rise structures are similar to those for low- and medium-rise buildings. The spanning members of the floor and roof systems help to tie the vertical structure together and serve as horizontal diaphragms. The most common floor system for steel-framed high-rise structures is corrugated metal decking with a lightweight concrete fill. This provides spaces for the distribution of power and communication wiring as well as small service ducts throughout the floor.

In reinforced concrete high-rise structures, it can be economical to use a framework of beams and girders supporting a lightweight structural concrete slab.

Trussed joists for long-span designs can be economical, even if the floor systems are deeper than normal. The mechanical systems can pass through the open web areas of the joists without any additional floor depth required below the bottom chord of the trusses.

In residential high-rise buildings, a post-tensioned flat slab design is often used for spans not exceeding 25 to 30 feet (7.6 to 9.1 m) with slab thicknesses in the range of 6 to 7 inches (150 to 180) or at most 8 inches (205). The flat slabs are supported directly by columns without any supporting beams, resulting in minimal structural floor depth. However, any mechanical and electrical services would have to be suspended below the slab.

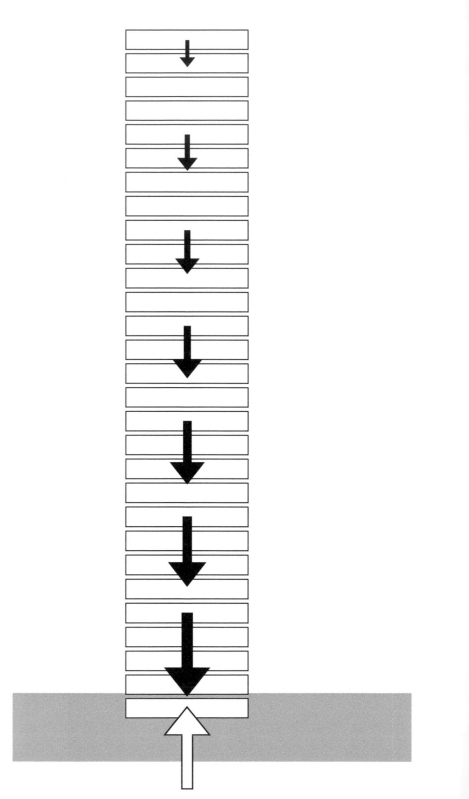

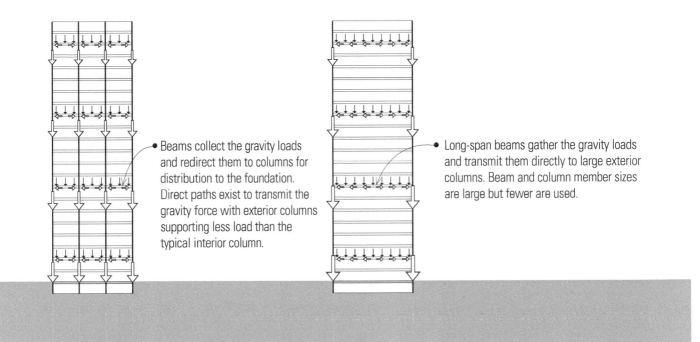

• Beams collect the gravity loads and redirect them to columns for distribution to the foundation. Direct paths exist to transmit the gravity force with exterior columns supporting less load than the typical interior column.

• Long-span beams gather the gravity loads and transmit them directly to large exterior columns. Beam and column member sizes are large but fewer are used.

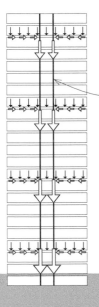

• A central core is used to collect loads from cantilevered floor systems. Since the core is responsible for supporting all of the gravity and lateral loads, the core plan area and wall thicknesses will be more substantial.

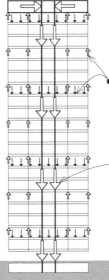

• Floor loads are initially supported by beams attached to suspension cables that redirect the loads upward to major trusses or a space frame at the roof level. The loads are then transmitted to the central core and directed down to the foundation. Again, this represents a system where all gravity and lateral loads are essentially resisted by the core.

In designing for safety, the aim is to reduce the likelihood of building collapse from wind and seismic forces. Secondarily, consideration must be given to the potential failure of cladding materials, architectural elements, utilities, and services.

Except for high-risk seismic zones, wind is the force that most affects the design of high-rise buildings. Wind loads acting on the overall structure are generally given as stepped increments of wind pressure, increasing in magnitude as the height above ground increases. These wind loads are assumed to act normal to the vertical surfaces of the building, with consideration also given to the effect of quartering wind.

Under a steady wind, a high-rise structure deflects like a vertical cantilever beam that is fixed at the ground level. However, wind gusts on the building can oscillate and the smaller modal deflections can also cause vibrations in the building. Small oscillations may contribute to some occupants feeling uncomfortable and insecure. The inherent stiffness and damping characteristics of most high-rise buildings preclude the possibility of wind-induced resonance and aerodynamic instability.

Seismic movements in a building are different from those produced by wind. Under catastrophic earthquakes, a building will deflect much more and may deflect in random directions, with the challenge of avoiding movements large enough to produce collapse. The critical periods of vibration of earthquakes are generally in the range of fractions of a second while the period for flexible high-rise buildings will be several seconds. When the earthquake period is kept out of phase from the building period, the possibility of harmonic resonance is lessened. Harmonic resonance increases the amplitude of the displacement and can result in catastrophic movement. Tall buildings are designed to be relatively rigid under wind loading but certain parts of the structure may be allowed to yield or crack locally under earthquake loads to lengthen the building's period of vibration and increase its damping capability. This is done to resist catastrophic failure for very strong earthquakes. The ductility requirement for seismic design involves equipping buildings with reserve strength—through plastic yielding beyond the elastic limit—so that the building can sway without losing its structural integrity.

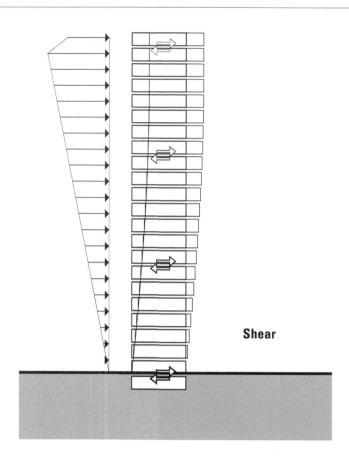

**Shear**

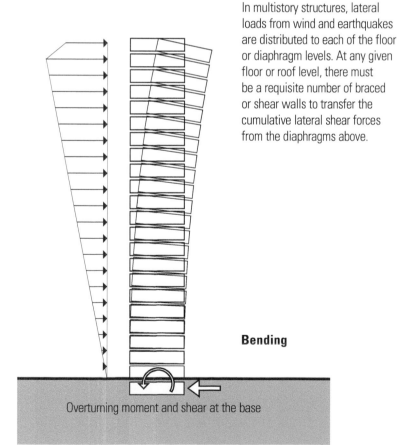

In multistory structures, lateral loads from wind and earthquakes are distributed to each of the floor or diaphragm levels. At any given floor or roof level, there must be a requisite number of braced or shear walls to transfer the cumulative lateral shear forces from the diaphragms above.

**Bending**

Overturning moment and shear at the base

In tall buildings, the overturning moment due to lateral loading is significant. It is advantageous for the floor system to distribute a major part of the gravity load of the building to the exterior resisting elements in order to stabilize them by precompression against tensile overturning force requirements. This can be achieved by eliminating as many interior columns as possible and using long-span floor systems capable of spanning from the central core to the exterior columns. This stronger floor can also make an appropriate contribution to resisting lateral shear forces.

• Braced core

A cap truss or outriggers at the roof level, tied to the core and combined with the exterior tie-down columns, serve to reduce the overturning moment and lateral drift in the building. The tie-downs are attached at every story and support gravity loads in addition to restraining the lateral movement of the frame.

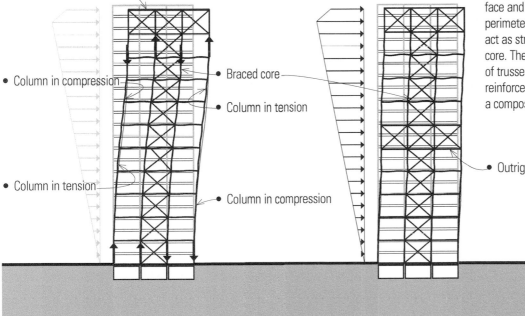

• Cap-truss structure

• Column in compression

• Column in tension

• Braced core

• Column in tension

• Column in compression

A variation of the cap truss and tie-down concept is the use of outriggers at various levels in the height of the building. The core is often centrally located with outriggers extending on both sides. When the shear core tries to bend, the outriggers act as lever arms that place direct axial loads, tension on one face and compression on the other, into the perimeter columns. These columns, in turn, act as struts to resist the deflection of the core. The outriggers generally are in the form of trusses in steel-frame structures or walls in reinforced concrete structures, or they may be a composite assembly of steel and concrete.

• Outrigger

Any lateral load applied at a distance above grade generates an overturning moment at the base of a structure. For equilibrium, the overturning moment must be counterbalanced by an external restoring moment and an internal resisting moment provided by forces developed in column members and shear walls. Tall, slender buildings with a high aspect (height-to-base width) ratio experience larger horizontal deflections at their tops and are especially susceptible to overturning moments.

While torsion may be present in buildings of any height, it can be particularly critical in high-rise structures. Due to the extreme height of high-rise buildings, a story torsion that would normally be considered acceptable in low- and midrise buildings can accumulate over many stories to cause a total rotation for the high-rise that would be unacceptable. The motions associated with torsion can add to the swaying motion along the building's axes, creating unacceptable translations and accelerations.

Multistory structures are generally braced with a minimum of four lateral-force-resisting planes per story, each wall being positioned to minimize torsional moments and displacement. Although it is desirable to position the lateral resisting planes in the same position at each floor level, it is not always necessary. The transfer of shear through any one level may be examined as an isolated problem. Torsional resistance is maximized by positioning lateral-force-resisting systems and cores in a balanced, symmetrical manner. This minimizes the possibility of the building's center of mass being offset or eccentric from its center of rigidity or resistance.

- Torsional resistance is enhanced by configuring braced frames, moment frames, or shear walls into a complete tube. Circulation cores using reinforced concrete or steel framing are also more effective when closed.

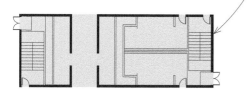

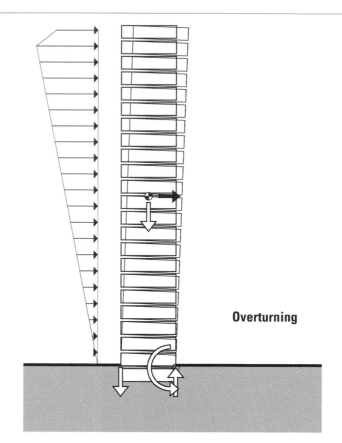

**Overturning**

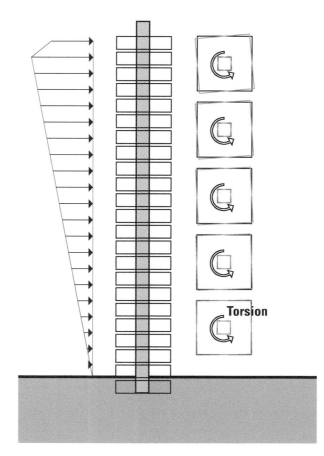

**Torsion**

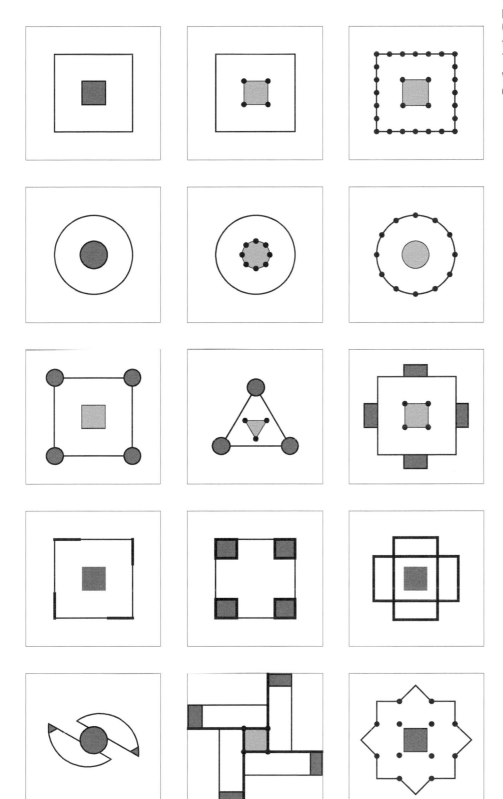

Illustrated on this page are inherently stable plan configurations for high-rise structures. Open forms of bracing are inherently weak in torsional stiffness and should be avoided. L-, T-, and X-shaped plan arrangements are the worst in torsional resistance while C and Z configurations are only slightly better.

# TYPES OF HIGH-RISE STRUCTURES

The proper choice of a lateral-force-resisting system can make or break a high-rise project in terms of constructibility, usefulness, and economics.

We can divide high-rise structures into two categories, based on the dominant location of the vertical lateral-resisting systems: interior structures and exterior structures.

### Interior Structures

Interior structures are high-rise structures that resist lateral loads primarily through lateral-force-resisting elements located within the interior of the structure, such as a rigid frame structure of steel or concrete, or a structure braced by a core consisting of braced frames, moment frames, or shear walls constructed into a closed system that acts as a structural tube.

### Exterior Structures

Exterior structures are high-rise structures that resist lateral loads primarily through lateral-force-resisting elements located along the perimeter of the structure.

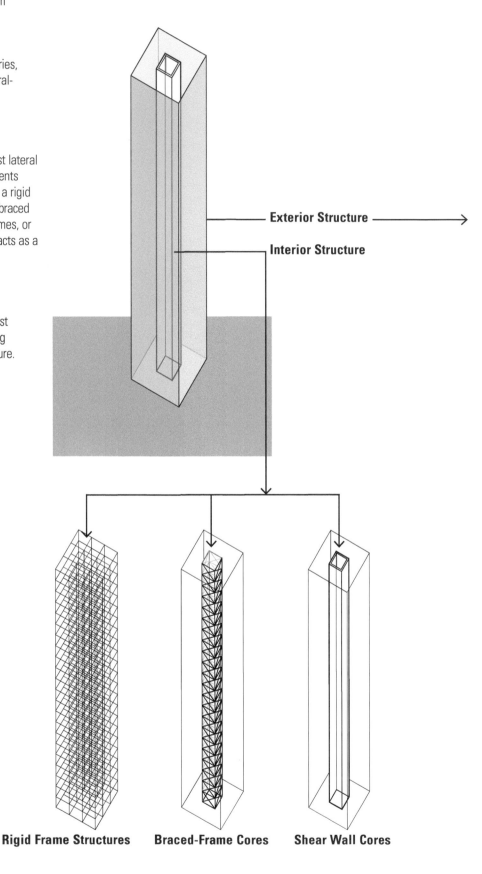

Exterior Structure →

Interior Structure

**Rigid Frame Structures**  **Braced-Frame Cores**  **Shear Wall Cores**

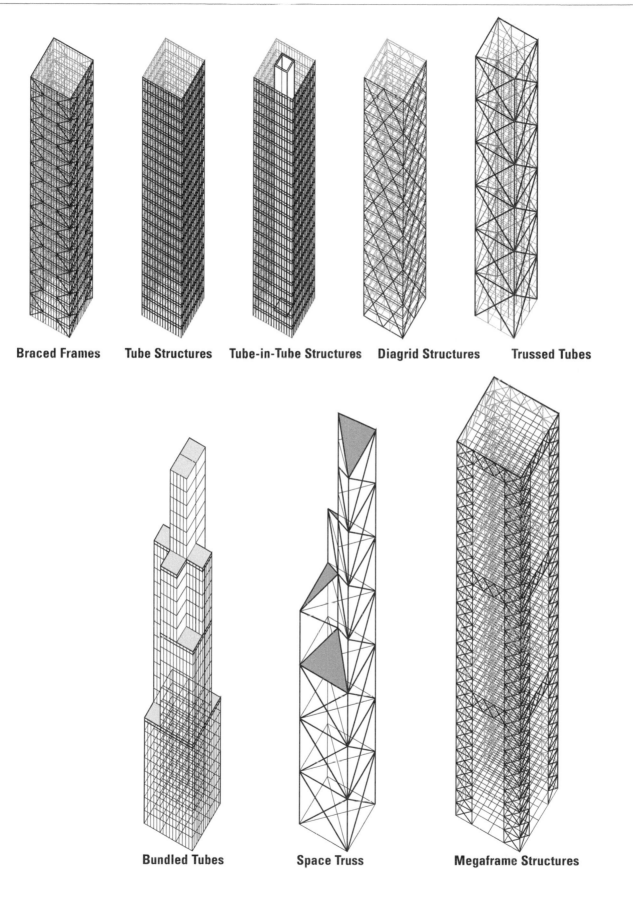

**Braced Frames**   **Tube Structures**   **Tube-in-Tube Structures**   **Diagrid Structures**   **Trussed Tubes**

**Bundled Tubes**   **Space Truss**   **Megaframe Structures**

# TYPES OF HIGH-RISE STRUCTURES

The graph on this and the facing page show the basic types of high-rise structures and the number of stories each type can reasonably attain.

Number of Stories

|  |  |  |  |  |  |
|---|---|---|---|---|---|
| Braced Hinge Frame Reference Structure | Rigid Frame | Braced Rigid Frame | Rigid Frame with Shear Walls | Outrigger Structure | Braced Frame |

←——————— **Interior Structures** ———————→        ←——

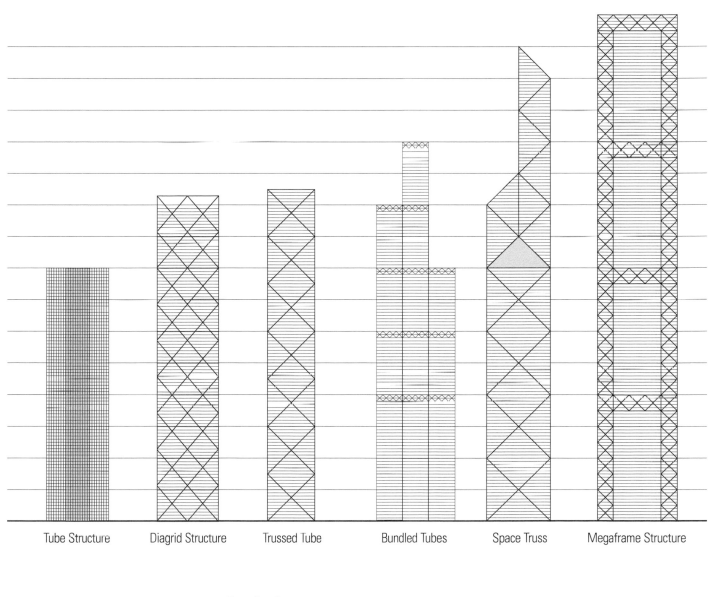

Tube Structure    Diagrid Structure    Trussed Tube    Bundled Tubes    Space Truss    Megaframe Structure

**←——— Exterior Structures ———→**

### Rigid Frame Structures

One of the primary and predominant structural systems employed for tall steel and concrete buildings through the 1960s was the conventional rigid frame. The structural framework represents a vertical cantilever beam with a fixed base at the ground.

Wind and earthquake loads are assumed to act laterally, generating shear and bending moments in addition to the vertical gravity loads. The floor framing system usually carries almost the same gravity loads at each floor but the girders along the column lines need to be progressively heavier toward the base of the building to resist the increasing lateral forces and to augment the building's stiffness.

Column sizes increase progressively toward the base of the building due to the accumulated increase in gravity loads transmitted from the floors above. Additionally, the columns toward the base need to be increased further to resist the accumulating lateral loads. The net result is that as a building's height increases and its sway from lateral forces becomes critical, there is a greater demand placed on the columns and girders that make up the rigid frame system to carry the lateral forces.

In rigid frame construction, the beams and girders spanning in both directions must be stiff enough to minimize the shear-racking or drift of the high-rise floors. This generally requires additional material for the beams and girders unless the floor drift can be controlled by other vertical elements, such as shear walls or structural cores. The quantity of materials required for resisting lateral loads could increase to such a degree that rigid frame systems would become cost-prohibitive for use in buildings exceeding 30 stories in height.

Vertical steel shear trusses or concrete shear walls alone are effective in providing lateral resistance for buildings from 10 to 35 stories high. However, when shear walls or shear trusses are combined with rigid, moment-resisting frames, the interaction of the two lateral-force-resisting systems can produce greater lateral rigidity for the building and increase its capability to rise as high as 60 stories.

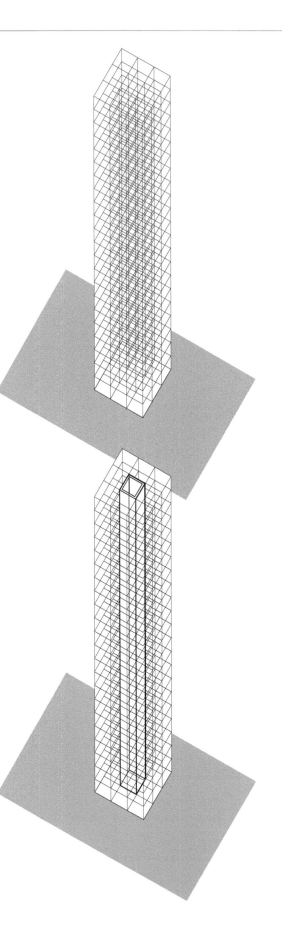

The vertical circulation cores for elevators and emergency egress stairways are usually constructed of reinforced concrete or braced steel frames, enabling them to be used as a major component of the gravity and lateral-force-resisting strategy for multistory buildings. The placement of the shear-resisting core is critical in minimizing the possibility of torsion due to lateral loads. A relatively symmetrical placement of structural cores and braced frames or shear walls can alleviate the eccentricity between the center of mass of a diaphragm level and the center of rigidity or resistance.

Regardless of core location, the preferred lateral resistance system is of the closed type, with the bracing or frame action forming a complete tube. Examples of this are tubular framed towers with continuous, moment-connected spandrels and columns around the building perimeter; braced cores with the core sides stiffened by diagonals or knee braces; and structural concrete cores with heavily reinforced lintel beams over doorways acting as links between wall segments. These closed forms are preferred because of their inherent torsional stiffness.

High-rise structures may contain a single or multiple cores. Large single-core structures may support cantilevered floor structures, or be combined with a top-hat structure or intermediate outriggers to provide column-free spaces at each floor level.

**Braced-Core Structures**

**Shear-Wall Core Structures**

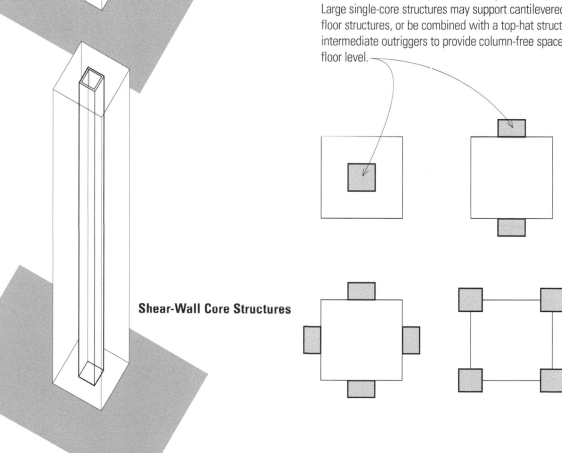

## Braced Frames

Braced-frame structures use vertical trusses to resist the lateral loads in tall buildings. These vertical trusses use the perimeter columns as chord members and K-, V-, or X-braces as web members, effectively eliminating bending in the columns under lateral loading. The columns, girders, and diagonal bracing can be simply connected with pin joints, making their fabrication and erection more economical than the moment-resisting connections required for rigid frame structures. The diagonal bracing increases the structure's stiffness, moderates drift, and enables greater overall heights. Braced frames are generally used in conjunction with other lateral-force-resisting systems for taller buildings.

Eccentrically braced frames use diagonal braces that are connected to the floor girders that form horizontal elements of the truss. The eccentricity of the axial offsets introduce bending and shear into the frame, lowering the stiffness of the frame but increasing its ductility, which is an advantage in seismic zones where ductility is an important requirement for structural design. Eccentrically braced frames also have the ability to accommodate wide door and window openings in their plane.

If the diagonal bracing members increase in scale to cross several floor levels, the system falls closer to the category of a megaframe structure.

## Shear Walls

Shear wall systems are often used for high-rise structures to provide the necessary strength and stiffness to resist the lateral forces caused by wind and earthquakes. Generally constructed of reinforced concrete, the shear walls are relatively thin and tend to have relatively high (height-to-width) aspect ratios.

Shear walls are treated as vertical cantilevers fixed at their base. When two or more shear walls in the same plane are connected by beams or slabs, as in the case of shear walls with window and door openings, the total stiffness of the system can exceed the sum of the individual wall stiffnesses. This occurs because the connecting beam forces the walls to act as a single unit (like a large rigid frame) by restraining the individual cantilever actions. When designed to act as a unit, the assembly is known as a coupled shear wall.

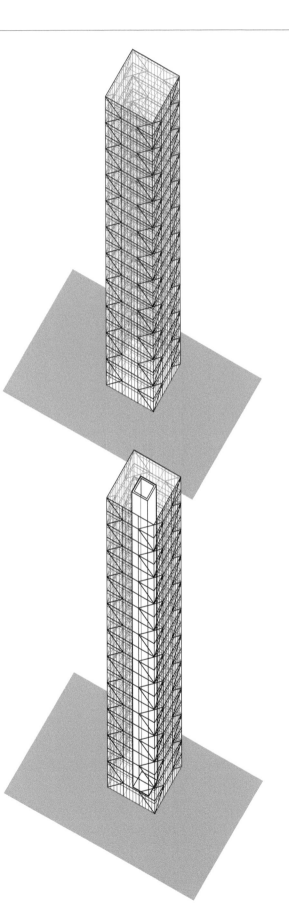

## Tube Structures

A framed-tube structure utilizes the entire building perimeter to resist lateral loads. The basic tubular structure is best viewed as a hollow, cantilevered box beam fixed at the ground level, with exterior frames constructed of closely spaced columns rigidly connected to deep spandrel beams. Previous examples of framed-tube systems, like the former World Trade Center Towers, used columns spaced from 4 to 15 feet (1.2 to 4.6 m) on center and spandrel beams from 2 to 4 feet (610 to 1220) deep.

The tube can be rectangular, circular, or other relatively regular shape. Since the exterior walls resist all or most of the lateral loads, much or all of the interior diagonals and shear walls are eliminated. The stiffness of the facade can be further enhanced by adding diagonal braces to create a trussing action.

When a building bends as a cantilever beam would under lateral loading, the racking of the structural frame causes an uneven distribution of axial column loads. The corner columns experience larger loads and the distribution is nonlinear from each corner toward the middle. Since the framed tube's behavior is somewhere between that of a pure cantilever and a pure frame, the sides of the tube parallel to the lateral load tend to act as independent multibay rigid frames due to the flexibility of the columns and spandrel beams. This causes the columns toward the middle of the frames to lag behind those near the corners, unlike the behavior of a true tube. This phenomenon is known as shear lag.

Designers have developed various techniques for reducing the effects of shear lag. Among these, the most notable is the use of belt trusses. Belt trusses are placed on the exterior wall planes, often at mechanical floors, to assist in equalizing the tension and compression forces due to shear lag.

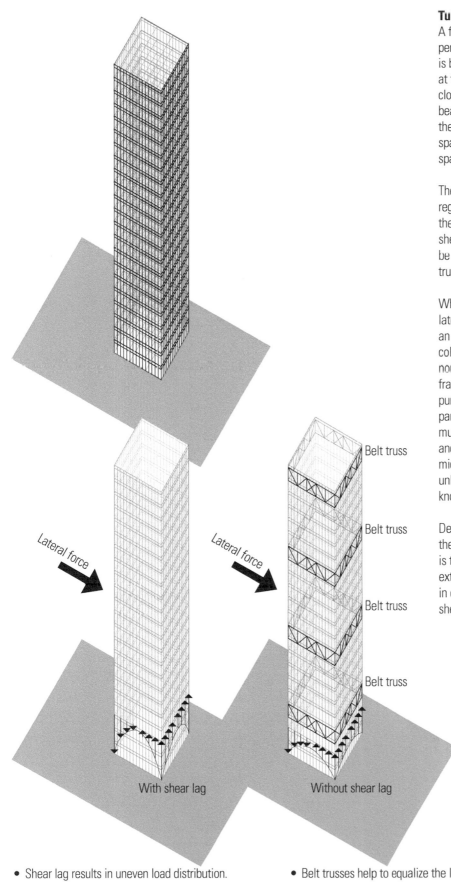

Lateral force

Lateral force

Belt truss

Belt truss

Belt truss

Belt truss

With shear lag

Without shear lag

- Shear lag results in uneven load distribution.
- Belt trusses help to equalize the load distribution.

### Tube-in-Tube Structures

The stiffness of framed tubes can be improved considerably by using a structural core to not only resist gravity loads but to resist lateral loads as well. The floor diaphragms tie the exterior and interior tubes together, allowing the two tubes to resist lateral forces as a unit. This system is known as a tube-in-tube structure.

The exterior tube, with its larger plan dimensions, can resist the overturning forces quite efficiently, however, the openings required in this tube compromise its capacity to resist shear, particularly at the lower levels. On the other hand, the solidity of the inner tube, which can be constructed of shear walls, braced frames, or moment frames, can better resist the story shear.

### Braced-Tube Structures

An inherent weakness of framed-tube structures lies in the flexibility of their spandrel beams. Framed tubes can be stiffened by adding large diagonals to the exterior wall frame, as at the 100-story John Hancock Center in Chicago. When diagonals are added to a framed-tube structure, it is called a braced-tube structure.

The large diagonal braces together with the spandrel beams create a wall-like rigidity against lateral loads. This stiffening of the perimeter frames overcomes the shear lag problem faced by framed-tube structures. The diagonals support lateral load forces primarily through axial action and also act as inclined columns in resisting gravity floor loads, allowing the exterior columns to be spaced farther apart.

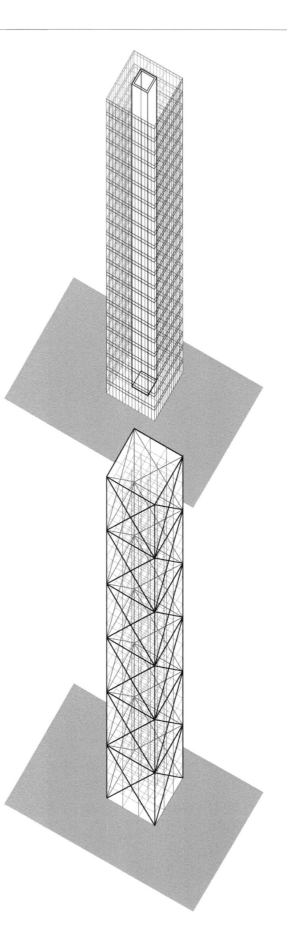

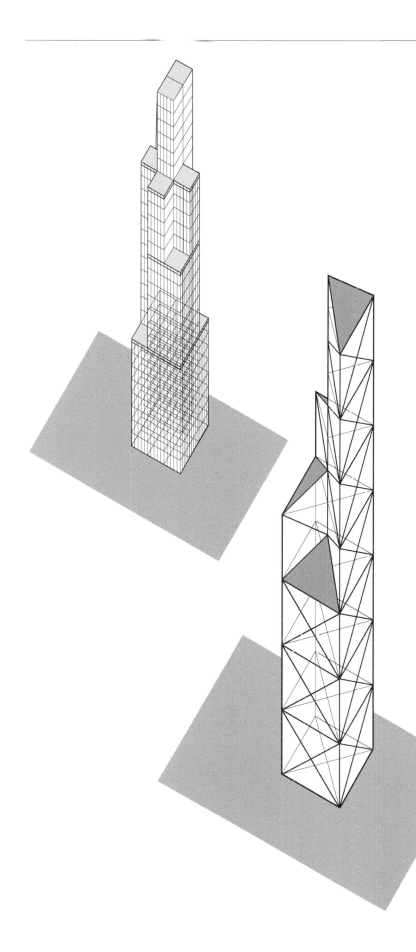

## Bundled-Tube Structures

A bundled-tube structure is a cluster of individual tubes tied together to act as a single unit. Single framed tubes are restricted in height by their slenderness (height-to-width ratio). Combining several tubes to act in unison with each other adds considerably to their stiffness and moderates the sway at the upper floors. A special weakness of this system is the differential column shortening.

Chicago's 110-story Sears Tower, designed by SOM, consists of nine framed steel tubes, each with its own structural integrity. Because each of the individual tubes are independently strong with respect to wind load, they can be bundled into varying configurations and terminated at various levels. Only two of the modules rise to the full 1450-foot (440-meter) height of the structure. Two drop off at the 50th floor, two more at the 66th, and three at the 90th. Dropping off modules reduces wind sway by breaking the flow of the wind. The nine modules are each 75 by 75 feet (22 by 22 meters) square and have common interior columns that make up two diaphragms trisecting the building in two directions and thereby stiffening the structure. The interior diaphragms act as webs of a huge cantilever beam in resisting shear forces, thus minimizing shear lag.

## Space-Truss Structures

A space-truss structure is a modified braced tube based on the idea of stacking triangulated prisms which contain diagonals connecting the exterior with the interior frame. The space truss resists both lateral and vertical loads. Unlike the more typical braced-tube structure with diagonals placed on the exterior wall planes, the space-truss system introduces diagonals that become an integral part of the interior space.

A prominent example of a space-truss system is the 72-story Bank of China Building in Hong Kong, designed by I.M. Pei, consisting of triangular prisms of different heights, which transfers internal loads to the building corners at 13-story intervals. The space truss resists the lateral loads and transfers almost the entire weight of the building onto the four super-columns at the corners.

## Megaframe Structures

As buildings rise above the 60-story range, megaframe or superframe structures become a viable possibility. Megaframe structures use megacolumns comprising the chords of oversized braced frames at the building corners, which are linked by multistory trusses at 15- to 20-story intervals; these are often the mechanical floor levels. The entire story depth of the mechanical floors can be used to construct a strong and stiff horizontal subsystem. Linking these very large girders or space trusses to the megacolumns produces a rigid megaframe that can be infilled with a lighter secondary frame of standard design.

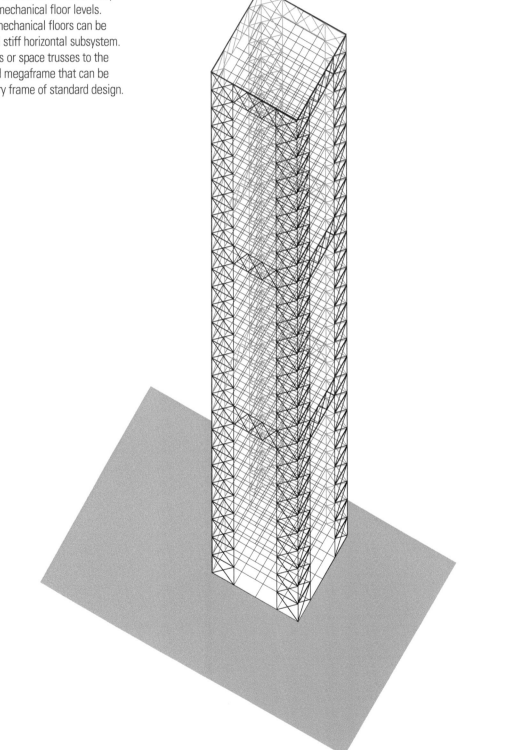

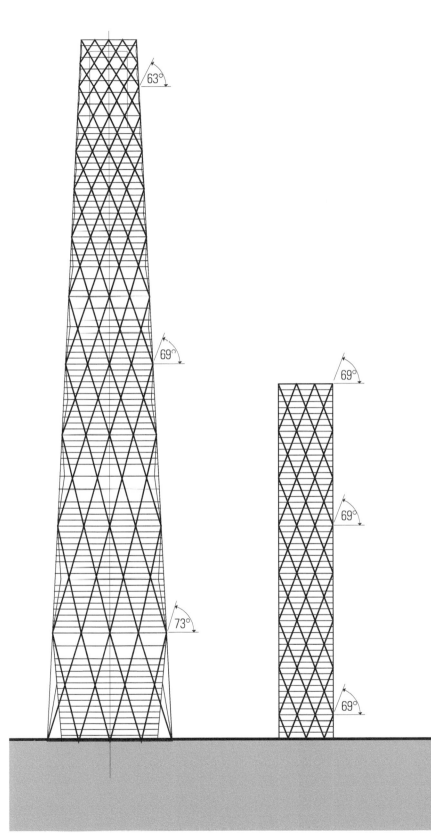

### Diagrid Structures

A fairly recent application of a lattice-like framework on the exterior surface of the building to resist both lateral and gravity loads is the diagrid (diagonal grid) system. Diagrid structures differ from conventional braced frames in their ability to resist gravity loads, which is so effective that vertical columns are virtually eliminated.

The diagonal members in the diagrid system carry both gravity and lateral loads through triangulation, which results in a relatively uniform load distribution. Shear deformation is minimized very effectively because the diagonals resist the shear through axial action rather than by bending of vertical columns and horizontal spandrels. Diagrids provide both shear and bending rigidity to resist the effects of drift and overturning moment. Diagrid systems are also highly redundant and can transfer loads through multiple paths in case of a localized structural failure. See page 186.

The most common structural material used in diagrids is steel. Because of their structural efficiency, diagrids generally require less steel than other types of high-rise structures.

- The diagrid structural system can accommodate a variety of open floor plans. Beside the service core, the typical floor plan can be free of columns and other structural elements.

- Design studies indicate that using variable-angle diagrids for very tall buildings with height:width aspect ratios over 7 results in structural efficiency. However, using uniform-angle diagrids for buildings with height:width ratios lower than 7 reduces the amount of steel required.

The Hearst Tower has 46 stories, stands 597 feet (182 m) tall, and contains 860,000 sf (80,000 m²) of office space. Because the triangulated three-dimensional form of the steel diagrid structure is capable of both supporting gravity loads and resisting lateral wind forces, there is no need for exterior vertical columns. The diagrid structure reportedly used 20% less steel than a conventionally framed high-rise of similar size.

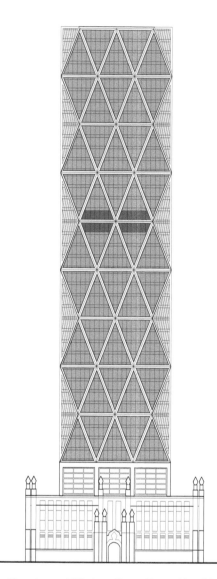

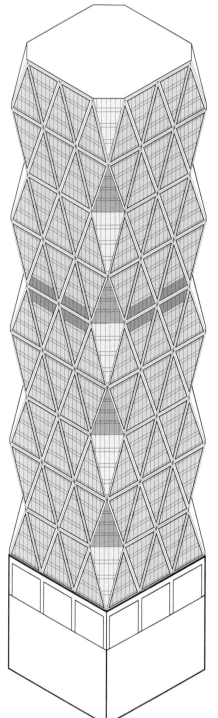

Elevation and 3D view: Hearst Tower, New York, New York, 2000–2006, Norman Foster/Foster + Partners

30 St. Mary Axe—informally known as The Gherkin and previously, the Swiss Re Building—is a skyscraper in London's financial district. With 41 floors, the tower is 591 feet (180 m) tall and stands on the site of the former Baltic Exchange, which was extensively damaged in 1992 by the explosion of a bomb placed by the Provisional IRA. After plans to build the Millennium Tower were dropped, 30 St. Mary Axe was erected, soon becoming an iconic symbol of London and one of the city's more widely recognized examples of modern architecture.

The shape of the tower was partially influenced by the need to have a smooth flow of wind around the building and minimize its impact on the local wind environment. Across this curved surface the diagrid structure is formed by generating a pattern of intersecting diagonals spiraling in two directions.

The unusual geometry of the tower gives rise to significant horizontal forces at each node level where the diagonal columns intersect, which are resisted by perimeter hoops. As with dome structures, the hoops in the upper region are in compression while those at the middle and lower levels are subject to significant tensile forces. The hoops also serve to transform the diagrid into a very stiff triangulated shell, freeing the interior core from the need to resist lateral wind forces. Foundation loads are also reduced when compared with a high-rise structure stabilized by its core.

Typical floor plan and section: 30 St. Mary Axe (The Gherkin), London, England, 2001–2003, Norman Foster/ Foster + Partners

## STABILIZING HIGH-RISE STRUCTURES

This elevation represents the most recent redesign of Tower Verre—a slender, 75-story steel-framed skyscraper that is shorter than the originally planned 1050-foot (320-m), 78 story high-rise. As opposed to the regular geometry of both the Hearst Tower and St. Mary Axe, Tower Verre uses an irregular diagrid structure to compose its faceted exterior that tapers to a set of three distinct asymmetrical, crystalline peaks at the apex of the tower.

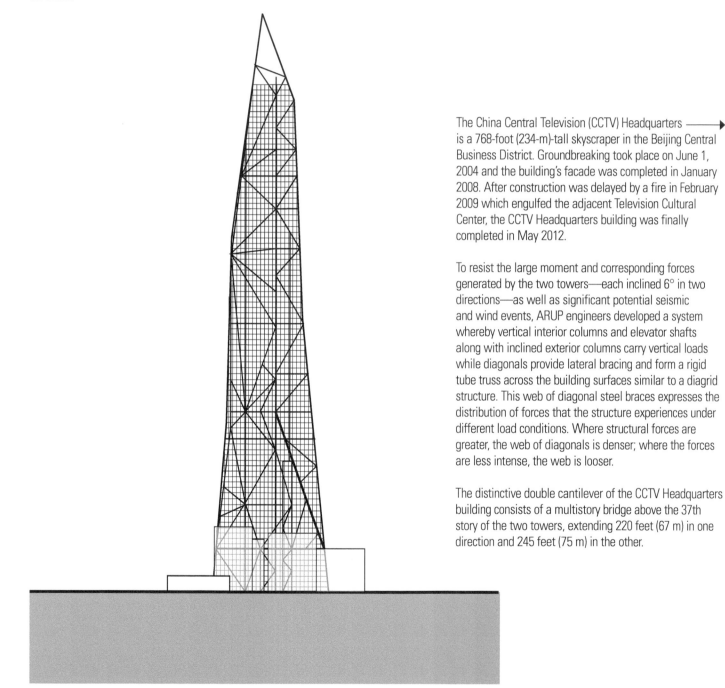

The China Central Television (CCTV) Headquarters ⟶ is a 768-foot (234-m)-tall skyscraper in the Beijing Central Business District. Groundbreaking took place on June 1, 2004 and the building's facade was completed in January 2008. After construction was delayed by a fire in February 2009 which engulfed the adjacent Television Cultural Center, the CCTV Headquarters building was finally completed in May 2012.

To resist the large moment and corresponding forces generated by the two towers—each inclined 6° in two directions—as well as significant potential seismic and wind events, ARUP engineers developed a system whereby vertical interior columns and elevator shafts along with inclined exterior columns carry vertical loads while diagonals provide lateral bracing and form a rigid tube truss across the building surfaces similar to a diagrid structure. This web of diagonal steel braces expresses the distribution of forces that the structure experiences under different load conditions. Where structural forces are greater, the web of diagonals is denser; where the forces are less intense, the web is looser.

The distinctive double cantilever of the CCTV Headquarters building consists of a multistory bridge above the 37th story of the two towers, extending 220 feet (67 m) in one direction and 245 feet (75 m) in the other.

Elevation: Tower Verre, New York, New York, under design review, Jean Nouvel

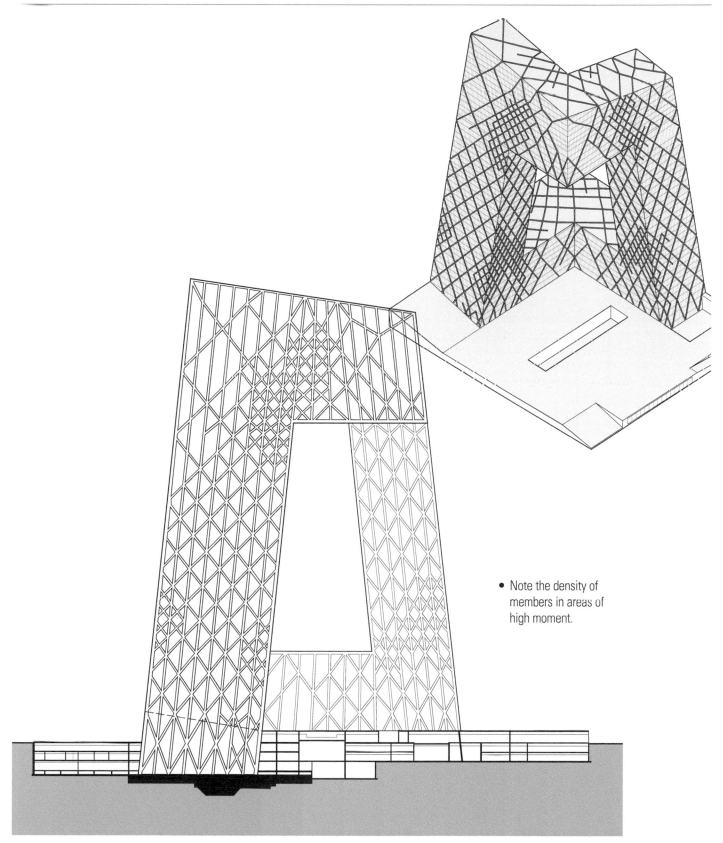

• Note the density of members in areas of high moment.

Elevation and aerial view: China Central Television Headquarters (CCTV), Beijing, China, 2004–2012, Rem Koolhaas and Ole Scheeren/OMA, Structural Engineer: Arup

Although stiffening a tall structure to reduce sway and limit deflections and deformation under lateral loading, large increases in structural size relative to those required for strength alone are often required to achieve satisfactory dynamic performance. A more cost-effective approach is to use damping systems that mitigate the effects of wind-induced vibration and earthquake shaking on tall structures, as well as on its nonstructural architectural elements and mechanical components. By absorbing and dissipating a significant portion of the energy transmitted to the building during high winds or a seismic event, damping systems limit excessive motion and deflections, moderate structural member sizes, and add to occupants' comfort level against sway perception.

The base isolation system described in Chapter 5 is an effective damping system for stiff buildings up to seven stories in height. For taller buildings subject to overturning, there are three types of damping systems used to control excessive motions and deflections and ensure occupancy comfort. These are active damping systems, passive damping systems, and aerodynamic damping.

### Active Damping Systems

Damping systems that require power for motors, sensors, and computer controls are known as active systems; those that do not are passive systems. The most significant drawback to active damping systems is that external power is required to regulate their movement and may be undependable during a seismic event when the power supply could be disrupted. For this reason, actively controlled dampers are more suitable for tall buildings subject to wind-induced loading rather than the more unpredictable cyclic loading caused by earthquakes.

Semi-active damping systems combine the features of passive and active damping systems. Rather than push on a building's structure, they use a controlled resistive force to reduce motion. They are fully controllable yet require little input power.

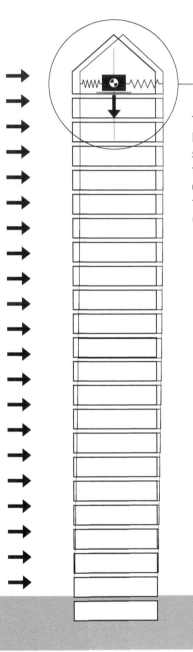

Tuned mass and tuned liquid dampers, located near the top of the building structure, act as force generators that actively push on the structure to counteract a disturbance. They are fully controllable and require a great deal of power.

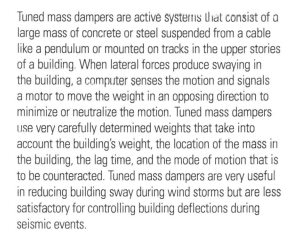

Tuned mass dampers are active systems that consist of a large mass of concrete or steel suspended from a cable like a pendulum or mounted on tracks in the upper stories of a building. When lateral forces produce swaying in the building, a computer senses the motion and signals a motor to move the weight in an opposing direction to minimize or neutralize the motion. Tuned mass dampers use very carefully determined weights that take into account the building's weight, the location of the mass in the building, the lag time, and the mode of motion that is to be counteracted. Tuned mass dampers are very useful in reducing building sway during wind storms but are less satisfactory for controlling building deflections during seismic events.

Tuned liquid dampers use water or other liquid in a tank designed to give the desired natural frequency of water motion. When the building moves under wind loading, the water in the tank moves back and forth in the opposing direction, transferring its momentum to the building and counteracting the effects of the wind vibration. A benefit of using a tuned liquid damping system is the availability of the water in the tank for firefighting.

An active tendon damping system uses a computerized controller that responds to building movement by actuating tension-adjusting members which are connected to an array of steel tendons disposed adjacent to the structure's main support members. The tension-adjusting members apply tensile force to the tendons to counter the force causing the deflection of the structure and dampening the oscillation of the structure. Active pulse systems use hydraulic pistons in the foundation or between the stories of a building to significantly reduce the lateral forces acting on a structure. Both active and tendon systems can also be used to counteract the effects of torsion by being placed off center in the structure.

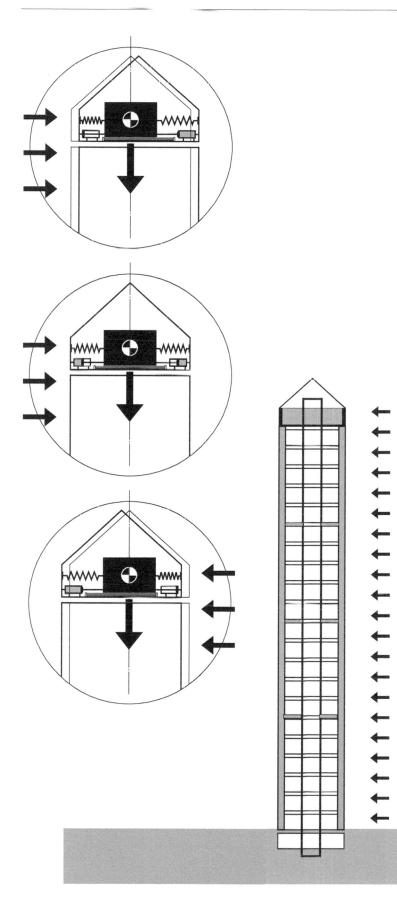

# DAMPING MECHANISMS

## Passive Damping Systems

Passive damping systems are incorporated within a structure to absorb a portion of the wind-induced or seismic energy, reducing the need for primary structural elements to dissipate energy. There are a number of manufactured dampers available, using a variety of materials to obtain different levels of stiffness and damping. Some of these include viscoelastic, viscous fluid, friction, and metallic-yield dampers.

Viscoelastic and viscous dampers act as large shock absorbers to dissipate energy over a broad range of frequencies. They can be designed for integration into structural components and connections to control both wind and seismic responses in tall buildings.

Friction dampers dissipate energy only when the slip force of two surfaces rubbing against each other is reached and exceeded. Metallic-yield dampers dissipate energy through the inelastic deformation of the material. Both friction and metallic-yield dampers are developed for earthquake engineering applications and are unsuitable for mitigating wind-induced motion.

## Aerodynamic Damping

The wind-induced motion of tall buildings has primarily three modes of action: drag (along with the wind), cross-wind (transverse to the wind direction), and torsion. Of these, cross-wind pressures alternating between the two walls of a building parallel to the wind direction, caused by vortex shedding, can induce transverse vibrations large enough to affect the occupants' comfort.

Aerodynamic damping refers to how buildings can be shaped to affect the airflow around it, modify the pressures acting on its surfaces, and mitigate resulting motion of the structure. In general, objects having the smoothest aerodynamic shape, such as a circular plan building, will impede the airflow much less than a comparable structure with a rectangular plan, resulting in a lessening of the wind effect. Because wind-induced forces become greater with building elevation, the aerodynamic shaping of a high-rise building is one approach which can be used to improve its performance against wind loading and motion. These modifications include rounded and tapered plan sections, setbacks, sculpted tops, modified corner geometry, and the addition of openings through the building.

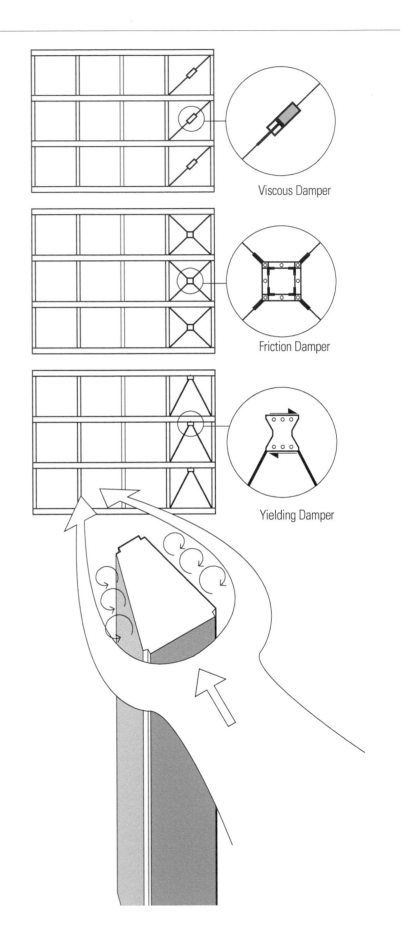

Viscous Damper

Friction Damper

Yielding Damper

# 8
# Systems Integration

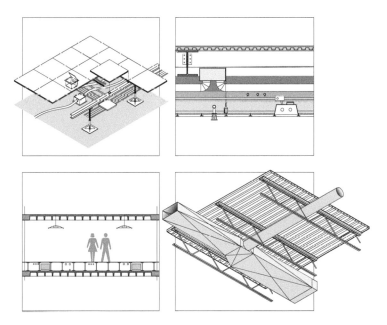

This chapter discusses the integration of the mechanical, electrical, and plumbing systems with the structural systems of buildings. These systems, which are integral to maintaining a comfortable, healthy, and safe building environment for the occupants, will typically include:

- Heating, ventilation, and air-conditioning (HVAC) systems that provide conditioned air to the interior spaces of a building. Conditioning may include ventilation, heating, cooling, humidification, and filtration.

- Electrical systems that provide power for lighting, electrical motors, appliances, and voice and data communications.

- Plumbing systems that provide a potable water supply, dispose of wastewater and sewage, control stormwater, and supply water to the fire suppression system.

The equipment and hardware of these systems require both considerable space and continuous distribution paths throughout a building. They are normally hidden from view within concealed construction spaces or special rooms but they require access for inspection and maintenance. Meeting these criteria requires careful coordination and integration in the planning and layout of the systems in relation to the structural system.

In addition to shafts and space for HVAC, electrical, and plumbing systems, the circulation system that provides access and emergency egress must also penetrate the structural system of multistory buildings. Providing shafts and space for corridors, stairways, elevators and escalators will not only influence the layout of the structural system but may, in some cases, become an integral part of the structure.

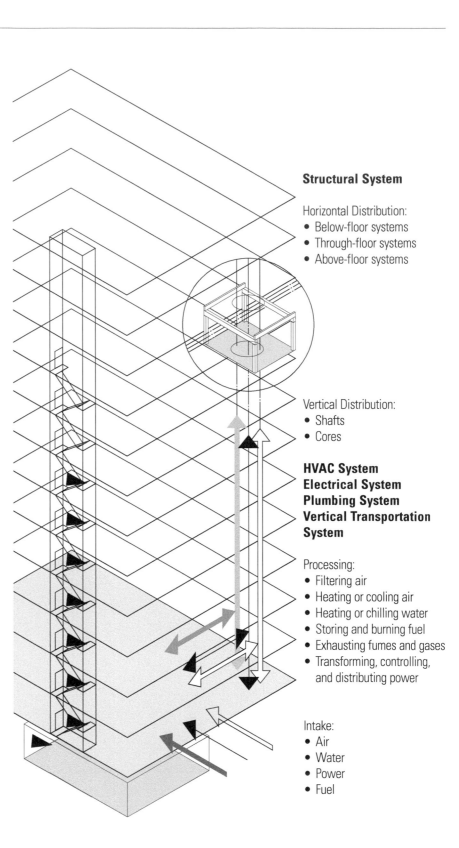

**Structural System**

Horizontal Distribution:
- Below-floor systems
- Through-floor systems
- Above-floor systems

Vertical Distribution:
- Shafts
- Cores

**HVAC System**
**Electrical System**
**Plumbing System**
**Vertical Transportation System**

Processing:
- Filtering air
- Heating or cooling air
- Heating or chilling water
- Storing and burning fuel
- Exhausting fumes and gases
- Transforming, controlling, and distributing power

Intake:
- Air
- Water
- Power
- Fuel

## Water Supply Systems

Water supply systems operate under pressure. The service pressure of a water supply system must be great enough to absorb pressure losses due to vertical travel and friction as the water flows through pipes and fittings, and still satisfy the pressure requirement of each plumbing fixture. Public water systems usually supply water at about 50 psi (345 kPa), which is sufficient for upfeed distribution in low-rise buildings up to six stories in height. For taller buildings, or where the water service pressure is insufficient to maintain adequate fixture service, water is pumped up to an elevated or rooftop storage tank for gravity downfeed. Part of this water is often used as a reserve for fire-protection systems.

The pressurized water supply side of the plumbing system results in smaller piping and more flexible distribution layouts. The water supply lines can usually be accommodated within floor and wall construction spaces without too much difficulty. It should be coordinated with the building structure and other systems, such as the parallel but bulkier sanitary drainage system. Water supply pipes should be supported at every story vertically and every 6 to 10 feet (1830 to 3050) horizontally. Adjustable hangers can be used to ensure proper pitch along horizontal runs for drainage.

- Water heaters are electric or gas appliances for heating water and storing it for use. Additional dispersed hot-water storage tanks may be required for large installations and widespread fixture groupings. Alternatively, in-line, on-demand water heaters that heat water at the time and point of use may be used. These systems alleviate the need for a storage tank but will require a flue if they burn fuel. Solar heating is also a possibility, either as a primary source of hot water in sunny climates or as a preheating system backed up by a standard water-heating system.

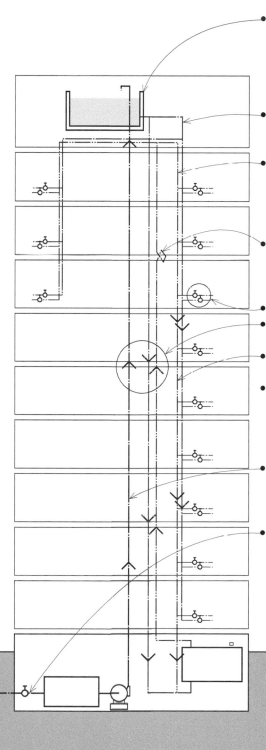

- Gravity downfeed system sets a water source at a height sufficient to maintain adequate supply pressure throughout the water distribution system.

- Cold-water supply pipes should be insulated to prevent heat flow into the water from the warmer surrounding air.

- Hot-water pipes should be insulated against heat loss and should be no closer than 6" (150) to parallel cold-water pipes.

- Expansion bends permit thermal expansion to occur in long runs of hot-water piping.

- Branch lines
- Risers

- Hot-water return line to heater or storage tank in two-pipe systems.

- If a water supply pipe must be located in an exterior wall, it should be placed on the warm side of the wall insulation.

- Upfeed system distributes water from a water main or an enclosed storage tank under pressure from compressed air.

- Service pipe connects the building to a water main with a building shutoff valve.

### Sanitary Sewage Systems

The water supply system terminates at each plumbing fixture. After water has been drawn and used, it enters the sanitary sewage system. The primary objective of this drainage system is to dispose of fluid waste and organic matter as quickly as possible. Because a sanitary drainage system relies on gravity for its discharge, its pipes are much larger than the water supply lines, which are under pressure. Sanitary drain lines are sized according to their location in the system and the total number and types of fixtures served.

The layout of the sanitary drainage system should be as direct and straightforward as possible to prevent the deposit of solids and clogging. Cleanouts should be located to allow pipes to be easily cleaned if they do clog.

- Branch drains connect one or more fixtures to a soil or waste stack.
- Horizontal drain lines should slope 1/8" per foot (1:100) for pipes up to 3" (75) ø, and 1/4" per foot (1:50) for pipes larger than 3" (75) ø.
- Fixture drains extend from the trap of a plumbing fixture to a junction with a waste or soil stack.
- Soil stacks carry the discharge from water closets or urinals to the building drain or building sewer.
- Waste stacks carry the discharge from plumbing fixtures other than water closets or urinals.
- Minimize bends in all stacks.
- The building drain is the lowest part of a drainage system that receives the discharge from soil and waste stacks inside the walls of a building and conveys it by gravity to the building sewer.
- Fresh-air inlets admit fresh air into the drainage system of a building, connected to the building drain at or before the building trap.
- The building sewer connects a building drain to a public sewer or private treatment facility.

### Storm Drain Systems

The storm drain system conveys rainfall drained from roofs and paved surfaces as well as the outfall from the building foundation to the municipal storm drain or to holding ponds or tanks for irrigation use. Storm drains, like sanitary drains, have a prescribed slope to ensure proper drainage.

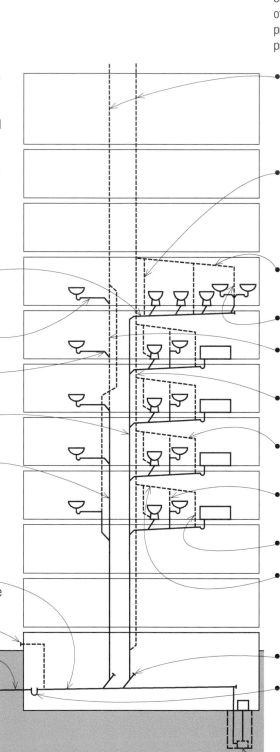

### Vent Systems

The vent system permits septic gases to escape to the outside and supplies a flow of fresh air into the drainage system to protect trap seals from siphonage and back pressure.

- Stack vents are extensions of a soil or waste stack above the highest horizontal drain connected to the stack; they should extend well above the roof surface and be distant from vertical surfaces, operable skylights, and roof windows.
- Relief vents provide circulation of air between a drainage and a venting system by connecting a vent stack to a horizontal drain between the first fixture and the soil or waste stack.

- Loop vents are circuit vents that loop back and connect with a stack vent instead of a vent stack.
- Common vents serve two fixture drains connected at the same level.
- Wet vents are oversized pipes functioning both as a soil or waste pipe and a vent.
- Vent stacks are vertical vents installed primarily to provide circulation of air to or from any part of a drainage system.
- Branch vents connect one or more individual vents with a vent stack or stack vent.
- Continuous vents are formed by a continuation of the drain line to which they connect.
- Back vents are installed on the sewer side of a trap.
- Circuit vents serve two or more traps and extend from in front of the last fixture connection of a horizontal branch to the vent stack.

- Cleanouts

- A building trap is installed in the building drain to prevent the passage of sewer gases from the building sewer to the drainage system of a building. Not all building codes require a building trap.
- A sump pump for removing the accumulations of liquid from a sump pit is required for fixtures located below the street sewer.

## Fire Protection Systems

In large commercial and institutional buildings where public safety is an issue, building codes often require a fire sprinkler system to extinguish a fire before it can spread out of control; some codes allow an increase in floor area if an approved sprinkler system is installed. Some jurisdictions require the installation of fire sprinkler systems in multifamily housing as well.

Fire sprinkler systems consist of pipes that are located in or below ceilings, connected to a suitable water supply, and supplied with valves or sprinkler heads made to open automatically at a certain temperature. Specific requirements for the use and location of the sprinkler heads make the planning and coordination of the system a priority in the design of ceilings and underfloor cavities.

The two major types of sprinkler systems are wet-pipe systems and dry-pipe systems.

- Wet-pipe systems contain water at sufficient pressure to provide an immediate, continuous discharge through sprinkler heads that open automatically in the event of a fire.
- Dry-pipe systems contain pressurized air that is released when a sprinkler head opens in the event of fire, allowing water to flow through the piping and out the opened nozzle. Dry-pipe systems are used where the piping is subject to freezing.
- Preaction systems are dry-pipe sprinkler systems through which water flow is controlled by a valve operated by fire-detection devices more sensitive than those in the sprinkler heads. Preaction systems are used when an accidental discharge would damage valuable materials.
- Deluge systems have sprinkler heads open at all times, through which water flow is controlled by a valve operated by a heat-, smoke-, or flame-sensing device.

- Sprinkler heads are nozzles for dispersing a stream or spray of water, usually controlled by a fusible link that melts at a predetermined temperature.
- Standpipes are water pipes extending vertically through a building to supply fire hoses at every floor.
- Dry standpipes contain air that is displaced by water when they are put to use; wet standpipe systems contain water at all times.
- Class I systems provide large 2 1/2"- (64-) diameter hose connections for use by firefighters trained in the use of the heavy flow these connections provide.

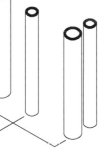

- Class II systems provide 1 1/2"- (38-) diameter fittings and hoses for use by both untrained building occupants and first responders.
- Class III standpipe systems provide access to both sizes of connections to allow use by either building occupants or firefighters.
- Water pressure for a standpipe or sprinkler system may be provided by a municipal water main or a pumper truck, augmented by a fire pump or rooftop water tank.

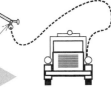

Water main

- A Siamese pipe fitting is installed close to the ground on the exterior of a building, providing two or more connections through which the fire department can pump water to a standpipe or sprinkler system.

## Electrical Systems

Utility companies transmit electrical power at high voltage to minimize voltage drop and conductor size in the transmission systems. For safety, transformers step this voltage down to lower voltages at the point of use. There are three different electrical system voltages commonly used in buildings:

- 120/240-volt, single-phase electrical power is typical for smaller-scale buildings and almost all residences. The utility owns and maintains transformers that provide 120/240-volt power from the high-voltage distribution line. The building requires only a meter, main disconnect, and distribution panel.
- 120/208-volt, three-phase electrical power is used in medium-sized buildings for the efficient operation of large motors used for fans, elevators, escalators; 120-volt power is provided as well for lighting and outlets. Such facilities would have a dry transformer to step down a high-supply voltage, located either outside of the building or inside as a unit substation.
- 277/480-volt, three-phase electrical power is used in large commercial buildings that will purchase their power at high voltage. These buildings require a large transformer along with a transformer vault. In addition there will be a separate switchboard room to partition the power to major users. Large motors in the building will use three-phase power while fluorescent lighting will use 277-volt, single-phase power. Electric closets will typically be required throughout the building, typically on each floor, to house smaller dry transformers to produce 120-volt, single-phase power for electrical outlets.

The electrical system of a building supplies power for lighting, heating, and the operation of electrical equipment and appliances. Generator sets may be required to supply emergency electrical power for exit lighting, alarm systems, elevators, telephone systems, fire pumps, and medical equipment in hospitals.

The service connection may be overhead or underground. Overhead service is less expensive, easily accessible for maintenance, and can carry high voltages over long runs. Underground service is more expensive but is used in high-load-density situations such as urban areas. The service cables are run in pipe conduit or raceways for protection and to allow for future replacement. Direct burial cable may be used for residential service connections.

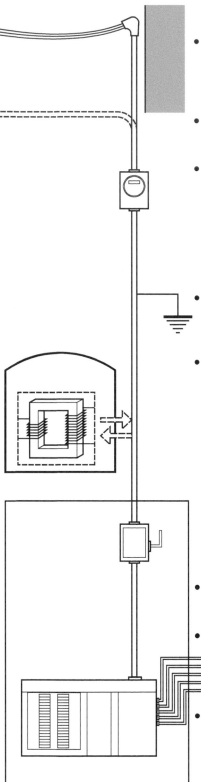

- Service conductors extend from a main power line or transformer to the service equipment of a building.
- The service drop is the overhead portion of service conductors extending from the nearest utility pole to a building. The service lateral is the underground equivalent extending from a main power line or transformer to a building.
- A service entrance conductor extends from a service drop or service lateral to the service equipment of a building.
- A watt-hour meter measures and records the quantity of electric power consumed with respect to time. Supplied by the public utility, it is always placed ahead of the main disconnect switch so that it cannot be disconnected; for multiple-occupancy buildings, banks of meters are installed so that each unit can be metered independently.
- A grounding rod or electrode is firmly embedded in the earth to establish a ground connection.

- Transformers step down a high-supply voltage to the service voltage of medium-sized and large buildings. To reduce costs, maintenance, and noise and heat problems, a transformer may be placed on an outdoor pad. If located within a building, oil-filled transformers require a well-ventilated, fire-rated vault with two exits and located on an exterior wall adjacent to the switchgear room. Dry-type transformers used in small- and medium-sized buildings may be placed together with a disconnect switch and switchgear in a unit substation.

- The service switch is the main disconnect for the entire electrical system of a building, except for any emergency power systems.
- Switchgear room

- The main switchboard is a panel on which are mounted switches, overcurrent devices, metering instruments, and busbars for controlling, distributing, and protecting a number of electric circuits. It should be located as close as possible to the service connection to minimize voltage drop and for wiring economy.

### Electrical Circuits

Once the electrical power requirements for the various areas of a building are determined, wiring circuits must be laid out to distribute the power to the points of use. Separate wiring circuits are required for the sound and signal equipment of telephone, cable, intercom, and security or fire alarm systems.

### Electrical Wiring

Conduit provides support for wires and cables and protects them against physical damage and corrosion. Metal conduit also provides a continuous grounded enclosure for the wiring. For fireproof construction, rigid metal conduit, electrical metallic tubing, or flexible metal conduit can be used. For frame construction, armored or nonmetallic sheathed cable is used. Plastic tubing and conduits are most commonly used for underground wiring.

Being relatively small, conduit can be easily accommodated in most construction systems. Conduit should be adequately supported and laid out as directly as possible. Codes generally restrict the radius and number of bends a run of conduit may have between junction or outlet boxes. Coordination with a building's mechanical and plumbing systems is required to avoid conflicting paths.

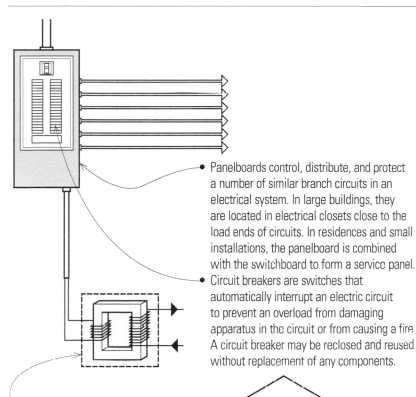

- Panelboards control, distribute, and protect a number of similar branch circuits in an electrical system. In large buildings, they are located in electrical closets close to the load ends of circuits. In residences and small installations, the panelboard is combined with the switchboard to form a service panel.
- Circuit breakers are switches that automatically interrupt an electric circuit to prevent an overload from damaging apparatus in the circuit or from causing a fire. A circuit breaker may be reclosed and reused without replacement of any components.

- Low-voltage circuits carry alternating current below 50 volts, supplied by a step-down transformer from the normal line voltage. These circuits are used in residential systems to control doorbells, intercoms, heating and cooling systems, and remote lighting fixtures. Low-voltage wiring does not require a protective raceway.

- Trench header perpendicular to raceways
- Floor outlets are located on a preset module.

- Cellular steel floor decking

Electrical conductors are often run within the raceways of cellular steel decking to allow for the flexible placement of power, signal, and telephone outlets in office buildings. Flat conductor cable systems are also available for installation directly under carpet tiles.

For exposed installations, special conduit, raceways, troughs, and fittings are available. As with exposed mechanical systems, the layout should be visually coordinated with the physical elements of the space.

- Low-voltage switching is used when a central control point is desired from which all switching may take place. The low-voltage switches control relays that do the actual switching at the service outlets.

- Carpet squares
- 1, 2, or 3 flat circuit conductor cables with low-profile outlets

## Heating, Ventilating, and Air-Conditioning Systems

Heating, ventilating, and air-conditioning (HVAC) systems simultaneously control the temperature, humidity, purity, distribution, and motion of the air in the interior spaces of a building.

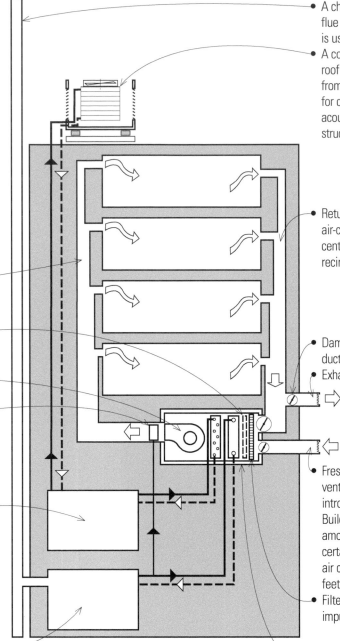

- Heating and cooling energy can be distributed by air, water, or a combination of both.

- Preheaters heat outside cold air as necessary in advance of other processing.
- Blowers supply air at a moderate pressure to supply forced drafts in a HVAC system.
- Humidifiers maintain or increase the amount of water vapor in the supply air.

- A chilled water plant, powered by electricity, steam, or gas, delivers chilled water to the air-handling equipment for cooling, and pumps condenser water to the cooling tower for the disposal of heat.

- A boiler produces hot water or steam for heating. Boilers require fuel (gas or oil) and an air supply for combustion. Oil-fired boilers also need an on-site storage tank. Electric boilers, which may be feasible if electricity costs are low, eliminate the need for combustion air and a chimney. If hot water or steam can be supplied by a central plant, a boiler is not required.

- A chimney is required to exhaust flue gases if a fuel-burning boiler is used.
- A cooling tower, usually on the roof of a building, extracts heat from water that has been used for cooling. They should be acoustically isolated from the structural frame of the building.

- Return air is conveyed from an air-conditioned space back to the central plant for processing and recirculation.

- Dampers regulate the draft in air ducts, intakes, and outlets.
- Exhaust air

- Fresh air. Typically 20% of ventilation air will be new air introduced from the outside. Building codes specify the amount of ventilation required for certain uses and occupancies in air changes per hour or in cubic feet per minute per person.
- Filters remove suspended impurities from the air supply.

- Fan rooms contain the air-handling equipment in large buildings. A single fan room should be located to minimize the distance conditioned air must travel to the farthest air-conditioned space. Individual fan rooms can also be distributed to serve individual zones of a building or be located on each floor to minimize vertical duct runs.

- Air-handling units contain the fans, filters, and other components necessary to treat and distribute conditioned air.

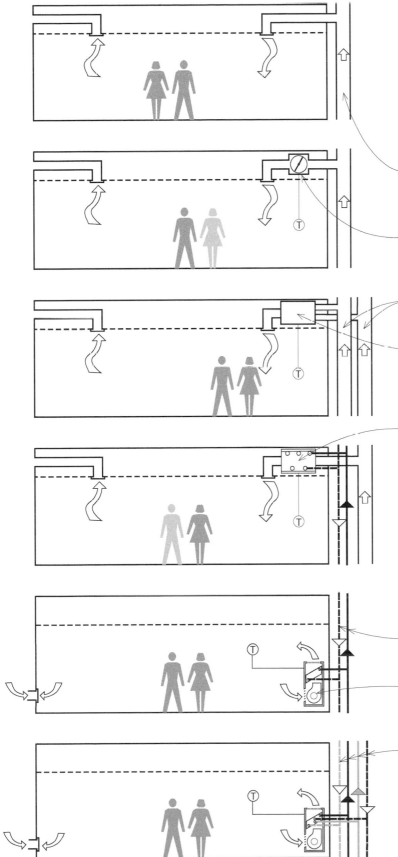

### All-Air HVAC Systems

The air treatment and refrigeration source in all-air systems may be located in a central location some distance from the conditioned spaces. Only the final heating-cooling medium (air) is brought into the conditioned space through ducts and distributed within the space through outlets or mixing terminal-outlets. All-air systems can not only provide heat and cooling but also clean the air and control humidity. Air is returned to the central unit and mixed with outside air for ventilation.

- Multizone systems supply a single air stream to each space or zone through finger ducts at normal velocity. Cold and warm air are premixed centrally using dampers controlled by room thermostats.
- Single-duct, variable-air-volume (VAV) uses dampers at the terminal outlets to control the flow of conditioned air according to the temperature requirements of each zone or space.
- Dual-duct systems use separate ducts to deliver warm air and cool air to mixing boxes, which contain thermostatically controlled dampers.
- The mixing boxes proportion and blend the warm and cold air to reach the desired temperature before distributing the blended air to each zone or space. This is usually a high-velocity system [2400 fpm (730 m/min) or higher] to reduce duct sizes and installation space.
- Terminal reheat systems offer more flexibility in meeting changing space requirements. It supplies air at about 55°F (13°C) to terminals equipped with electric or hot-water reheat coils, which regulate the temperature of the air being furnished to each individually controlled zone or space.

### All-Water HVAC Systems

All-water systems supply hot or chilled water from a central location to fan-coil units located in the conditioned spaces through pipes, which require less installation space than air ducts.

- A two-pipe system uses one pipe to supply hot or chilled water to each fan-coil unit and another to return it to the boiler or chilled water plant.
- Fan-coil units contain an air filter and a centrifugal fan for drawing in a mixture of room air and outside air over coils of heater or chilled water and then blowing it back into the space.
- A four-pipe system uses two separate piping circuits— one for hot water and one for chilled water—to provide simultaneous heating and cooling as needed to the various zones of a building.
- Ventilation is provided through wall openings, by infiltration, or separate ventilation units.

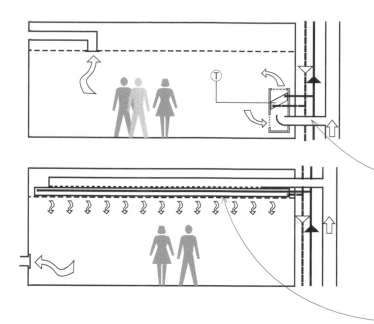

## Air-Water HVAC Systems

In air-water systems, the air treatment and refrigeration source may be separated from the served spaces. However, the temperature of the air delivered to the conditioned spaces is primarily balanced by warm or cool water circulated in an induction unit or radiant panel in the conditioned spaces. Air may be returned to the central unit or exhausted directly. Common types of air-water systems include:

- Induction systems use high-velocity ducts to supply conditioned primary air from a central plant to each zone or space, where it mixes with room air and is further heated or cooled in induction units. The primary air draws in room air through a filter and the mixture passes over coils that are heated or chilled by secondary water piped from a boiler or chilled-water plant. Local thermostats control water flow over the coils to regulate air temperature.
- Radiant panel systems provide heating or cooling from radiant panels in the wall or ceiling, while a constant-volume air supply provides ventilation and humidity control.

## Packaged HVAC Systems

Packaged systems are self-contained, weatherproof units incorporating a fan, filters, compressor, condenser, and evaporator coils for cooling. For heating, the unit may operate as a heat pump or contain auxiliary heating elements. Packaged systems are powered by electricity or by a combination of electricity and gas.

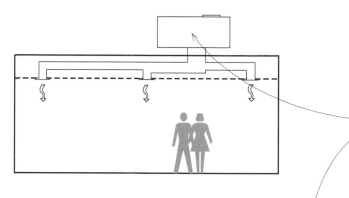

- Packaged systems may be mounted as a single piece of equipment on the roof or on a concrete pad alongside an exterior wall of a building.

- Rooftop packaged units may be placed at intervals to serve long buildings.
- Packaged systems with vertical shafts that connect to horizontal branch ducts can serve buildings up to four or five stories in height.

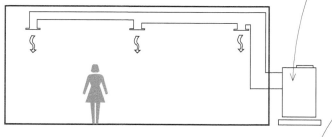

- Split-packaged systems consist of an outdoor unit incorporating the compressor and condenser and an indoor unit that contains the cooling and heating coils and the circulating fan. Insulated refrigerant tubing and control wiring connect the two parts.

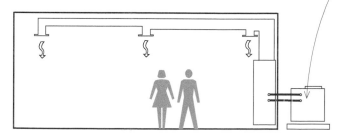

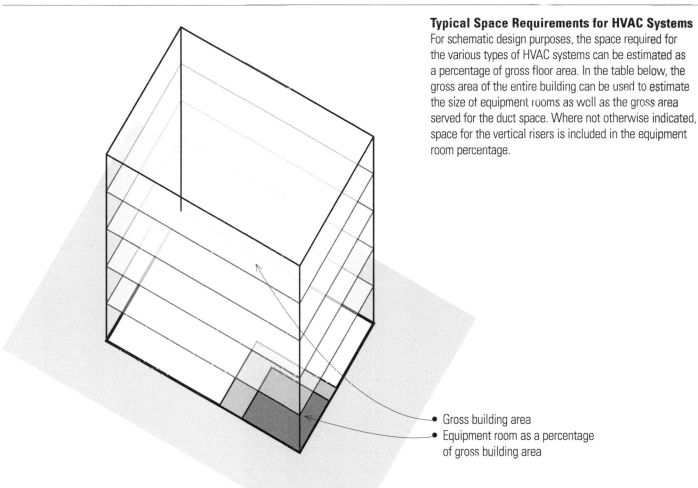

### Typical Space Requirements for HVAC Systems

For schematic design purposes, the space required for the various types of HVAC systems can be estimated as a percentage of gross floor area. In the table below, the gross area of the entire building can be used to estimate the size of equipment rooms as well as the gross area served for the duct space. Where not otherwise indicated, space for the vertical risers is included in the equipment room percentage.

- Gross building area
- Equipment room as a percentage of gross building area

| HVAC System | Equipment Room | | Ductwork Distribution | |
| --- | --- | --- | --- | --- |
| | Air Handling %* | Refrigeration %* | Vertical Risers* | Horizontal Runs* |
| Conventional: Low Velocity | 2.2–3.5 | 0.2–1.0 | | 0.7–0.9 |
| Conventional: High Velocity | 2.0–3.3 | 0.2–1.0 | | 0.4–0.5 |
| Terminal Reheat: Hot Water | 2.0–3.3 | 0.2–1.0 | | 0.4–0.5 |
| Terminal Reheat: Electric | 2.0–3.3 | 0.2–1.0 | | 0.4–0.5 |
| Variable-Air-Volume | | 0.2–1.0 | | 0.1–0.2 |
| Multizone | | 0.2–1.0 | | 0.7–0.9 |
| Dual Duct | 2.2–3.5 | 0.2–1.0 | | 0.6–0.8 |
| All-Air Induction | 2.0–3.3 | 0.2–1.0 | | 0.4–0.5 |
| Air-Water Induction: 2 Pipe | 0.5–1.5 | 0.2–1.0 | 0.25–0.35 | |
| Air-Water Induction: 4 Pipe | 0.5–1.5 | 0.2–1.0 | 0.3–0.4 | |
| Fan-Coil Units: 2 Pipe | — | 0.2–1.0 | — | — |
| Fan-Coil Units: 4 Pipe | — | 0.2–1.0 | — | — |

*Percentage of gross building area

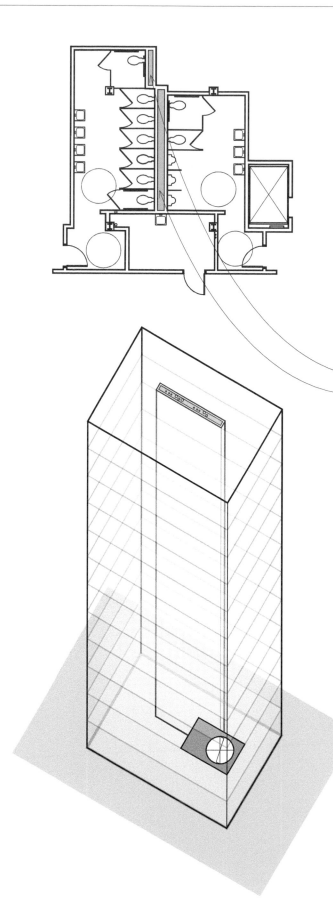

## Plumbing Chases

Plumbing chases provide the space necessary for the water supply and sanitary sewage lines in a building. They are almost invariably associated with lavatories, kitchens, and laboratories. Potential conflicts between a building structure and plumbing lines can be avoided by restricting supply and drainage piping to vertical plumbing chases.

- For reasons of economy and access, it is desirable to arrange the plumbing waste and vent stacks in a vertical chase extending through all of the floors of multistory buildings.
- Locating rooms that require plumbing above one another with the fixtures backed up to a common plumbing wall or chase creates room for the waste and vent stacks and for the plumbing runs that often must cross the stacks horizontally.

- Plumbing chases provide easier access for maintenance.
- Plumbing or wet walls behind fixtures should be deep enough to accommodate branch lines, fixture runouts, and air chambers.
- 12" (305) wide for single-loaded plumbing walls
- 18" (455) wide for double-loaded plumbing walls

- Horizontal sanitary sewage and stormwater lines must be sloped to drain and thus have priority in the planning of the horizontal mechanical space.

Although the use of plumbing chases is less critical in low-rise buildings, it is a particularly efficient approach to organizing and laying out the plumbing systems of certain building types, such as high-rise structures, hotels, hospitals, and dormitories.

## Fan Rooms

While it is more efficient to locate a fan room in a central location to reduce the length of air supply ducts, it may be located anywhere in a building that provides an outside air source and exhaust, and from which vertical shafts can accommodate the necessary supply and return air ducts.

- In large buildings, it may be economical to use multiple fan rooms for different zones of service.
- Air handlers are limited in forcing air up or down through a maximum of 10 to 15 floors. In taller buildings, multiple fan rooms are required, resulting in mechanical floors spaced 20 to 30 floors apart. Some tall buildings eliminate the need for vertical shafts by locating a fan room on each floor.

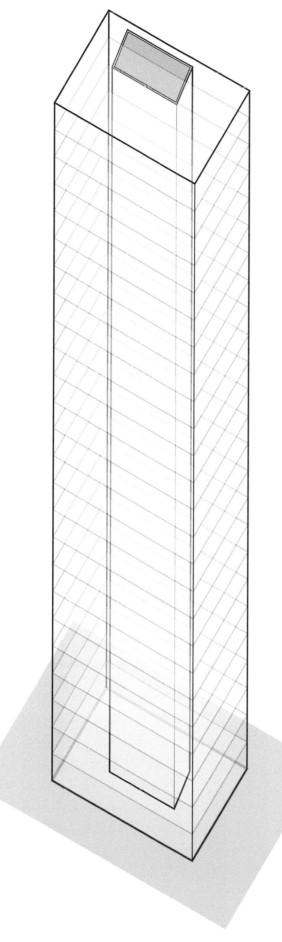

### Cores

In buildings two to three stories high, vertical chases for mechanical services are often located wherever they can be accommodated within the floor plans and provide service where it is needed. Without careful planning, this can result in weaving ductwork, piping, and wiring in and around the building structure, making access for maintenance or alterations difficult and reducing the efficiency of the systems.

In large and tall buildings, mechanical chases are often located with other shafts, such as those enclosing exit stairways, elevators, and plumbing risers. This naturally leads to the grouping of these facilities into one or more efficient cores that extend vertically through the height of the building. Because these cores are continuous as they rise through multiple floors—and additional fire protection is required in their construction—they can also serve as shear walls to help resist lateral loads as well as bearing walls to assist in carrying gravity loads.

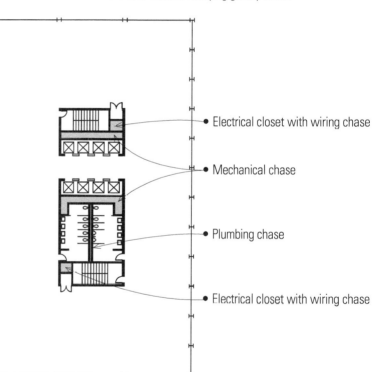

- Electrical closet with wiring chase
- Mechanical chase
- Plumbing chase
- Electrical closet with wiring chase

## Core Locations

The service core or cores of a building house the vertical distribution of mechanical and electrical services, elevator shafts, and exit stairways. These cores must be coordinated with the structural layout of columns, bearing walls, and shear walls or lateral bracing as well as with the desired patterns of space, use, and activity.

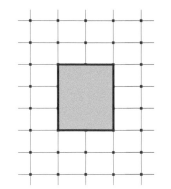

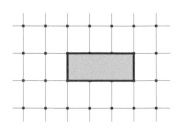

The building type and configuration will influence the location of vertical cores.

• A single core is often used in high-rise office buildings to leave a maximum amount of unobstructed rentable area.

• Central locations are ideal for short horizontal runs and efficient distribution patterns.

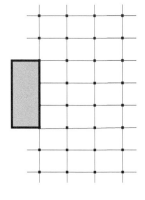

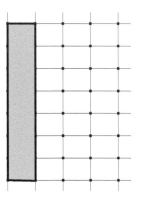

• Placing the core along an edge leaves an unobstructed floor space but occupies a portion of the daylit perimeter.

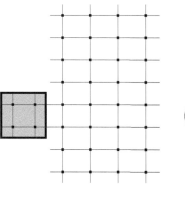

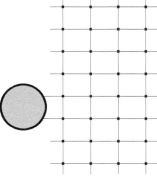

• Detached cores leave a maximum amount of floor space but require long service runs and cannot contribute lateral bracing to the building.

• Two cores may be symmetrically placed to reduce service runs and to serve effectively as lateral bracing, but the remaining floor area loses some flexibility in layout and use.

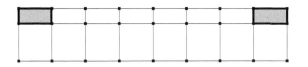

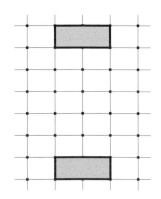

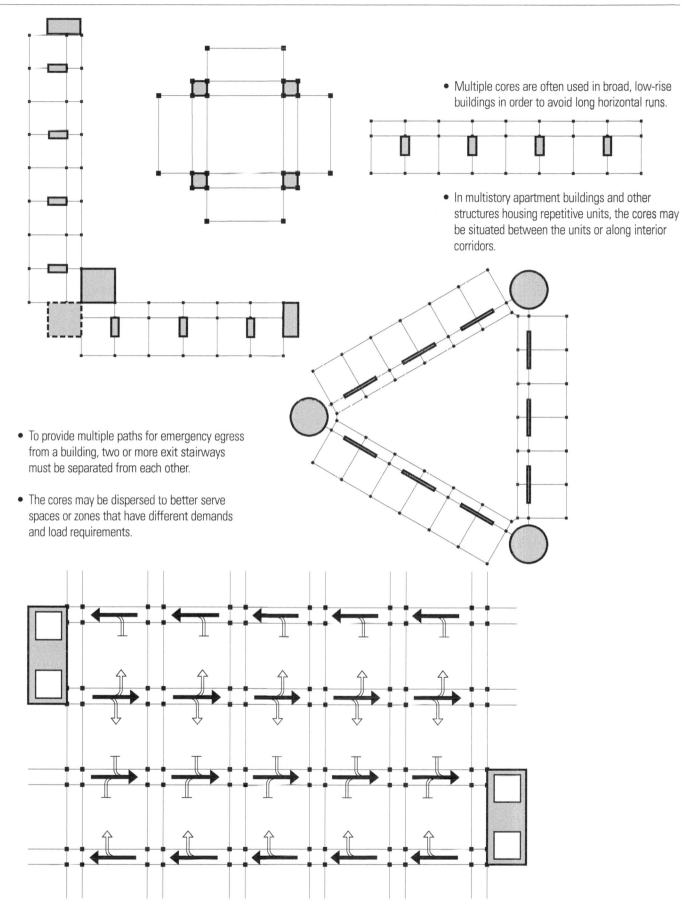

- Multiple cores are often used in broad, low-rise buildings in order to avoid long horizontal runs.

- In multistory apartment buildings and other structures housing repetitive units, the cores may be situated between the units or along interior corridors.

- To provide multiple paths for emergency egress from a building, two or more exit stairways must be separated from each other.

- The cores may be dispersed to better serve spaces or zones that have different demands and load requirements.

## Horizontal Distribution of Mechanical Services

Mechanical services are distributed to and from vertical shafts and chases in a horizontal manner through the floor-ceiling assemblies of a building. The manner in which these services relate to the depth of the structural spanning system determines the vertical extent of the floor-ceiling assemblies, which in turn has a significant effect on the overall height of a building.

There are three fundamental ways in which to distribute the horizontal runs of mechanical services:

- Above the spanning structure
- Through the spanning structure
- Below the spanning structure

Wiring and supply pipes require little space and can readily be run in small chases and floor or ceiling cavities. Distributing air, however, requires supply and return ducts of significant size. This is particularly true of systems where reduced noise is important and air is supplied at a low velocity, or where a small differential between a desired temperature and that of the supplied air requires a high volume of air movement. HVAC systems, therefore, pose the greatest potential conflict with both the horizontal and vertical dimensions of a building structure.

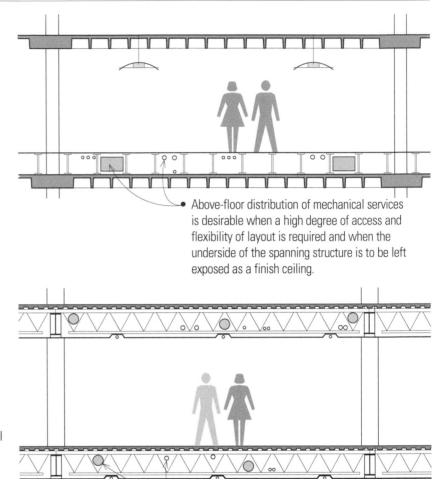

Above-floor distribution of mechanical services is desirable when a high degree of access and flexibility of layout is required and when the underside of the spanning structure is to be left exposed as a finish ceiling.

Through-floor distribution of mechanical services is appropriate when the spanning elements are deep and incorporate openings large enough for the passage of ducts and piping.

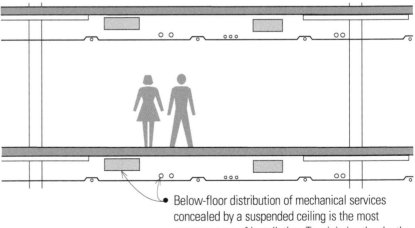

Below-floor distribution of mechanical services concealed by a suspended ceiling is the most common type of installation. To minimize the depth of the floor-ceiling assembly, below-floor distribution systems should be used with relatively shallow spanning structures, such as flat slabs and plates.

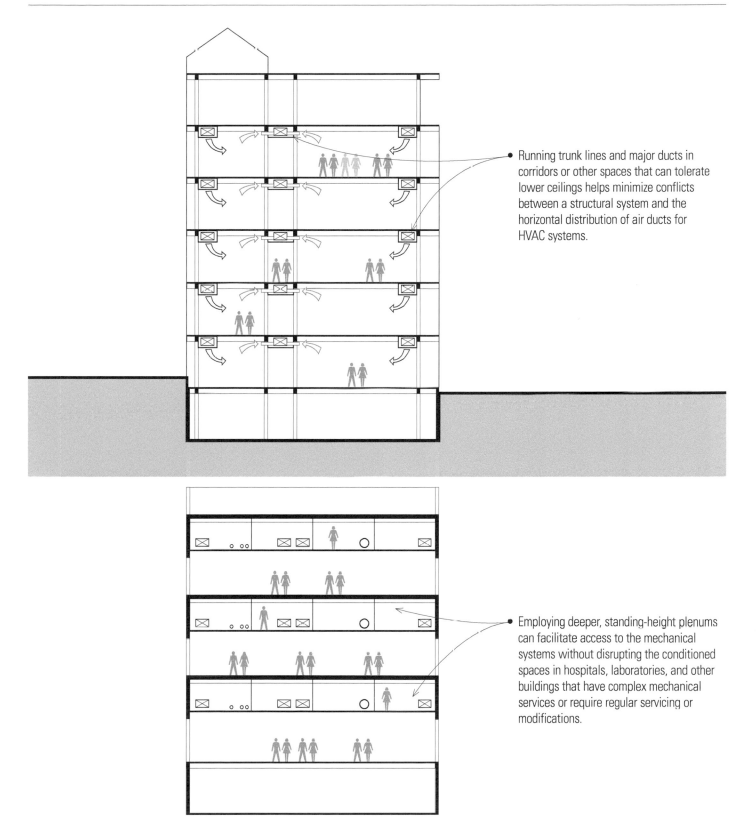

Running trunk lines and major ducts in corridors or other spaces that can tolerate lower ceilings helps minimize conflicts between a structural system and the horizontal distribution of air ducts for HVAC systems.

Employing deeper, standing-height plenums can facilitate access to the mechanical systems without disrupting the conditioned spaces in hospitals, laboratories, and other buildings that have complex mechanical services or require regular servicing or modifications.

## Horizontal Distribution of Mechanical Services Through the Floor Structure

The horizontal distribution of mechanical services through a spanning structure is made possible by the openings inherent in certain structural elements, such as steel and wood trusses, light-gauge steel joists, hollow-core concrete planks, cellular steel decking, and wood I-joists.

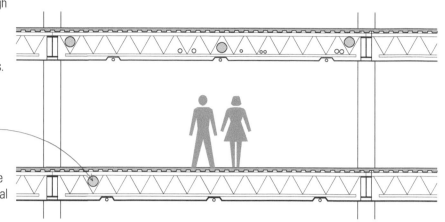

- Running air ducts within the depth of a spanning structure will constrain their maximum size. For example, the maximum diameter of an air duct passing through a series of open-web joists is one-half the joist depth.
- Running air ducts through floor trusses or in the space between joists reduces the flexibility of the mechanical system to accommodate change.

- The girders and beams of steel and timber structures can occupy separate layers to allow mechanical services to be woven through the structural system.

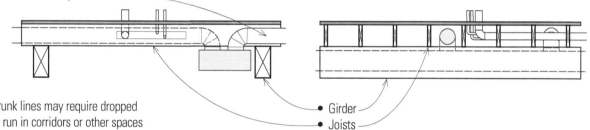

- Girder
- Joists

- Large ducts such as trunk lines may require dropped ceilings and are often run in corridors or other spaces where the ceiling height can be reduced.
- Note that it is sometimes difficult to run rigid elements of mechanical systems through openings in structural members within the sequence of construction.

Specialized building systems have been developed to accommodate integrating some mechanical systems with the structural system.

- Raceways for wiring may be cast into structural or topping slabs. The raceways can, in some cases, reduce the effective slab thickness.
- Some steel decking allows the underside of the corrugations to be used as a raceway for electrical wiring.

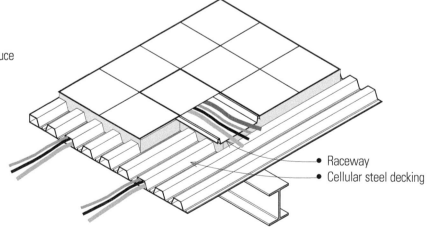

- Raceway
- Cellular steel decking

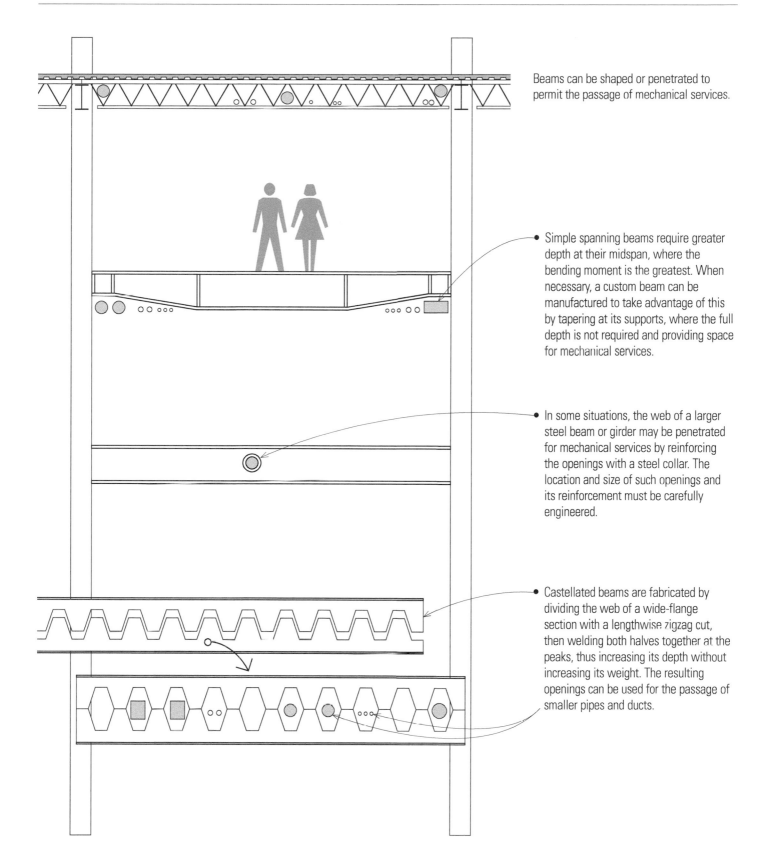

Beams can be shaped or penetrated to permit the passage of mechanical services.

• Simple spanning beams require greater depth at their midspan, where the bending moment is the greatest. When necessary, a custom beam can be manufactured to take advantage of this by tapering at its supports, where the full depth is not required and providing space for mechanical services.

• In some situations, the web of a larger steel beam or girder may be penetrated for mechanical services by reinforcing the openings with a steel collar. The location and size of such openings and its reinforcement must be carefully engineered.

• Castellated beams are fabricated by dividing the web of a wide-flange section with a lengthwise zigzag cut, then welding both halves together at the peaks, thus increasing its depth without increasing its weight. The resulting openings can be used for the passage of smaller pipes and ducts.

### Horizontal Distribution of Mechanical Services Below the Structural Floor

When the mechanical systems are located below the floor structure, the horizontal zone layer immediately below the structure is reserved for the distribution of air ducts. For maximum efficiency, the main or trunk lines of air ducts should run parallel to the girders or main beams. Where necessary, the smaller branch ducts cross under the girders to minimize the total floor depth. The lowest layer is typically reserved for lighting fixtures and the sprinkler system that extend through the ceiling.

- Suspended ceiling systems, electrical components, ductwork, and access floors must be braced to resist displacement under lateral loading as well as against the upward forces during a seismic event that can dislodge systems not braced for reversal of gravity loads.

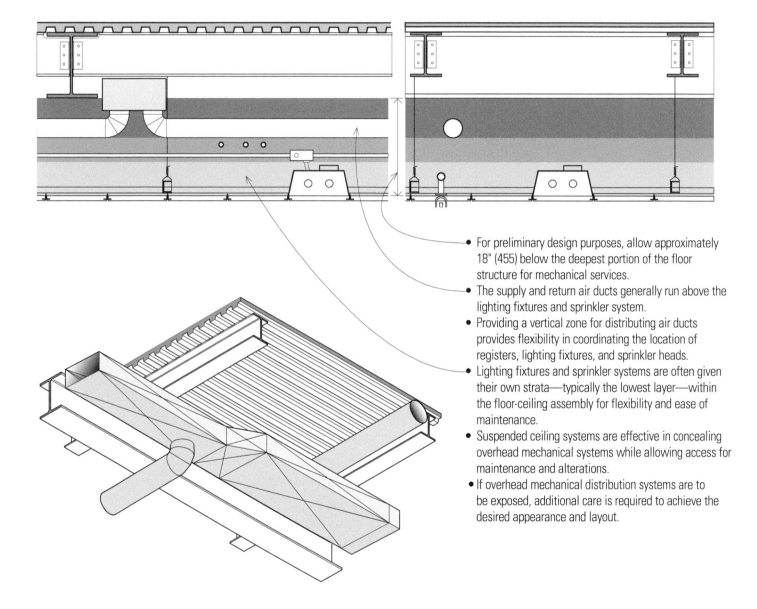

- For preliminary design purposes, allow approximately 18" (455) below the deepest portion of the floor structure for mechanical services.
- The supply and return air ducts generally run above the lighting fixtures and sprinkler system.
- Providing a vertical zone for distributing air ducts provides flexibility in coordinating the location of registers, lighting fixtures, and sprinkler heads.
- Lighting fixtures and sprinkler systems are often given their own strata—typically the lowest layer—within the floor-ceiling assembly for flexibility and ease of maintenance.
- Suspended ceiling systems are effective in concealing overhead mechanical systems while allowing access for maintenance and alterations.
- If overhead mechanical distribution systems are to be exposed, additional care is required to achieve the desired appearance and layout.

## Horizontal Distribution of Mechanical Services Above the Structural Floor

Access flooring systems are typically used in office spaces, hospitals, laboratories, computer rooms, and television and communication centers to provide accessibility and flexibility in the placement of desks, workstations, and equipment. Equipment can be moved and reconnected fairly easily with modular wiring systems. They are also a desirable option when the underside of the spanning structure, such as a waffle slab, is to be exposed as a finish ceiling.

- Access flooring systems consist essentially of removable and interchangeable floor panels supported on adjustable pedestals to allow free access to the space beneath. The floor panels are typically 24 inches (610) square and constructed of steel, aluminum, a wood core encased in steel or aluminum, or lightweight reinforced concrete. The panels may be finished with carpet tile, vinyl tile, or high-pressure laminate; fire-rated and electrostatic-discharge-control coverings are also available.

- The pedestals are adjustable to provide finished floor heights from 12" to 30" (305 to 760); a minimum finished floor height as low as 8" (205) is also available.
- Systems using stringers have greater lateral stability than stringerless systems; seismic pedestals are available to meet building code requirements for lateral stability.
- Design loads range from 250 to 625 psf (12 to 30 kPa), but are available up to 1125 psf (54 kPa) to accommodate heavier loadings.
- The underfloor space is used for the installation of electrical conduit, junction boxes, and the cables for computer, security, and communication systems.
- It may still be necessary for sprinkler systems, power for lighting, and air-handling equipment to penetrate the spanning structural floors.

- The space can also be used as a plenum to distribute the supply air of the HVAC system, allowing the ceiling plenum to be used only for return air. Separating cool supply air from warmer return air in this manner can reduce energy consumption. Lowering the overall height of service plenums also reduces the floor-to-floor height of new construction.

### Flat Plates and Slabs

- Due to the unobstructed space below flat plates and between the drop panels of flat slabs, mechanical services may run in both directions in all areas, providing the greatest flexibility and adaptability in laying out mechanical services.

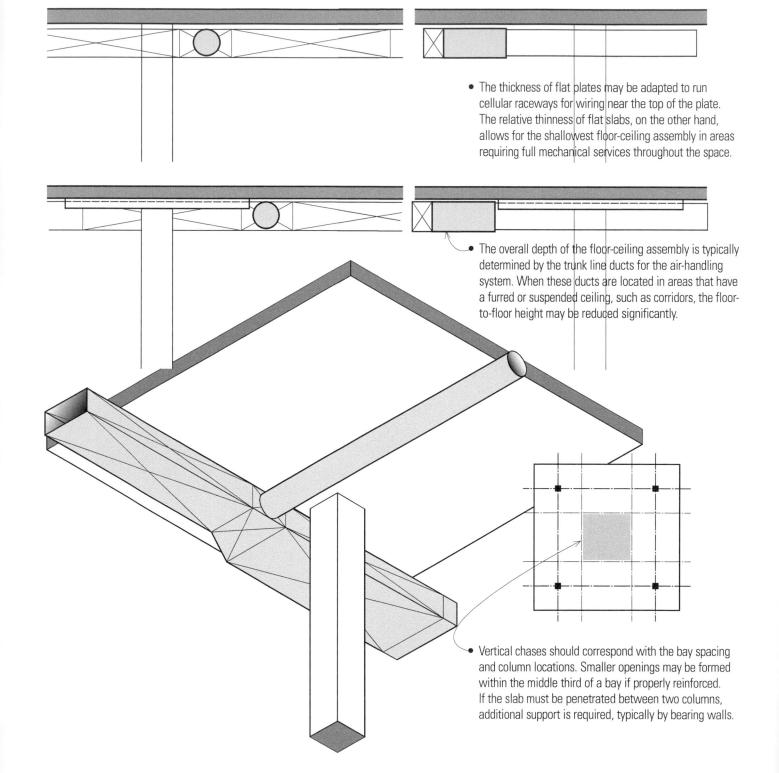

- The thickness of flat plates may be adapted to run cellular raceways for wiring near the top of the plate. The relative thinness of flat slabs, on the other hand, allows for the shallowest floor-ceiling assembly in areas requiring full mechanical services throughout the space.

- The overall depth of the floor-ceiling assembly is typically determined by the trunk line ducts for the air-handling system. When these ducts are located in areas that have a furred or suspended ceiling, such as corridors, the floor-to-floor height may be reduced significantly.

- Vertical chases should correspond with the bay spacing and column locations. Smaller openings may be formed within the middle third of a bay if properly reinforced. If the slab must be penetrated between two columns, additional support is required, typically by bearing walls.

### One-Way Slab and Beams

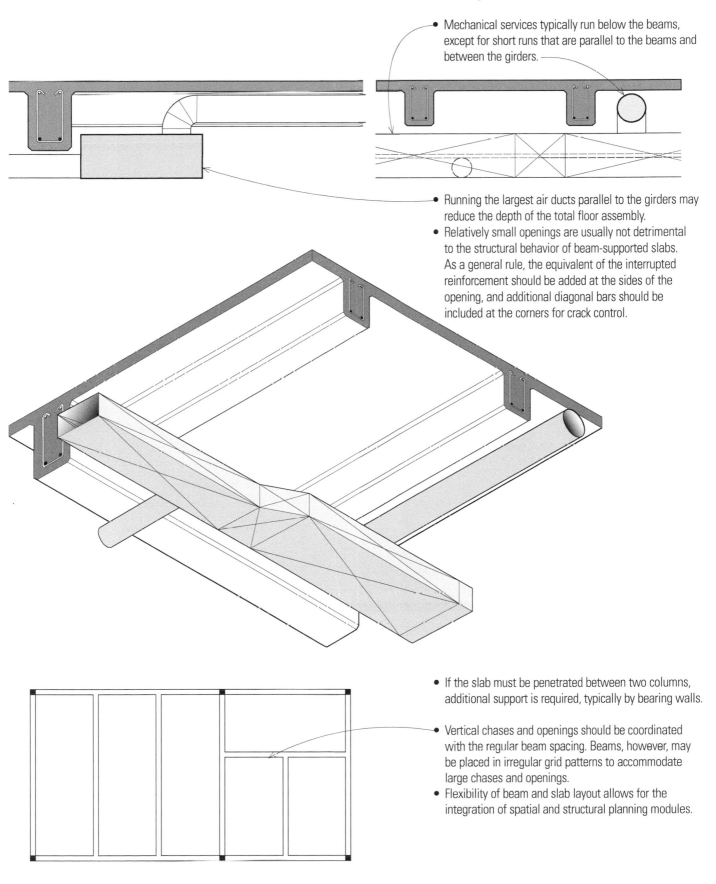

- Mechanical services typically run below the beams, except for short runs that are parallel to the beams and between the girders.

- Running the largest air ducts parallel to the girders may reduce the depth of the total floor assembly.
- Relatively small openings are usually not detrimental to the structural behavior of beam-supported slabs. As a general rule, the equivalent of the interrupted reinforcement should be added at the sides of the opening, and additional diagonal bars should be included at the corners for crack control.

- If the slab must be penetrated between two columns, additional support is required, typically by bearing walls.

- Vertical chases and openings should be coordinated with the regular beam spacing. Beams, however, may be placed in irregular grid patterns to accommodate large chases and openings.
- Flexibility of beam and slab layout allows for the integration of spatial and structural planning modules.

## Joist and Waffle Slabs

- Mechanical services generally run below the joist or waffle slab. If the pan joists or coffers are exposed as the finish ceiling, mechanical services may be run in an accessible floor system above the slab.

- The pans of joist slabs can provide space for short plumbing runs between the joist bands.

- Large vertical chases and openings should be accommodated and framed within the column grid. Smaller openings should be coordinated with the joist or rib spacing.

- Small holes can be cut in the slab between the joists or ribs. However, mechanical services should not penetrate the joists, ribs, or solid bands of joist and waffle slabs.

- The location of ceiling fixtures, such as luminaires and fire sprinklers, require careful integration with the coffers of waffle slabs.

### Precast Concrete Planks

- Mechanical services run below the support beams, except for short runs that can run parallel to the beams.

- Running the largest air ducts parallel to the girders may reduce the depth of the total floor assembly.
- Small openings for plumbing supply lines may be cut in the field.

- The precast voids in hollow-core planks may be used for electrical chases with perpendicular wiring chases cast into the slab topping.

- If the concrete planks are exposed as the finish ceiling, additional care is required in locating and installing the exposed air ducts for the desired appearance. The exposed planks may also dictate the use of surface wiring with exposed conduit and exposing horizontal plumbing runs that may not be desirable.

- Vertical chases should be coordinated with the beam spacing. Openings the width of a single plank can be created by hanging the cut plank off of adjacent planks; wider openings must be supported on additional beams or bearing walls.

### Structural Steel Framing

• When steel beams and girders are framed in-plane, air ducts may run between the beams but must be located below a supporting girder to cross the girder. Locating the girder below the beams allows mechanical services to pass over it but increases the depth of the floor assembly.

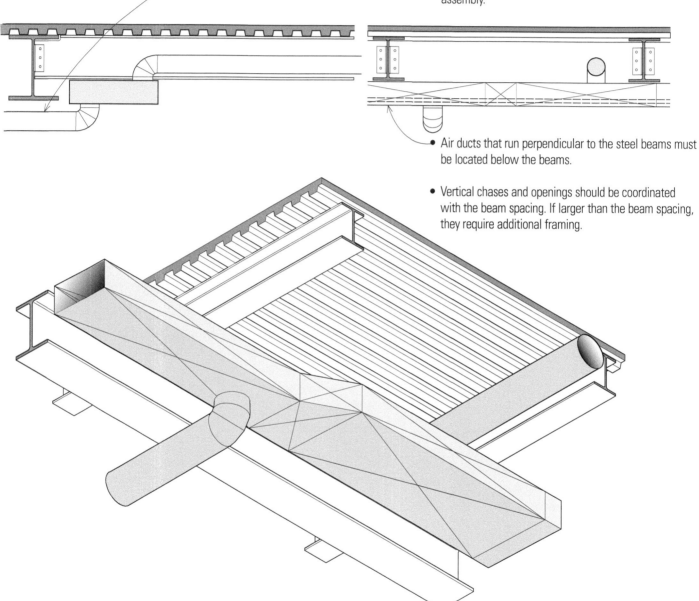

• Air ducts that run perpendicular to the steel beams must be located below the beams.

• Vertical chases and openings should be coordinated with the beam spacing. If larger than the beam spacing, they require additional framing.

• When necessary, structural steel beams can be modified and reinforced to accommodate mechanical services within their webs. Custom-fabricated steel beams can also be tapered, haunched, or castellated to provide space for mechanical services. See page 323.

### Post-and-Beam Construction

- In-plane framing between secondary beams and girder beams require that air ducts and drainage lines cross over below the girder beams.
- Air ducts running perpendicular to secondary beams must run below the beams.

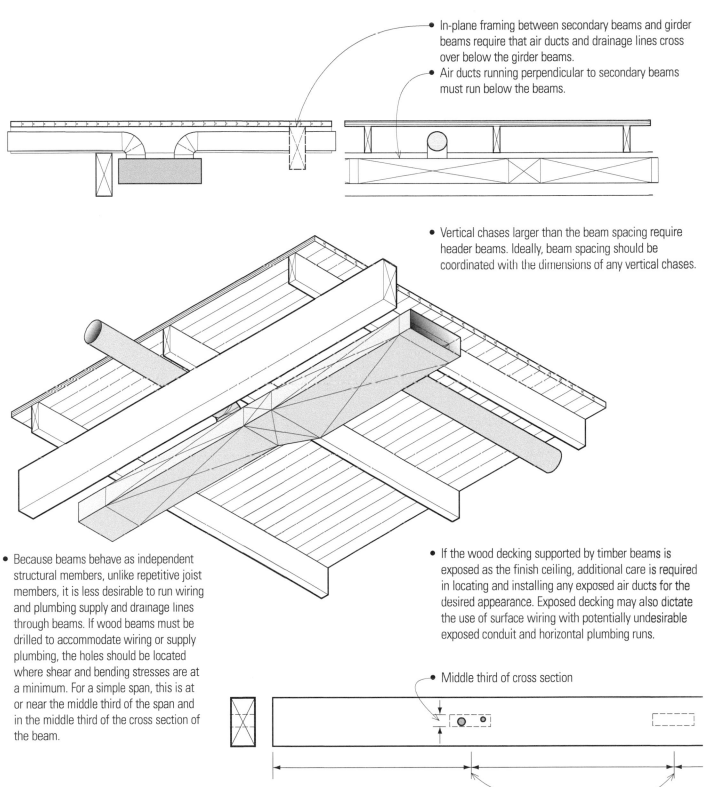

- Vertical chases larger than the beam spacing require header beams. Ideally, beam spacing should be coordinated with the dimensions of any vertical chases.

- Because beams behave as independent structural members, unlike repetitive joist members, it is less desirable to run wiring and plumbing supply and drainage lines through beams. If wood beams must be drilled to accommodate wiring or supply plumbing, the holes should be located where shear and bending stresses are at a minimum. For a simple span, this is at or near the middle third of the span and in the middle third of the cross section of the beam.

- If the wood decking supported by timber beams is exposed as the finish ceiling, additional care is required in locating and installing any exposed air ducts for the desired appearance. Exposed decking may also dictate the use of surface wiring with potentially undesirable exposed conduit and horizontal plumbing runs.

- Middle third of cross section

- Third points of span

### Open-Web Steel Joists

- Open-web steel joists permit the passage of mechanical services through the webs as well as parallel to the joists.

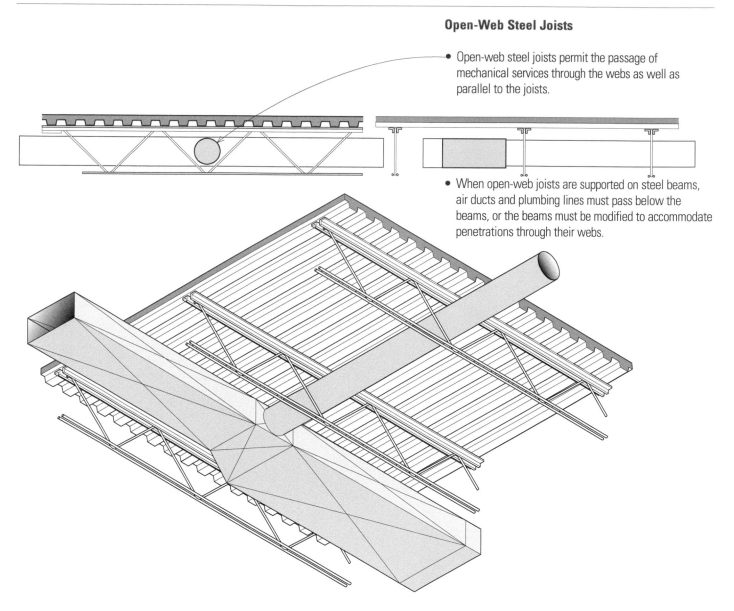

- When open-web joists are supported on steel beams, air ducts and plumbing lines must pass below the beams, or the beams must be modified to accommodate penetrations through their webs.

- Supporting open-web joists on girder trusses may allow mechanical services to pass through the girders when running parallel to the open-web joists. Note that a girder truss is typically deeper than a steel beam carrying an equivalent load, creating a deeper floor construction.

- Small vertical openings may be framed with steel angle headers supported by trimmer joists. Large openings, however, require structural steel framing.

**Light Frame Construction**

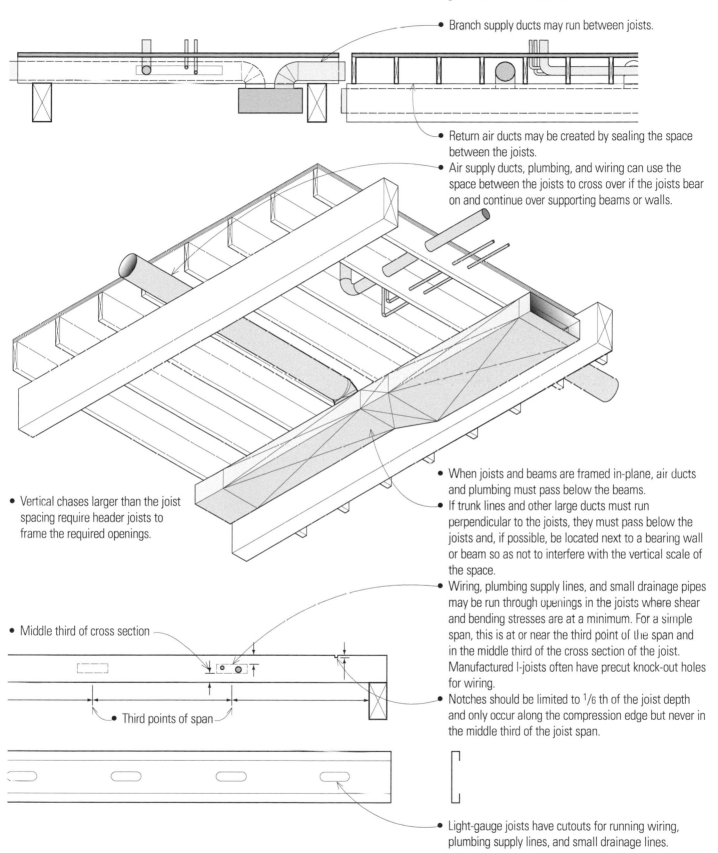

- Branch supply ducts may run between joists.

- Return air ducts may be created by sealing the space between the joists.
- Air supply ducts, plumbing, and wiring can use the space between the joists to cross over if the joists bear on and continue over supporting beams or walls.

- Vertical chases larger than the joist spacing require header joists to frame the required openings.

- When joists and beams are framed in-plane, air ducts and plumbing must pass below the beams.
- If trunk lines and other large ducts must run perpendicular to the joists, they must pass below the joists and, if possible, be located next to a bearing wall or beam so as not to interfere with the vertical scale of the space.
- Wiring, plumbing supply lines, and small drainage pipes may be run through openings in the joists where shear and bending stresses are at a minimum. For a simple span, this is at or near the third point of the span and in the middle third of the cross section of the joist. Manufactured I-joists often have precut knock-out holes for wiring.
- Notches should be limited to $1/6$ th of the joist depth and only occur along the compression edge but never in the middle third of the joist span.

- Middle third of cross section

- Third points of span

- Light-gauge joists have cutouts for running wiring, plumbing supply lines, and small drainage lines.

# Bibliography

Allen, Edward and Joseph Iano. *The Architect's Studio Companion: Rules of Thumb for Preliminary Design*, 5th Edition. Hoboken, New Jersey: John Wiley and Sons, 2011

Ambrose, James. *Building Structures Primer*. Hoboken, New Jersey: John Wiley and Sons,1981

Ambrose, James. *Building Structures*, 2nd Edition. Hoboken, New Jersey: John Wiley and Sons, 1993

The American Institute of Architects. *Architectural Graphic Standards*, 11th Edition. Hoboken, New Jersey: John Wiley and Sons, 2007

Arnold, Christopher, Richard Eisner, and Eric Elsesser. *Buildings at Risk: Seismic Design Basics for Practicing Architects*. Washington, DC: AIA/ACSA Council on Architectural Research and NHRP (National Hazards Research Program), 1994

Bovill, Carl. *Architectural Design: Integration of Structural and Environmental Systems*. New York: Van Nostrand Reinhold, 1991

Breyer, Donald. *Design of Wood Structures-ASD/LRFD*, 7th Edition. New York: McGraw-Hill, 2013

Charleson, Andrew. *Structure as Architecture–A Source Book for Architects and Structural Engineers*. Amsterdam: Elsevier, 2005

Ching, Francis D. K. *A Visual Dictionary of Architecture*, 2nd Edition. Hoboken, New Jersey: John Wiley and Sons, 2011

Ching, Francis D. K. and Steven Winkel. *Building Codes Illustrated—A Guide to Understanding the 2012 International Building Code*, 4th Edition. Hoboken, New Jersey: John Wiley and Sons, 2012

Ching, Francis D. K. *Building Construction Illustrated*, 4th Edition. Hoboken, New Jersey: John Wiley and Sons, 2008

Ching, Francis D. K. *Architecture—Form, Space, and Order*, 3rd Edition. Hoboken, New Jersey: John Wiley and Sons, 2007

Ching, Francis D. K., Mark Jarzombek, and Vikramaditya Prakash. *A Global History of Architecture*, 2nd Edition. Hoboken, New Jersey: John Wiley and Sons, 2010

Corkill, P. A., H. L. Puderbaugh, and H.K. Sawyers. *Structure and Architectural Design*. Davenport, Iowa: Market Publishing, 1993

Cowan, Henry and Forrest Wilson. *Structural Systems*. New York: Van Nostrand Reinhold, 1981

Crawley, Stan and Delbert Ward. *Seismic and Wind Loads in Architectural Design: An Architect's Study Guide*. Washington, DC: The American Institute of Architects, 1990

Departments of the Army, the Navy and the Air Force. *Seismic Design for Buildings—TM 5-809-10/Navfac P-355*. Washington, DC: 1973

Engel, Heino. *Structure Systems*, 3rd Edition. Germany: Hatje Cantz, 2007

Fischer, Robert, ed. *Engineering for Architecture*. New York: McGraw-Hill, 1980

Fuller Moore. *Understanding Structures*. Boston: McGraw-Hill, 1999

Goetz, Karl-Heinz., et al. *Timber Design and Construction Sourcebook*. New York: McGraw-Hill, 1989

Guise, David. *Design and Technology in Architecture*. Hoboken, New Jersey: John Wiley and Sons, 2000

Hanaor, Ariel. *Principles of Structures*. Cambridge, UK: Wiley-Blackwell, 1998

Hart, F., W. Henn, and H. Sontag. *Multi-Storey Buildings in Steel*. London: Crosby Lockwood and Staples, 1978

# BIBLIOGRAPHY

Hilson, Barry. *Basic Structural Behaviour—Understanding Structures from Models*. London: Thomas Telford,1993

Howard, H. Seymour, Jr. *Structure—An Architect's Approach*. New York: McGraw-Hill, 1966

Hunt, Tony. *Tony Hunt's Sketchbook*. Oxford, UK: Architectural Press, 1999

Hunt, Tony. *Tony Hunt's Structures Notebook*. Oxford, UK: Architectural Press, 1997

Johnson, Alford, et. al. *Designing with Structural Steel: A Guide for Architects*, 2nd Edition. Chicago: American Institute of Steel Construction, 2002

Kellogg, Richard. *Demonstrating Structural Behavior with Simple Models*. Chicago: Graham Foundation, 1994

Levy, Matthys, and Mario Salvadori. *Why Buildings Fall Down: How Structures Fail*. New York: W.W. Norton & Co., 2002

Lin, T. Y. and Sidney Stotesbury. *Structural Concepts and Systems for Architects and Engineers*. Hoboken, New Jersey: John Wiley and Sons, 1981

Lindeburg, Michael and Kurt M. McMullin. *Seismic Design of Building Structures*, 10th Edition. Belmont, California: Professional Publications, Inc., 1990

Macdonald, Angus. *Structural Design for Architecture*. Oxford, UK: Architectural Press, 1997

McCormac, Jack C. and Stephen F. Csernak. *Structural Steel Design*, 5th Edition. New York: Prentice-Hall, 2011

Millais, Malcolm. *Building Structures—From Concepts to Design*, 2nd Edition. Oxford, UK: Taylor & Francis, 2005

Nilson, Arthur et. al. *Design of Concrete Structures*. 14th Edition. New York: McGraw-Hill, 2009

Onouye, Barry and Kevin Kane. *Statics and Strength of Materials for Architecture and Building Construction*, 4th Edition. New Jersey: Prentice Hall, 2011

Popovic, O. Larsen and A. Tyas. *Conceptual Structural Design: Bridging the Gap Between Architects and Engineers*. London: Thomas Telford Publishing, 2003

Reid, Esmond. *Understanding Buildings—A Multidisciplinary Approach*. Cambridge, Massachusetts: MIT Press, 1984

Salvadori, Mario and Robert Heller. *Structure in Architecture: The Building of Buildings*. New Jersey: Prentice Hall, 1986

Salvadori, Mario. *Why Buildings Stand Up: The Strength of Architecture*. New York: W.W. Norton & Co., 2002

Schodek, Daniel and Martin Bechthold. *Structures*, 6th Edition. New Jersey: Prentice Hall, 2007

Schueller, Wolfgang. *Horizontal Span Building Structures*. Hoboken, New Jersey: John Wiley and Sons, 1983

Schueller, Wolfgang. *The Design of Building Structures*. New Jersey: Prentice Hall, 1996

Siegel, Curt. *Structure and Form in Modern Architecture*. New York: Reinhold Publishing Corporation, 1962

White, Richard and Charles Salmon, eds. *Building Structural Design Handbook*. Hoboken, New Jersey: John Wiley and Sons, 1987

Williams, Alan. *Seismic Design of Buildings and Bridges for Civil and Structural Engineers*. Austin, Texas: Engineering Press, 1998

# Index